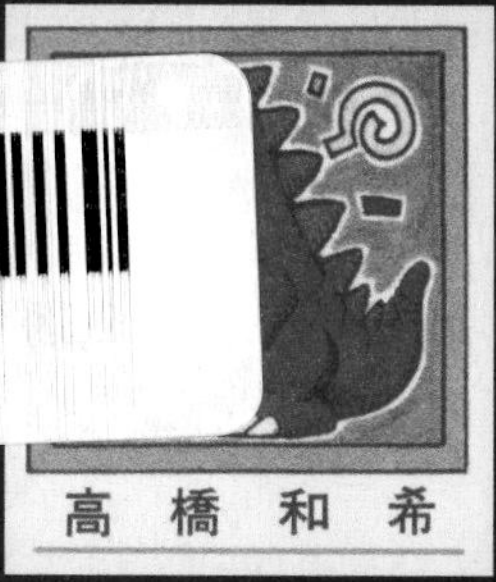
高橋和希

OH, HE CAME FROM THE SANDS OF TIME
HE'S THE KING OF GAMES, LEGENDS COME ALIVE
EVILDOERS WILL HIDE IN SHAME
WHEN THEY TASTE JUSTICE
IN A SHADOW GAME
(SHADOW!)
OH, BUT EVEN A KING HAS A HEART
AND THE DOOR TO THAT HEART, IT OPENS, IT PARTS
THERE IS ALWAYS A FRIEND IN YOUR HEART!
YUGI! YUGI! YU-GI-OH!

THIS IS A ***YU-GI-OH!*** THEME SONG I WROTE AND COMPOSED MYSELF (IN A SAMBA RHYTHM).

KAZUKI TAKAHASHI, 1997

Artist/author Kazuki Takahashi first tried to break into the manga business in 1982, but success eluded him until **Yu-Gi-Oh!** debuted in the Japanese **Weekly Shonen Jump** magazine in 1996. **Yu-Gi-Oh!**'s themes of friendship and fighting, together with Takahashi's weird and wonderful art, soon became enormously successful, spawning a real-world card game, video games, and two anime series. A lifelong gamer, Takahashi enjoys Shogi (Japanese chess), Mahjong, card games, and tabletop RPGs, among other games.

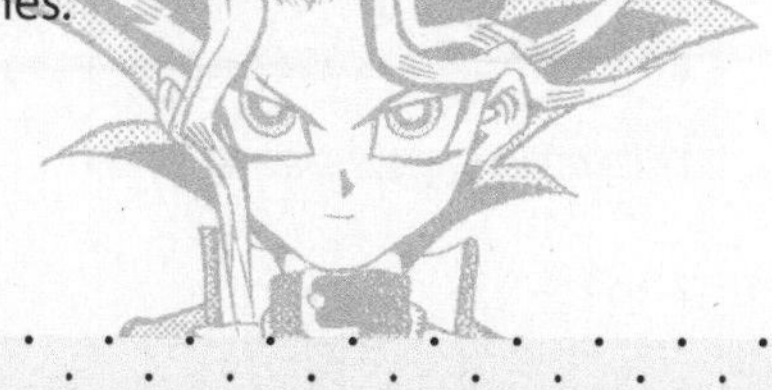

YU-GI-OH! VOL. 5
SHONEN JUMP Manga Edition

This graphic novel contains material that was originally published in English
in **SHONEN JUMP** #13 to #17.

STORY AND ART BY
KAZUKI TAKAHASHI

Translation & English Adaptation/Anita Sengupta
Touch-Up Art & Lettering/Kelle Han
Cover & Graphics Design/Sean Lee
Senior Editor/Jason Thompson

Printed in the U.S.A.

Published by VIZ Media, LLC
P.O. Box 77010
San Francisco, CA 94107

10 9 8 7 6 5 4
First printing, May 2004
Fourth printing, September 2013

www.viz.com

THE WORLD'S
MOST POPULAR MANGA
SHONEN JUMP
www.shonenjump.com

SHONEN JUMP MANGA

Vol. 5
THE HEART OF THE CARDS

STORY AND ART BY
KAZUKI TAKAHASHI

THE STORY SO FAR...

When Yugi beat his classmate Seto Kaiba at the collectible card game "Duel Monsters," he didn't know the lengths to which Kaiba would go to get revenge! The insane super-genius Kaiba spent $85 million to build a *Theme Park of Death* to torture Yugi and his friends, with death traps, chain-saw-wielding maniacs, and hitmen for play partners! Now, Yugi, Jonouchi and Anzu have made it almost to the end of the line—but their friend Honda, trapped in the "room of falling blocks," wasn't so lucky...

DARK YUGI

武藤遊戯
YUGI MUTOU

The main character. When he solved the ancient Egyptian Millennium Puzzle, he developed an alter ego, the King of Games, which emerges in times of stress. Afterwards, the regular Yugi doesn't remember what happened.

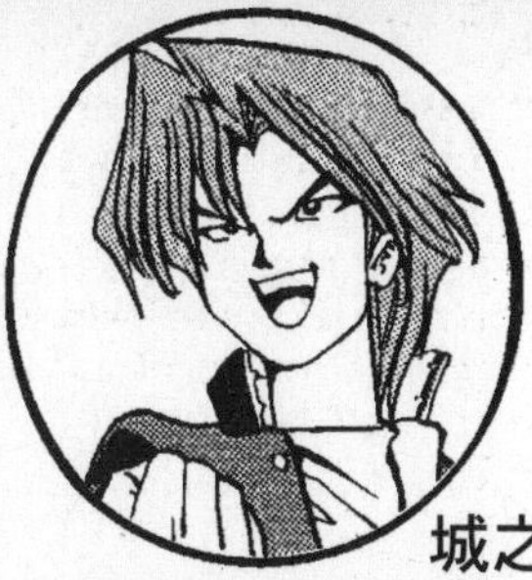

城之内克也

KATSUYA JONOUCHI

Yugi's classmate, a tough guy who gets in lots of fights. He used to think Yugi was a wimp, but now they are good friends. In the English anime he's known as "Joey Wheeler."

真崎杏子

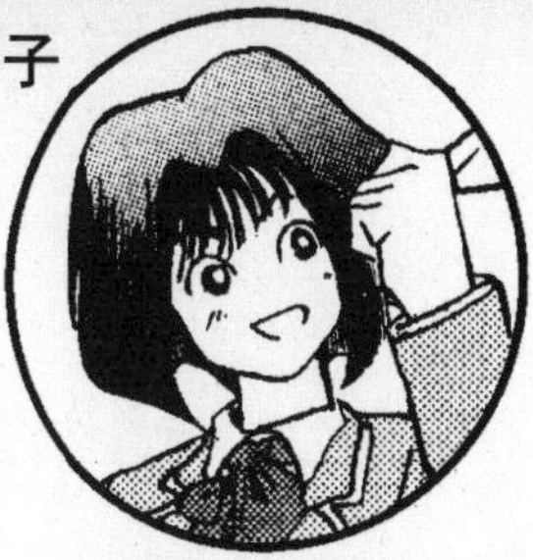

ANZU MAZAKI

Yugi's classmate and childhood friend. She fell in love with the charismatic voice of Yugi's alter ego, but doesn't know that they're the same person. Her first name means "Peach." In the English anime she's known as "Téa Gardner."

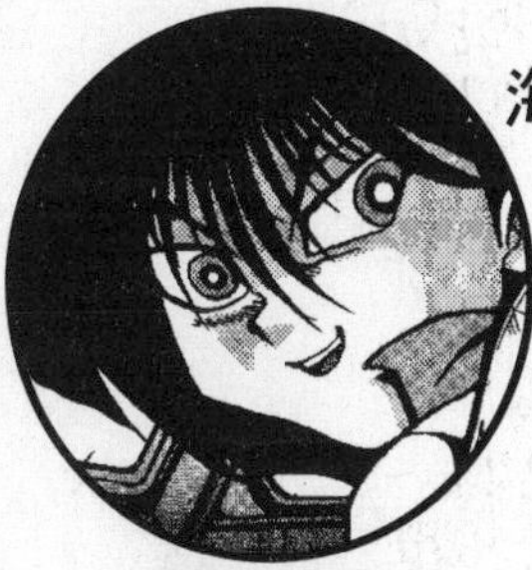

海馬モクバ

MOKUBA KAIBA

Seto's little brother. He's lost to Yugi twice at different games. His favorite game is the collectible miniatures game "Capsule Monster Chess."

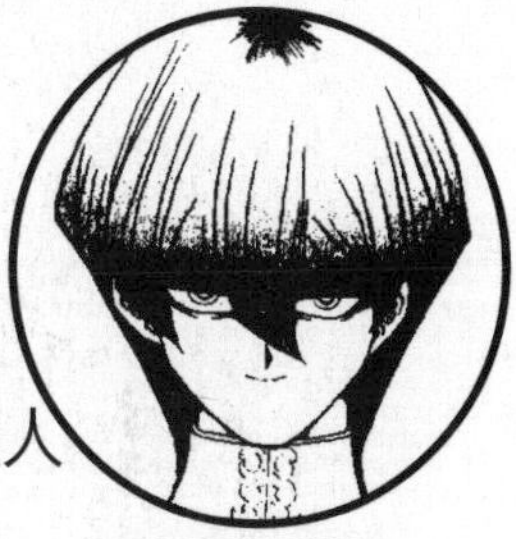

海馬瀬人

SETO KAIBA

Heir to Japan's biggest gaming empire, Kaiba is an expert at the American collectible card game "Duel Monsters." After losing to Yugi, he kidnapped Yugi's grandfather and forced him to play a duel in a prototype "Virtual Reality Simulation Box," which was so realistic it gave Yugi's grandfather a heart attack.

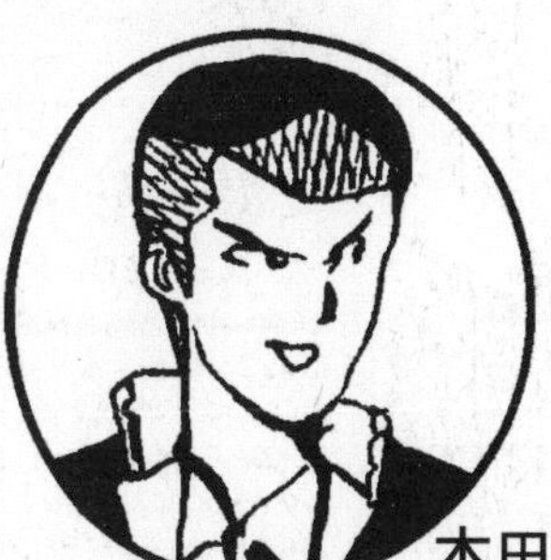

本田ヒロト

HIROTO HONDA

Yugi's classmate, a friend of Jonouchi. He was babysitting his nephew Johji, a talking baby, when he got caught up in the Theme Park of Death. In the English anime he's known as "Tristan Taylor."

武藤双六

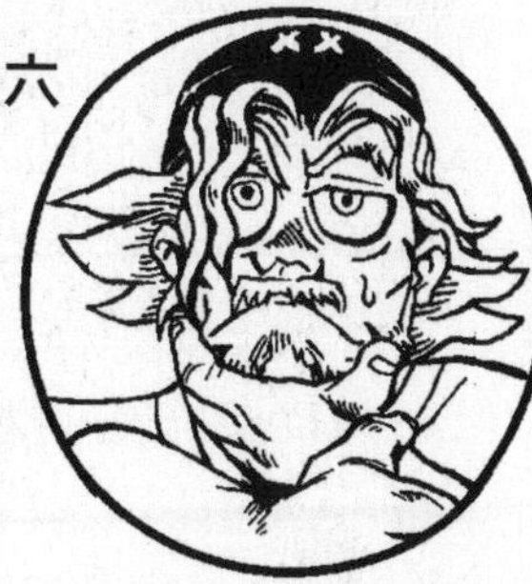

SUGOROKU MUTOU

Yugi's grandfather, the owner of the Kame ("Turtle") game store. Currently in the hospital undergoing heart surgery.

Yu-Gi-Oh!

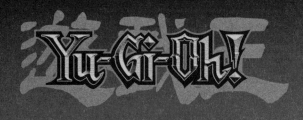

Vol. 5

CONTENTS

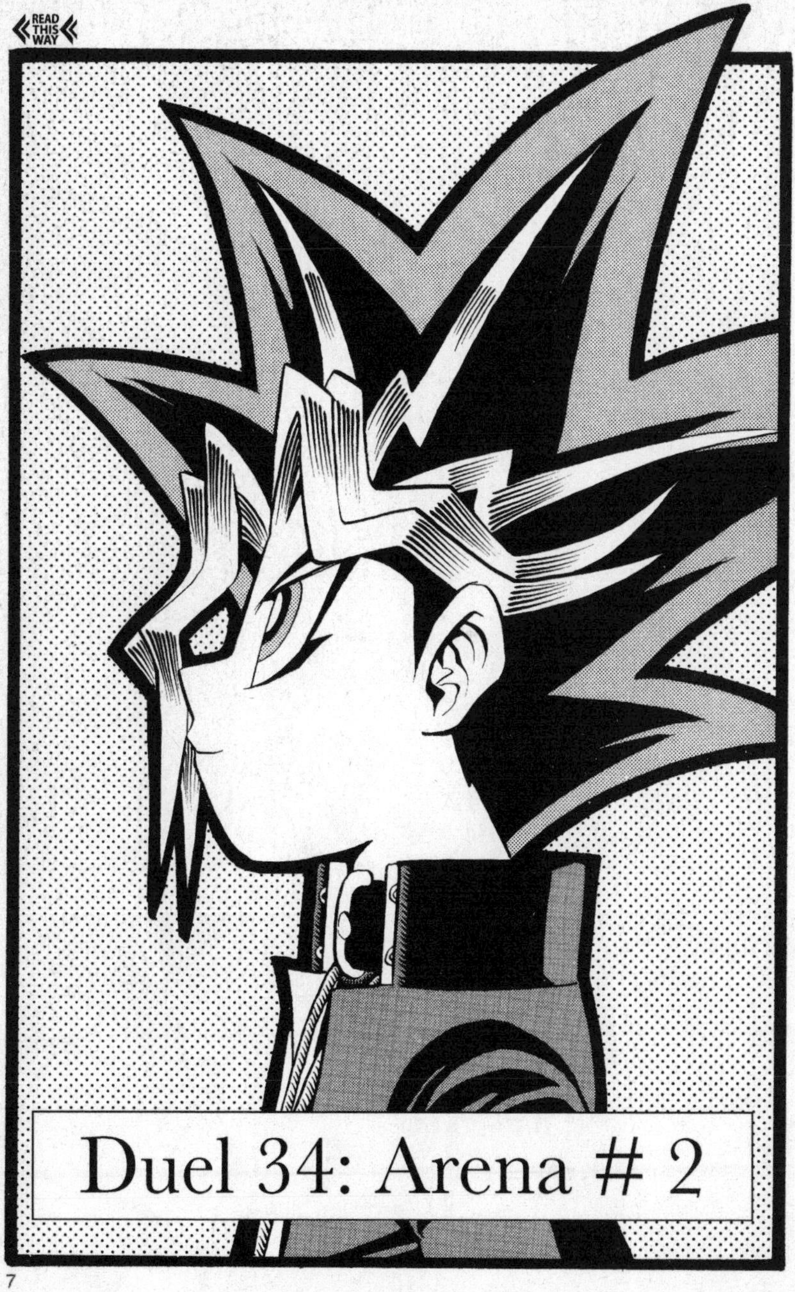
READ THIS WAY
Duel 34: Arena # 2

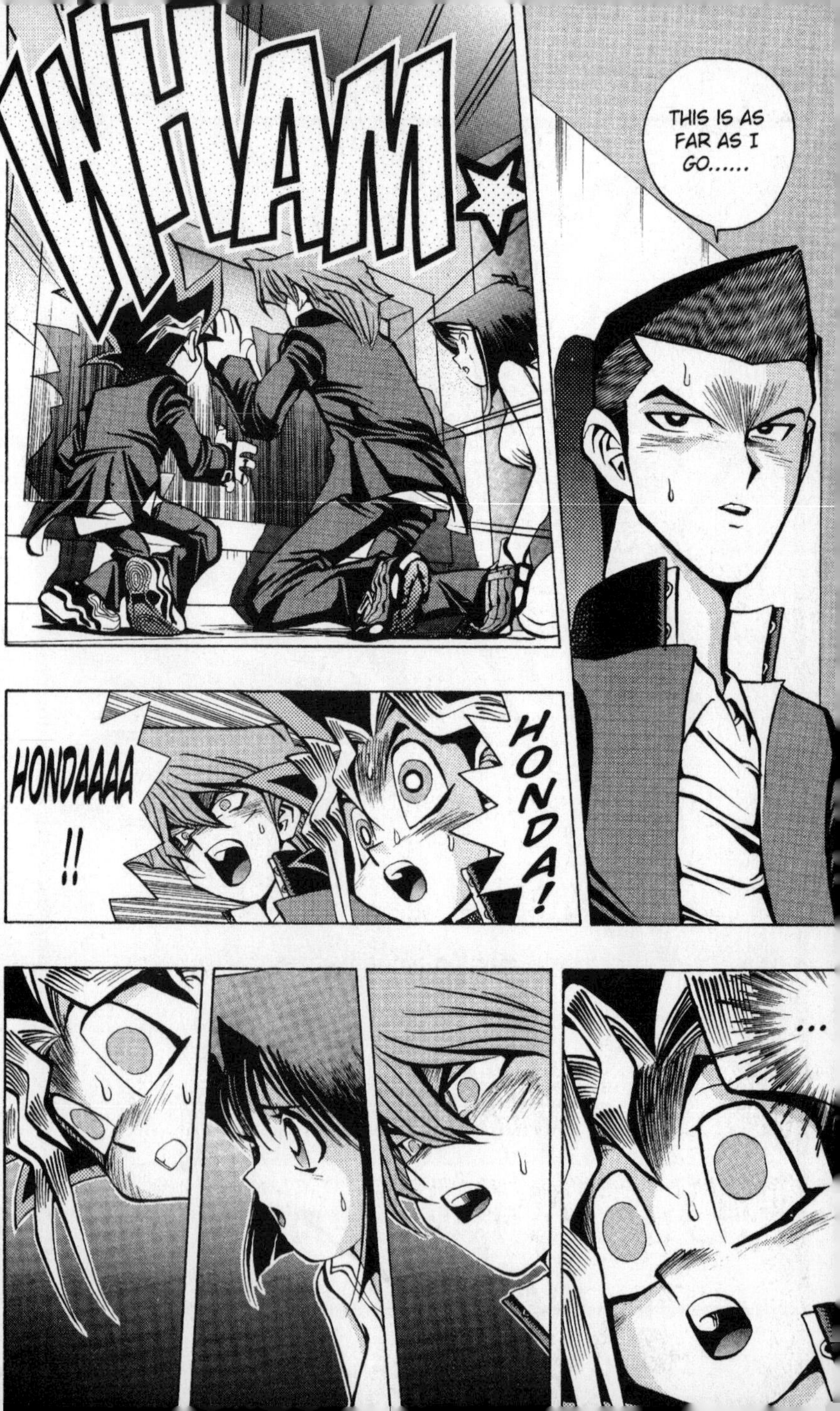
THIS IS AS FAR AS I GO......
WHAM
HONDA!
HONDAAAA !!
...

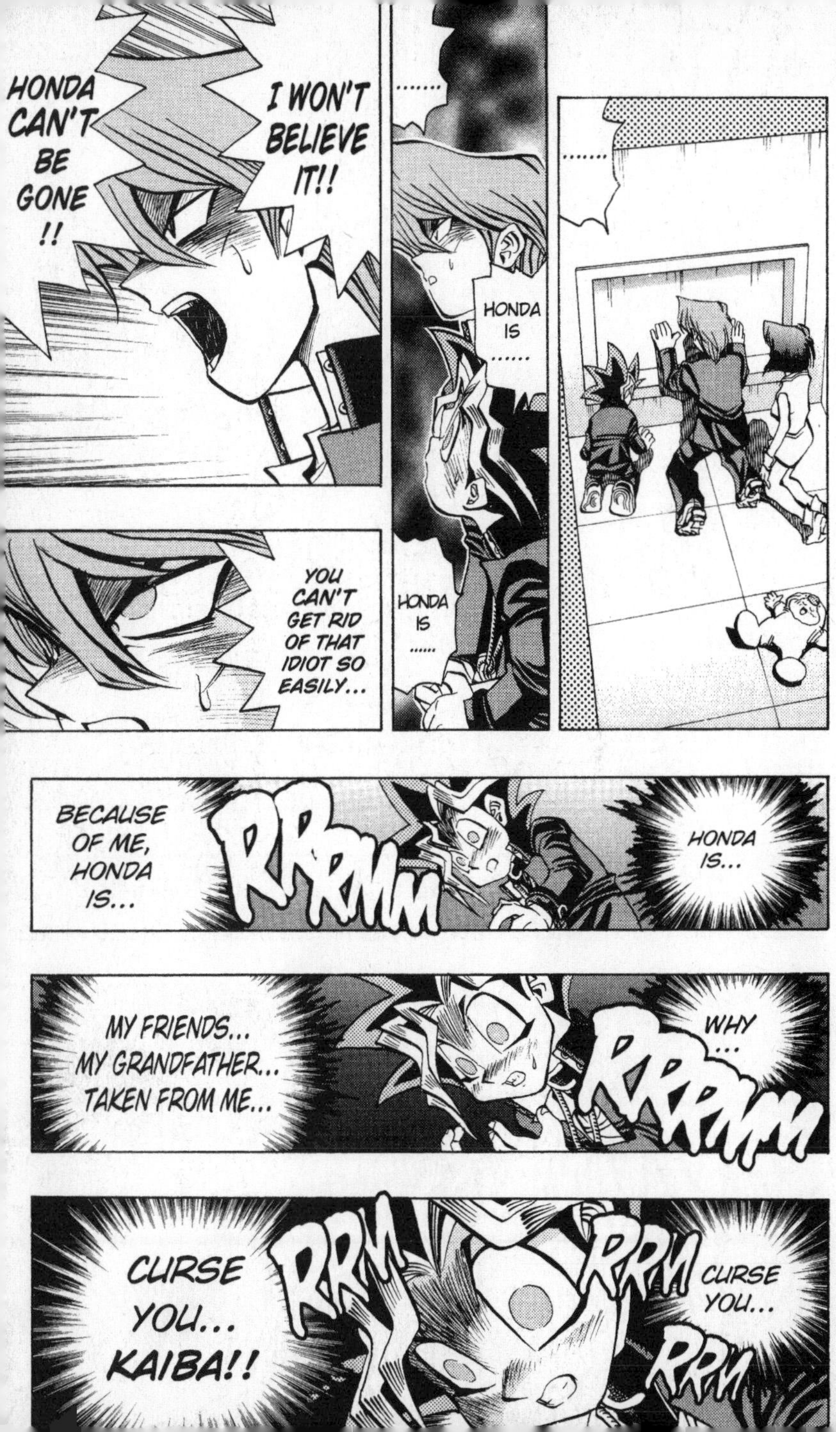
......
......
HONDA IS ......
HONDA IS ......
I WON'T BELIEVE IT!!
HONDA CAN'T BE GONE!!
YOU CAN'T GET RID OF THAT IDIOT SO EASILY...
HONDA IS...
RRRMM
BECAUSE OF ME, HONDA IS...
WHY ...
RRRMM
MY FRIENDS... MY GRANDFATHER... TAKEN FROM ME...
CURSE YOU...
RRM
RRM
RRM
CURSE YOU... KAIBA!!

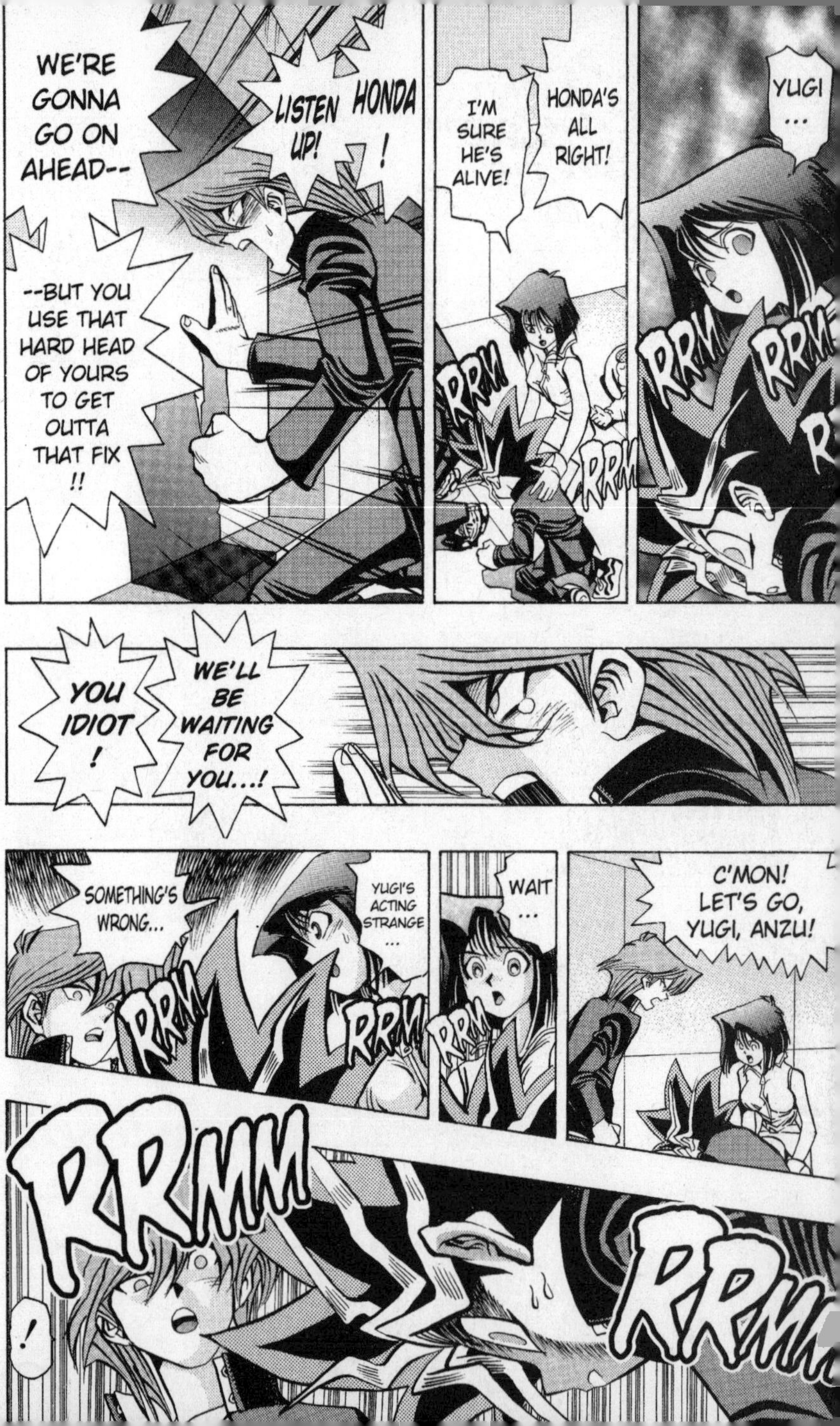
YUGI ...
RRM RRM
RRM
HONDA'S ALL RIGHT!
I'M SURE HE'S ALIVE!
RRM
RRM
HONDA !
LISTEN UP!
WE'RE GONNA GO ON AHEAD--
--BUT YOU USE THAT HARD HEAD OF YOURS TO GET OUTTA THAT FIX !!
WE'LL BE WAITING FOR YOU...!
YOU IDIOT !
C'MON! LET'S GO, YUGI, ANZU!
WAIT ...
RRM
RRM
YUGI'S ACTING STRANGE ...
SOMETHING'S WRONG...
RRM
RRMM
RRMM
!

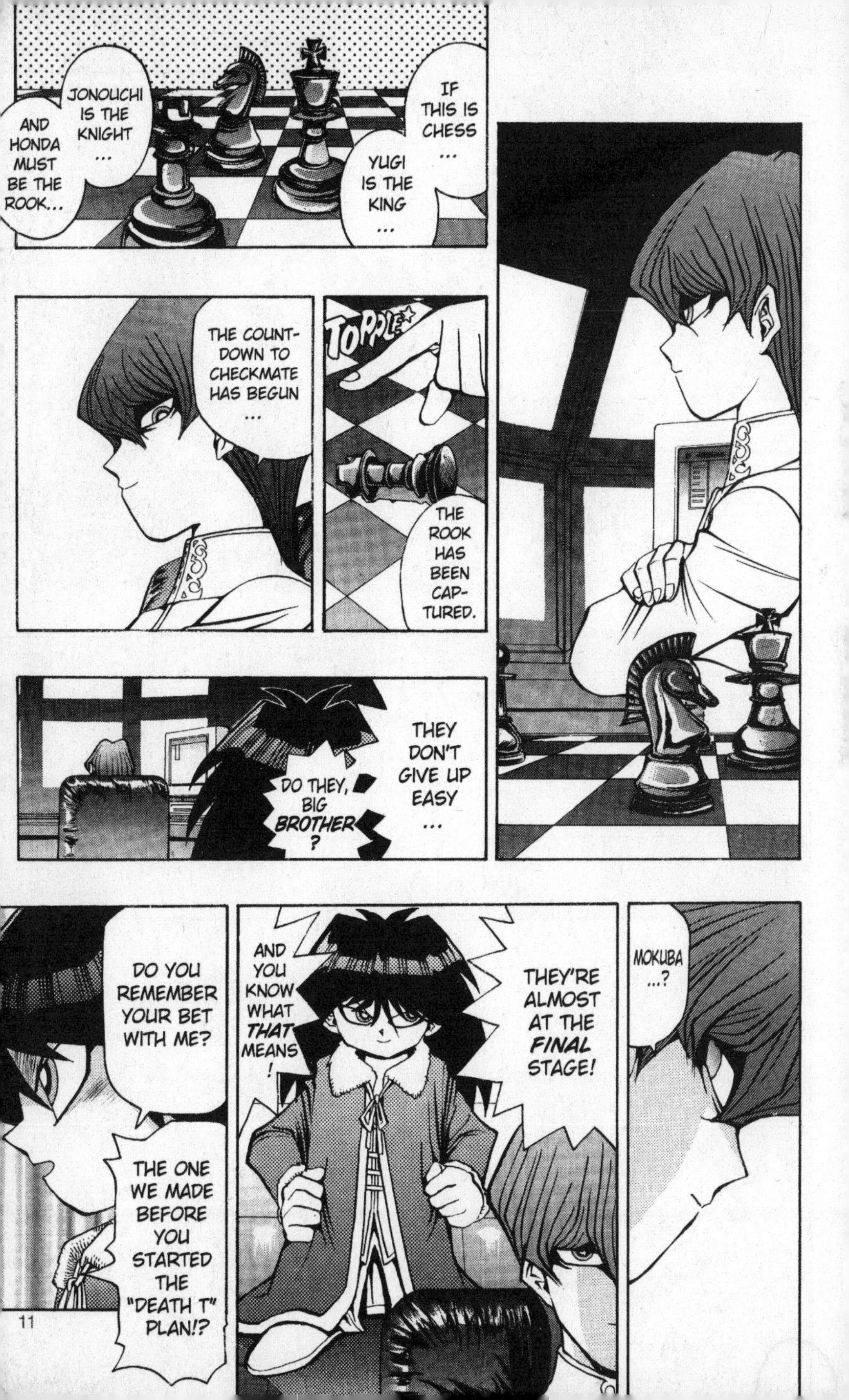
IF THIS IS CHESS ...
YUGI IS THE KING ...
JONOUCHI IS THE KNIGHT ...
AND HONDA MUST BE THE ROOK...
TOPPLE
THE ROOK HAS BEEN CAPTURED.
THE COUNT-DOWN TO CHECKMATE HAS BEGUN ...
THEY DON'T GIVE UP EASY ...
DO THEY, BIG BROTHER?
MOKUBA ...?
THEY'RE ALMOST AT THE FINAL STAGE!
AND YOU KNOW WHAT THAT MEANS!
DO YOU REMEMBER YOUR BET WITH ME?
THE ONE WE MADE BEFORE YOU STARTED THE "DEATH T" PLAN!?

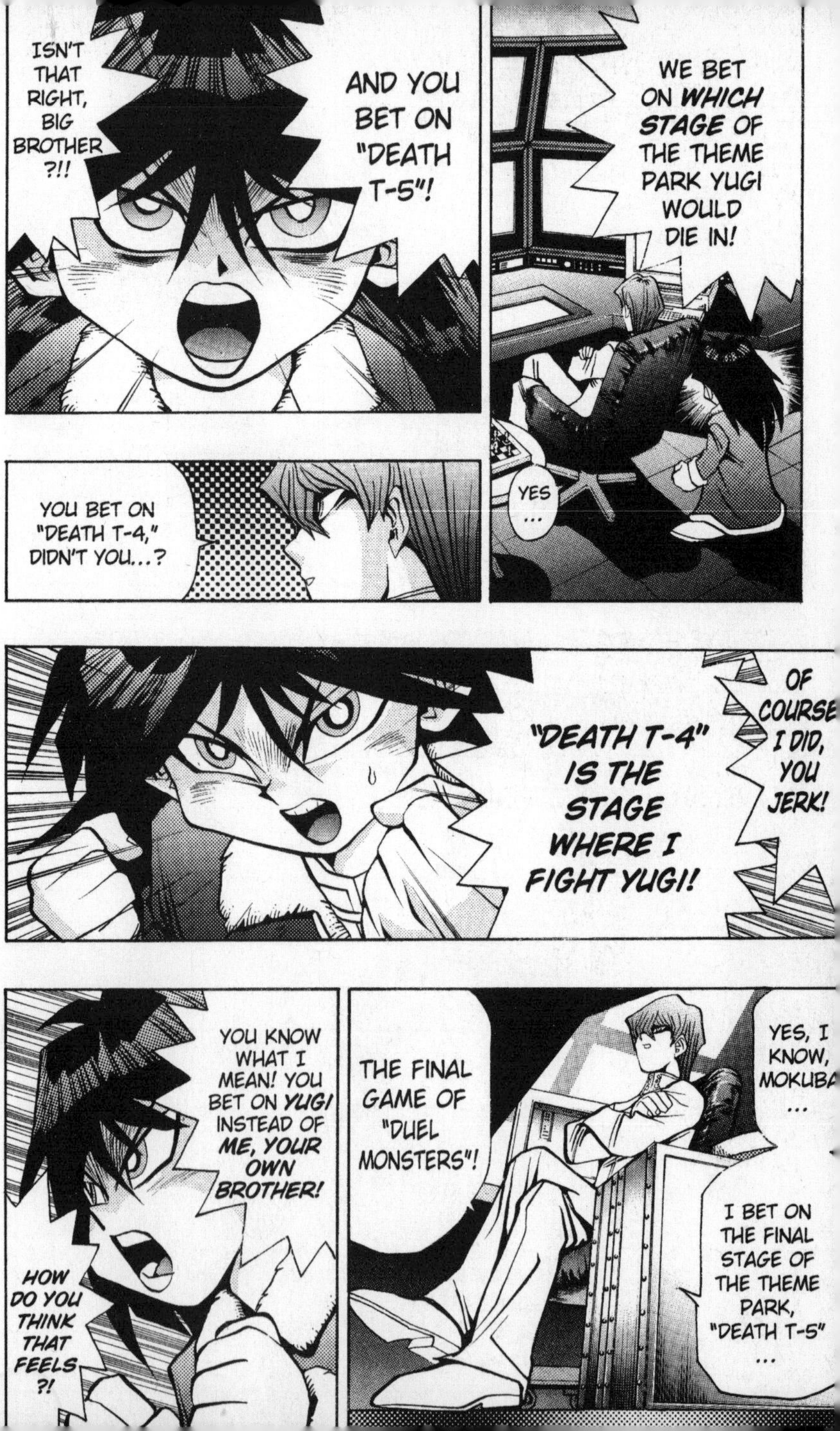
WE BET ON WHICH STAGE OF THE THEME PARK YUGI WOULD DIE IN!
YES ...
AND YOU BET ON "DEATH T-5"!
ISN'T THAT RIGHT, BIG BROTHER?!!
YOU BET ON "DEATH T-4," DIDN'T YOU...?
OF COURSE I DID, YOU JERK!
"DEATH T-4" IS THE STAGE WHERE I FIGHT YUGI!
YES, I KNOW, MOKUBA ...
I BET ON THE FINAL STAGE OF THE THEME PARK, "DEATH T-5" ...
THE FINAL GAME OF "DUEL MONSTERS"!
YOU KNOW WHAT I MEAN! YOU BET ON YUGI INSTEAD OF ME, YOUR OWN BROTHER!
HOW DO YOU THINK THAT FEELS?!

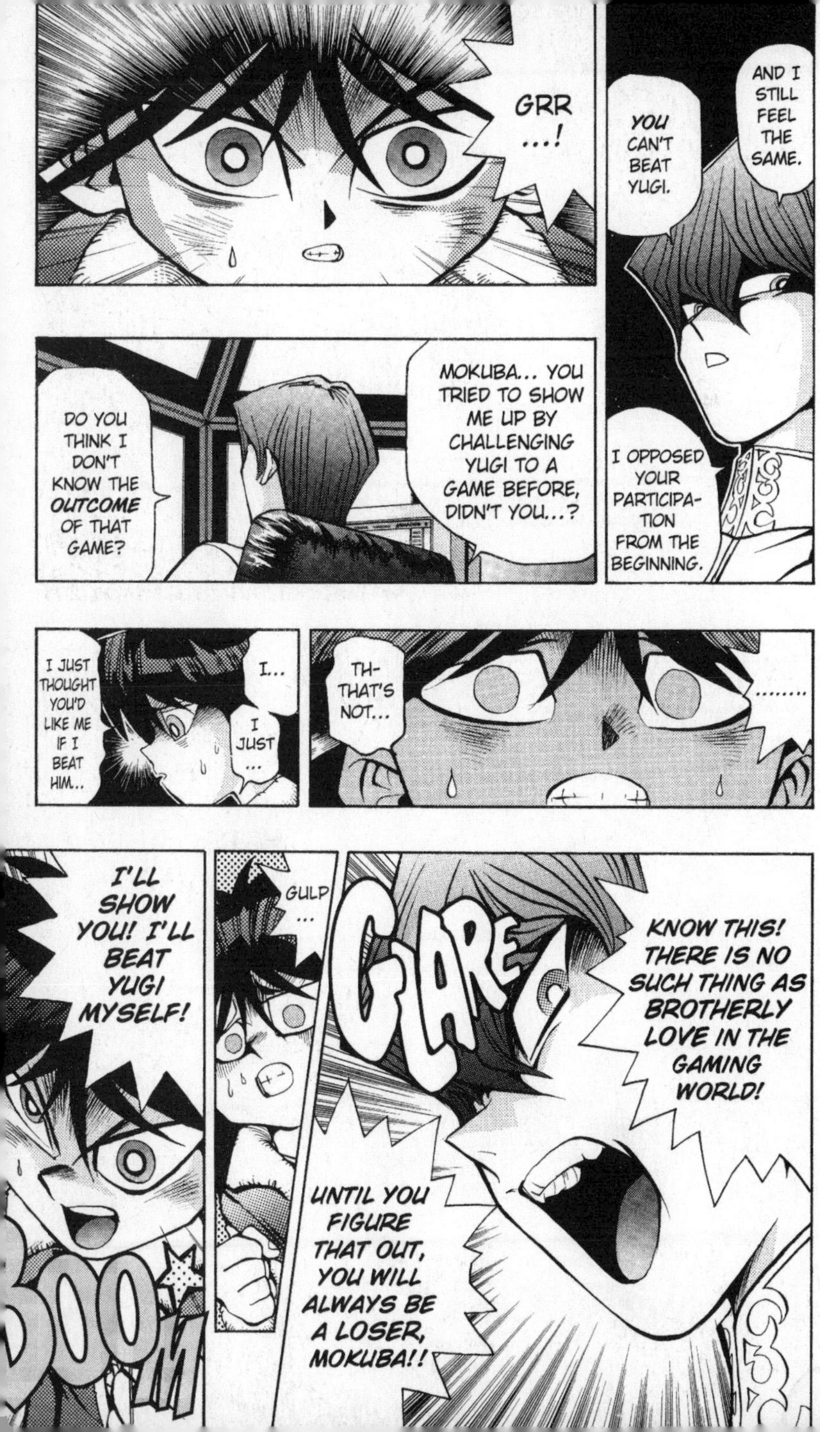
AND I STILL FEEL THE SAME.
YOU CAN'T BEAT YUGI.
I OPPOSED YOUR PARTICIPATION FROM THE BEGINNING.
GRR ...!
MOKUBA... YOU TRIED TO SHOW ME UP BY CHALLENGING YUGI TO A GAME BEFORE, DIDN'T YOU...?
DO YOU THINK I DON'T KNOW THE OUTCOME OF THAT GAME?
....
TH-THAT'S NOT...
I...
I JUST ...
I JUST THOUGHT YOU'D LIKE ME IF I BEAT HIM..
GLARE
KNOW THIS! THERE IS NO SUCH THING AS BROTHERLY LOVE IN THE GAMING WORLD!
UNTIL YOU FIGURE THAT OUT, YOU WILL ALWAYS BE A LOSER, MOKUBA!!
GULP ...
I'LL SHOW YOU! I'LL BEAT YUGI MYSELF!
BOOM

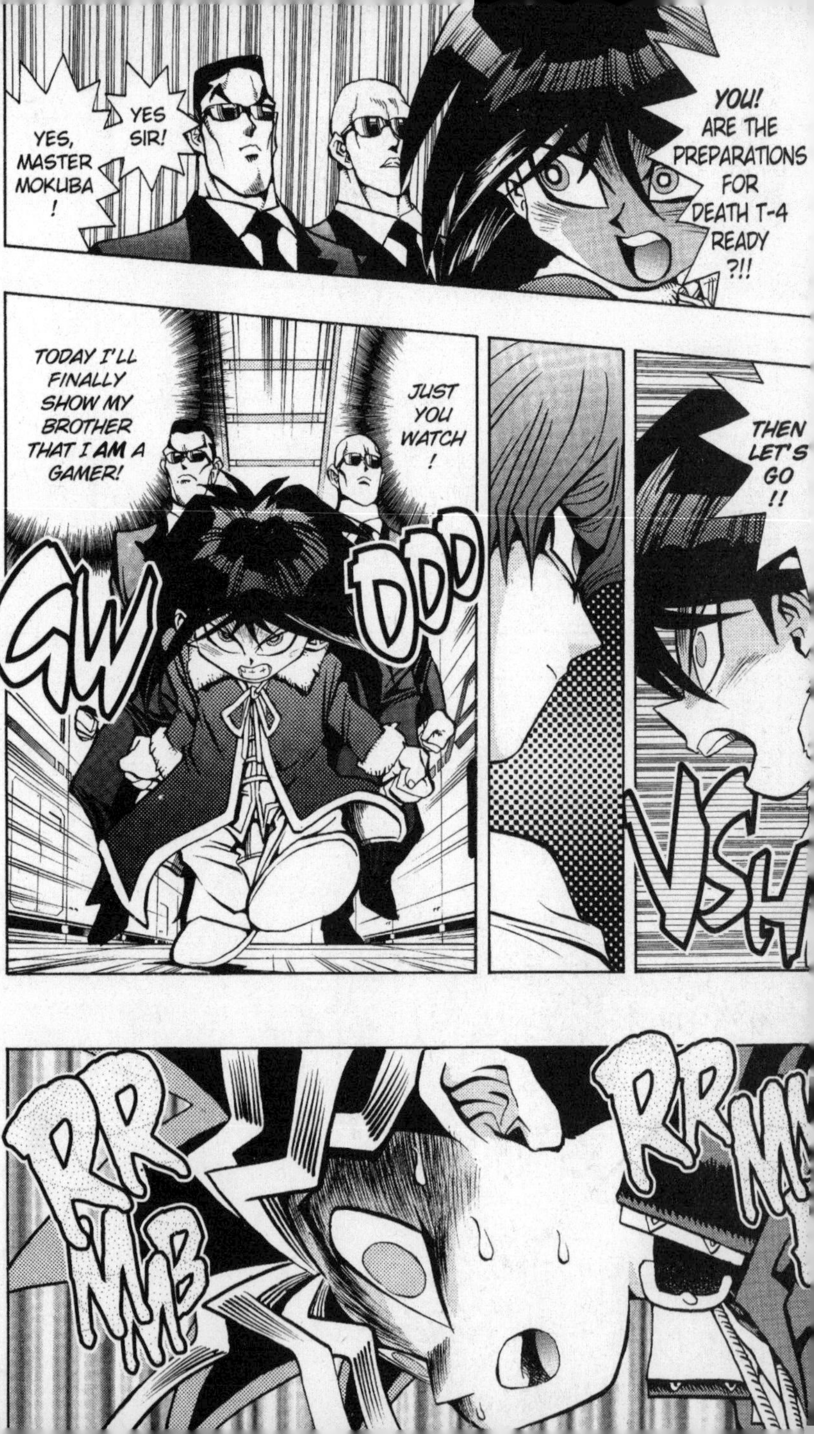
YOU! ARE THE PREPARATIONS FOR DEATH T-4 READY ?!!
YES SIR!
YES, MASTER MOKUBA !
THEN LET'S GO !!
VSH
JUST YOU WATCH !
TODAY I'LL FINALLY SHOW MY BROTHER THAT I **AM** A GAMER!
DDD
GW
RRMM
RRMMB

READ THIS WAY

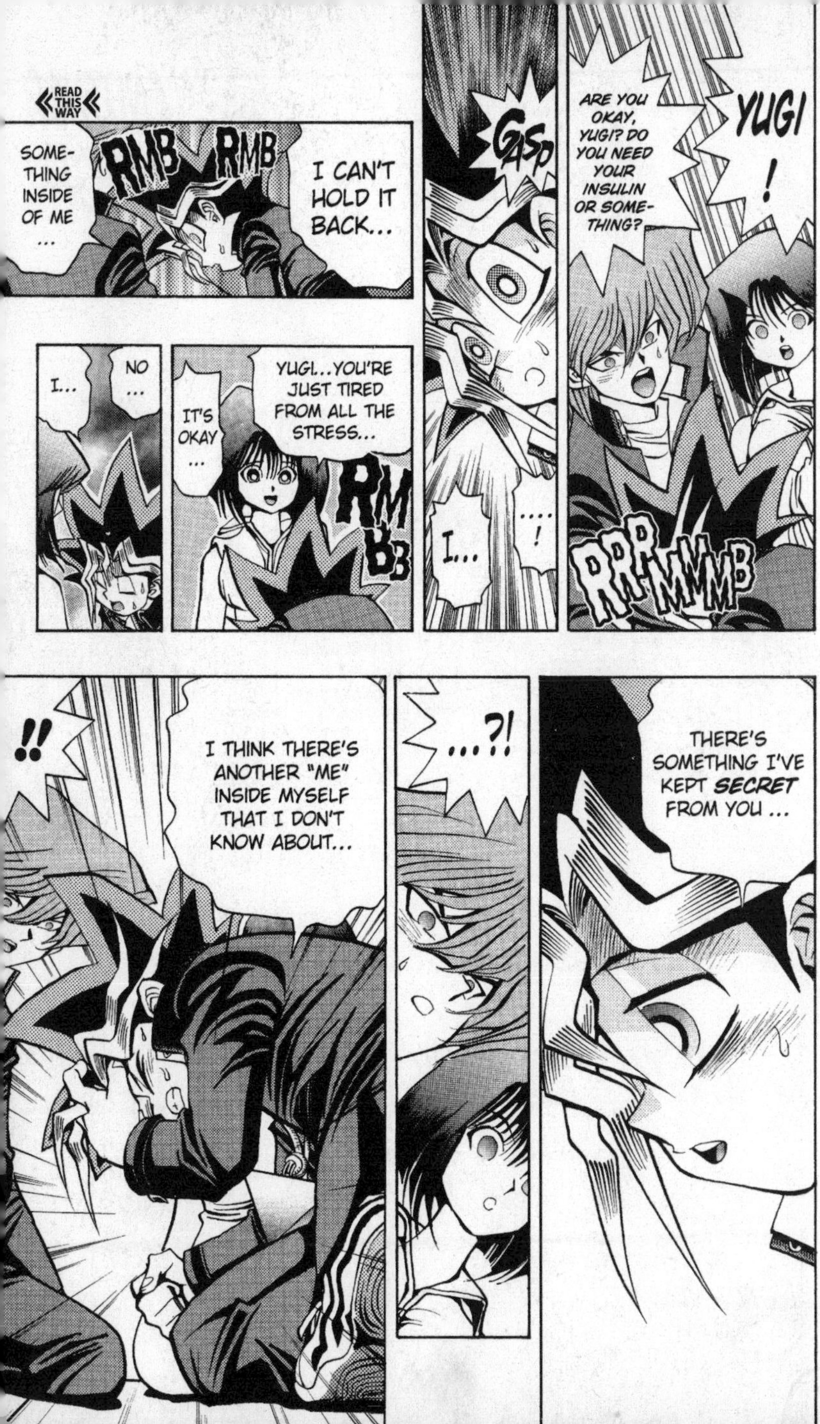
YUGI!
ARE YOU OKAY, YUGI? DO YOU NEED YOUR INSULIN OR SOMETHING?
RRRMMMB
GASP
....!
I...
I CAN'T HOLD IT BACK...
RMB RMB
SOME-THING INSIDE OF ME ...
YUGI...YOU'RE JUST TIRED FROM ALL THE STRESS...
IT'S OKAY ...
RMBB
NO ...
I...
THERE'S SOMETHING I'VE KEPT *SECRET* FROM YOU ...
...?!
I THINK THERE'S ANOTHER "ME" INSIDE MYSELF THAT I DON'T KNOW ABOUT...
!!

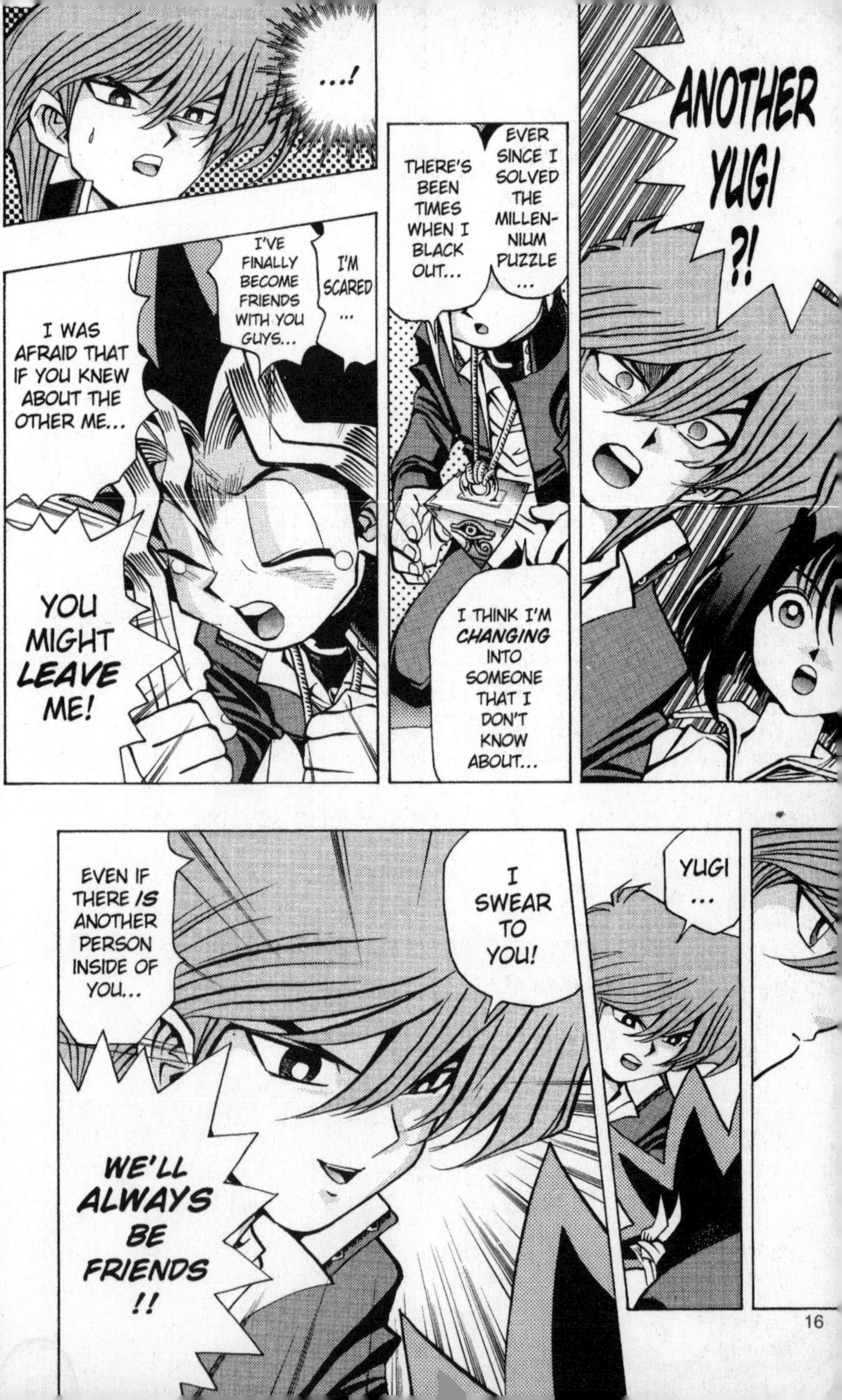
EVER SINCE I SOLVED THE MILLENNIUM PUZZLE...
THERE'S BEEN TIMES WHEN I BLACK OUT...
I THINK I'M *CHANGING* INTO SOMEONE THAT I DON'T KNOW ABOUT...
ANOTHER YUGI ?!
...!
I'M SCARED...
I'VE FINALLY BECOME FRIENDS WITH YOU GUYS...
I WAS AFRAID THAT IF YOU KNEW ABOUT THE OTHER ME...
YOU MIGHT *LEAVE* ME!
YUGI...
I SWEAR TO YOU!
EVEN IF THERE *IS* ANOTHER PERSON INSIDE OF YOU...
WE'LL ALWAYS BE FRIENDS !!

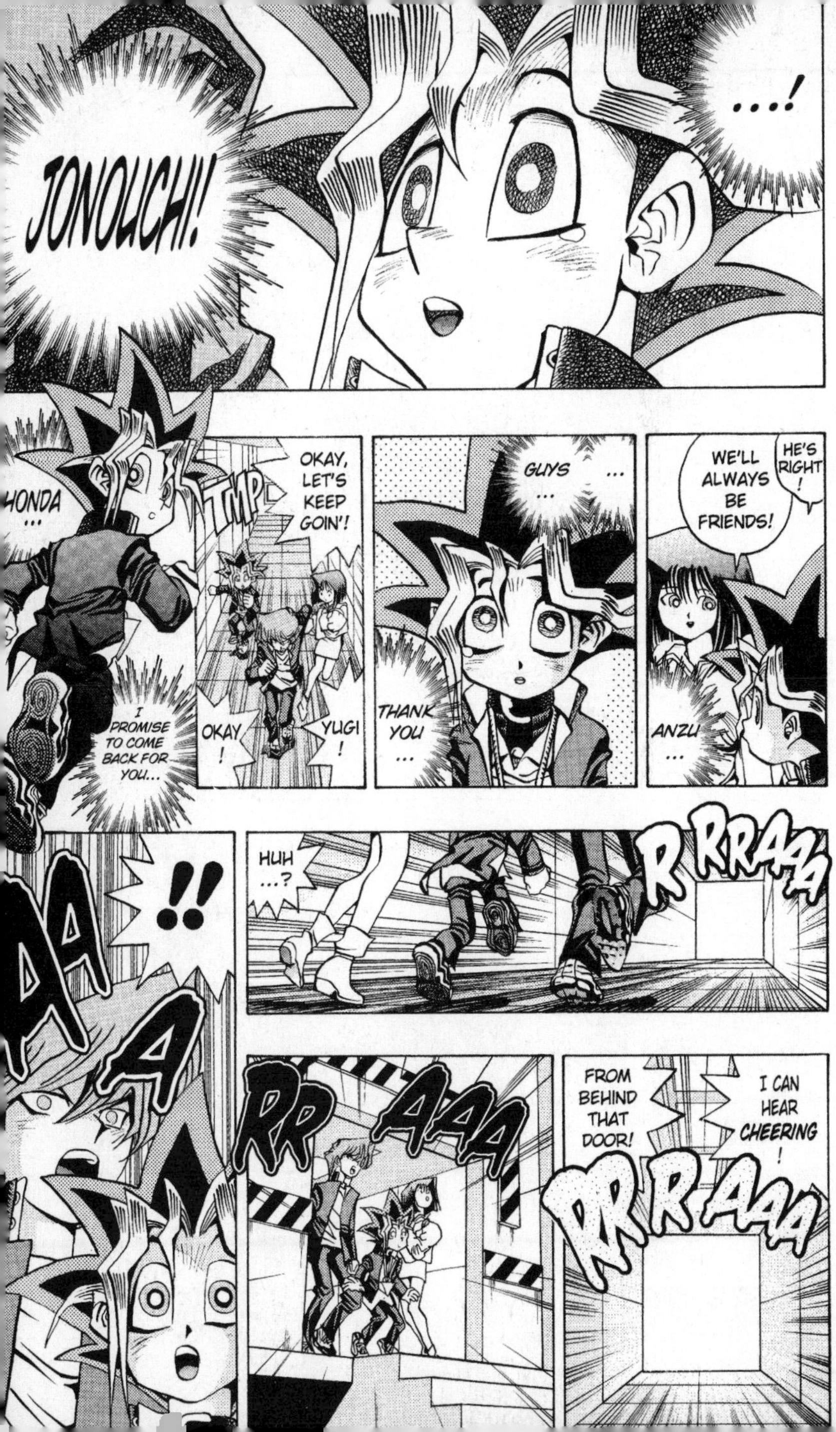
...!
JONOUCHI!
HE'S RIGHT!
WE'LL ALWAYS BE FRIENDS!
ANZU...
GUYS... ...
THANK YOU...
OKAY, LET'S KEEP GOIN'!
TMP
YUGI!
OKAY!
HONDA...
I PROMISE TO COME BACK FOR YOU...
RRRAAA
HUH...?
I CAN HEAR CHEERING!
FROM BEHIND THAT DOOR!
RRRAAA
RRAAA
!!
AAA

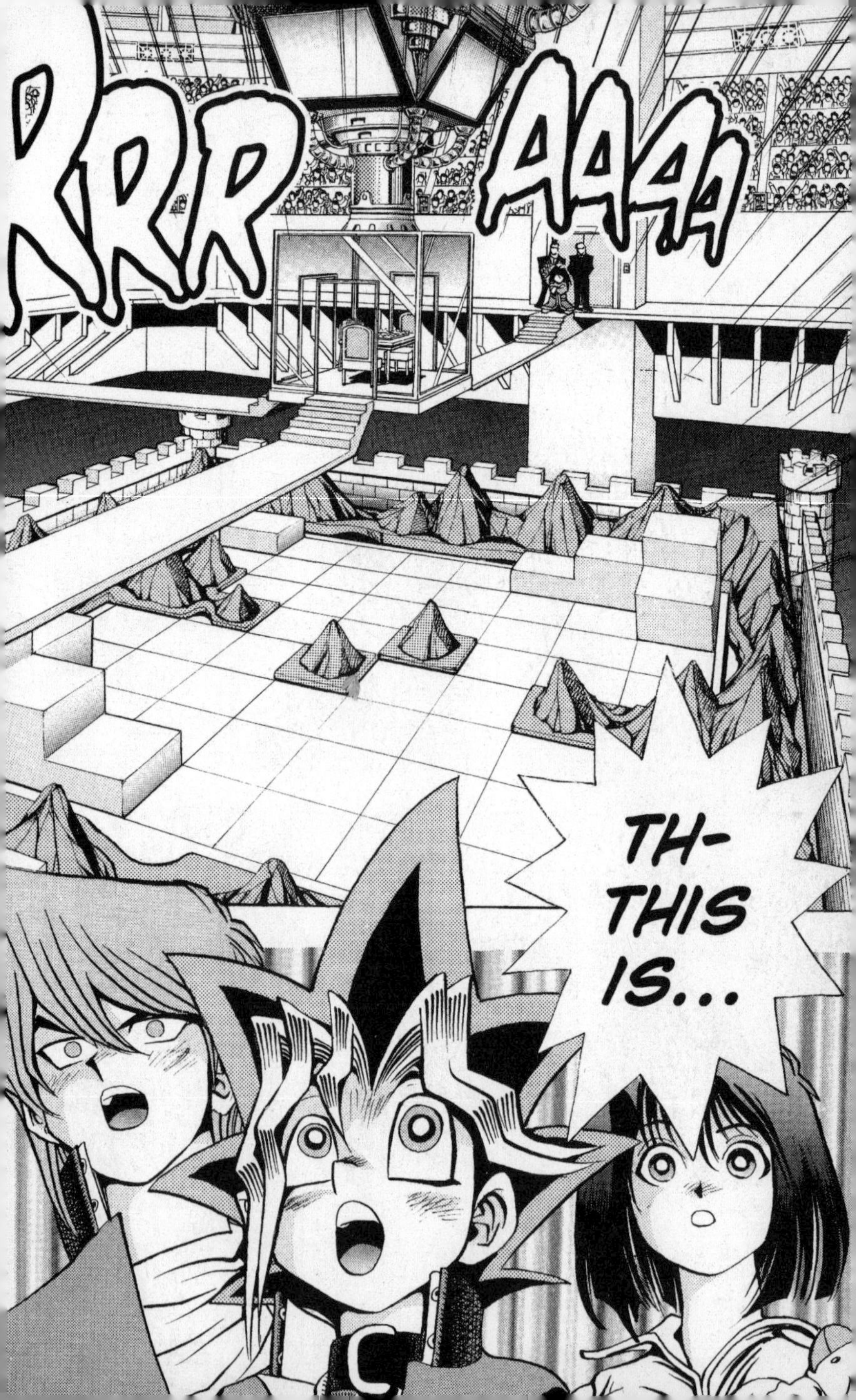
RRR AAAA
TH-
THIS
IS...

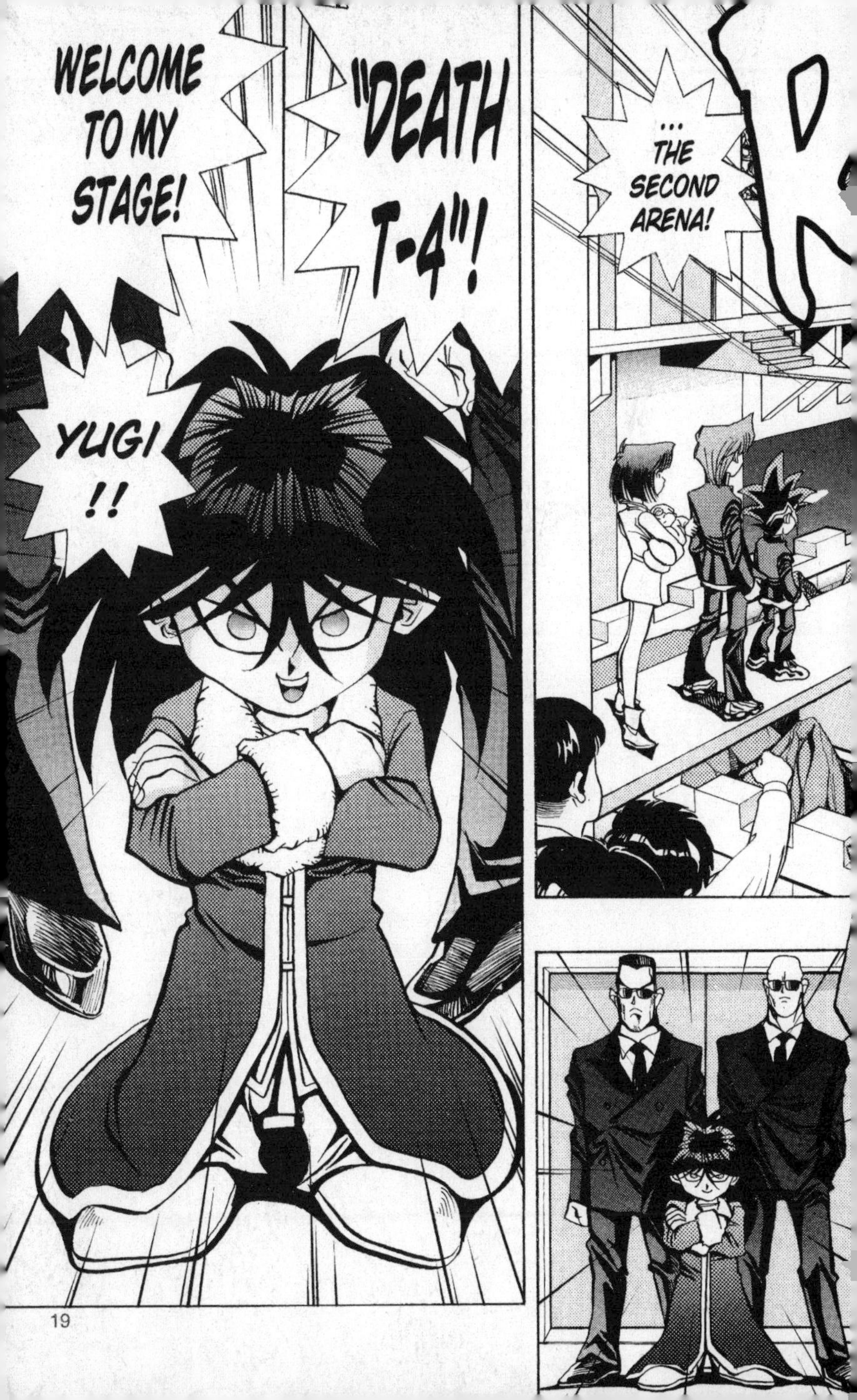
... THE SECOND ARENA!
"DEATH T-4"!
WELCOME TO MY STAGE!
YUGI !!

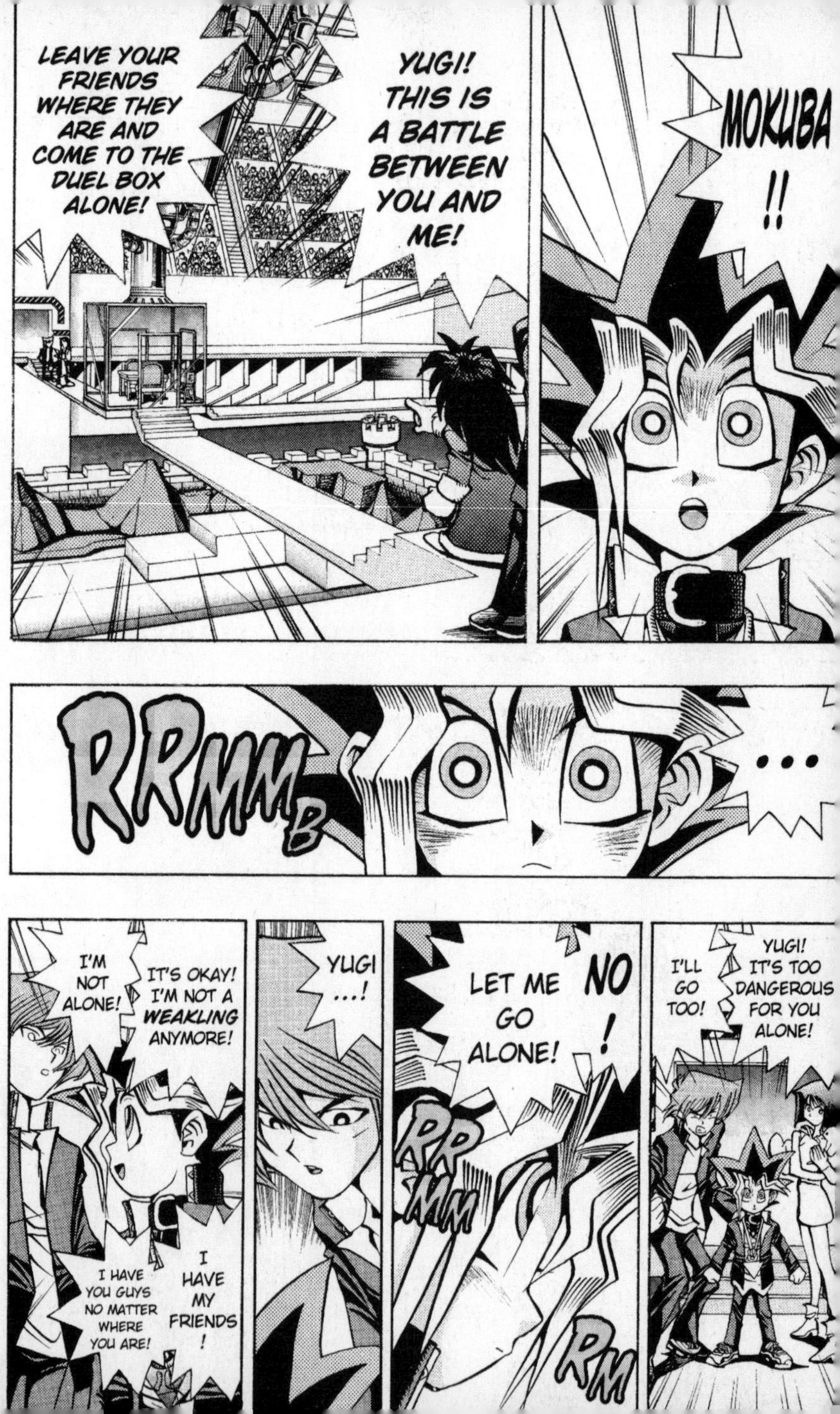
MOKUBA !!
YUGI! THIS IS A BATTLE BETWEEN YOU AND ME!
LEAVE YOUR FRIENDS WHERE THEY ARE AND COME TO THE DUEL BOX ALONE!
...
RRMMB
YUGI! IT'S TOO DANGEROUS FOR YOU ALONE!
I'LL GO TOO!
NO!
LET ME GO ALONE!
RRMM
RM
YUGI ...!
IT'S OKAY! I'M NOT A WEAKLING ANYMORE!
I'M NOT ALONE!
I HAVE MY FRIENDS!
I HAVE YOU GUYS NO MATTER WHERE YOU ARE!

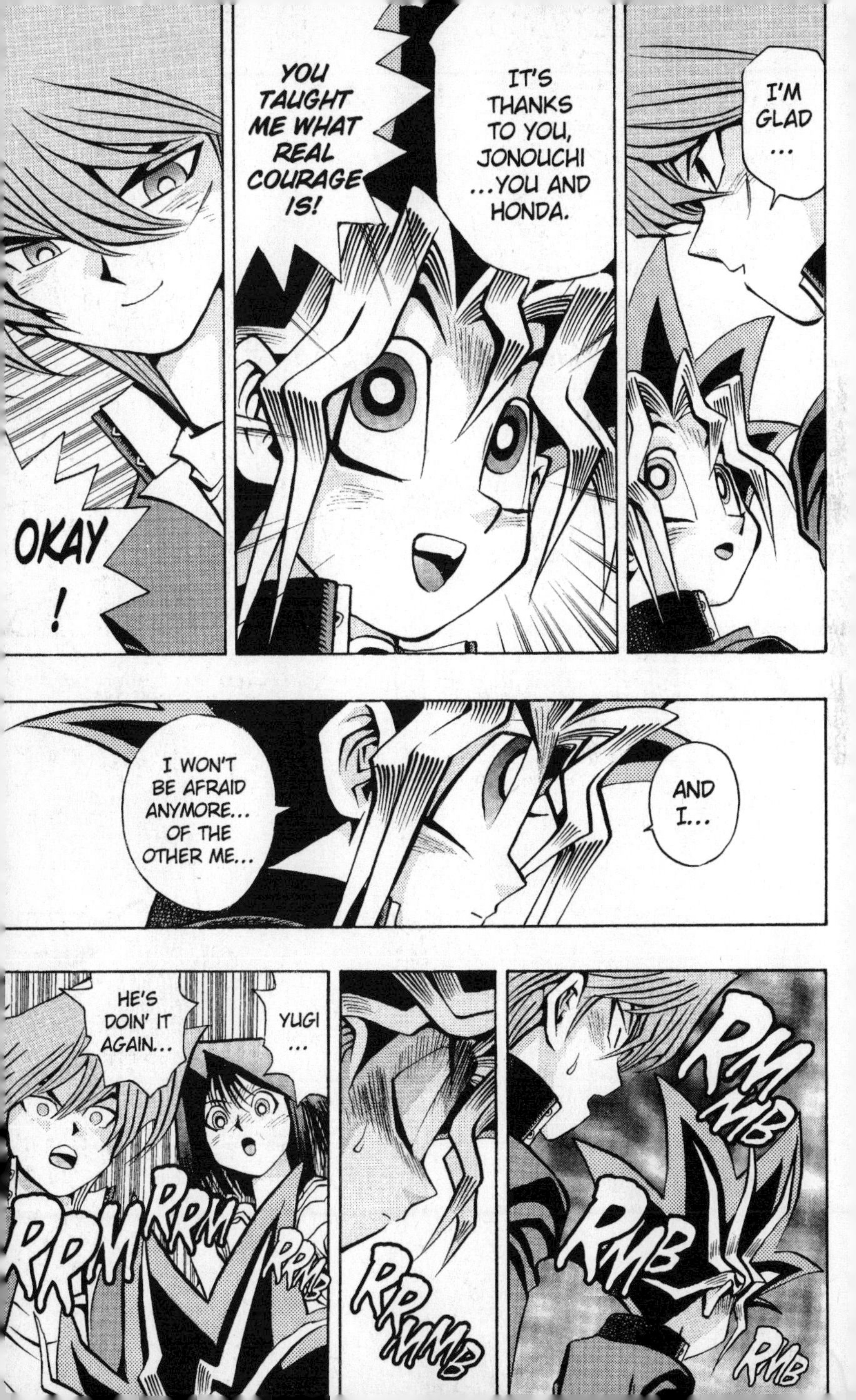
I'M GLAD ...
IT'S THANKS TO YOU, JONOUCHI ...YOU AND HONDA.
YOU TAUGHT ME WHAT REAL COURAGE IS!
OKAY !
AND I...
I WON'T BE AFRAID ANYMORE... OF THE OTHER ME...
YUGI ...
HE'S DOIN' IT AGAIN...

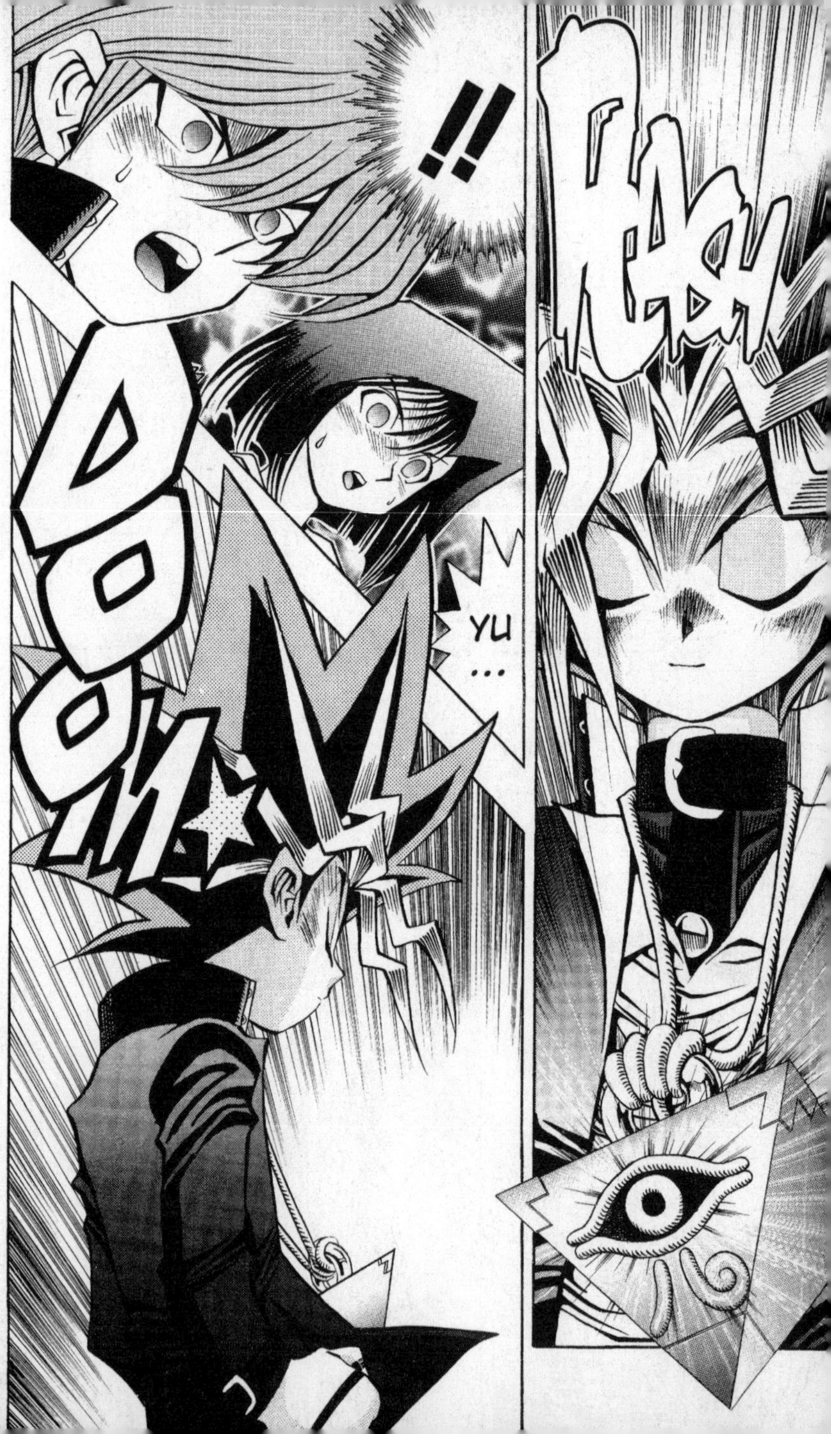
FLASH
!!
DOOM
YU ...

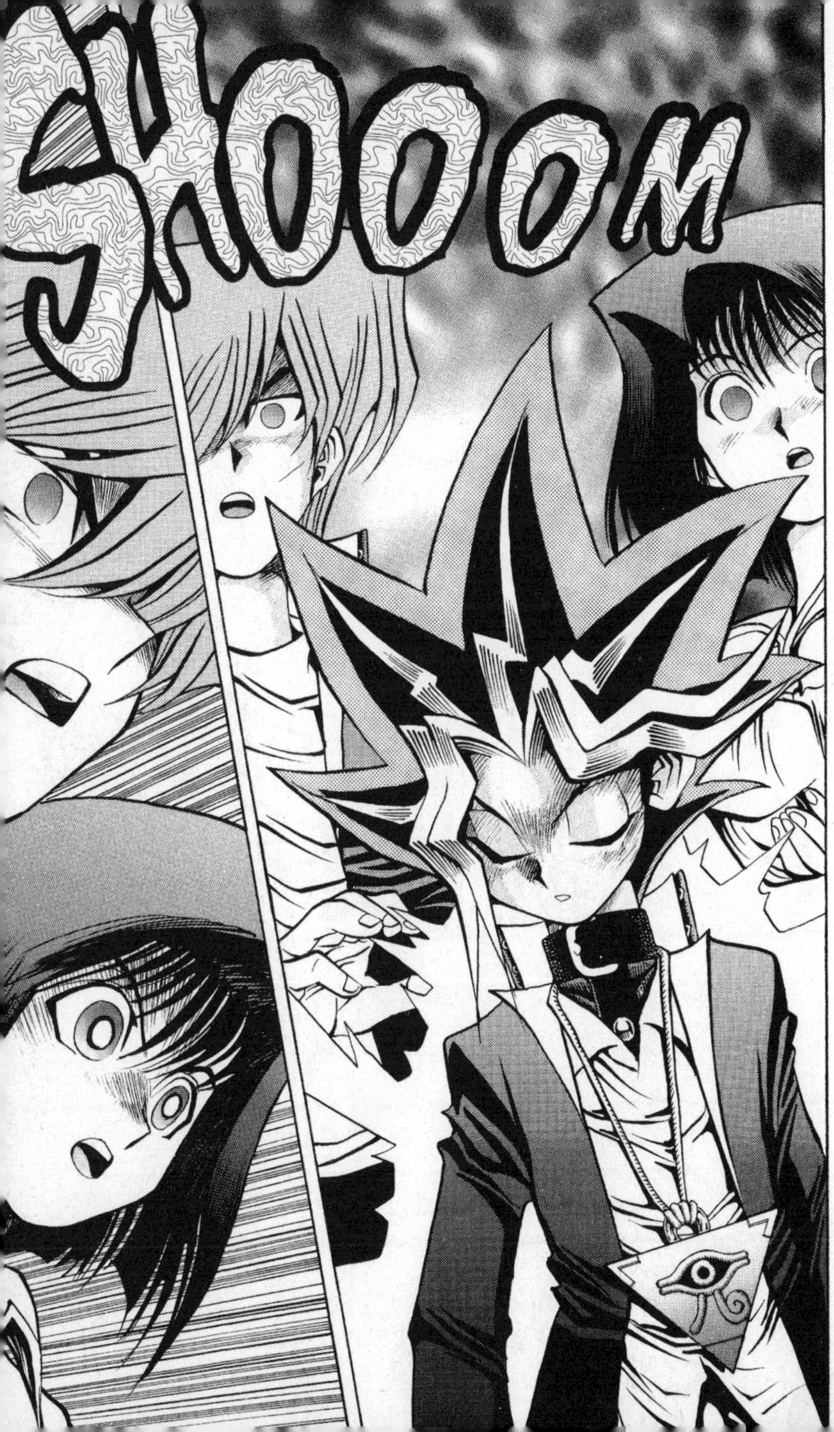
SHOOOM

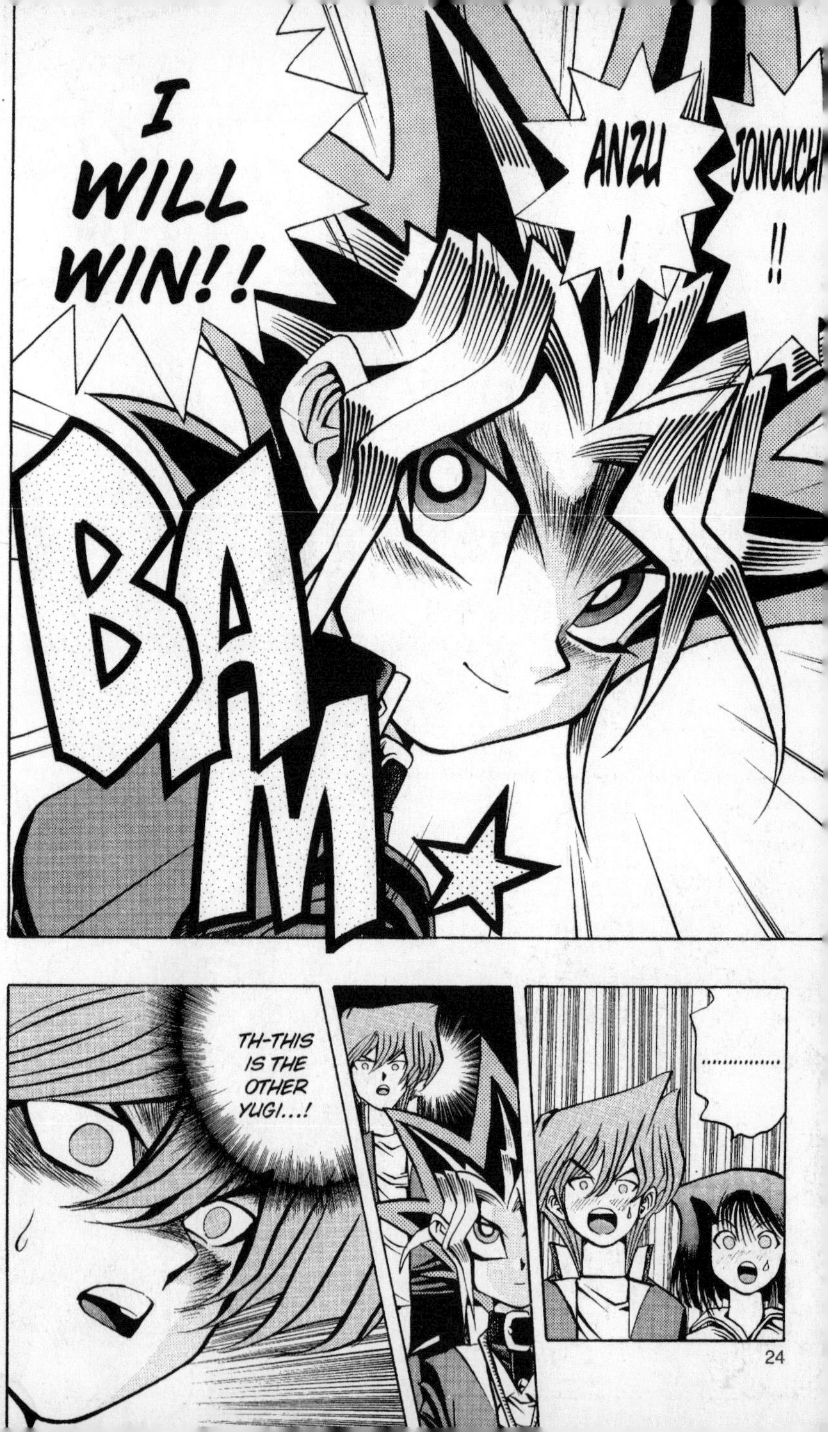
JONOUCHI !!
ANZU !
I WILL WIN!!
BAM
....
TH-THIS IS THE OTHER YUGI...!

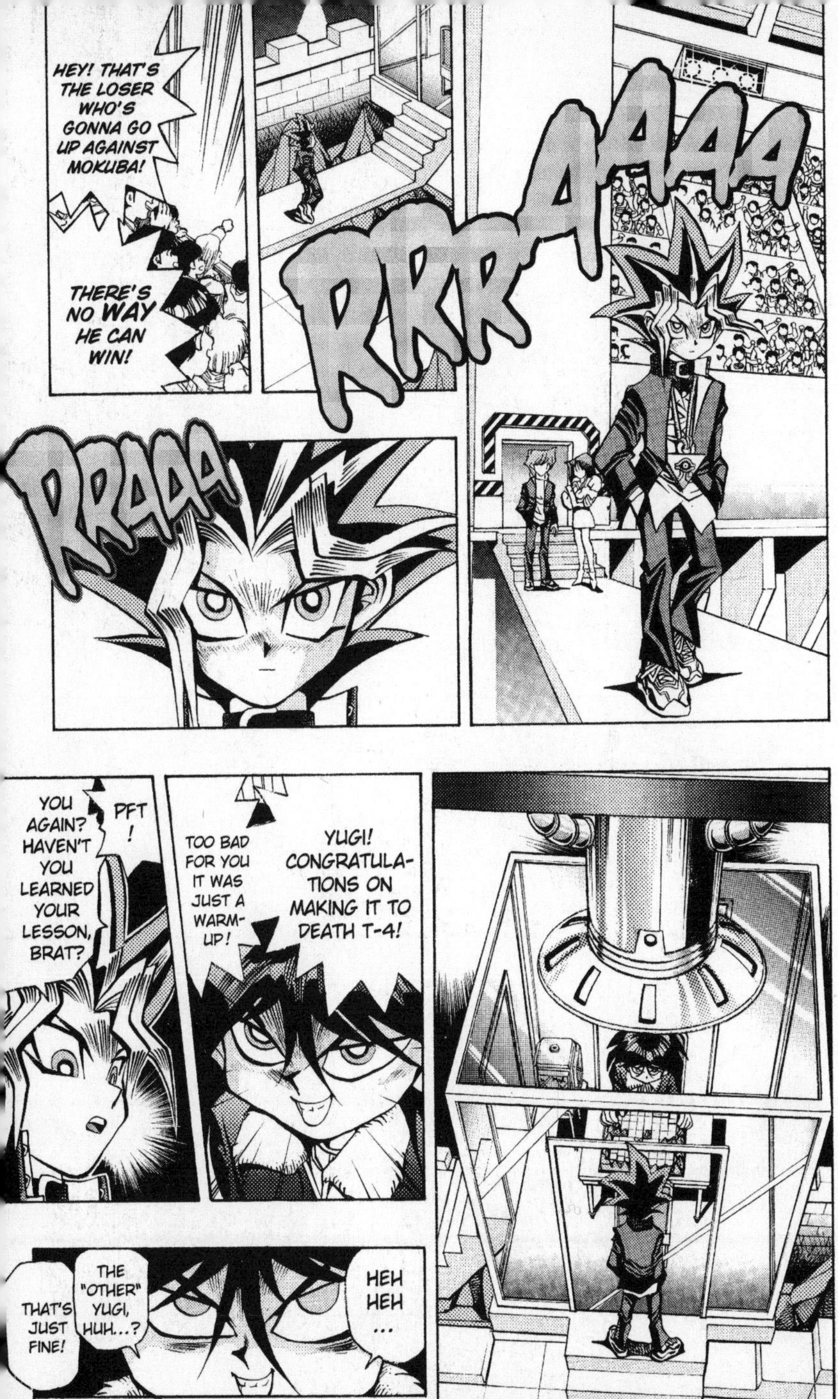
RRRAAAA
HEY! THAT'S THE LOSER WHO'S GONNA GO UP AGAINST MOKUBA!
THERE'S NO WAY HE CAN WIN!
RRAAA
YUGI! CONGRATULATIONS ON MAKING IT TO DEATH T-4!
TOO BAD FOR YOU IT WAS JUST A WARM-UP!
PFT!
YOU AGAIN? HAVEN'T YOU LEARNED YOUR LESSON, BRAT?
HEH HEH...
THE "OTHER" YUGI, HUH...?
THAT'S JUST FINE!

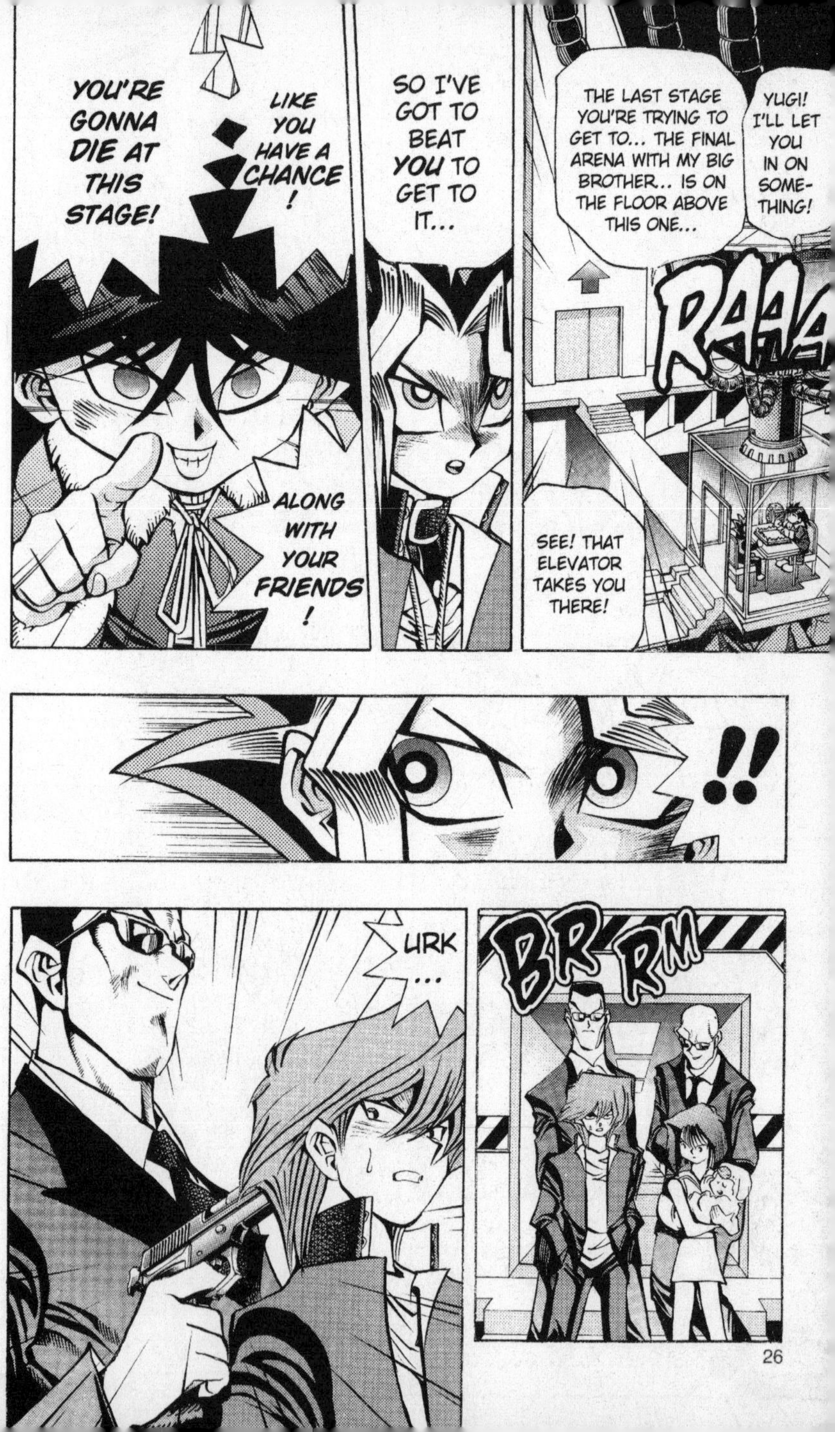
YUGI! I'LL LET YOU IN ON SOME-THING!
THE LAST STAGE YOU'RE TRYING TO GET TO... THE FINAL ARENA WITH MY BIG BROTHER... IS ON THE FLOOR ABOVE THIS ONE...
RAAA
SEE! THAT ELEVATOR TAKES YOU THERE!
SO I'VE GOT TO BEAT YOU TO GET TO IT...
LIKE YOU HAVE A CHANCE!
YOU'RE GONNA DIE AT THIS STAGE!
ALONG WITH YOUR FRIENDS!
!!
BR RM
URK...

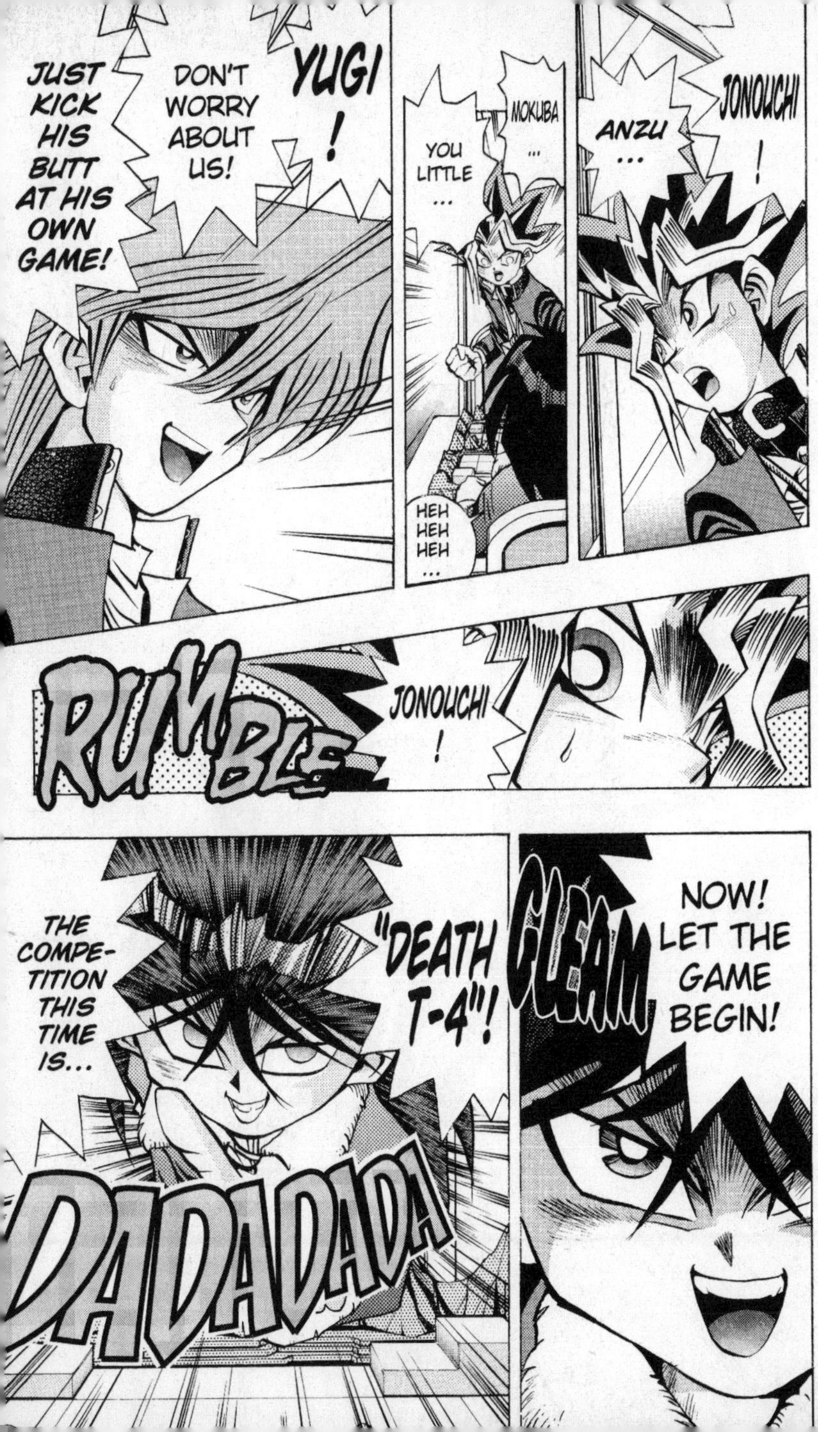
JONOUCHI!
ANZU...
MOKUBA...
YOU LITTLE...
HEH HEH HEH...
YUGI!
DON'T WORRY ABOUT US!
JUST KICK HIS BUTT AT HIS OWN GAME!
JONOUCHI!
RUMBLE
NOW! LET THE GAME BEGIN!
GLEAM
THE COMPETITION THIS TIME IS...
"DEATH T-4"!
DADADADA

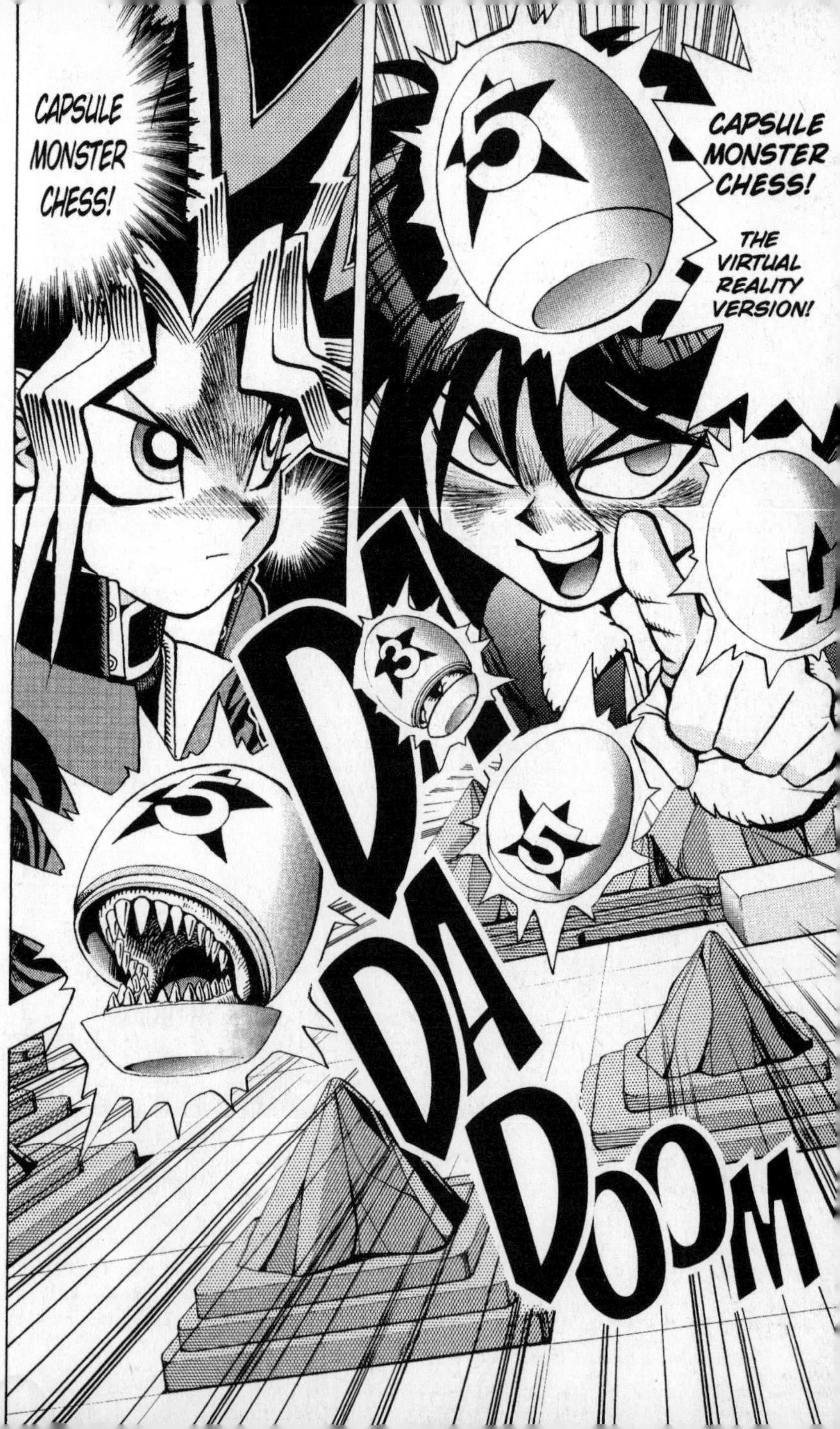
CAPSULE MONSTER CHESS!
THE VIRTUAL REALITY VERSION!
CAPSULE MONSTER CHESS!
D DA DOOM

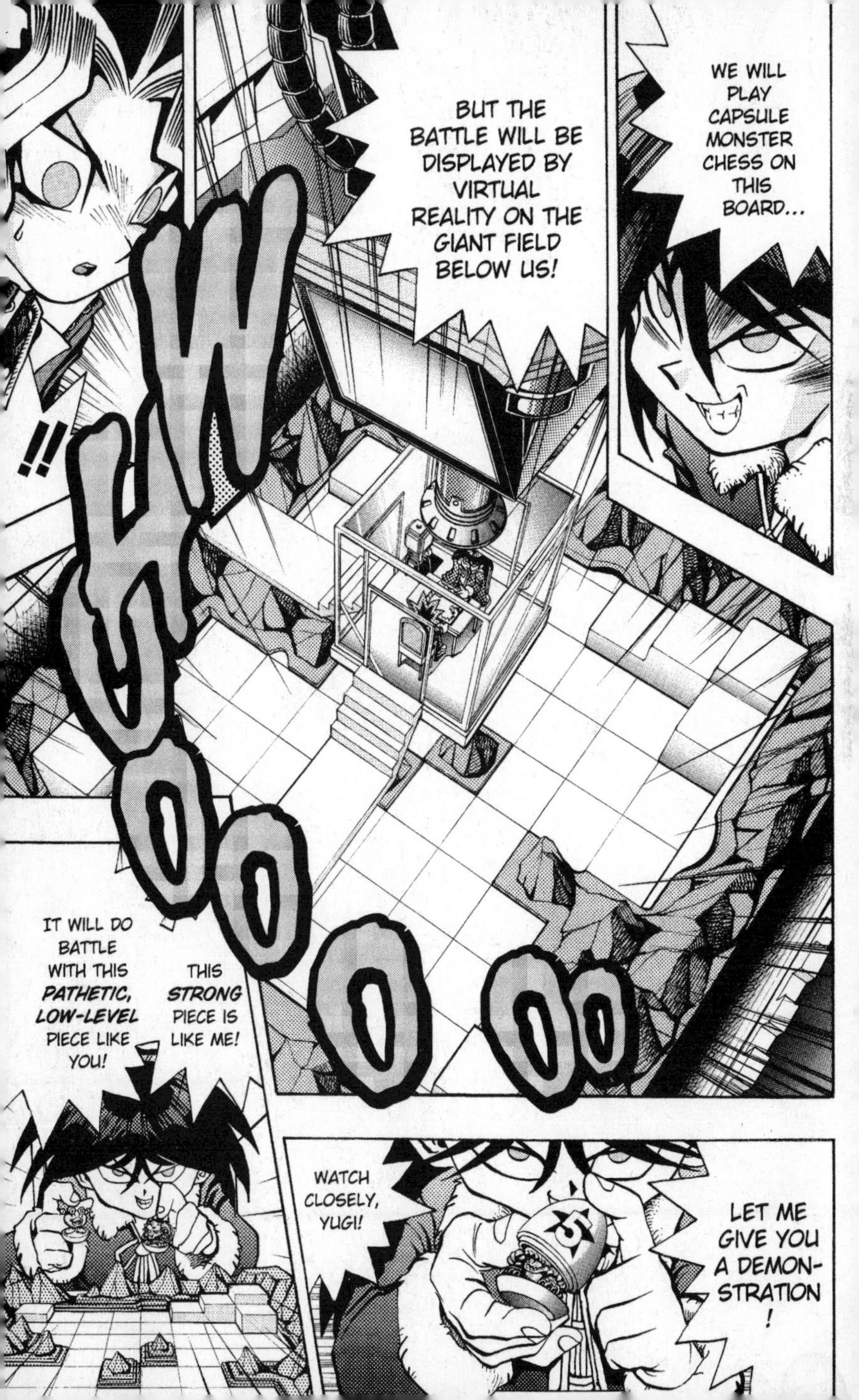
WE WILL PLAY CAPSULE MONSTER CHESS ON THIS BOARD...
BUT THE BATTLE WILL BE DISPLAYED BY VIRTUAL REALITY ON THE GIANT FIELD BELOW US!
!!
LET ME GIVE YOU A DEMON-STRATION!
WATCH CLOSELY, YUGI!
THIS *STRONG* PIECE IS LIKE ME!
IT WILL DO BATTLE WITH THIS *PATHETIC, LOW-LEVEL* PIECE LIKE YOU!

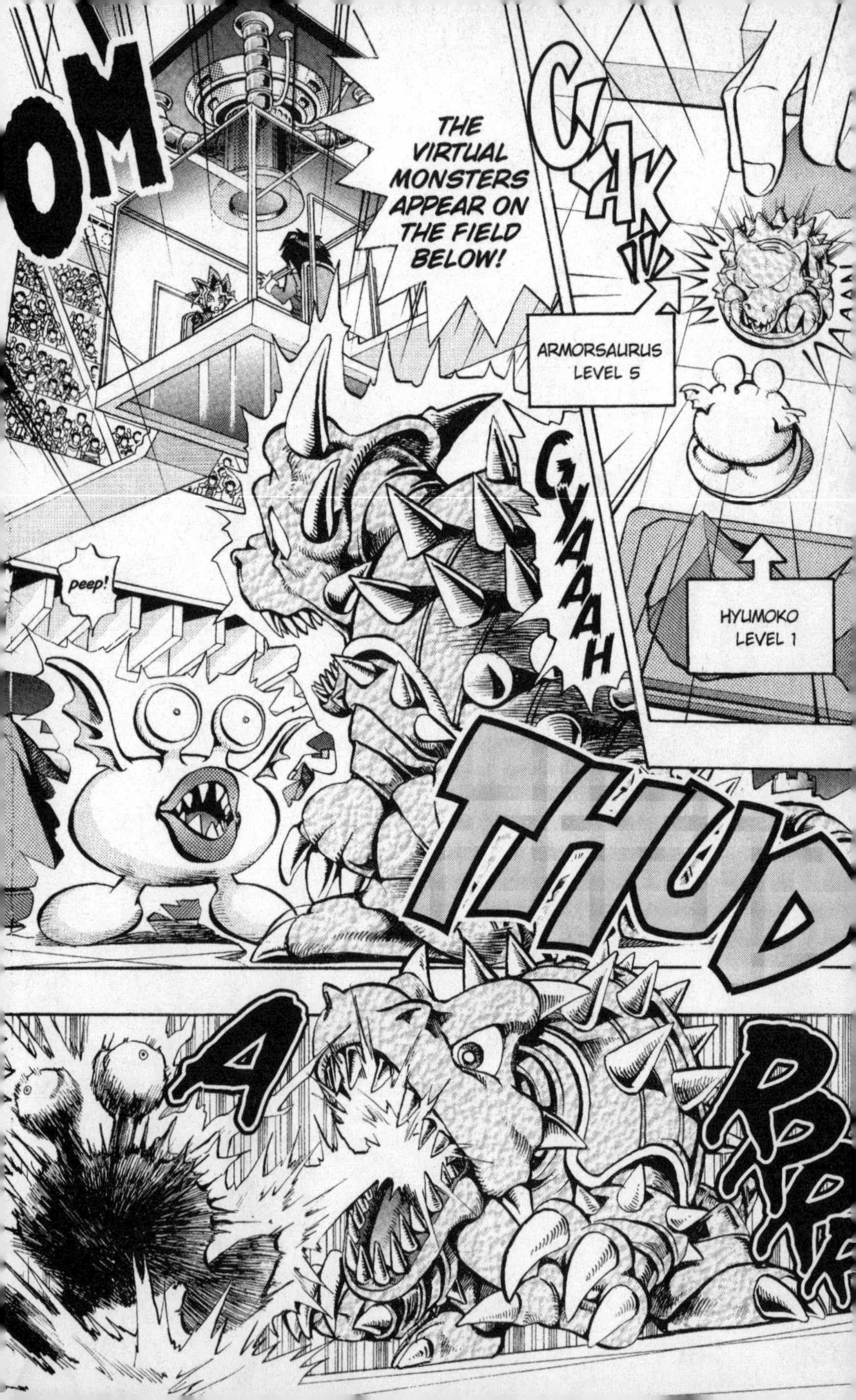
CLAK
ARMORSAURUS
LEVEL 5
HYUMOKO
LEVEL 1
OM
THE VIRTUAL MONSTERS APPEAR ON THE FIELD BELOW!
GYAAAH
peep!
THUD

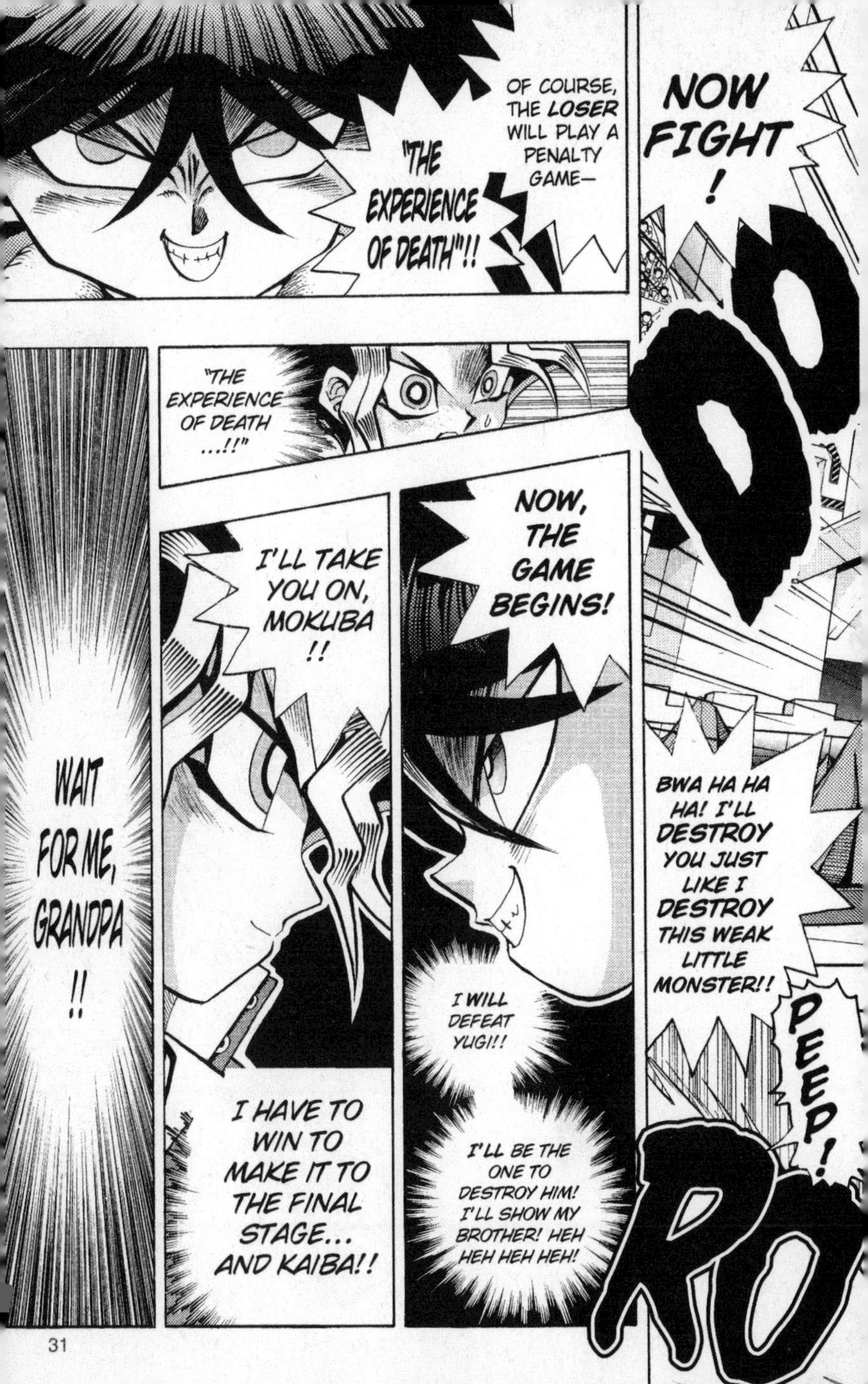
NOW FIGHT!
DO
BWA HA HA HA! I'LL DESTROY YOU JUST LIKE I DESTROY THIS WEAK LITTLE MONSTER!!
PEEP!
RO
OF COURSE, THE LOSER WILL PLAY A PENALTY GAME—
"THE EXPERIENCE OF DEATH"!!
"THE EXPERIENCE OF DEATH ...!!"
NOW, THE GAME BEGINS!
I WILL DEFEAT YUGI!!
I'LL BE THE ONE TO DESTROY HIM! I'LL SHOW MY BROTHER! HEH HEH HEH HEH!
I'LL TAKE YOU ON, MOKUBA!!
I HAVE TO WIN TO MAKE IT TO THE FINAL STAGE... AND KAIBA!!
WAIT FOR ME, GRANDPA!!

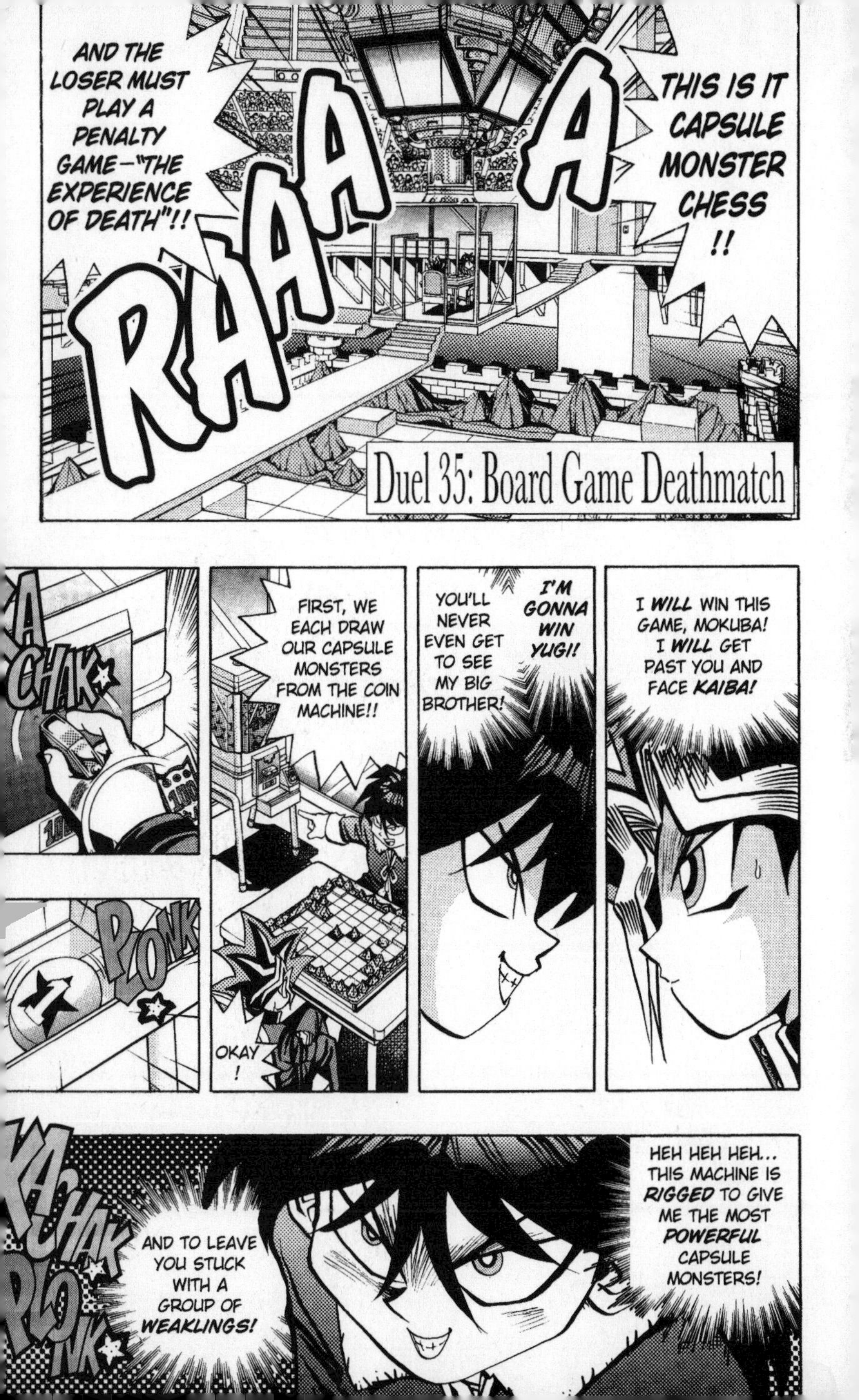
THIS IS IT CAPSULE MONSTER CHESS !!
RAAAA
AND THE LOSER MUST PLAY A PENALTY GAME—"THE EXPERIENCE OF DEATH"!!
Duel 35: Board Game Deathmatch
I WILL WIN THIS GAME, MOKUBA! I WILL GET PAST YOU AND FACE KAIBA!
I'M GONNA WIN YUGI!
YOU'LL NEVER EVEN GET TO SEE MY BIG BROTHER!
FIRST, WE EACH DRAW OUR CAPSULE MONSTERS FROM THE COIN MACHINE!!
OKAY!
KACHAK
PLONK
HEH HEH HEH... THIS MACHINE IS RIGGED TO GIVE ME THE MOST POWERFUL CAPSULE MONSTERS!
AND TO LEAVE YOU STUCK WITH A GROUP OF WEAKLINGS!
KACHAK
PLONK

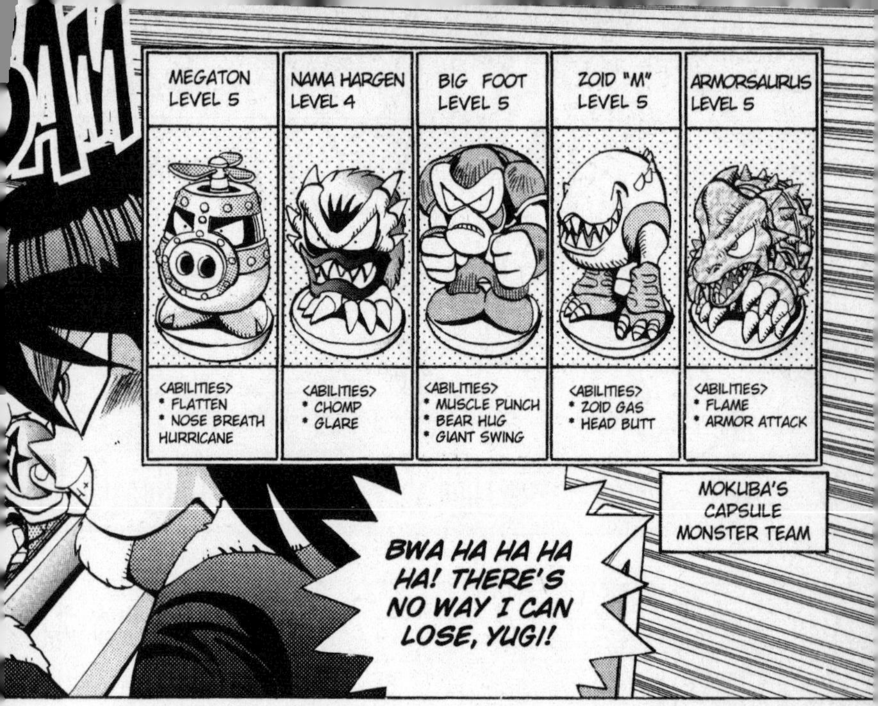
MEGATON LEVEL 5
<ABILITIES> * FLATTEN * NOSE BREATH HURRICANE
NAMA HARGEN LEVEL 4
<ABILITIES> * CHOMP * GLARE
BIG FOOT LEVEL 5
<ABILITIES> * MUSCLE PUNCH * BEAR HUG * GIANT SWING
ZOID "M" LEVEL 5
<ABILITIES> * ZOID GAS * HEAD BUTT
ARMORSAURUS LEVEL 5
<ABILITIES> * FLAME * ARMOR ATTACK
MOKUBA'S CAPSULE MONSTER TEAM
BWA HA HA HA HA! THERE'S NO WAY I CAN LOSE, YUGI!
BAM

Duel 35: Board Game Deathmatch

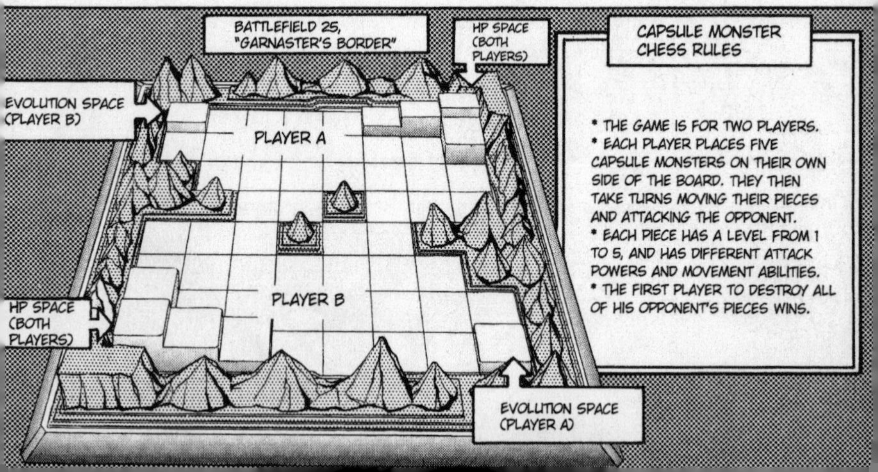
CAPSULE MONSTER CHESS RULES
* THE GAME IS FOR TWO PLAYERS.
* EACH PLAYER PLACES FIVE CAPSULE MONSTERS ON THEIR OWN SIDE OF THE BOARD. THEY THEN TAKE TURNS MOVING THEIR PIECES AND ATTACKING THE OPPONENT.
* EACH PIECE HAS A LEVEL FROM 1 TO 5, AND HAS DIFFERENT ATTACK POWERS AND MOVEMENT ABILITIES.
* THE FIRST PLAYER TO DESTROY ALL OF HIS OPPONENT'S PIECES WINS.
HP SPACE (BOTH PLAYERS)
BATTLEFIELD 25, "GARNASTER'S BORDER"
EVOLUTION SPACE (PLAYER B)
PLAYER A
PLAYER B
HP SPACE (BOTH PLAYERS)
EVOLUTION SPACE (PLAYER A)

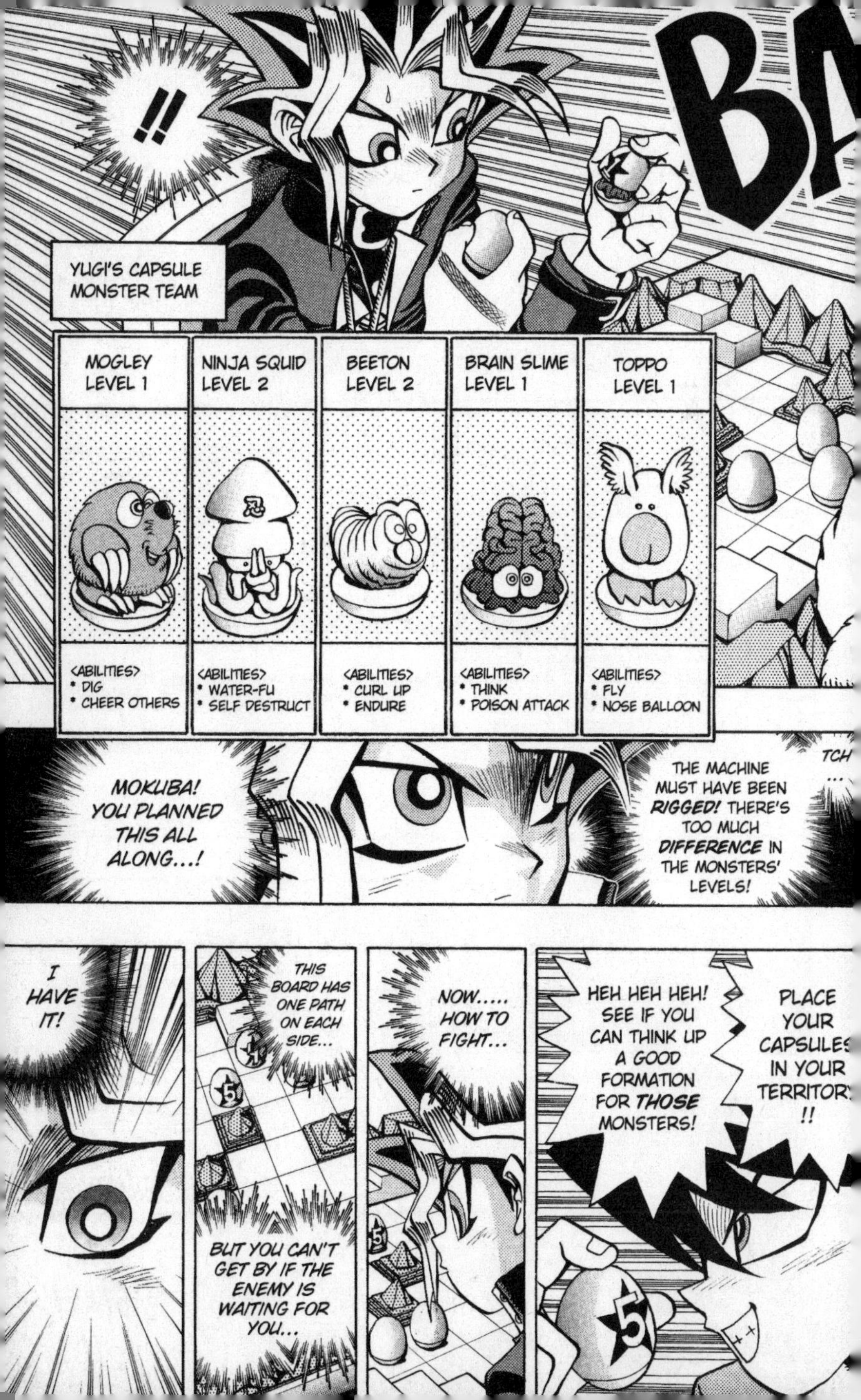
BA
!!
YUGI'S CAPSULE MONSTER TEAM
MOGLEY LEVEL 1
<ABILITIES> * DIG * CHEER OTHERS
NINJA SQUID LEVEL 2
<ABILITIES> * WATER-FU * SELF DESTRUCT
BEETON LEVEL 2
<ABILITIES> * CURL UP * ENDURE
BRAIN SLIME LEVEL 1
<ABILITIES> * THINK * POISON ATTACK
TOPPO LEVEL 1
<ABILITIES> * FLY * NOSE BALLOON
TCH ...
THE MACHINE MUST HAVE BEEN RIGGED! THERE'S TOO MUCH DIFFERENCE IN THE MONSTERS' LEVELS!
MOKUBA! YOU PLANNED THIS ALL ALONG...!
PLACE YOUR CAPSULES IN YOUR TERRITORY !!
HEH HEH HEH! SEE IF YOU CAN THINK UP A GOOD FORMATION FOR THOSE MONSTERS!
NOW..... HOW TO FIGHT...
THIS BOARD HAS ONE PATH ON EACH SIDE...
BUT YOU CAN'T GET BY IF THE ENEMY IS WAITING FOR YOU...
I HAVE IT!

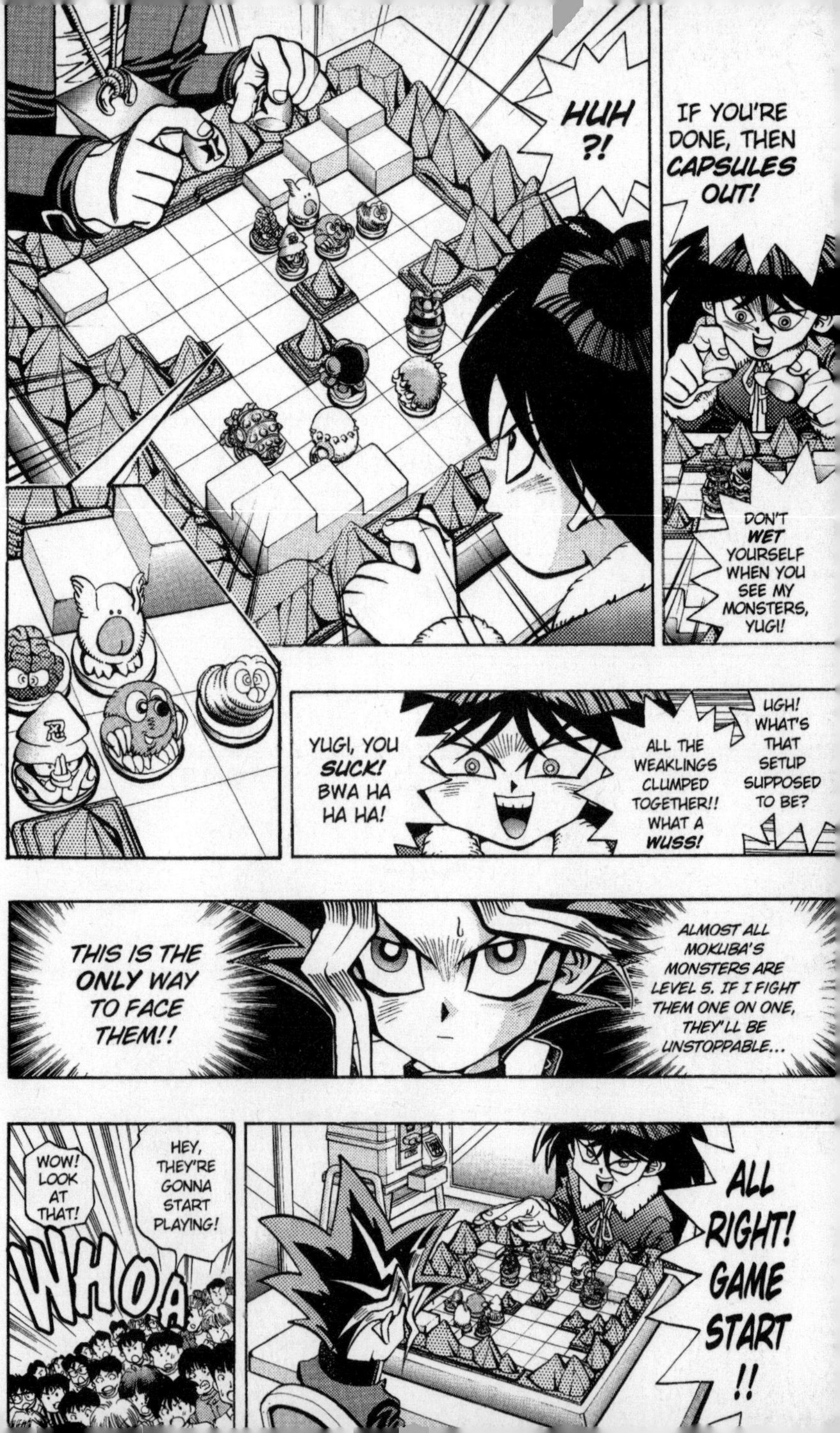

IF YOU'RE DONE, THEN CAPSULES OUT!
DON'T WET YOURSELF WHEN YOU SEE MY MONSTERS, YUGI!
HUH ?!
UGH! WHAT'S THAT SETUP SUPPOSED TO BE?
ALL THE WEAKLINGS CLUMPED TOGETHER!! WHAT A WUSS!
YUGI, YOU SUCK! BWA HA HA HA!
ALMOST ALL MOKUBA'S MONSTERS ARE LEVEL 5. IF I FIGHT THEM ONE ON ONE, THEY'LL BE UNSTOPPABLE...
THIS IS THE ONLY WAY TO FACE THEM!!
ALL RIGHT! GAME START !!
HEY, THEY'RE GONNA START PLAYING!
WOW! LOOK AT THAT!
WHOA

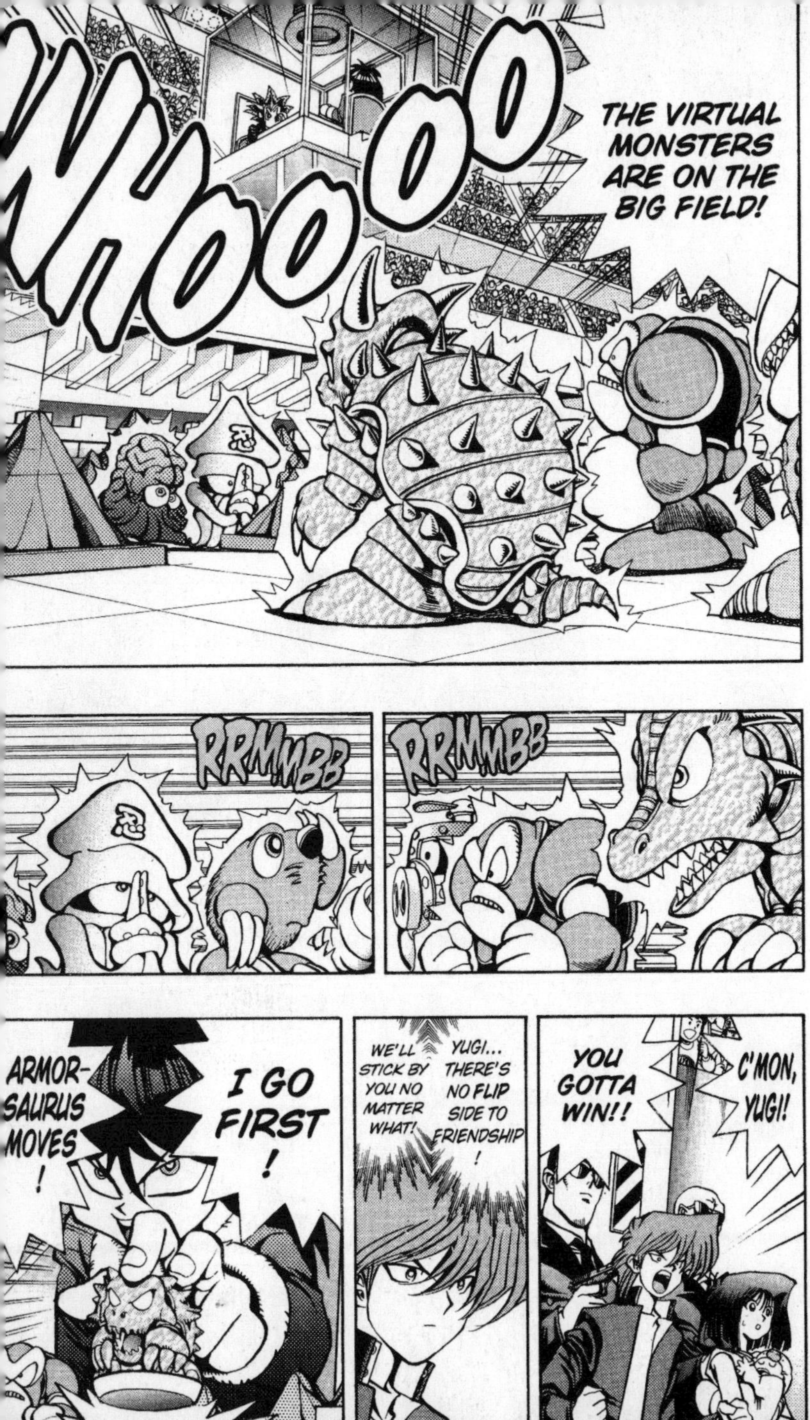
WHOOOOO
THE VIRTUAL MONSTERS ARE ON THE BIG FIELD!
RRMMBB
RRMMBB
C'MON, YUGI!
YOU GOTTA WIN!!
YUGI... THERE'S NO FLIP SIDE TO FRIENDSHIP!
WE'LL STICK BY YOU NO MATTER WHAT!
I GO FIRST!
ARMOR-SAURUS MOVES!

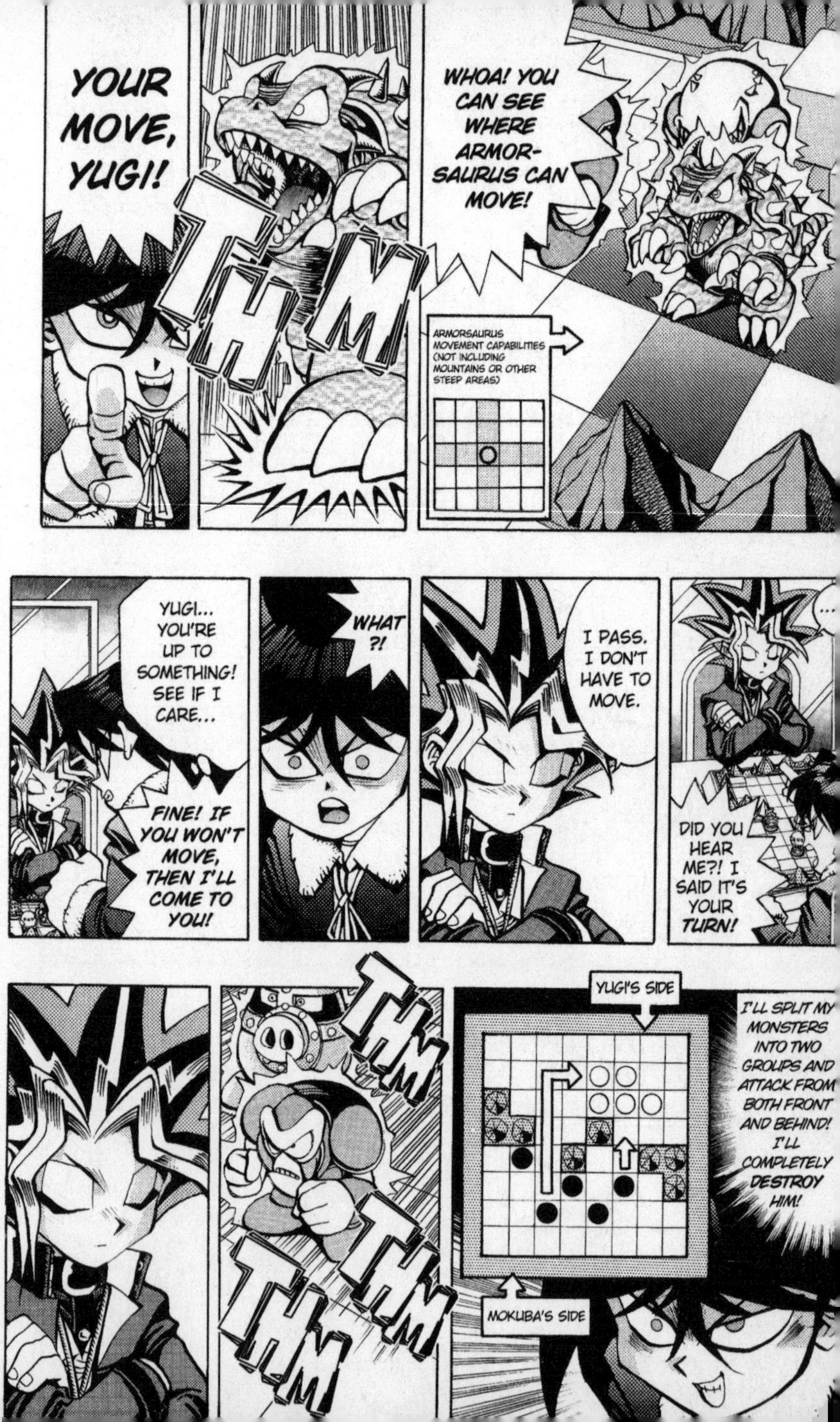
WHOA! YOU CAN SEE WHERE ARMOR-SAURUS CAN MOVE!
ARMORSAURUS MOVEMENT CAPABILITIES (NOT INCLUDING MOUNTAINS OR OTHER STEEP AREAS)
THM
YOUR MOVE, YUGI!
...
DID YOU HEAR ME?! I SAID IT'S YOUR TURN!
I PASS. I DON'T HAVE TO MOVE.
WHAT ?!
YUGI... YOU'RE UP TO SOMETHING! SEE IF I CARE...
FINE! IF YOU WON'T MOVE, THEN I'LL COME TO YOU!
YUGI'S SIDE
I'LL SPLIT MY MONSTERS INTO TWO GROUPS AND ATTACK FROM BOTH FRONT AND BEHIND! I'LL COMPLETELY DESTROY HIM!
MOKUBA'S SIDE
THM
THM
THM

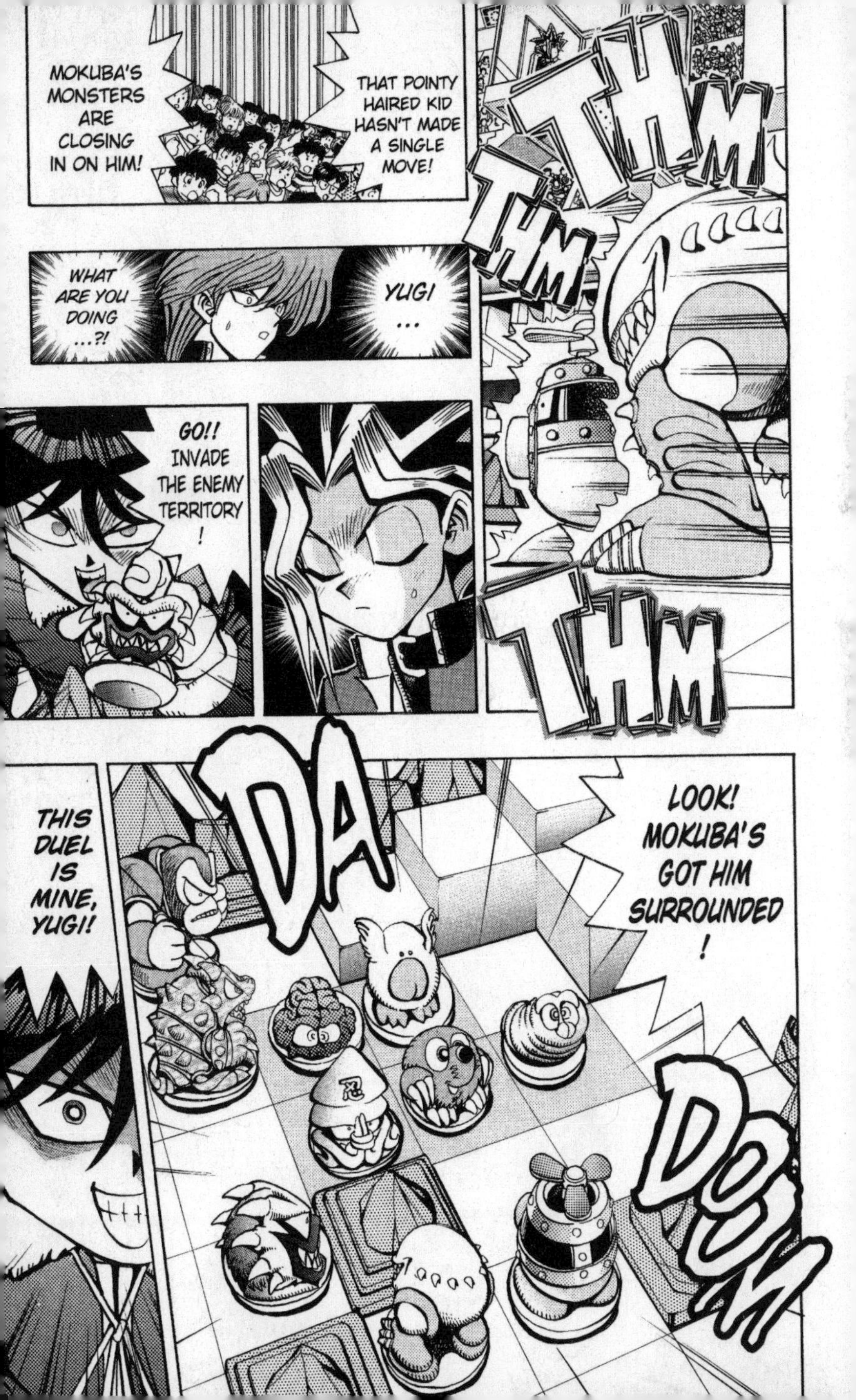
THM
THM
THM
THAT POINTY HAIRED KID HASN'T MADE A SINGLE MOVE!
MOKUBA'S MONSTERS ARE CLOSING IN ON HIM!
YUGI ...
WHAT ARE YOU DOING ...?!
GO!! INVADE THE ENEMY TERRITORY!
LOOK! MOKUBA'S GOT HIM SURROUNDED!
DOOM
DA
THIS DUEL IS MINE, YUGI!

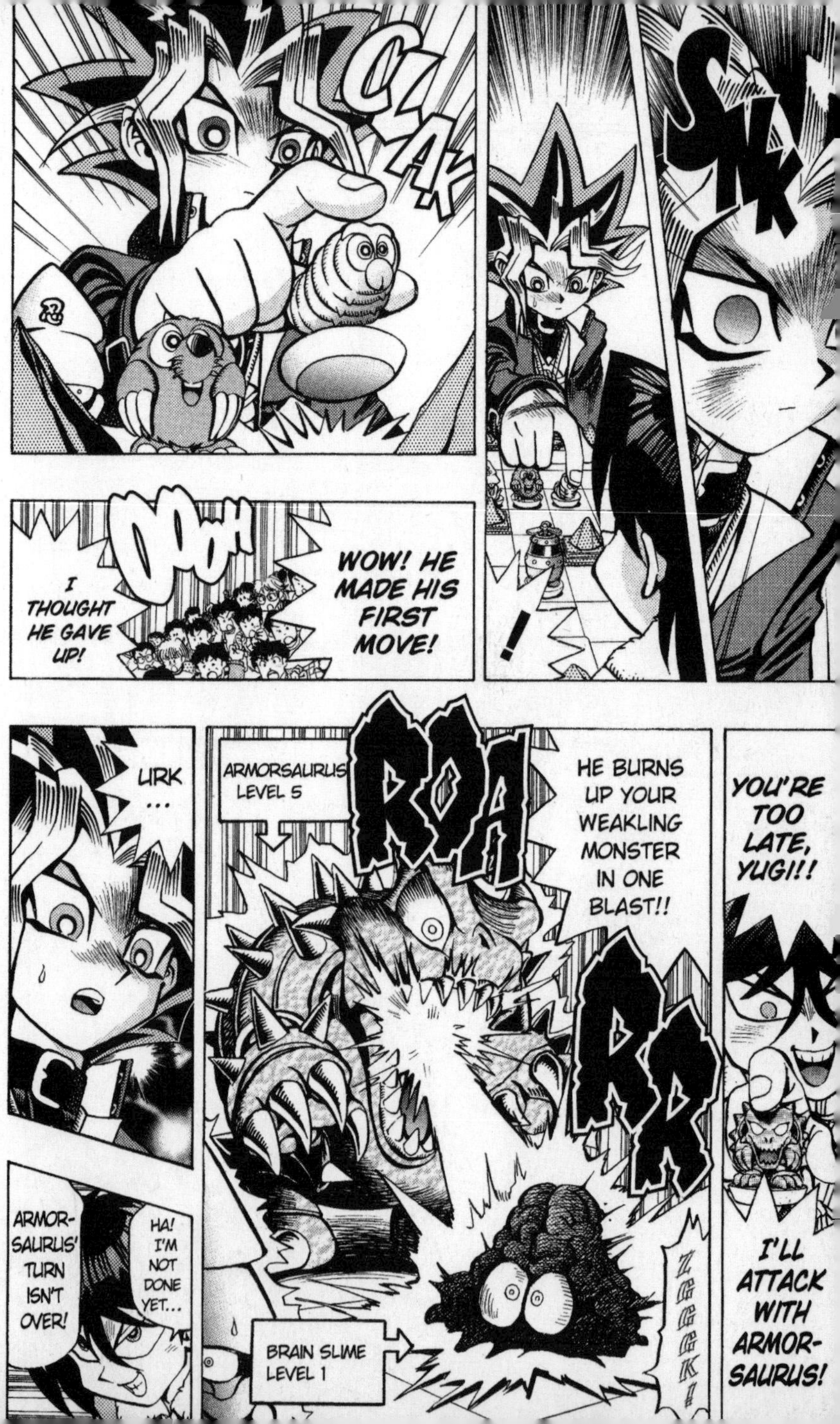
SHK
!
CLAK
WOW! HE MADE HIS FIRST MOVE!
OOOH
I THOUGHT HE GAVE UP!
YOU'RE TOO LATE, YUGI!!
I'LL ATTACK WITH ARMOR-SAURUS!
HE BURNS UP YOUR WEAKLING MONSTER IN ONE BLAST!!
ROA
ARMORSAURUS LEVEL 5
RR
ZGGGK!
BRAIN SLIME LEVEL 1
URK ...
HA! I'M NOT DONE YET...
ARMOR-SAURUS' TURN ISN'T OVER!

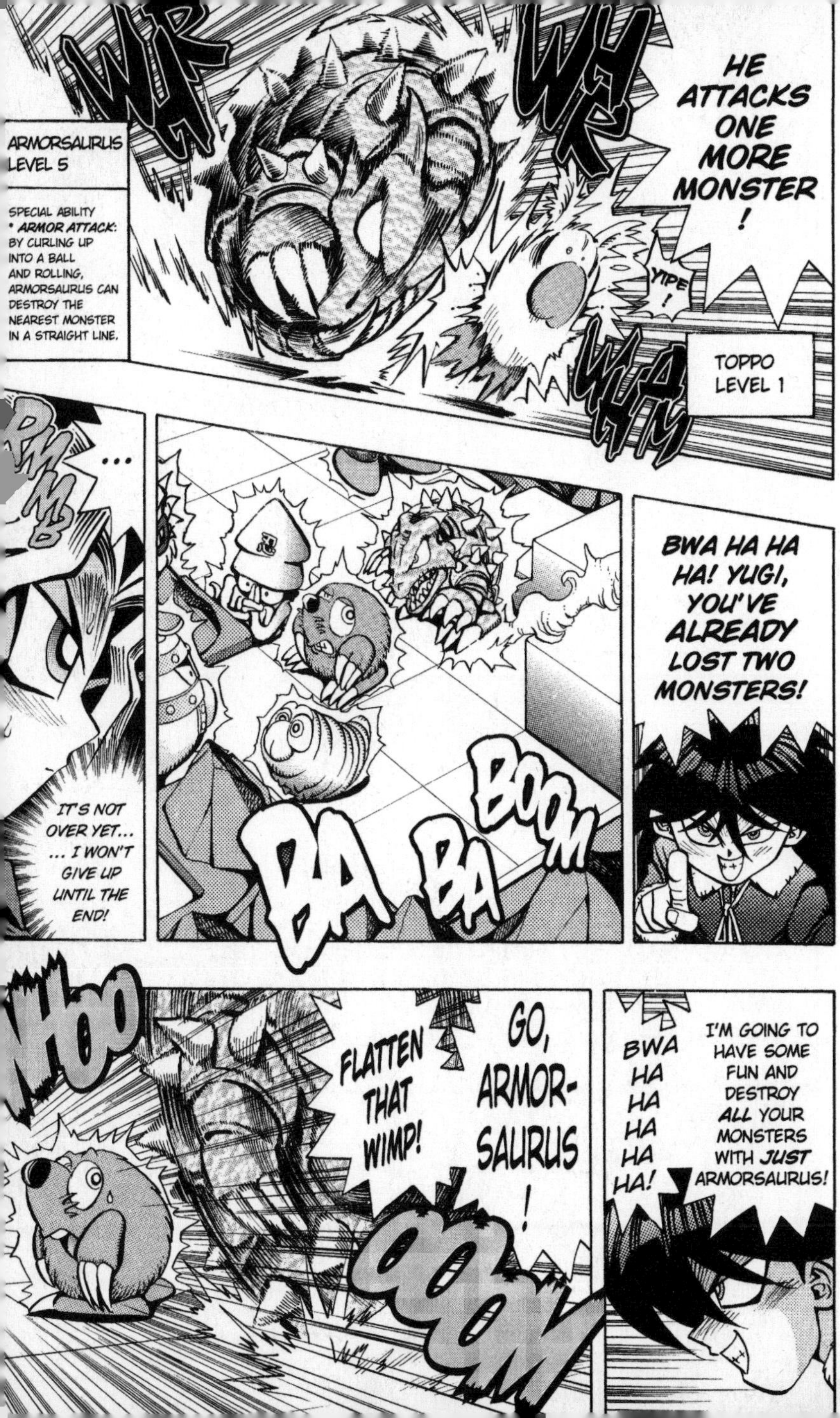
HE ATTACKS ONE MORE MONSTER!
WHR
WHR
YIPE!
WHAM
TOPPO LEVEL 1
ARMORSAURUS LEVEL 5
SPECIAL ABILITY
• ARMOR ATTACK: BY CURLING UP INTO A BALL AND ROLLING, ARMORSAURUS CAN DESTROY THE NEAREST MONSTER IN A STRAIGHT LINE.
BWA HA HA HA! YUGI, YOU'VE ALREADY LOST TWO MONSTERS!
BOOM
BA
BA
...
IT'S NOT OVER YET... ...I WON'T GIVE UP UNTIL THE END!
I'M GOING TO HAVE SOME FUN AND DESTROY ALL YOUR MONSTERS WITH JUST ARMORSAURUS!
BWA HA HA HA HA HA!
GO, ARMOR-SAURUS!
FLATTEN THAT WIMP!
OOOM
HOO

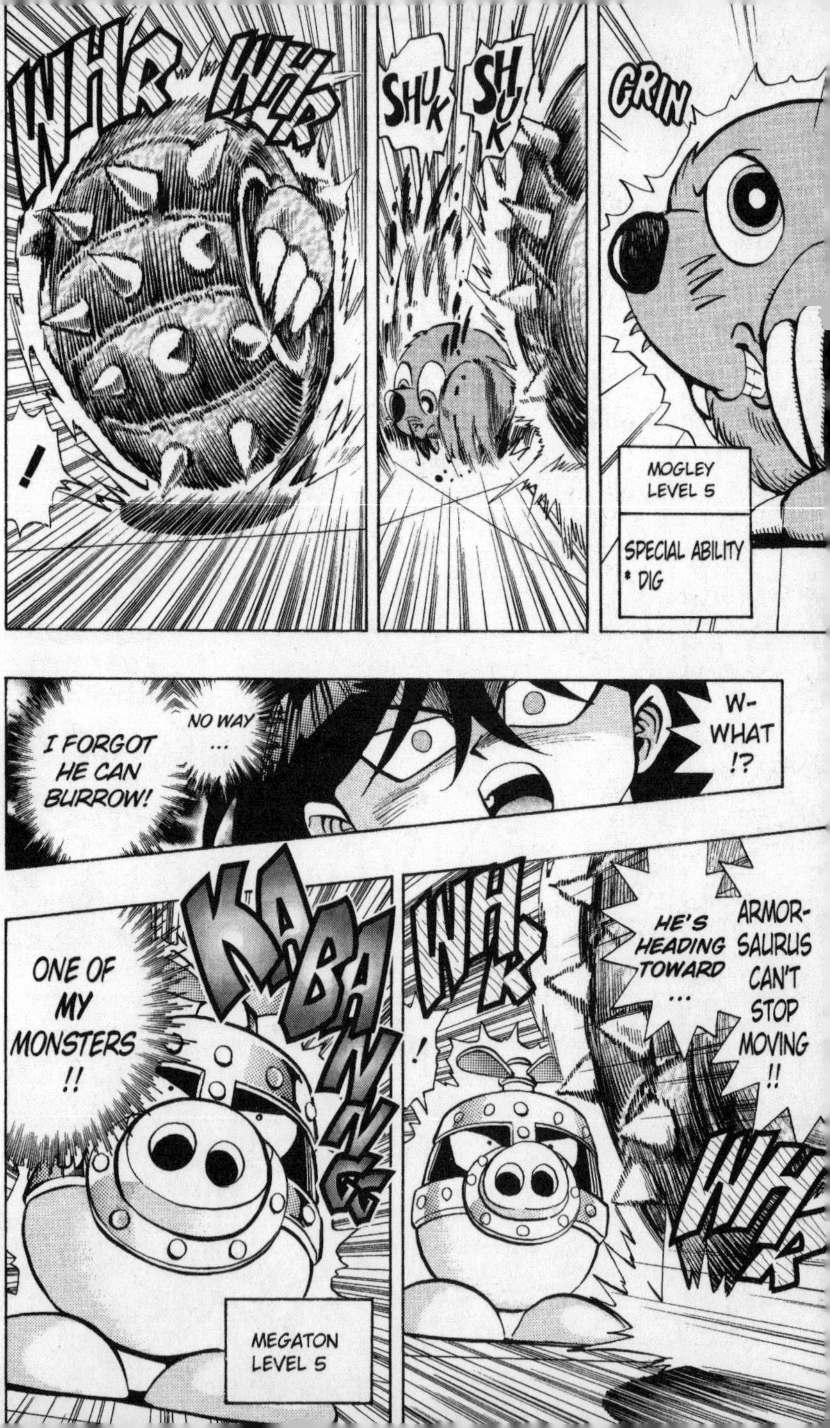
GRIN
MOGLEY LEVEL 5
SPECIAL ABILITY * DIG
SHUK SHUK
WHR WHR
!
W-WHAT !?
NO WAY ...
I FORGOT HE CAN BURROW!
ARMOR-SAURUS CAN'T STOP MOVING !!
HE'S HEADING TOWARD ...
WHR
!
WHR
KA-BANNG
ONE OF MY MONSTERS !!
MEGATON LEVEL 5

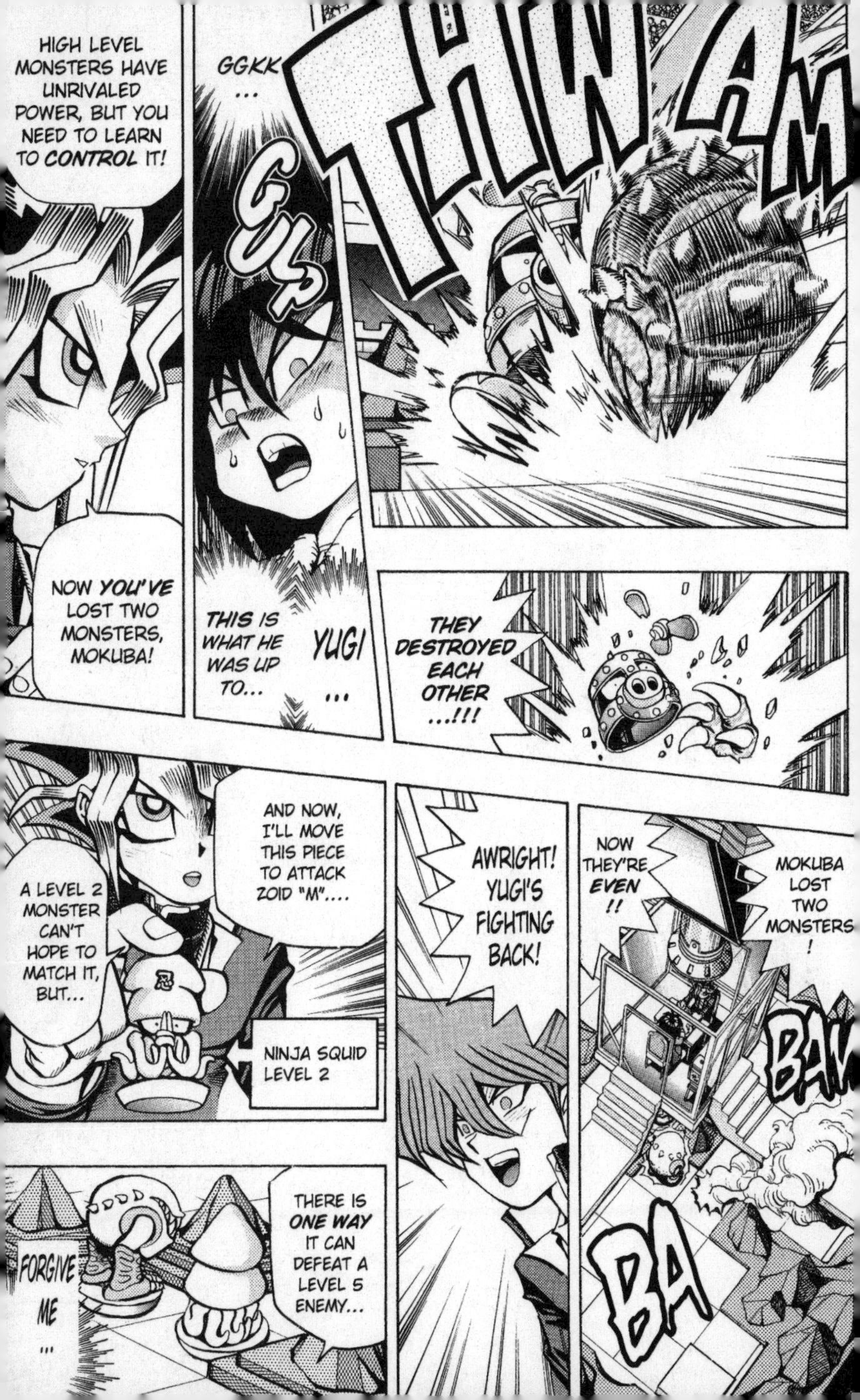
THWAM
THEY DESTROYED EACH OTHER ...!!!
GGKK ...
GULP
THIS IS WHAT HE WAS UP TO...
YUGI ...
HIGH LEVEL MONSTERS HAVE UNRIVALED POWER, BUT YOU NEED TO LEARN TO CONTROL IT!
NOW YOU'VE LOST TWO MONSTERS, MOKUBA!
MOKUBA LOST TWO MONSTERS!
NOW THEY'RE EVEN!!
BA
BA
AWRIGHT! YUGI'S FIGHTING BACK!
AND NOW, I'LL MOVE THIS PIECE TO ATTACK ZOID "M"....
A LEVEL 2 MONSTER CAN'T HOPE TO MATCH IT, BUT...
NINJA SQUID LEVEL 2
THERE IS ONE WAY IT CAN DEFEAT A LEVEL 5 ENEMY...
FORGIVE ME ...

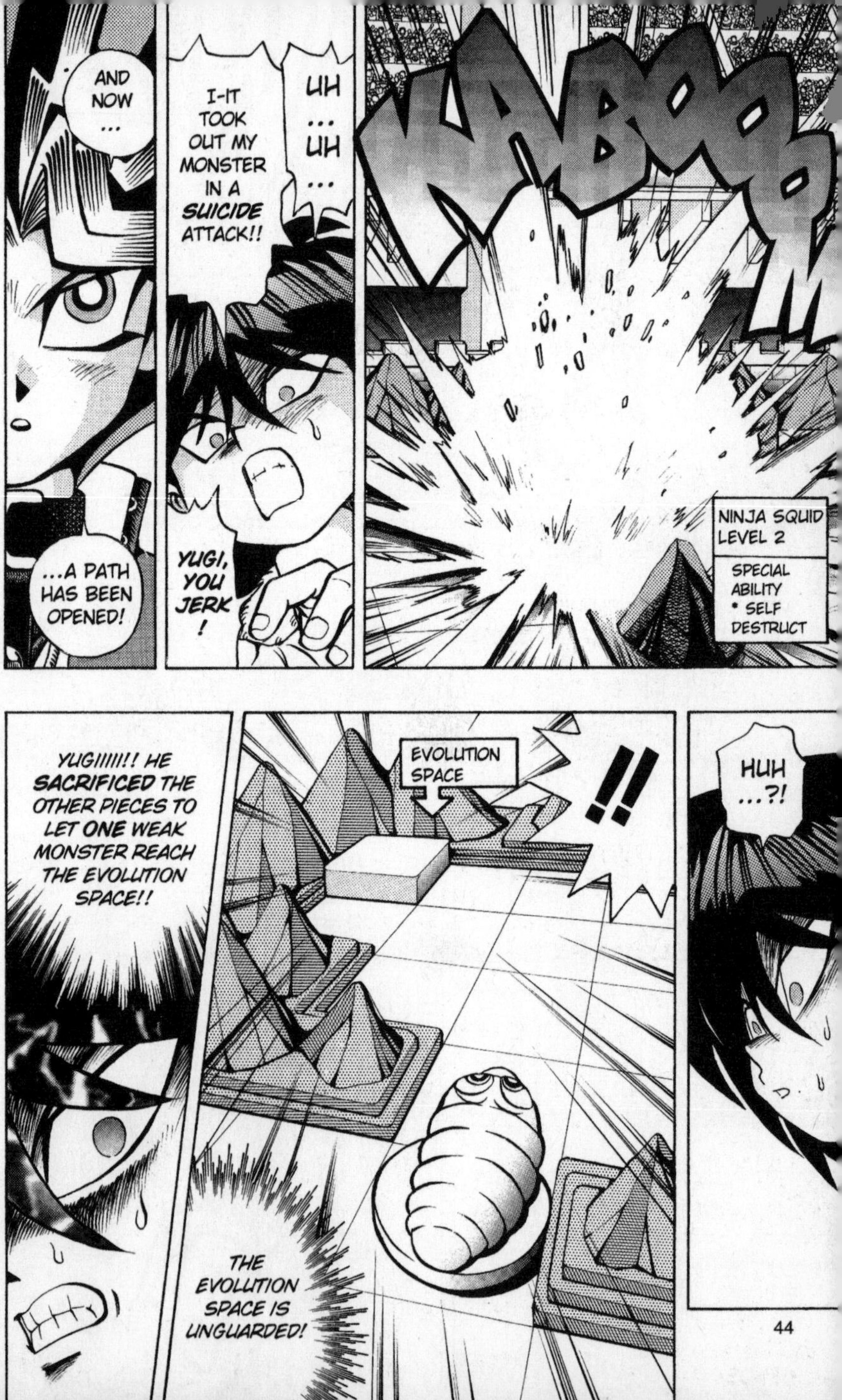
NINJA SQUID LEVEL 2
SPECIAL ABILITY * SELF DESTRUCT
UH ... UH ...
I-IT TOOK OUT MY MONSTER IN A SUICIDE ATTACK!!
YUGI, YOU JERK!
AND NOW ...
...A PATH HAS BEEN OPENED!
HUH ...?!
!!
EVOLUTION SPACE
THE EVOLUTION SPACE IS UNGUARDED!
YUGI!!!!!! HE SACRIFICED THE OTHER PIECES TO LET ONE WEAK MONSTER REACH THE EVOLUTION SPACE!!

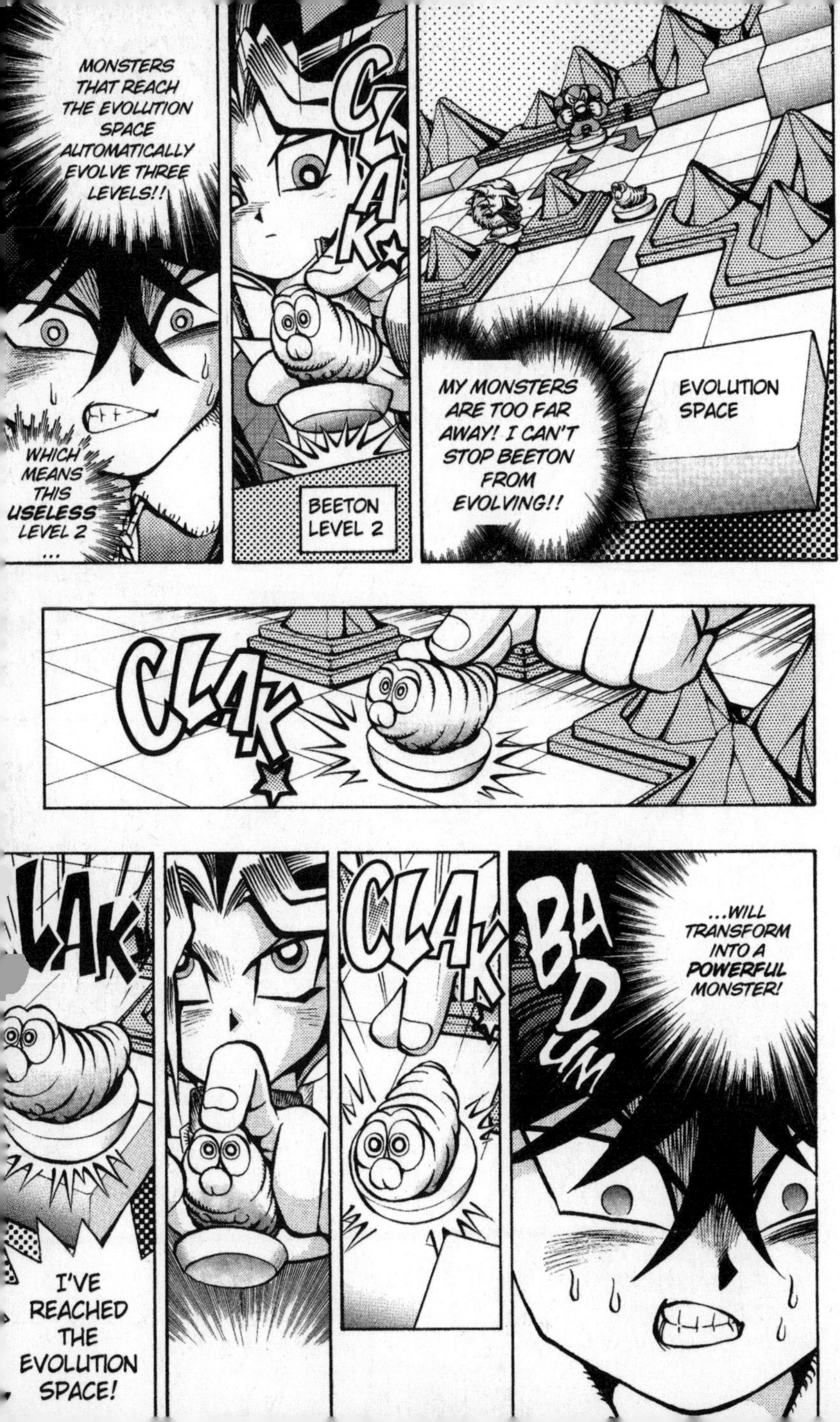
EVOLUTION SPACE
MY MONSTERS ARE TOO FAR AWAY! I CAN'T STOP BEETON FROM EVOLVING!!
CLAK
BEETON LEVEL 2
MONSTERS THAT REACH THE EVOLUTION SPACE AUTOMATICALLY EVOLVE THREE LEVELS!!
WHICH MEANS THIS USELESS LEVEL 2 ...
CLAK
BA DUM
...WILL TRANSFORM INTO A POWERFUL MONSTER!
CLAK
LAK
I'VE REACHED THE EVOLUTION SPACE!

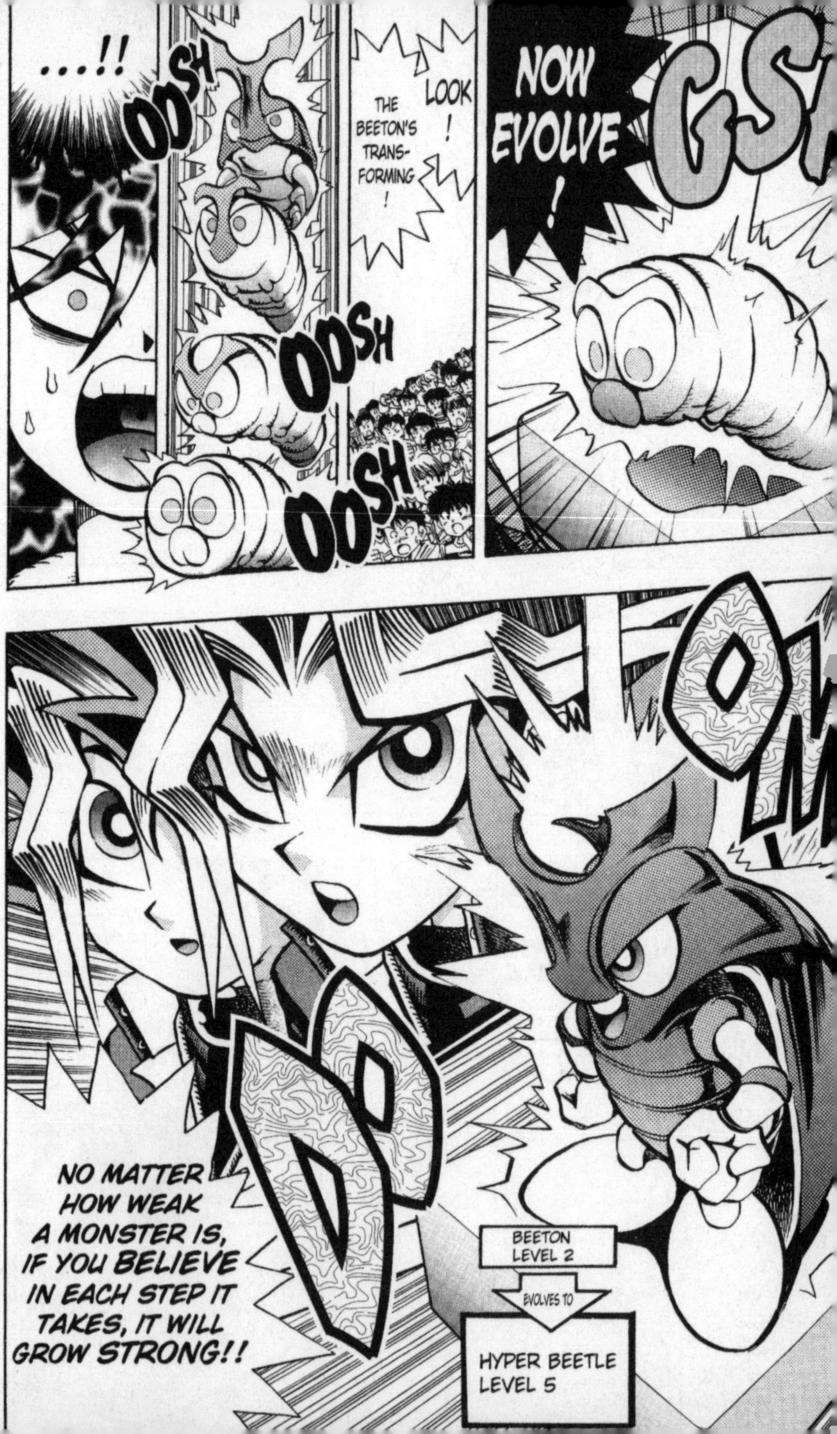
NOW EVOLVE!
LOOK!
THE BEETON'S TRANS-FORMING!
OOSH
OOSH
OOSH
OOSH
...!!
NO MATTER HOW WEAK A MONSTER IS, IF YOU BELIEVE IN EACH STEP IT TAKES, IT WILL GROW STRONG!!
BEETON LEVEL 2
EVOLVES TO
HYPER BEETLE LEVEL 5

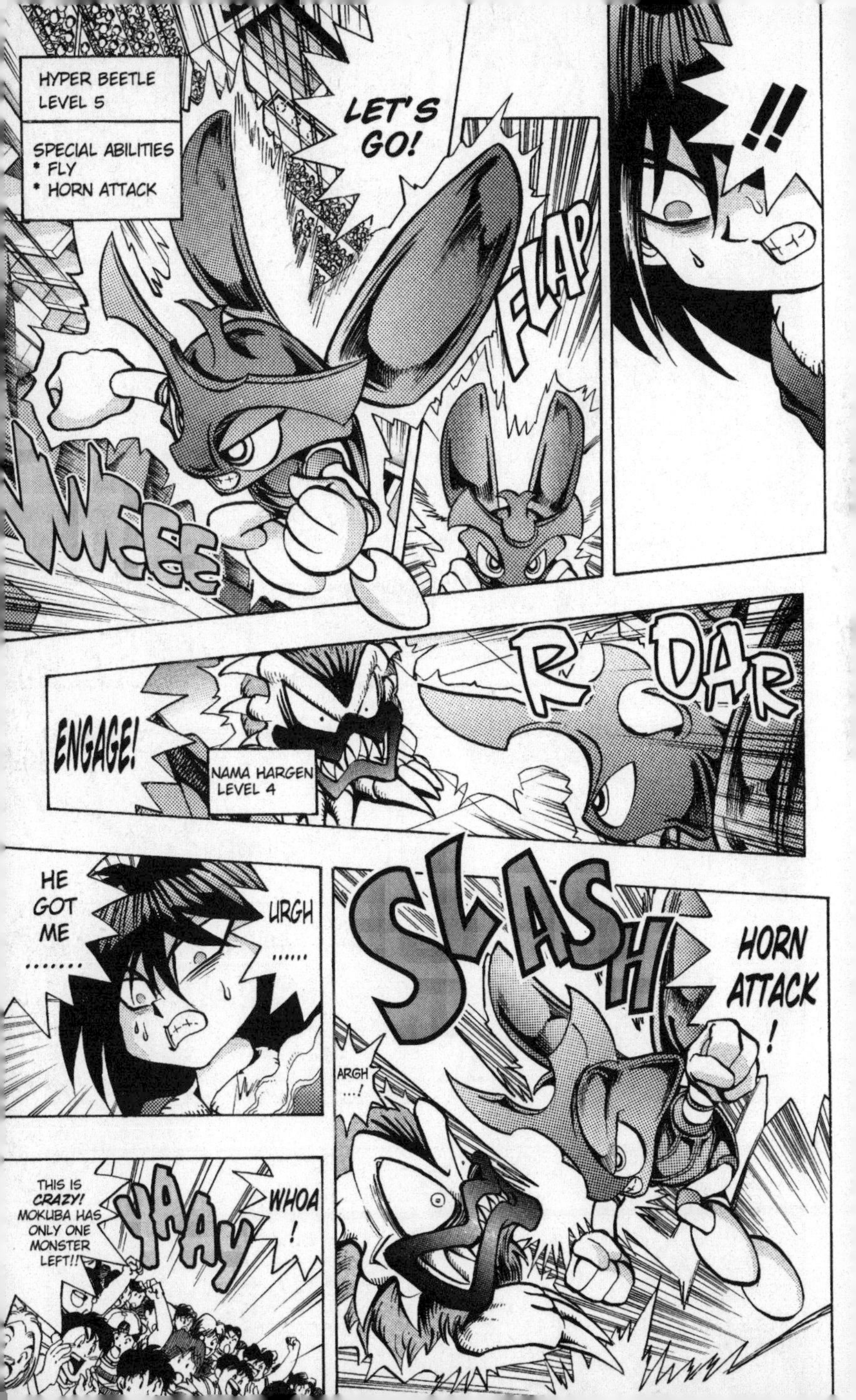
!!
LET'S GO!
FLAP
HYPER BEETLE LEVEL 5
SPECIAL ABILITIES
* FLY
* HORN ATTACK
WEEEE
R DAR
ENGAGE!
NAMA HARGEN LEVEL 4
SLASH
HORN ATTACK!
ARGH ...!
URGH ......
HE GOT ME ....
WHOA!
YAAY
THIS IS CRAZY! MOKUBA HAS ONLY ONE MONSTER LEFT!!

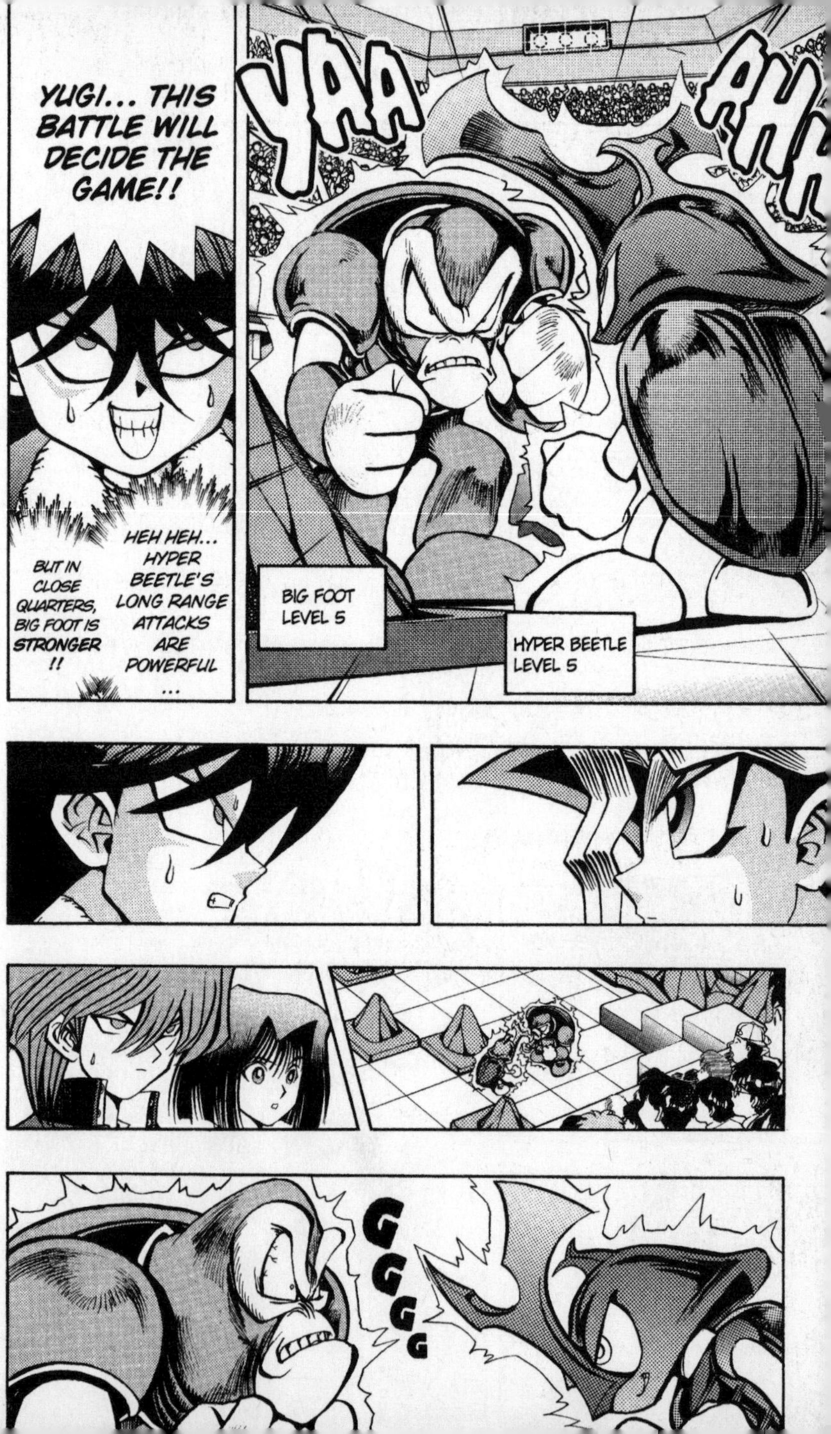
YAA AHH
HYPER BEETLE LEVEL 5
BIG FOOT LEVEL 5
YUGI... THIS BATTLE WILL DECIDE THE GAME!!
HEH HEH... HYPER BEETLE'S LONG RANGE ATTACKS ARE POWERFUL ...
BUT IN CLOSE QUARTERS, BIG FOOT IS STRONGER !!
GGGG

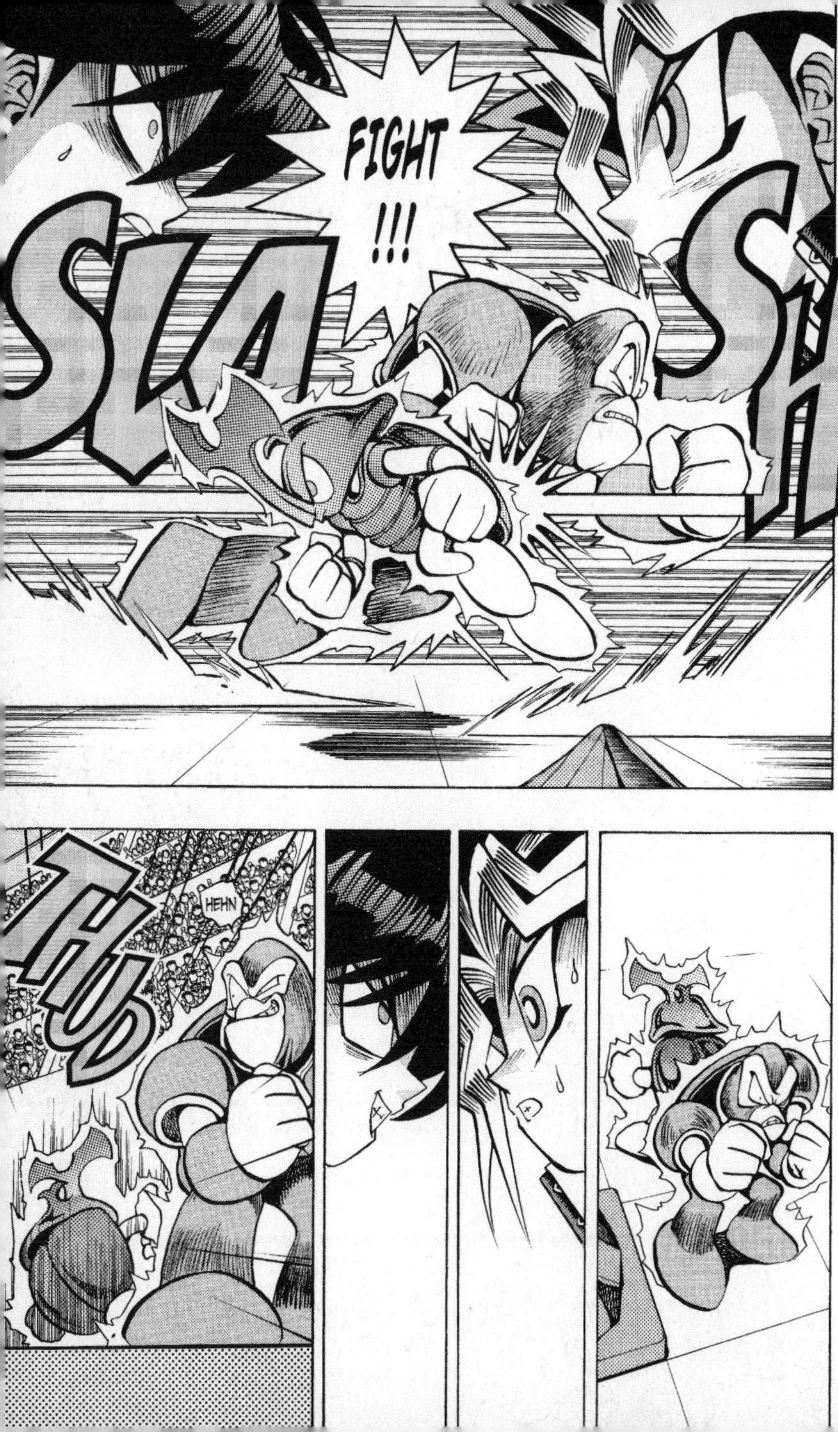
FIGHT !!!
SLASH
THUD
HEHN

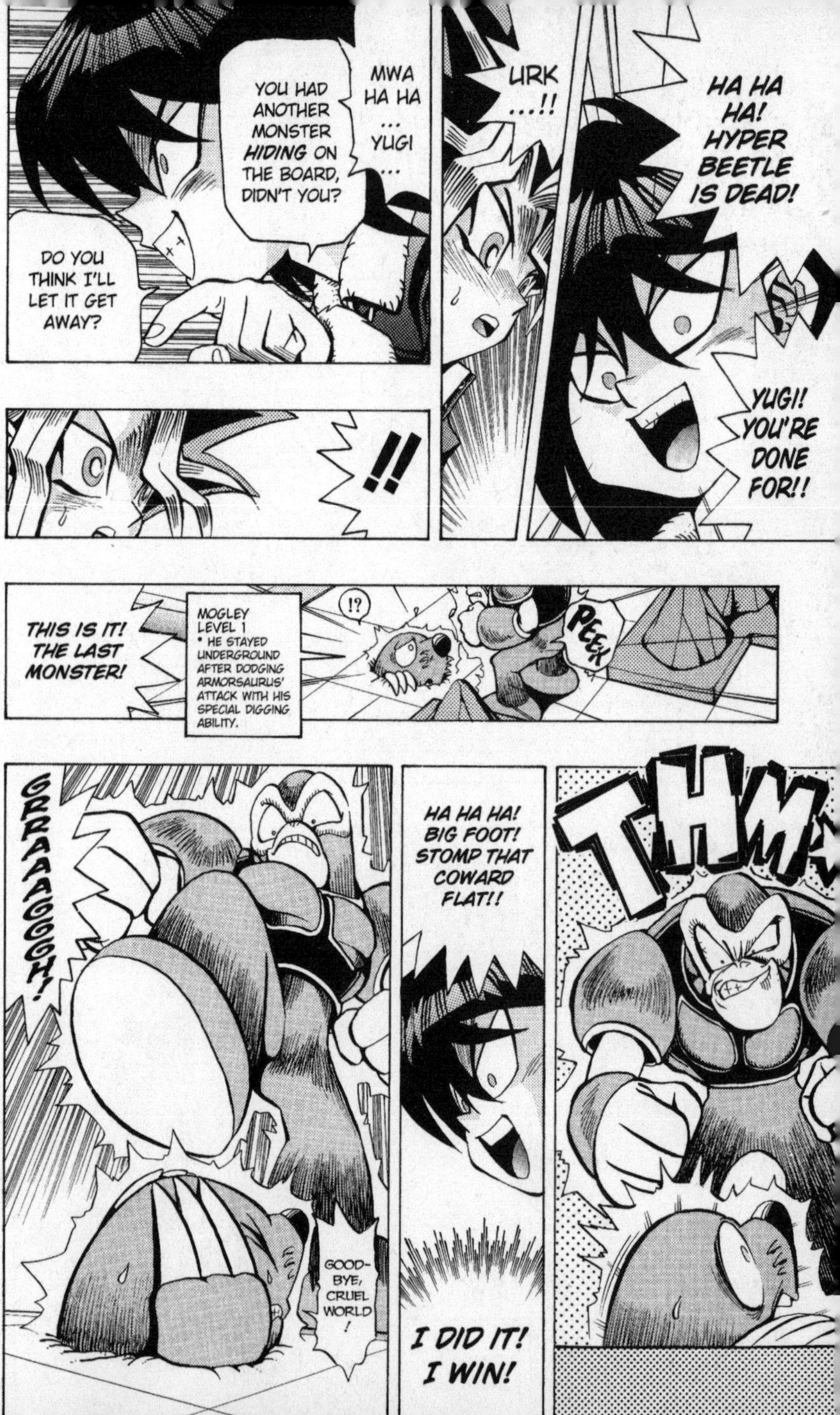
HA HA HA! HYPER BEETLE IS DEAD!
YUGI! YOU'RE DONE FOR!!
URK ...!!
MWA HA HA ... YUGI ...
YOU HAD ANOTHER MONSTER HIDING ON THE BOARD, DIDN'T YOU?
DO YOU THINK I'LL LET IT GET AWAY?
!!
PEEK
!?
MOGLEY LEVEL 1
• HE STAYED UNDERGROUND AFTER DODGING ARMORSAURUS' ATTACK WITH HIS SPECIAL DIGGING ABILITY.
THIS IS IT! THE LAST MONSTER!
THM
HA HA HA! BIG FOOT! STOMP THAT COWARD FLAT!!
I DID IT! I WIN!
GRRAAAAGGGH!
GOOD-BYE, CRUEL WORLD!

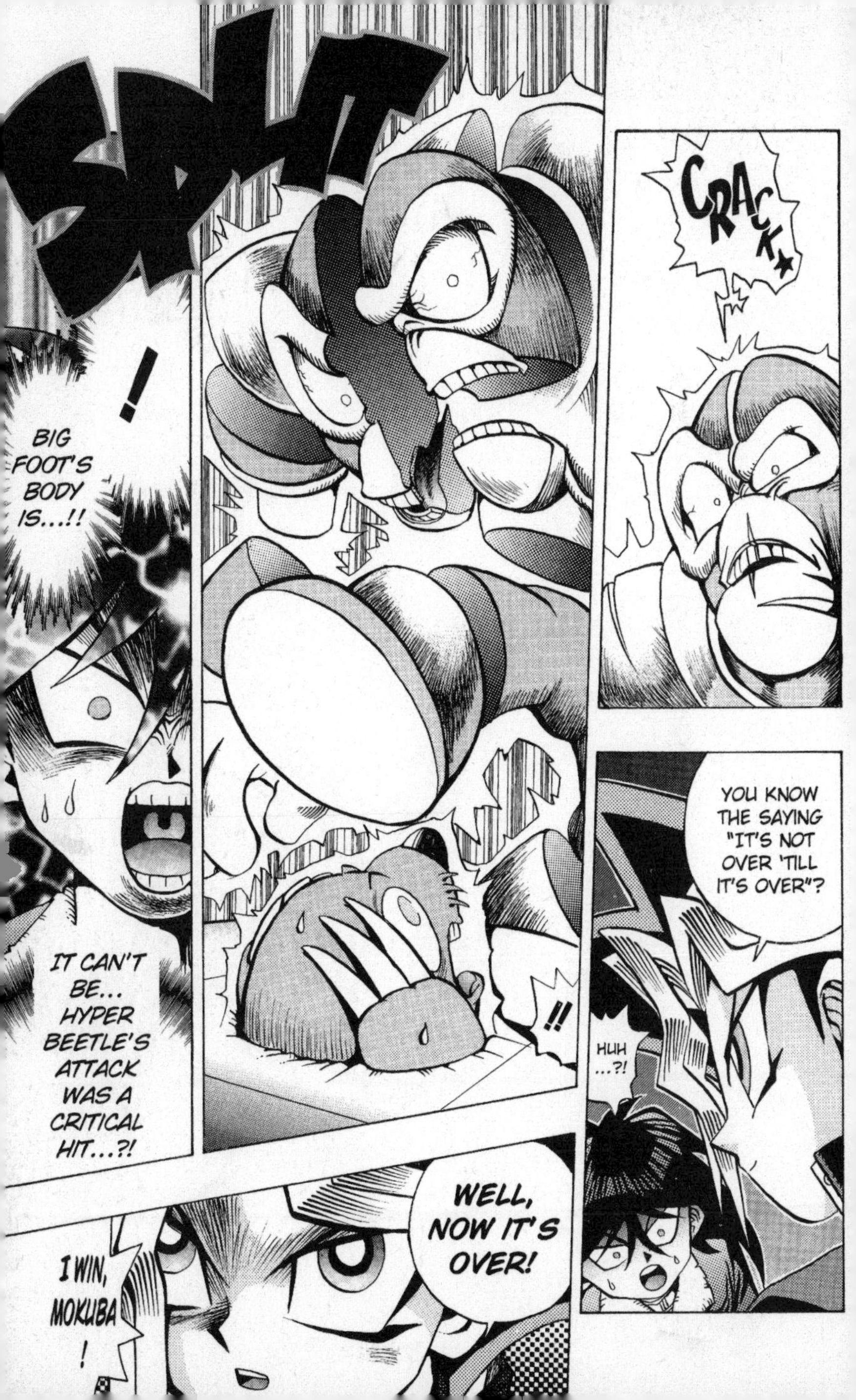
CRACK★
YOU KNOW THE SAYING "IT'S NOT OVER 'TILL IT'S OVER"?
HUH ...?!
!!
!
BIG FOOT'S BODY IS...!!
IT CAN'T BE... HYPER BEETLE'S ATTACK WAS A CRITICAL HIT...?!
WELL, NOW IT'S OVER!
I WIN, MOKUBA!

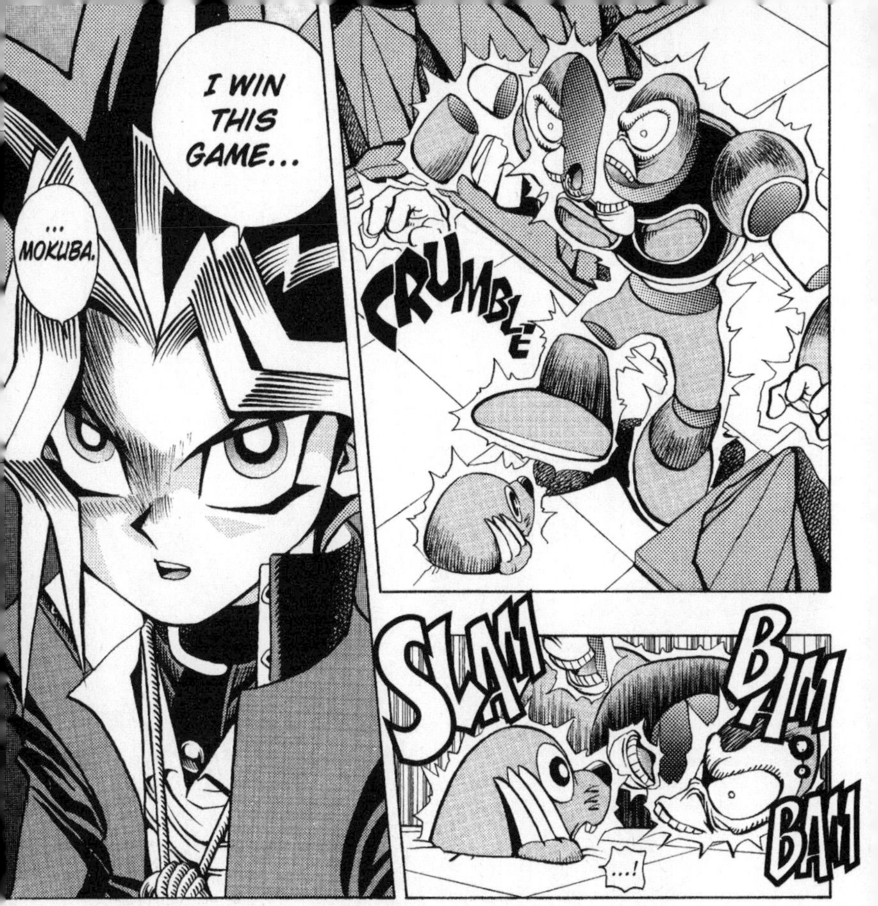
CRUMBLE
BAM
SLAM
BAM
...!
I WIN THIS GAME...
... MOKUBA.

Duel 36: Battle Beyond Hope

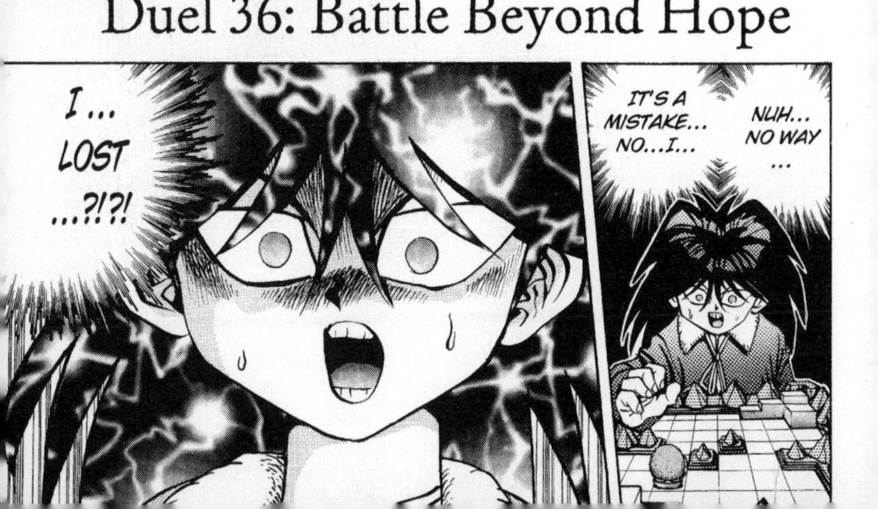
NUH... NO WAY ...
IT'S A MISTAKE... NO...I...
I ... LOST ...?!?!

Duel 36: Battle Beyond Hope

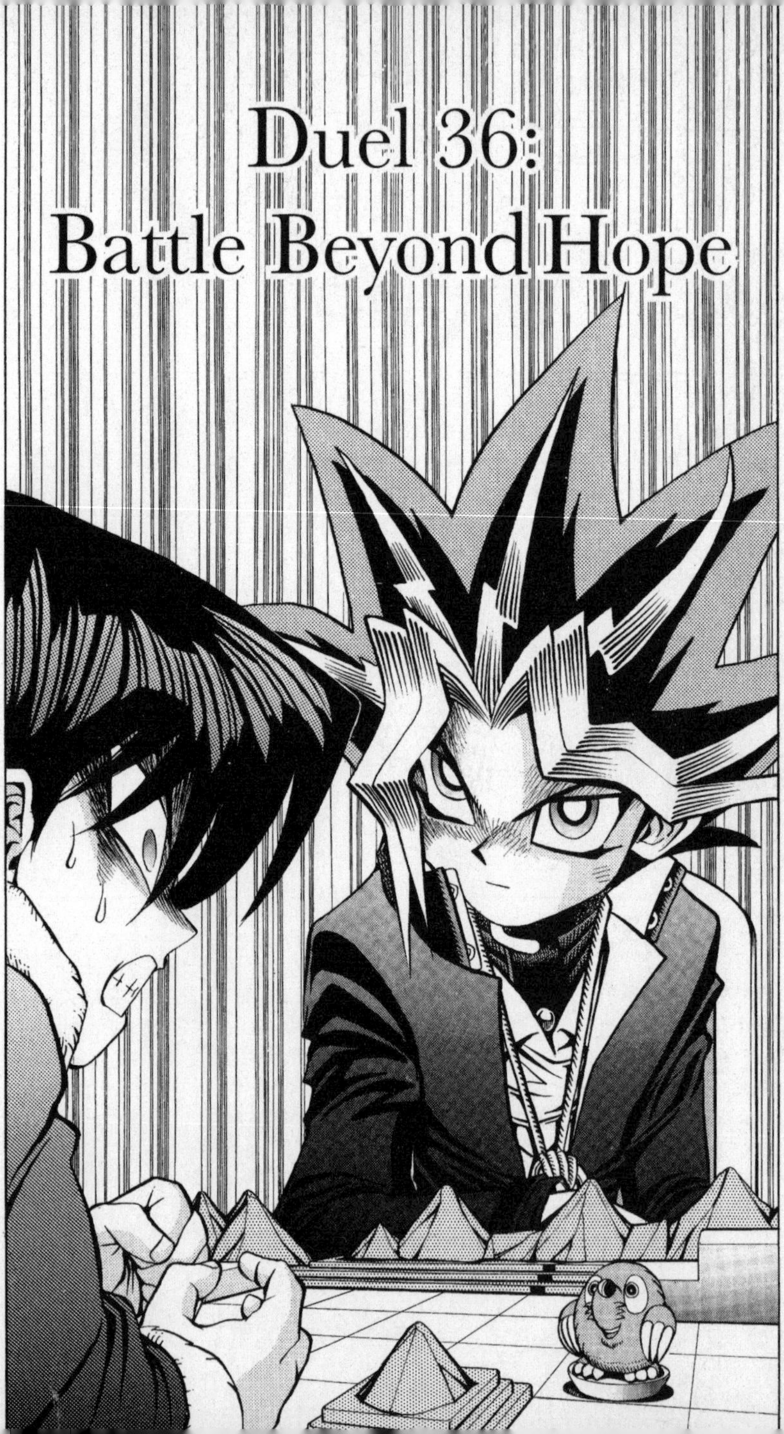

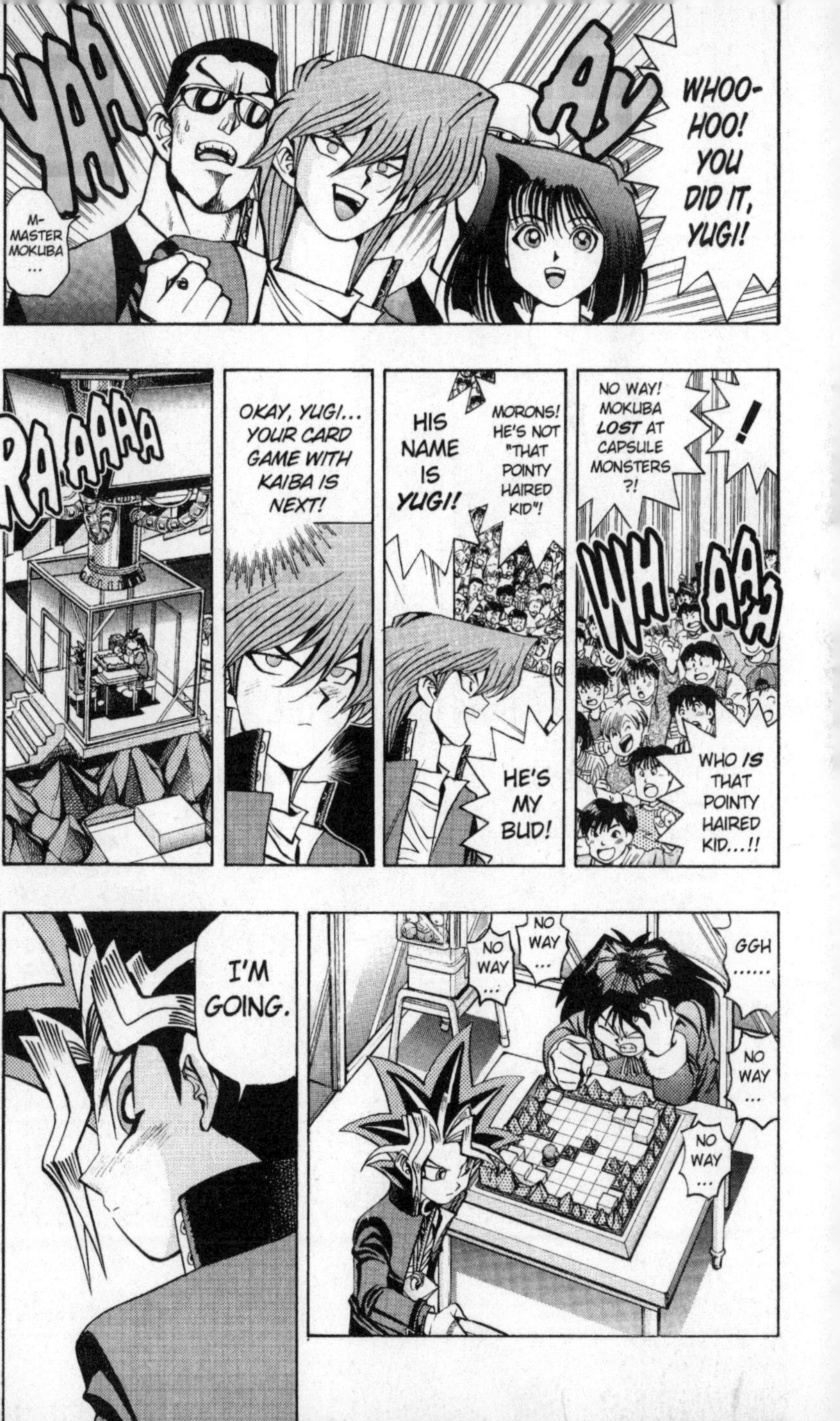
WHOO-HOO! YOU DID IT, YUGI!
AY
YAA
M-MASTER MOKUBA ...
NO WAY! MOKUBA LOST AT CAPSULE MONSTERS ?!
!
WH AAA
WHO IS THAT POINTY HAIRED KID...!!
MORONS! HE'S NOT "THAT POINTY HAIRED KID"!
HIS NAME IS YUGI!
HE'S MY BUD!
OKAY, YUGI... YOUR CARD GAME WITH KAIBA IS NEXT!
RA AAAA
GGH ......
NO WAY ...
NO WAY ...
NO WAY ...
NO WAY ...
I'M GOING.

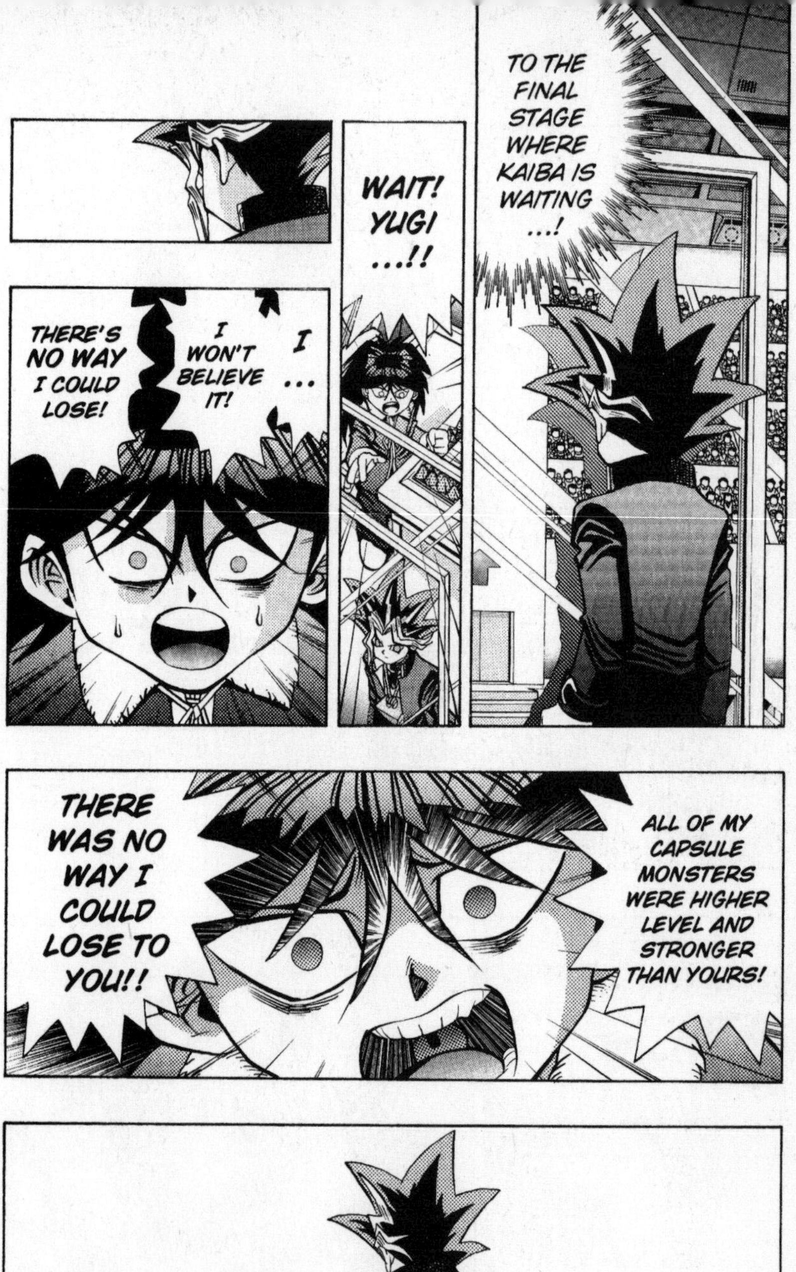
TO THE FINAL STAGE WHERE KAIBA IS WAITING ...!
WAIT! YUGI ...!!
I ...
I WON'T BELIEVE IT!
THERE'S NO WAY I COULD LOSE!
ALL OF MY CAPSULE MONSTERS WERE HIGHER LEVEL AND STRONGER THAN YOURS!
THERE WAS NO WAY I COULD LOSE TO YOU!!

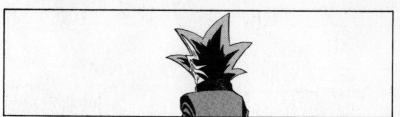

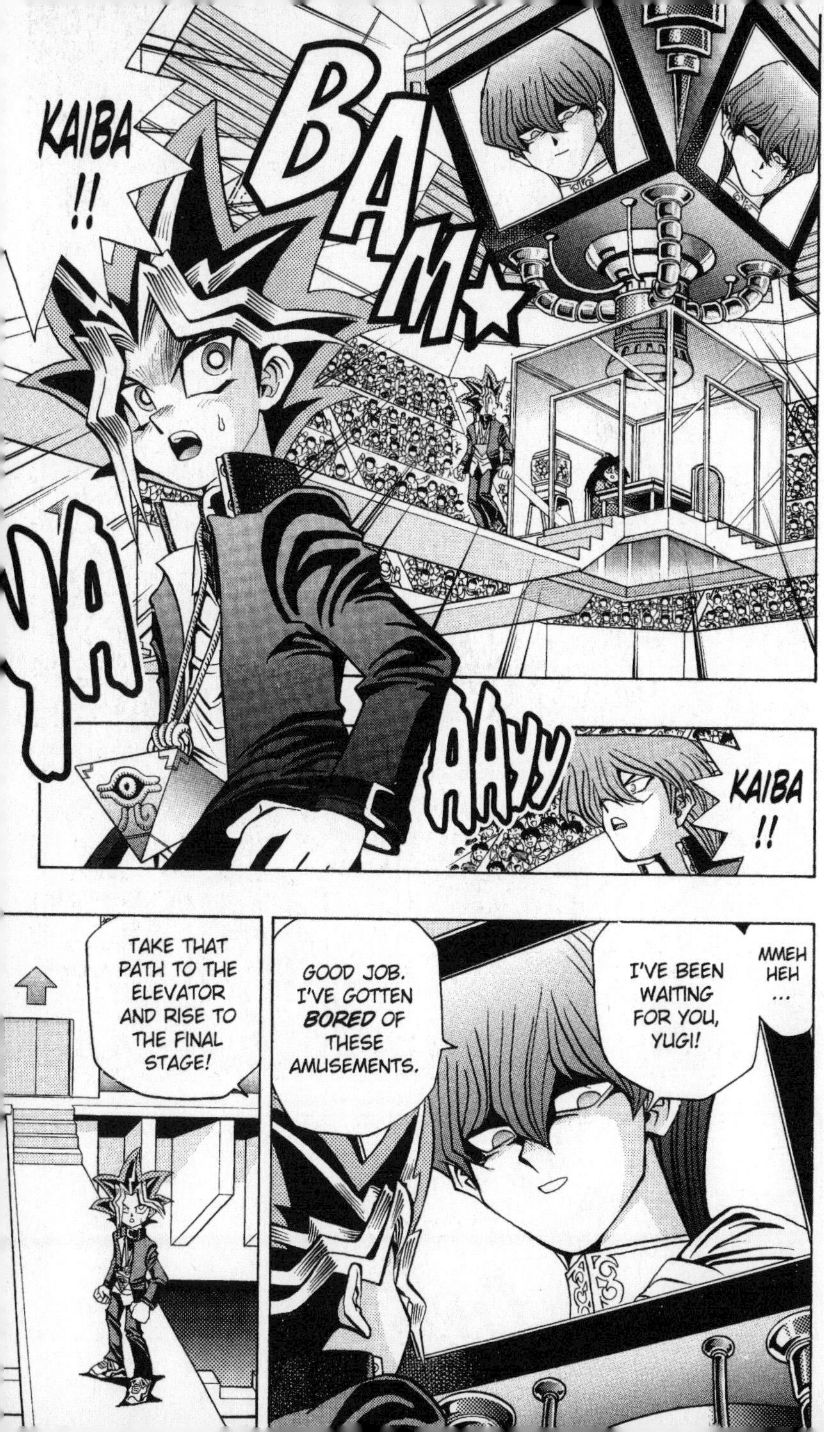
BAM
KAIBA!!
YAAAYY
KAIBA!!
MMEH HEH...
I'VE BEEN WAITING FOR YOU, YUGI!
GOOD JOB. I'VE GOTTEN **BORED** OF THESE AMUSEMENTS.
TAKE THAT PATH TO THE ELEVATOR AND RISE TO THE FINAL STAGE!

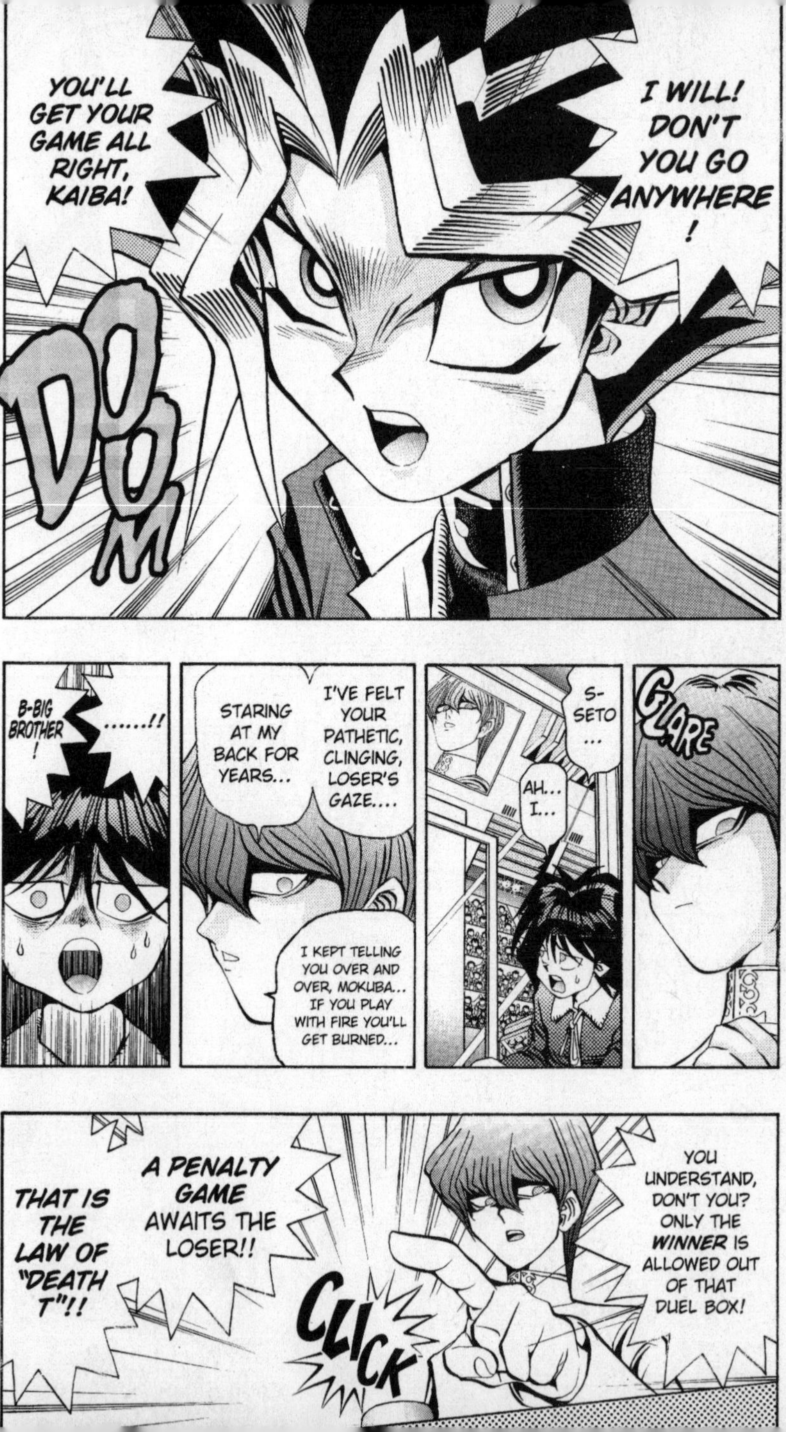
I WILL! DON'T YOU GO ANYWHERE!
YOU'LL GET YOUR GAME ALL RIGHT, KAIBA!
DOOM
GLARE
S-SETO...
AH... I...
I'VE FELT YOUR PATHETIC, CLINGING, LOSER'S GAZE....
STARING AT MY BACK FOR YEARS...
I KEPT TELLING YOU OVER AND OVER, MOKUBA... IF YOU PLAY WITH FIRE YOU'LL GET BURNED...
B-BIG BROTHER!
......!!
YOU UNDERSTAND, DON'T YOU? ONLY THE WINNER IS ALLOWED OUT OF THAT DUEL BOX!
CLICK
A PENALTY GAME AWAITS THE LOSER!!
THAT IS THE LAW OF "DEATH T"!!

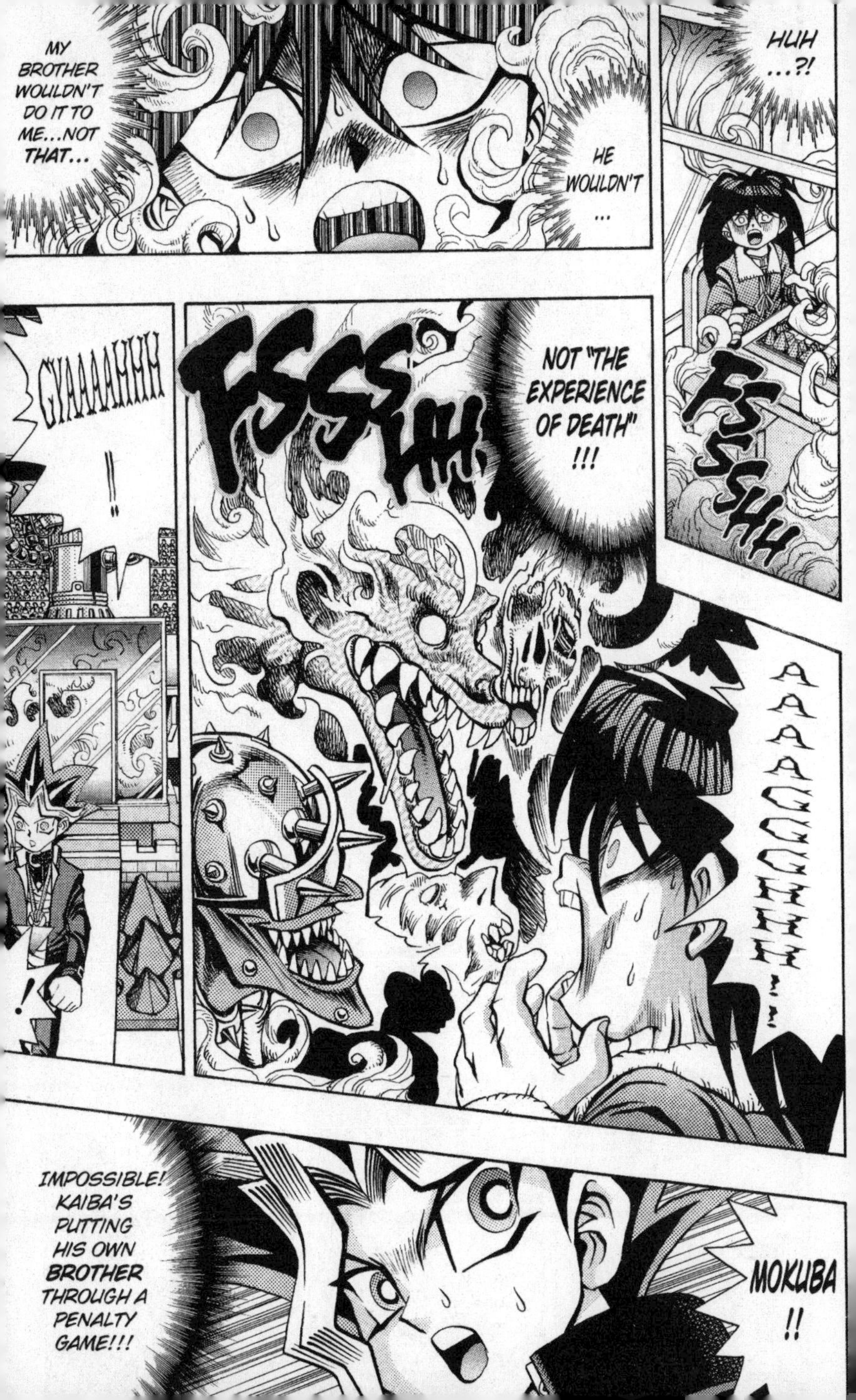

HUH ...?!
FSSSHH
MY BROTHER WOULDN'T DO IT TO ME...NOT THAT...
HE WOULDN'T ...
NOT "THE EXPERIENCE OF DEATH" !!!
FSSSHH
AAAAAGGGHHHH!!
GYAAAAHHH !!
MOKUBA !!
IMPOSSIBLE! KAIBA'S PUTTING HIS OWN BROTHER THROUGH A PENALTY GAME!!!

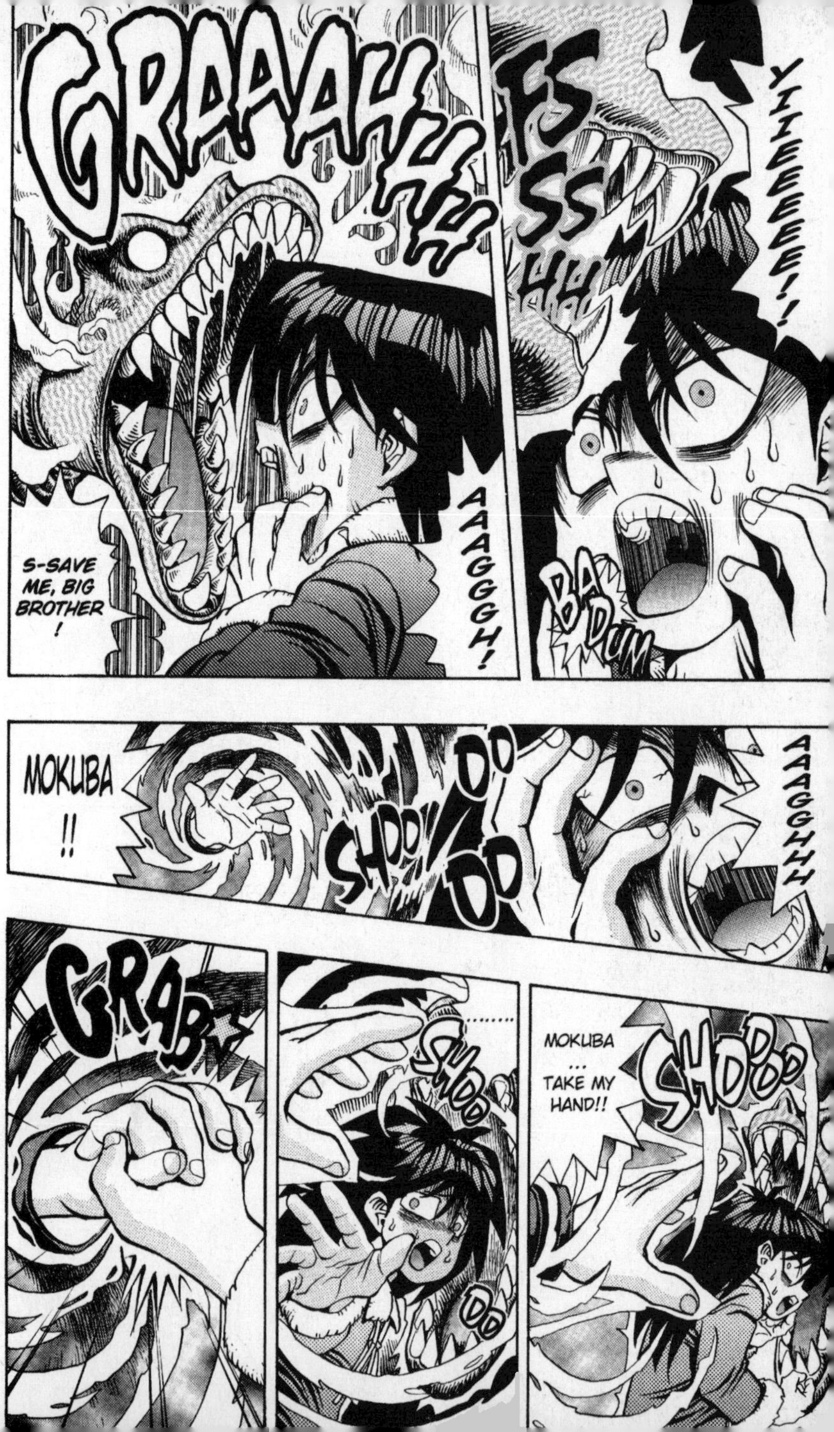
YIIEEEEEE!!
BA DUM
GRAAAHHH
AAAAGGGH!
S-SAVE ME, BIG BROTHER!
AAAAGGHHH
SHOOOO
MOKUBA!!
SHOOOO
MOKUBA ... TAKE MY HAND!!
....
SHOOOO
GRAB

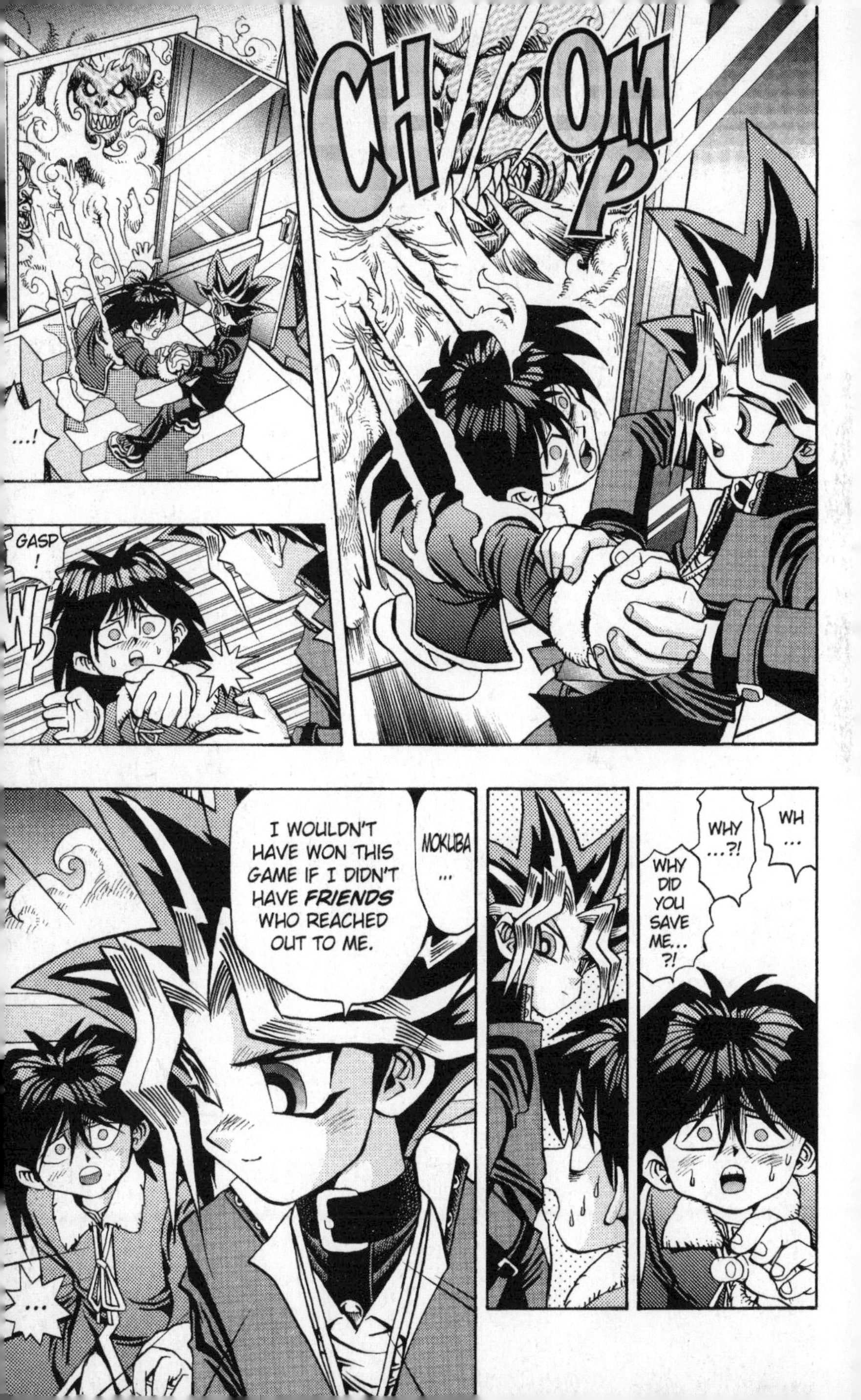
CH OMP
...!
GASP!
WH ...
WHY ...?!
WHY DID YOU SAVE ME... ?!
MOKUBA ...
I WOULDN'T HAVE WON THIS GAME IF I DIDN'T HAVE **FRIENDS** WHO REACHED OUT TO ME.
...

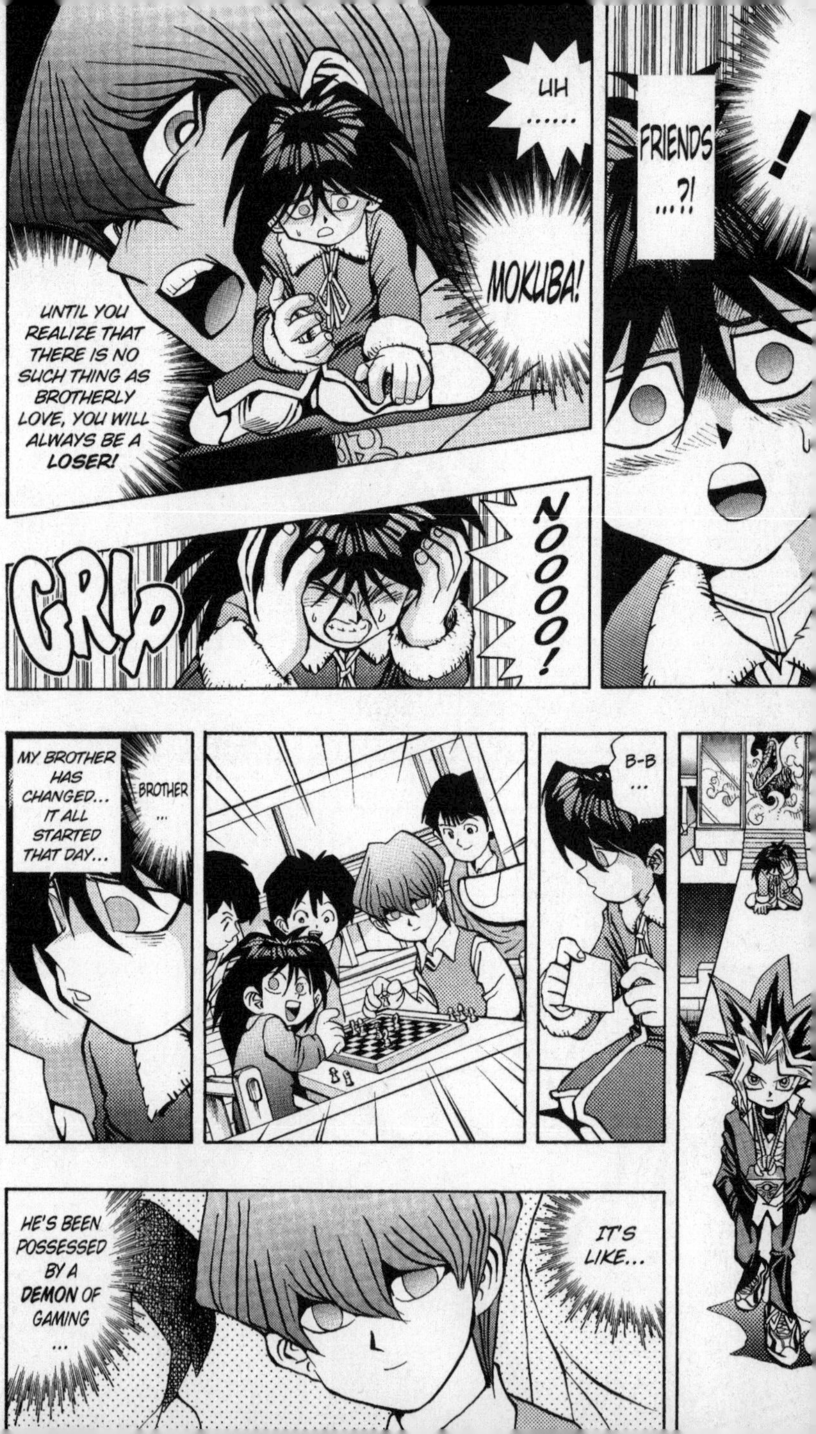
!
FRIENDS ...?!
UH ......
MOKUBA!
UNTIL YOU REALIZE THAT THERE IS NO SUCH THING AS BROTHERLY LOVE, YOU WILL ALWAYS BE A **LOSER!**
NOOOOO!
GRIP
B-B ...
BROTHER ...
MY BROTHER HAS CHANGED... IT ALL STARTED THAT DAY...
IT'S LIKE...
HE'S BEEN POSSESSED BY A **DEMON** OF GAMING ...

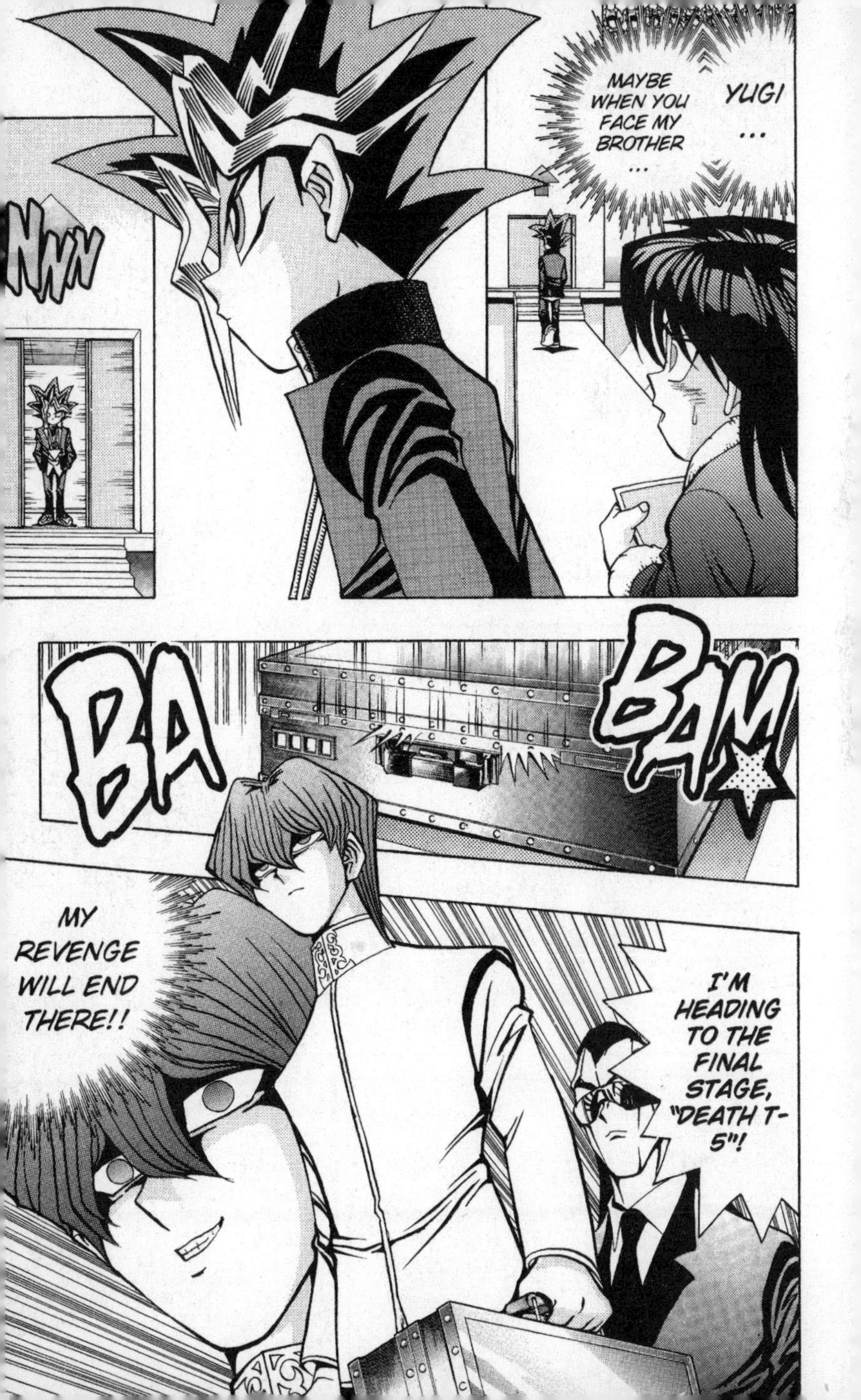
YUGI ...
MAYBE WHEN YOU FACE MY BROTHER ...
NNN
BA BAM
I'M HEADING TO THE FINAL STAGE, "DEATH T-5"!
MY REVENGE WILL END THERE!!

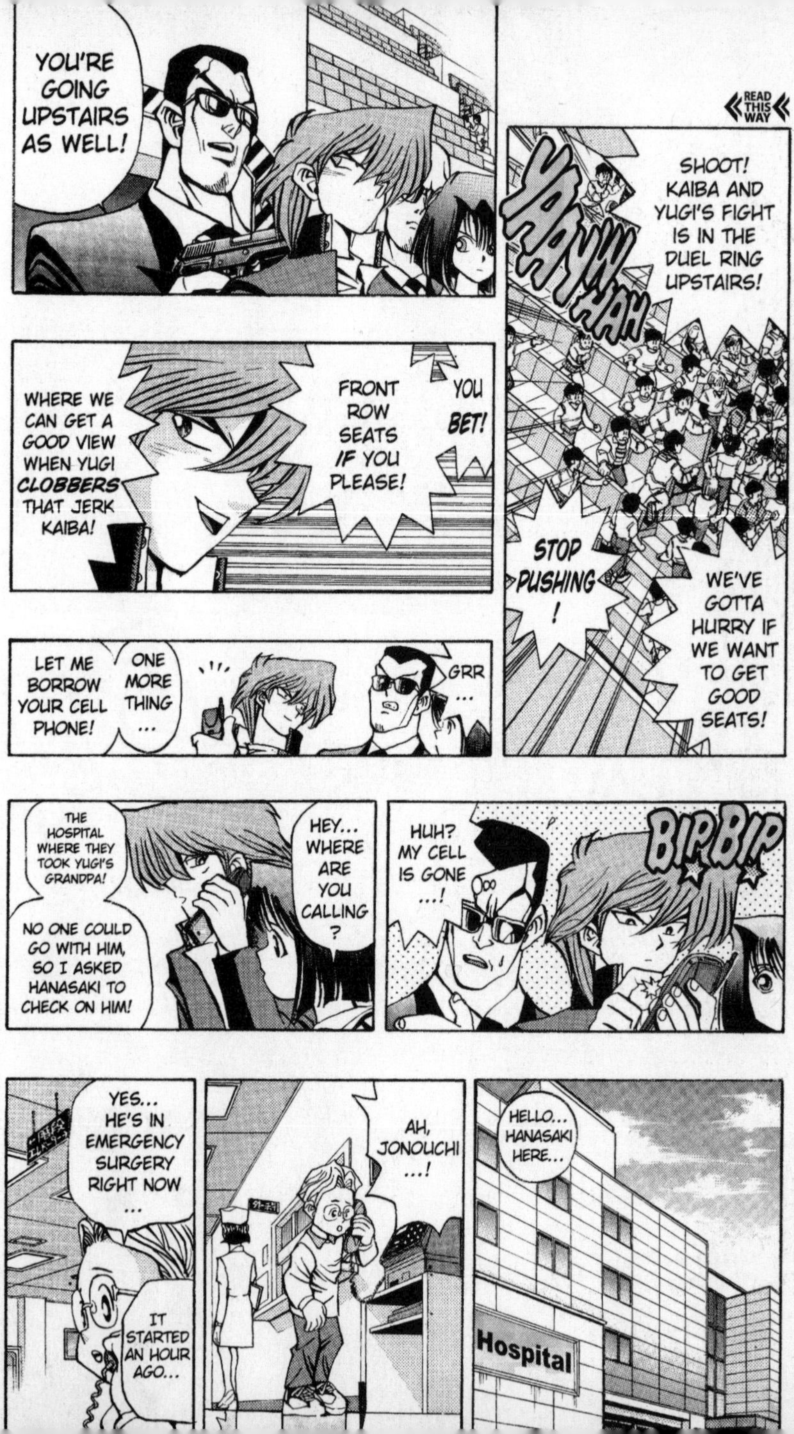
READ THIS WAY
SHOOT! KAIBA AND YUGI'S FIGHT IS IN THE DUEL RING UPSTAIRS!
STOP PUSHING!
WE'VE GOTTA HURRY IF WE WANT TO GET GOOD SEATS!
YOU'RE GOING UPSTAIRS AS WELL!
YOU BET!
FRONT ROW SEATS IF YOU PLEASE!
WHERE WE CAN GET A GOOD VIEW WHEN YUGI CLOBBERS THAT JERK KAIBA!
GRR...
ONE MORE THING...
LET ME BORROW YOUR CELL PHONE!
BIP BIP
HUH? MY CELL IS GONE...!
HEY... WHERE ARE YOU CALLING?
THE HOSPITAL WHERE THEY TOOK YUGI'S GRANDPA!
NO ONE COULD GO WITH HIM, SO I ASKED HANASAKI TO CHECK ON HIM!
HELLO... HANASAKI HERE...
Hospital
AH, JONOUCHI...!
YES... HE'S IN EMERGENCY SURGERY RIGHT NOW...
IT STARTED AN HOUR AGO...

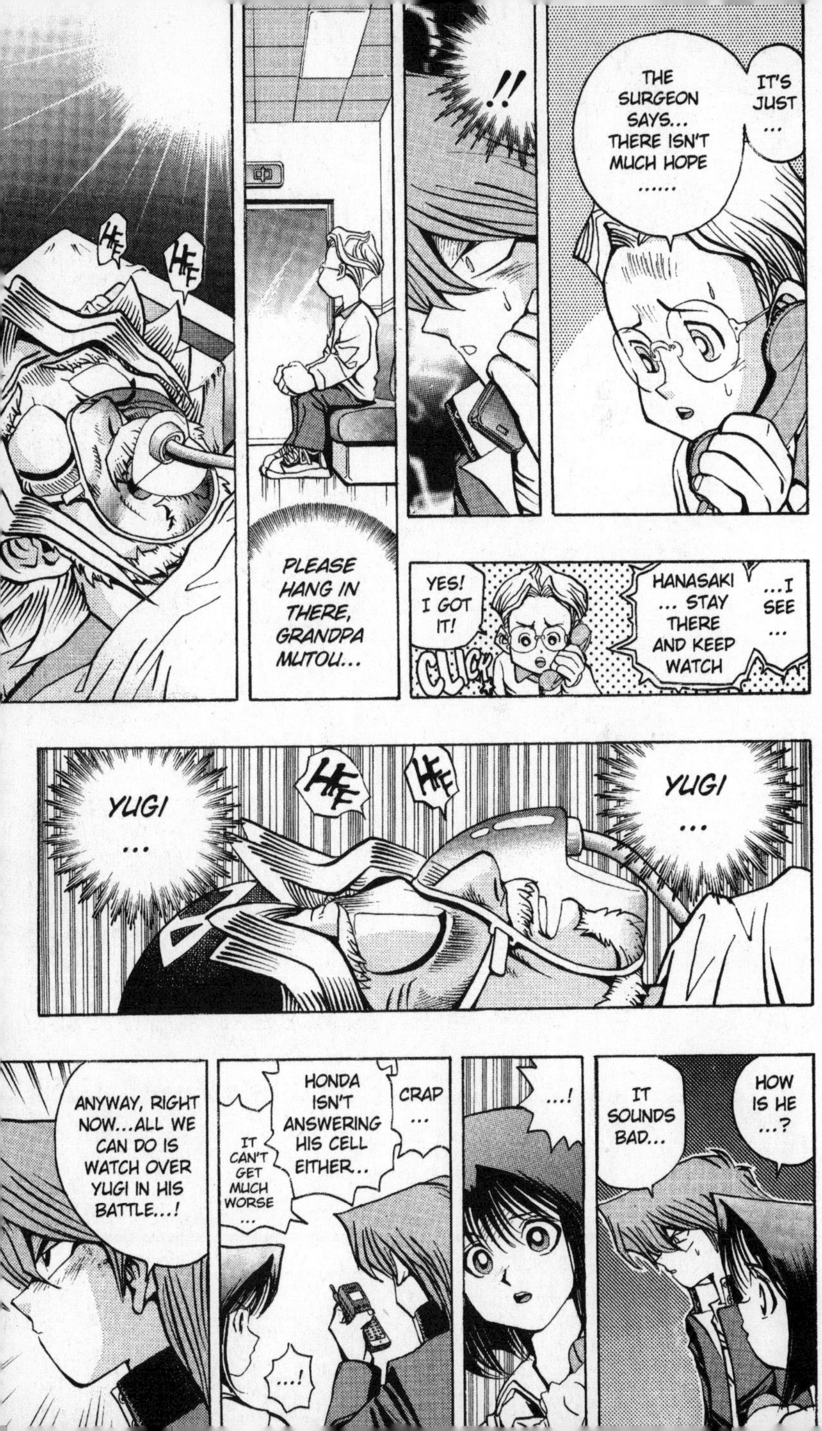
IT'S JUST ...
THE SURGEON SAYS... THERE ISN'T MUCH HOPE ......
!!
...I SEE ...
HANASAKI ... STAY THERE AND KEEP WATCH
YES! I GOT IT!
CLICK
PLEASE HANG IN THERE, GRANDPA MUTOU...
HEF
HEF
YUGI ...
HEF
HEF
YUGI ...
HOW IS HE ...?
IT SOUNDS BAD...
...!
CRAP ...
HONDA ISN'T ANSWERING HIS CELL EITHER...
IT CAN'T GET MUCH WORSE ...
...!
ANYWAY, RIGHT NOW...ALL WE CAN DO IS WATCH OVER YUGI IN HIS BATTLE...!

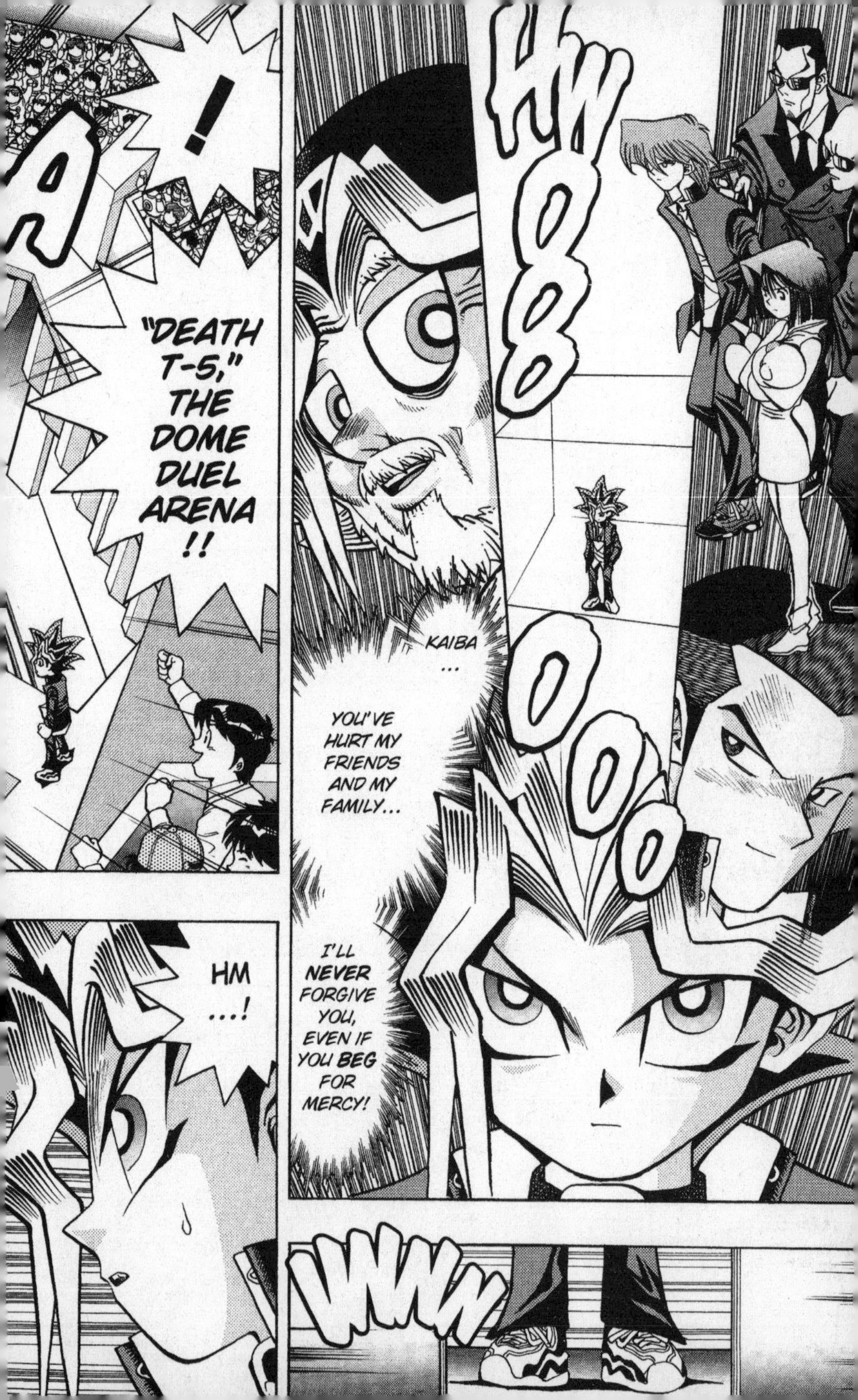
HWOOOOOOOO
KAIBA ...
YOU'VE HURT MY FRIENDS AND MY FAMILY...
I'LL NEVER FORGIVE YOU, EVEN IF YOU BEG FOR MERCY!
"DEATH T-5," THE DOME DUEL ARENA !!
HM ...!

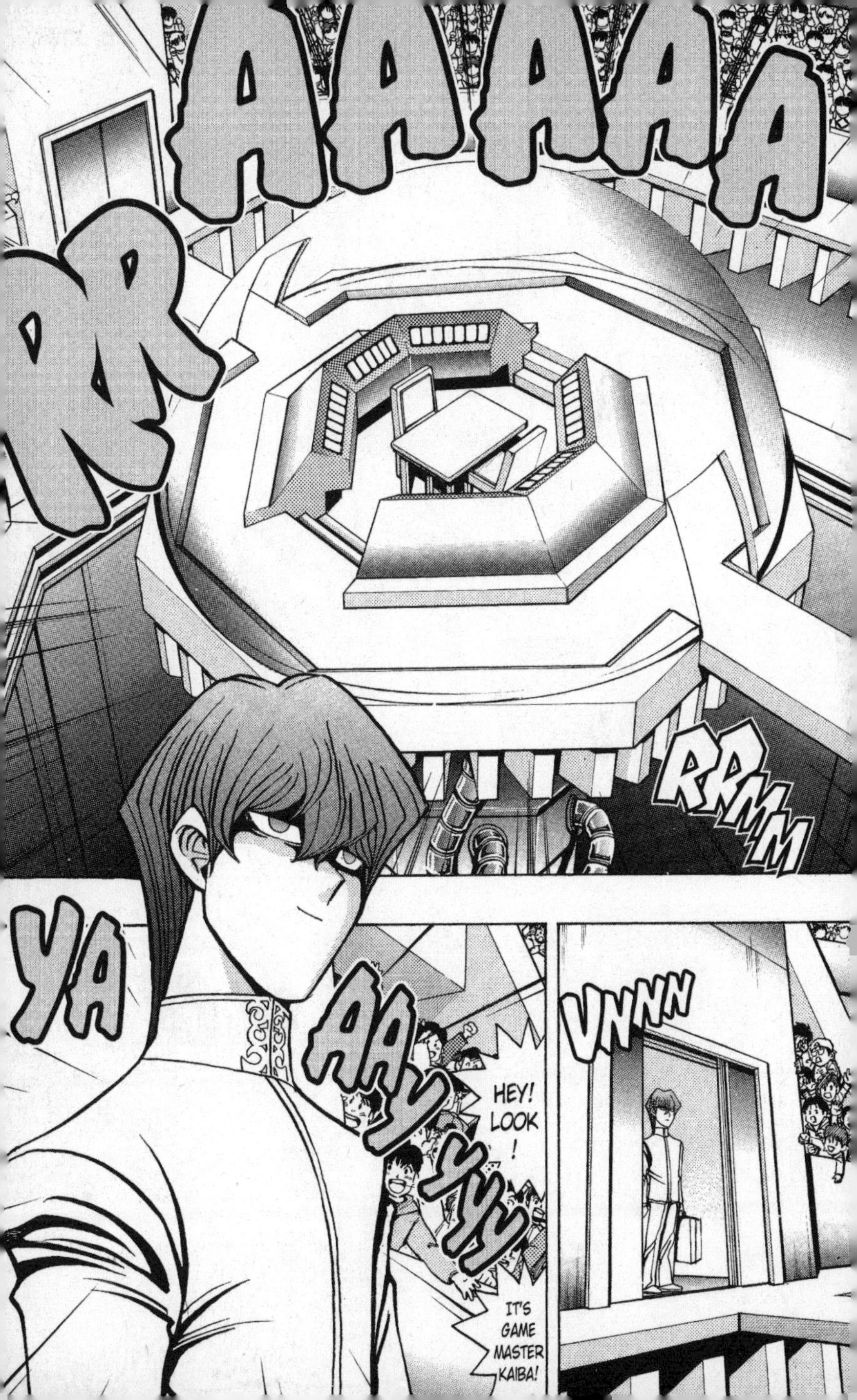
RRAAAAA
RRMMM
VNNNN
YAAAAYYY
HEY! LOOK!
IT'S GAME MASTER KAIBA!

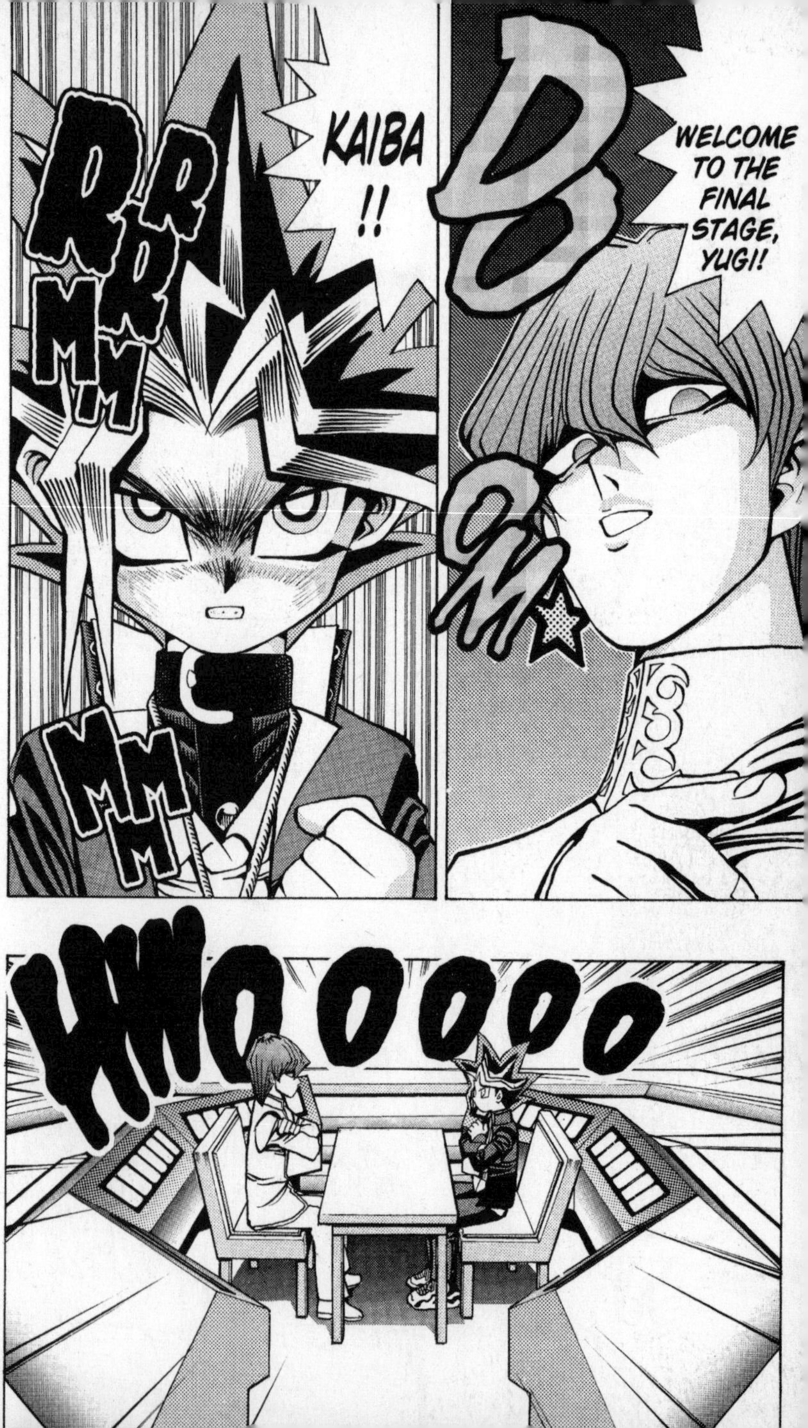
DOOM
WELCOME TO THE FINAL STAGE, YUGI!
KAIBA !!
RRRMMM
MMMM
VWOOOOO

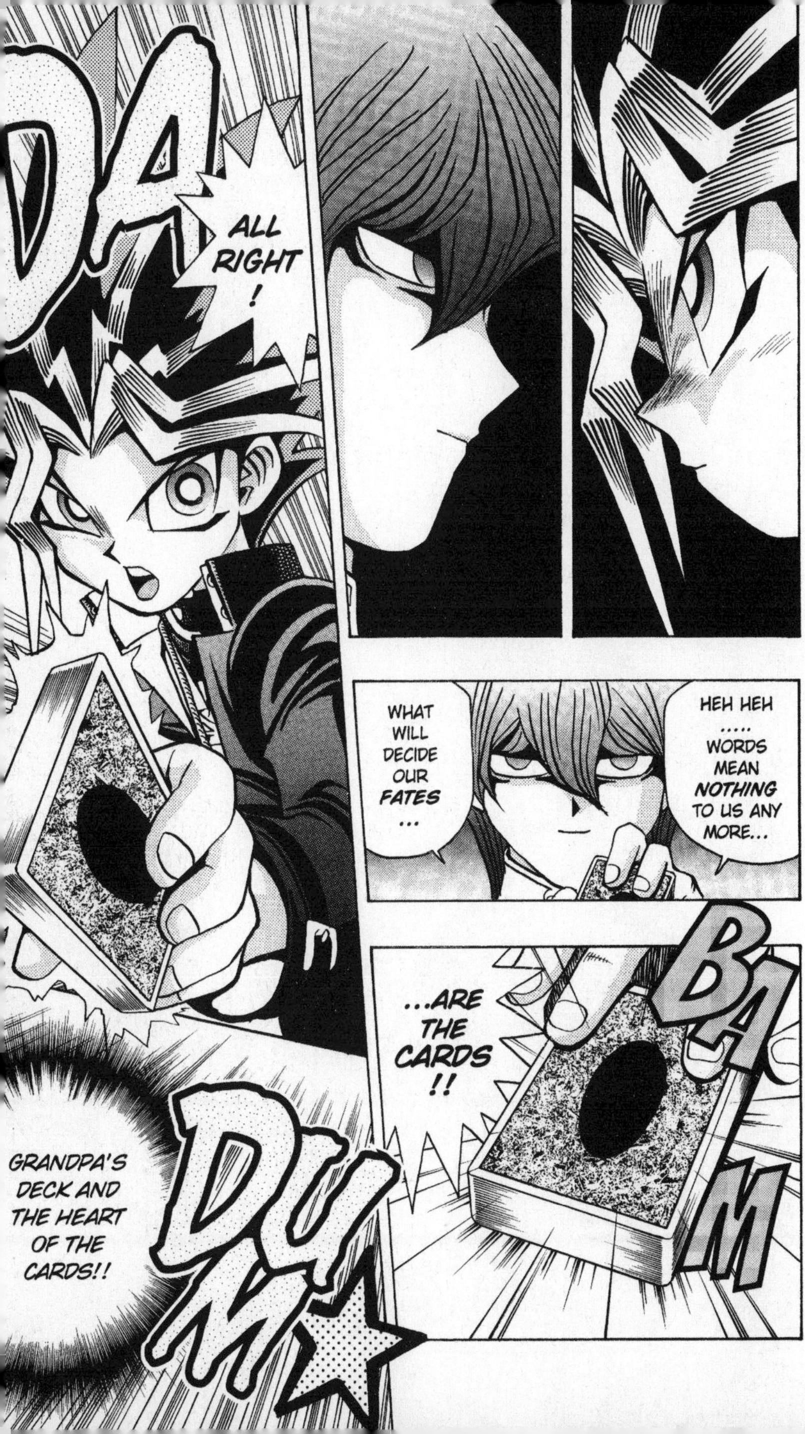
HEH HEH ..... WORDS MEAN NOTHING TO US ANY MORE...
WHAT WILL DECIDE OUR FATES ...
...ARE THE CARDS !!
BAM
DA
ALL RIGHT !
DUM
GRANDPA'S DECK AND THE HEART OF THE CARDS!!

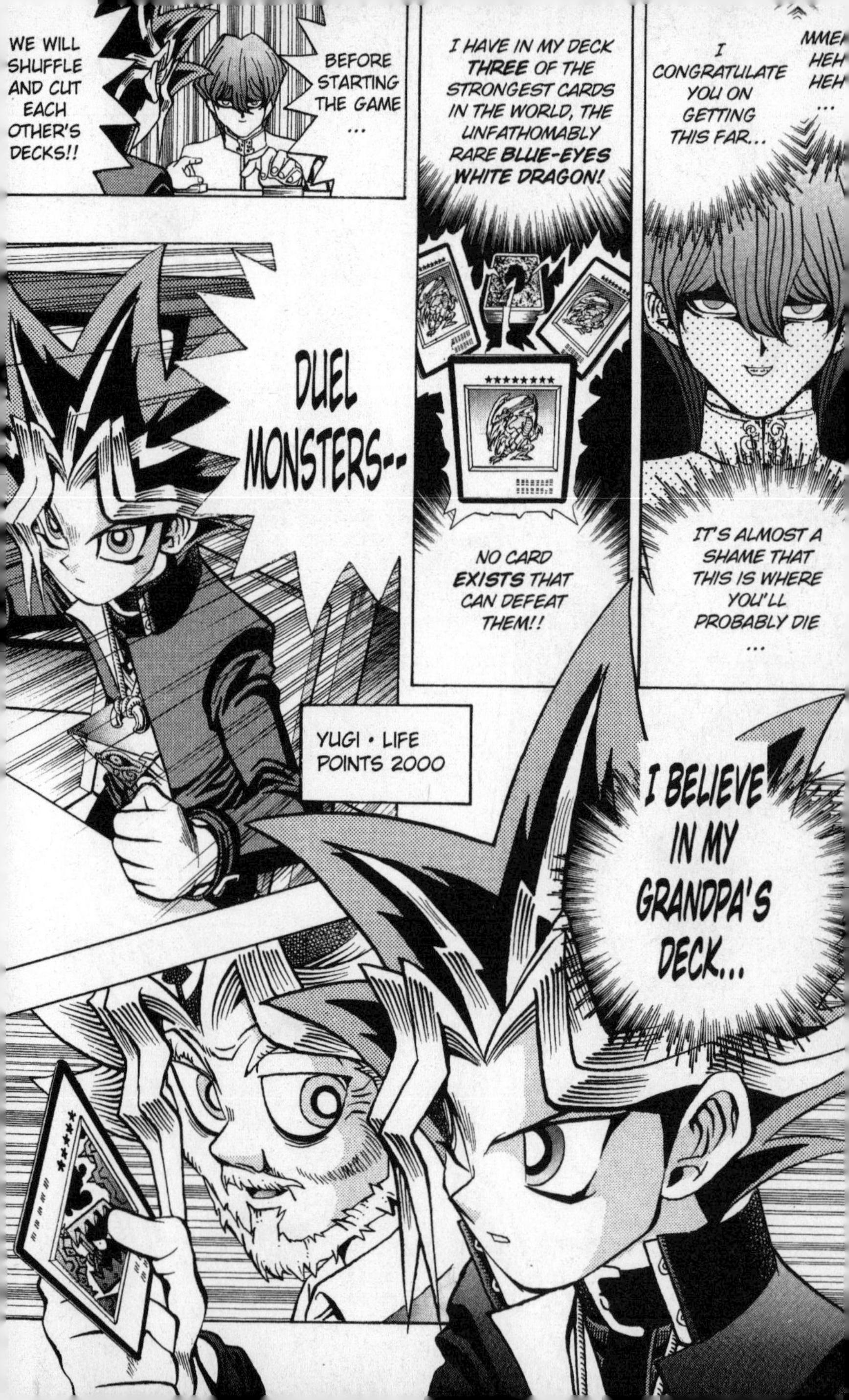

MME HEH HEH ...
I CONGRATULATE YOU ON GETTING THIS FAR...
IT'S ALMOST A SHAME THAT THIS IS WHERE YOU'LL PROBABLY DIE ...
I HAVE IN MY DECK THREE OF THE STRONGEST CARDS IN THE WORLD, THE UNFATHOMABLY RARE BLUE-EYES WHITE DRAGON!
NO CARD EXISTS THAT CAN DEFEAT THEM!!
BEFORE STARTING THE GAME ...
WE WILL SHUFFLE AND CUT EACH OTHER'S DECKS!!
DUEL MONSTERS--
YUGI • LIFE POINTS 2000
I BELIEVE IN MY GRANDPA'S DECK...

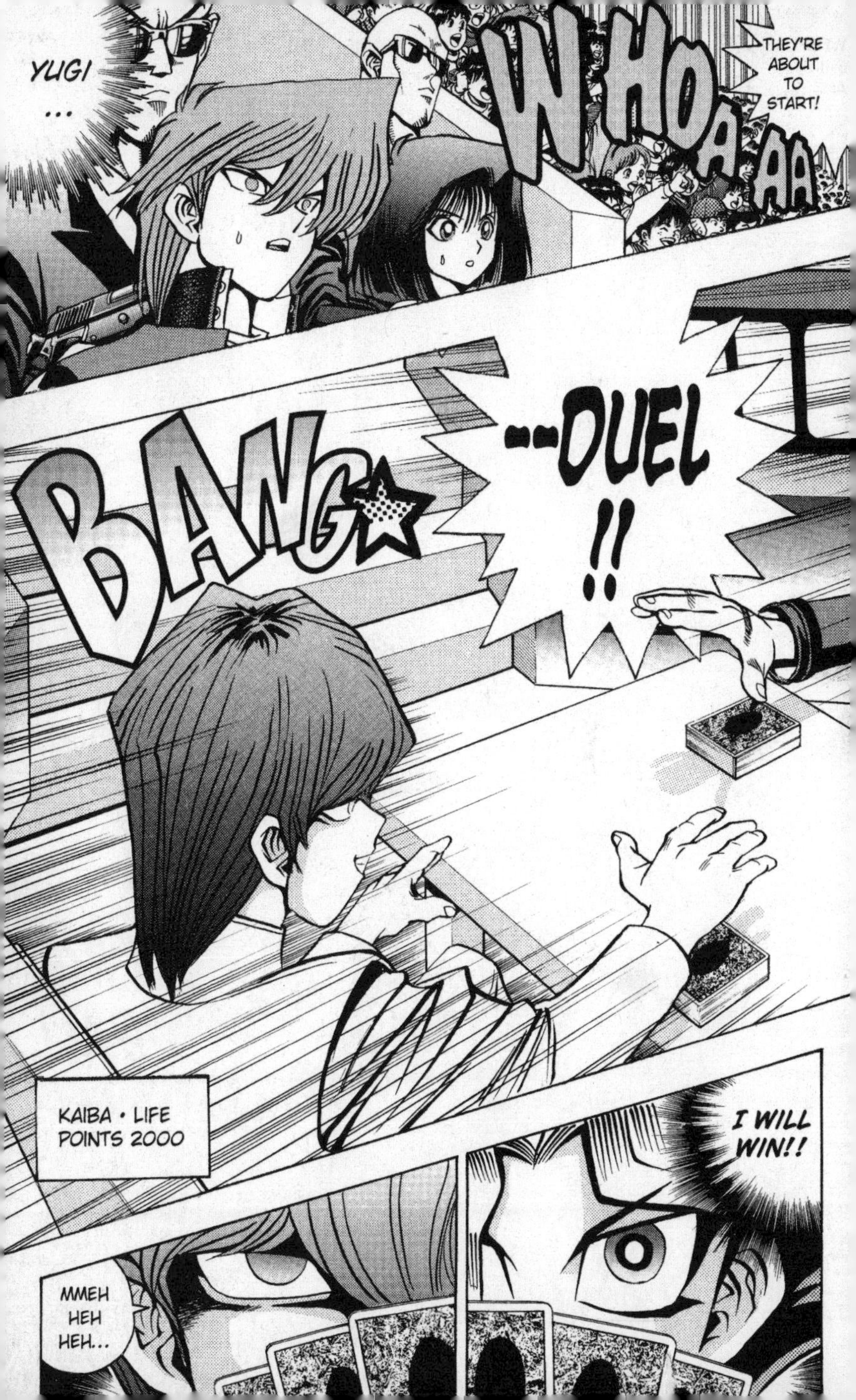
WHOA AA
THEY'RE ABOUT TO START!
YUGI ...
BANG
--DUEL !!
KAIBA • LIFE POINTS 2000
I WILL WIN!!
MMEH HEH HEH...

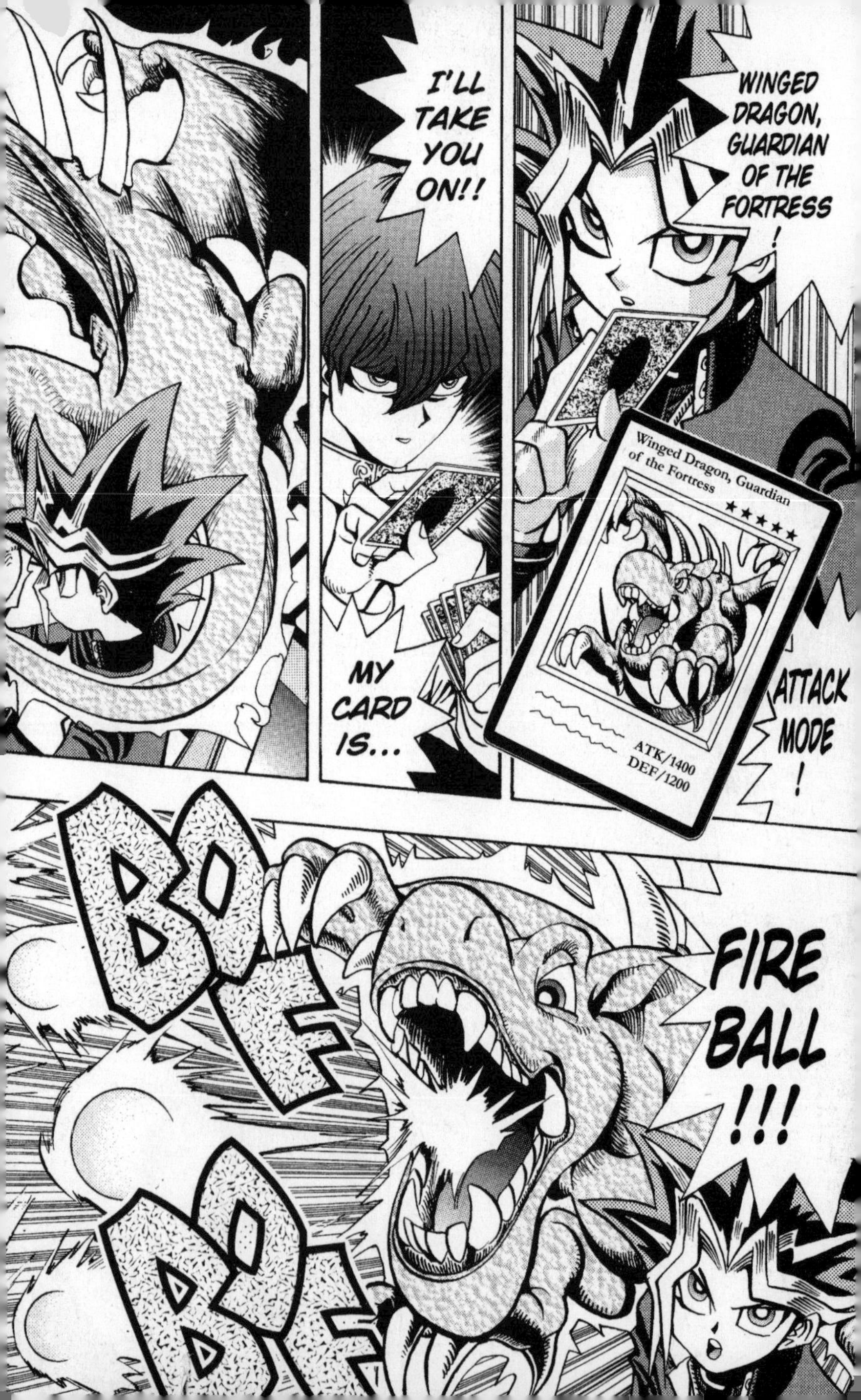
WINGED DRAGON, GUARDIAN OF THE FORTRESS!
Winged Dragon, Guardian of the Fortress
ATK/1400
DEF/1200
ATTACK MODE!
I'LL TAKE YOU ON!!
MY CARD IS...
FIRE BALL!!!
BOF
BOF

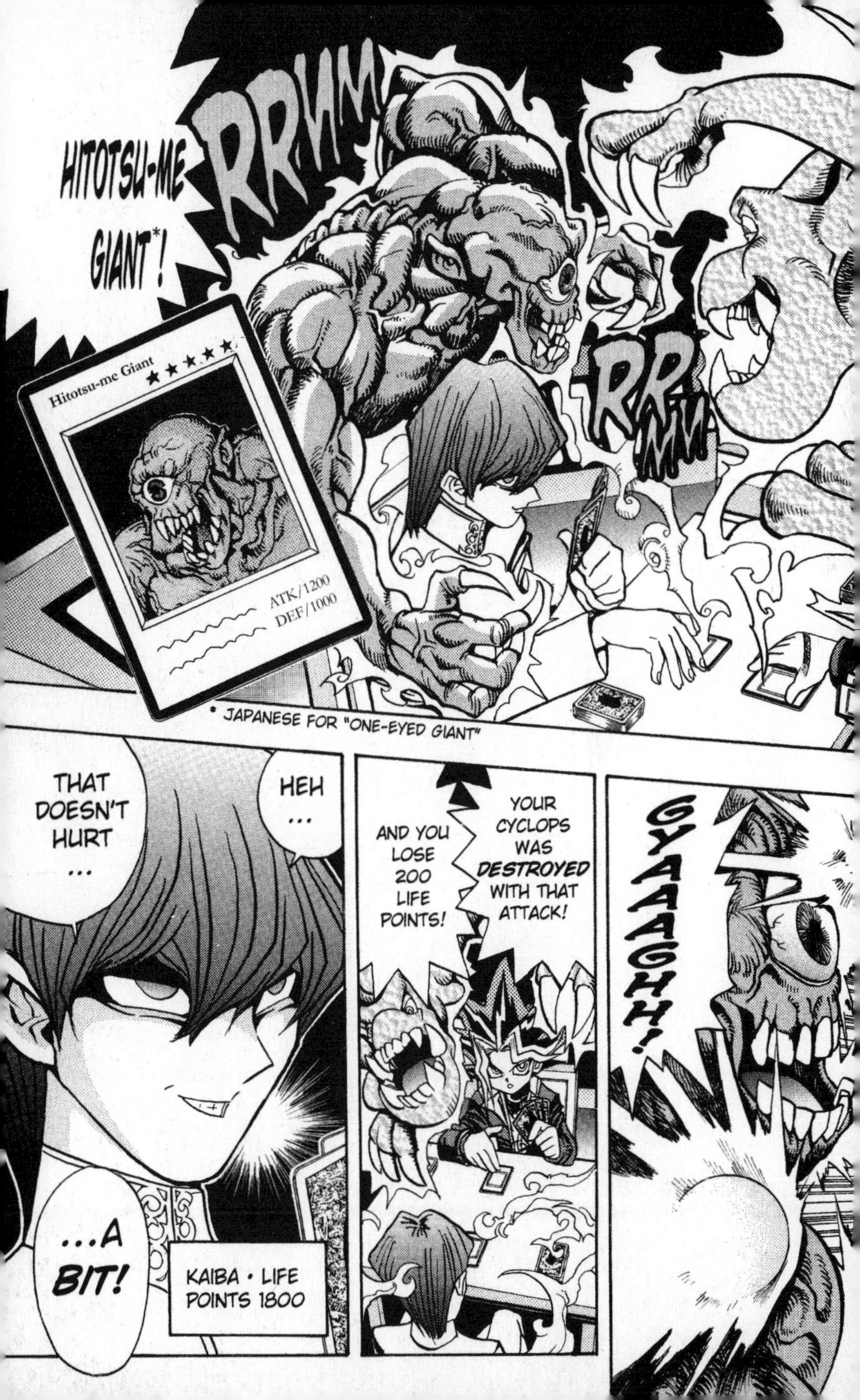
RRMM
HITOTSU-ME GIANT*!
RRMM
Hitotsu-me Giant
ATK/1200
DEF/1000
* JAPANESE FOR "ONE-EYED GIANT"
GYAAAAGHH!
YOUR CYCLOPS WAS DESTROYED WITH THAT ATTACK!
AND YOU LOSE 200 LIFE POINTS!
HEH ...
THAT DOESN'T HURT ...
...A BIT!
KAIBA • LIFE POINTS 1800

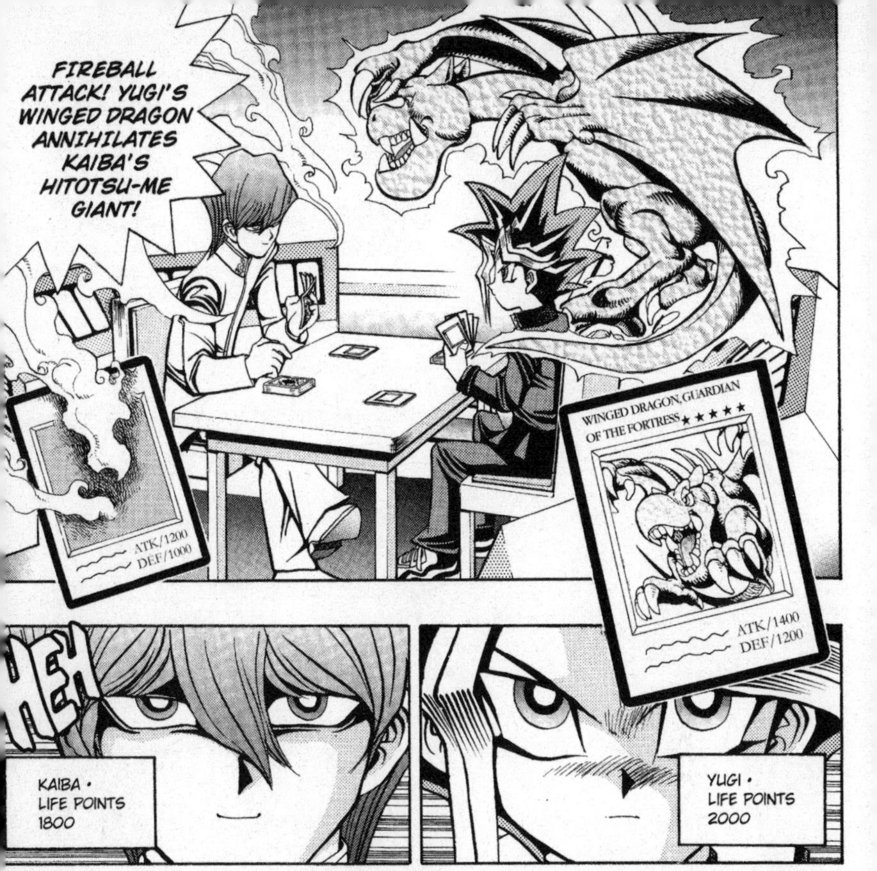
FIREBALL ATTACK! YUGI'S WINGED DRAGON ANNIHILATES KAIBA'S HITOTSU-ME GIANT!
WINGED DRAGON, GUARDIAN OF THE FORTRESS ★★★★★
ATK/1400
DEF/1200
ATK/1200
DEF/1000
YUGI • LIFE POINTS 2000
HEH
KAIBA • LIFE POINTS 1800

Duel 37: To the Death!

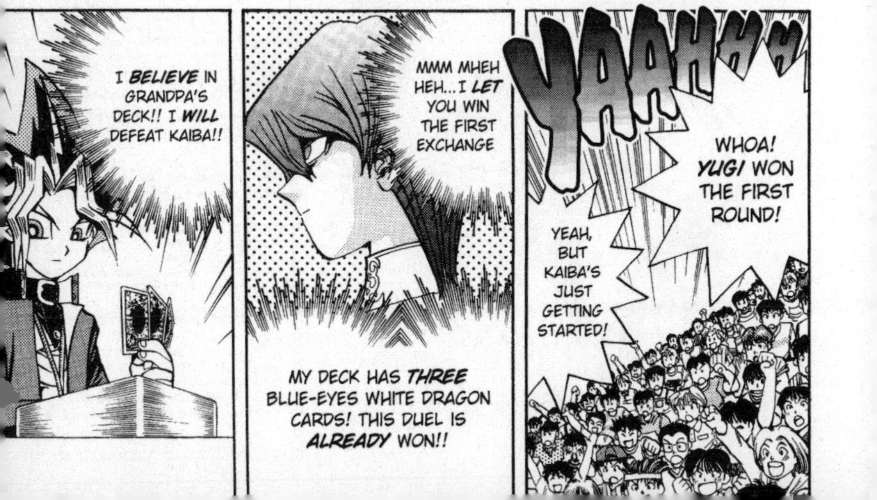
YAAHHH
WHOA! *YUGI* WON THE FIRST ROUND!
YEAH, BUT KAIBA'S JUST GETTING STARTED!
MMM MHEH HEH...I *LET* YOU WIN THE FIRST EXCHANGE
MY DECK HAS *THREE* BLUE-EYES WHITE DRAGON CARDS! THIS DUEL IS *ALREADY* WON!!
I *BELIEVE* IN GRANDPA'S DECK!! I *WILL* DEFEAT KAIBA!!

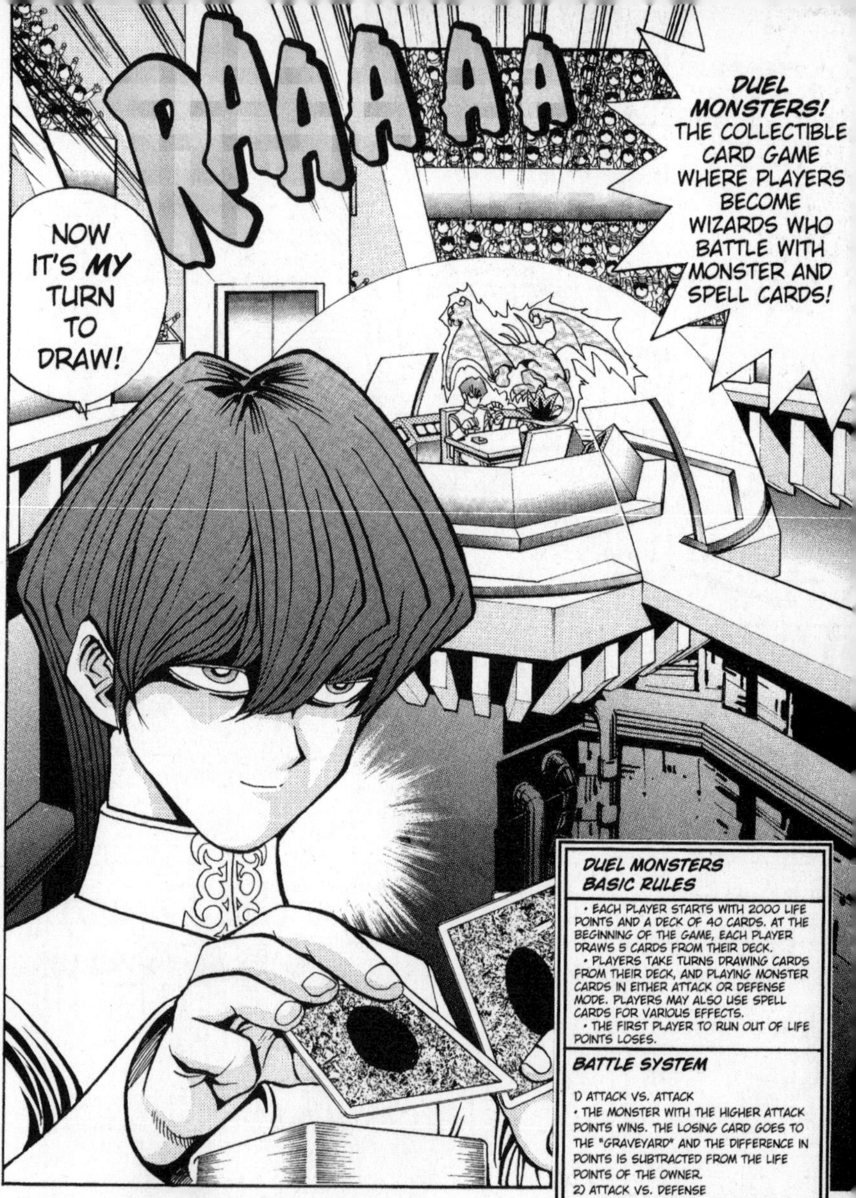
RAAAAA
DUEL MONSTERS! THE COLLECTIBLE CARD GAME WHERE PLAYERS BECOME WIZARDS WHO BATTLE WITH MONSTER AND SPELL CARDS!
NOW IT'S MY TURN TO DRAW!

DUEL MONSTERS BASIC RULES

- EACH PLAYER STARTS WITH 2000 LIFE POINTS AND A DECK OF 40 CARDS. AT THE BEGINNING OF THE GAME, EACH PLAYER DRAWS 5 CARDS FROM THEIR DECK.
- PLAYERS TAKE TURNS DRAWING CARDS FROM THEIR DECK, AND PLAYING MONSTER CARDS IN EITHER ATTACK OR DEFENSE MODE. PLAYERS MAY ALSO USE SPELL CARDS FOR VARIOUS EFFECTS.
- THE FIRST PLAYER TO RUN OUT OF LIFE POINTS LOSES.

BATTLE SYSTEM

1) ATTACK VS. ATTACK
- THE MONSTER WITH THE HIGHER ATTACK POINTS WINS. THE LOSING CARD GOES TO THE "GRAVEYARD" AND THE DIFFERENCE IN POINTS IS SUBTRACTED FROM THE LIFE POINTS OF THE OWNER.

2) ATTACK VS. DEFENSE
- IF THE ATTACKER'S ATTACK POINTS ARE HIGHER THAN THE DEFENDER'S DEFENSE, THE DEFENDING CARD GOES TO THE "GRAVEYARD." HOWEVER, THE OWNER'S LIFE POINTS ARE UNAFFECTED.
- IF THE DEFENDER'S DEFENSE IS HIGHER THAN THE ATTACKER'S ATTACK POINTS, THE DIFFERENCE IN POINTS IS SUBTRACTED FROM THE ATTACKING PLAYER'S LIFE POINTS. BOTH CARDS STAY PUT.

Duel 37: To The Death!

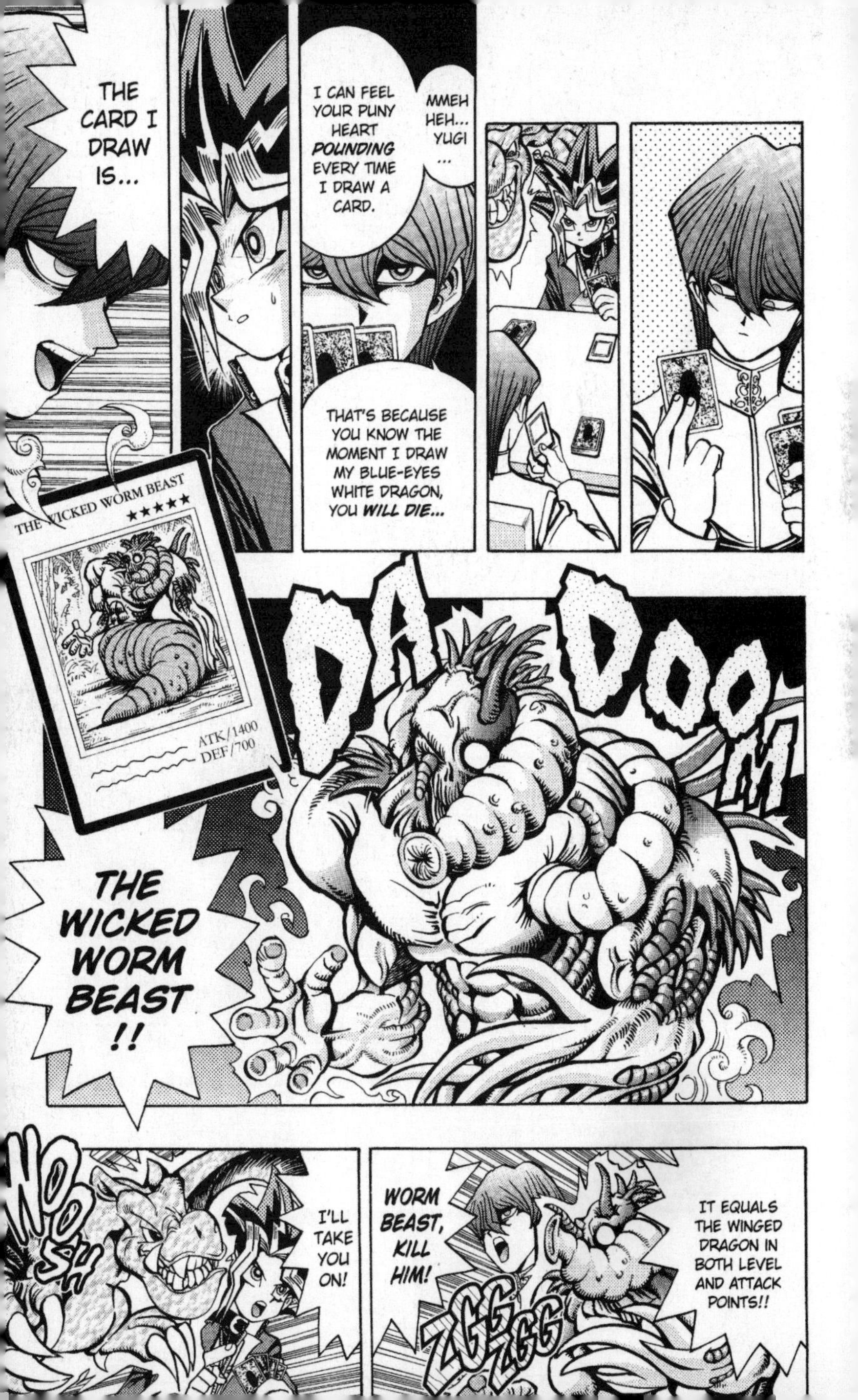
MMEH HEH... YUGI...
I CAN FEEL YOUR PUNY HEART POUNDING EVERY TIME I DRAW A CARD.
THAT'S BECAUSE YOU KNOW THE MOMENT I DRAW MY BLUE-EYES WHITE DRAGON, YOU WILL DIE...
THE CARD I DRAW IS...
DA DOOM
THE WICKED WORM BEAST
ATK/1400
DEF/700
THE WICKED WORM BEAST!!
IT EQUALS THE WINGED DRAGON IN BOTH LEVEL AND ATTACK POINTS!!
WORM BEAST, KILL HIM!
ZGG ZGG
I'LL TAKE YOU ON!
WOOOSH

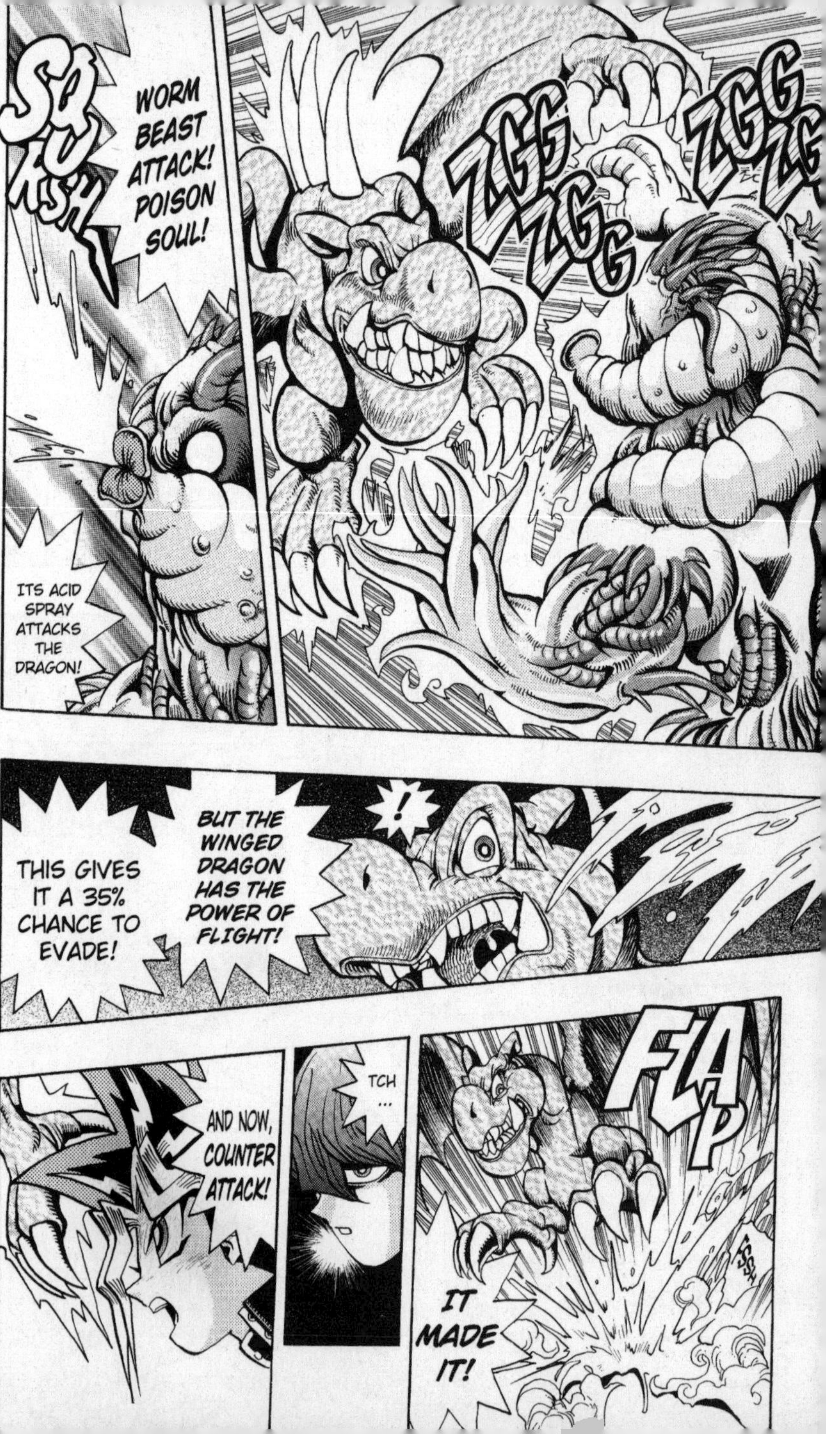
ZGG ZGG
ZGG ZG
SQUSH
WORM BEAST ATTACK! POISON SOUL!
ITS ACID SPRAY ATTACKS THE DRAGON!
!
BUT THE WINGED DRAGON HAS THE POWER OF FLIGHT!
THIS GIVES IT A 35% CHANCE TO EVADE!
FLAP
FSSH
IT MADE IT!
TCH ...
AND NOW, COUNTER ATTACK!

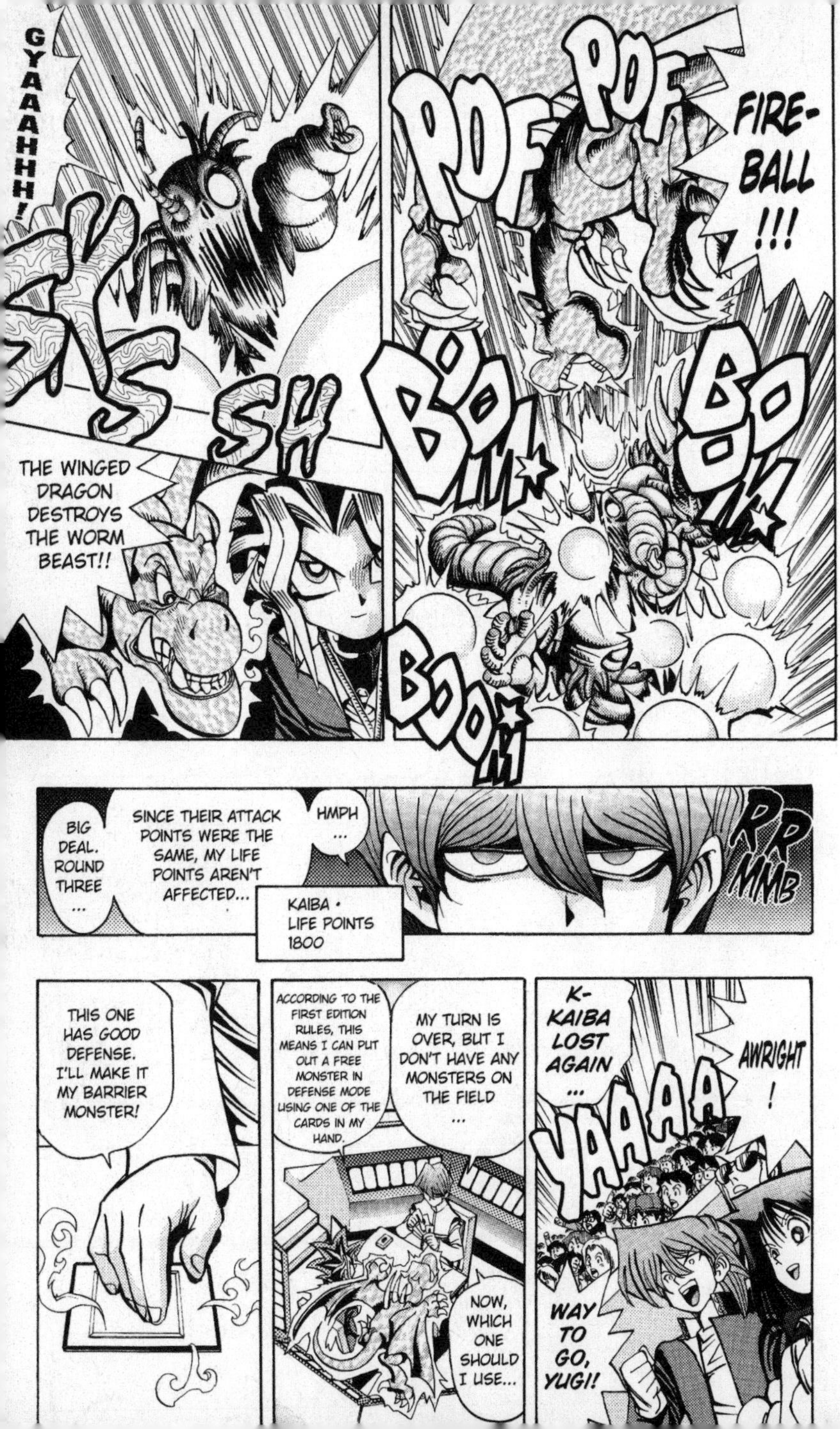
POF POF
FIRE-BALL!!!
BOOM
BOOM
BOOM
GYAAAAHHH!
SH
THE WINGED DRAGON DESTROYS THE WORM BEAST!!
RRMMB
HMPH...
SINCE THEIR ATTACK POINTS WERE THE SAME, MY LIFE POINTS AREN'T AFFECTED...
BIG DEAL. ROUND THREE...
KAIBA • LIFE POINTS 1800
AWRIGHT!
K-KAIBA LOST AGAIN...
YAAAA
WAY TO GO, YUGI!
MY TURN IS OVER, BUT I DON'T HAVE ANY MONSTERS ON THE FIELD...
ACCORDING TO THE FIRST EDITION RULES, THIS MEANS I CAN PUT OUT A FREE MONSTER IN DEFENSE MODE USING ONE OF THE CARDS IN MY HAND.
NOW, WHICH ONE SHOULD I USE...
THIS ONE HAS GOOD DEFENSE. I'LL MAKE IT MY BARRIER MONSTER!

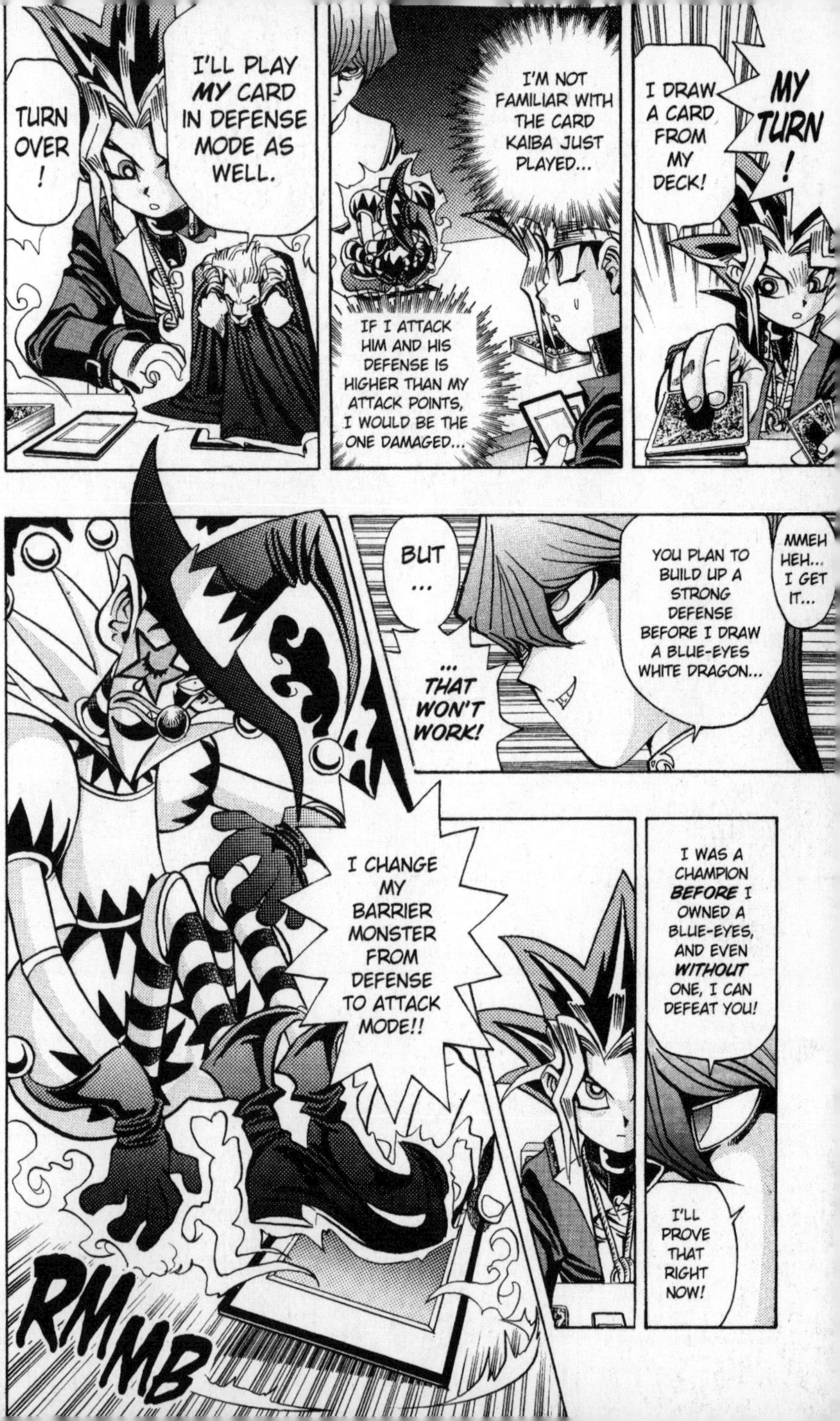
MY TURN!
I DRAW A CARD FROM MY DECK!
I'M NOT FAMILIAR WITH THE CARD KAIBA JUST PLAYED...
IF I ATTACK HIM AND HIS DEFENSE IS HIGHER THAN MY ATTACK POINTS, I WOULD BE THE ONE DAMAGED...
I'LL PLAY *MY* CARD IN DEFENSE MODE AS WELL.
TURN OVER!
MMEH HEH... I GET IT...
YOU PLAN TO BUILD UP A STRONG DEFENSE BEFORE I DRAW A BLUE-EYES WHITE DRAGON...
BUT...
...*THAT WON'T WORK!*
I WAS A CHAMPION *BEFORE* I OWNED A BLUE-EYES, AND EVEN *WITHOUT* ONE, I CAN DEFEAT YOU!
I'LL PROVE THAT RIGHT NOW!
I CHANGE MY BARRIER MONSTER FROM DEFENSE TO ATTACK MODE!!
RMMB

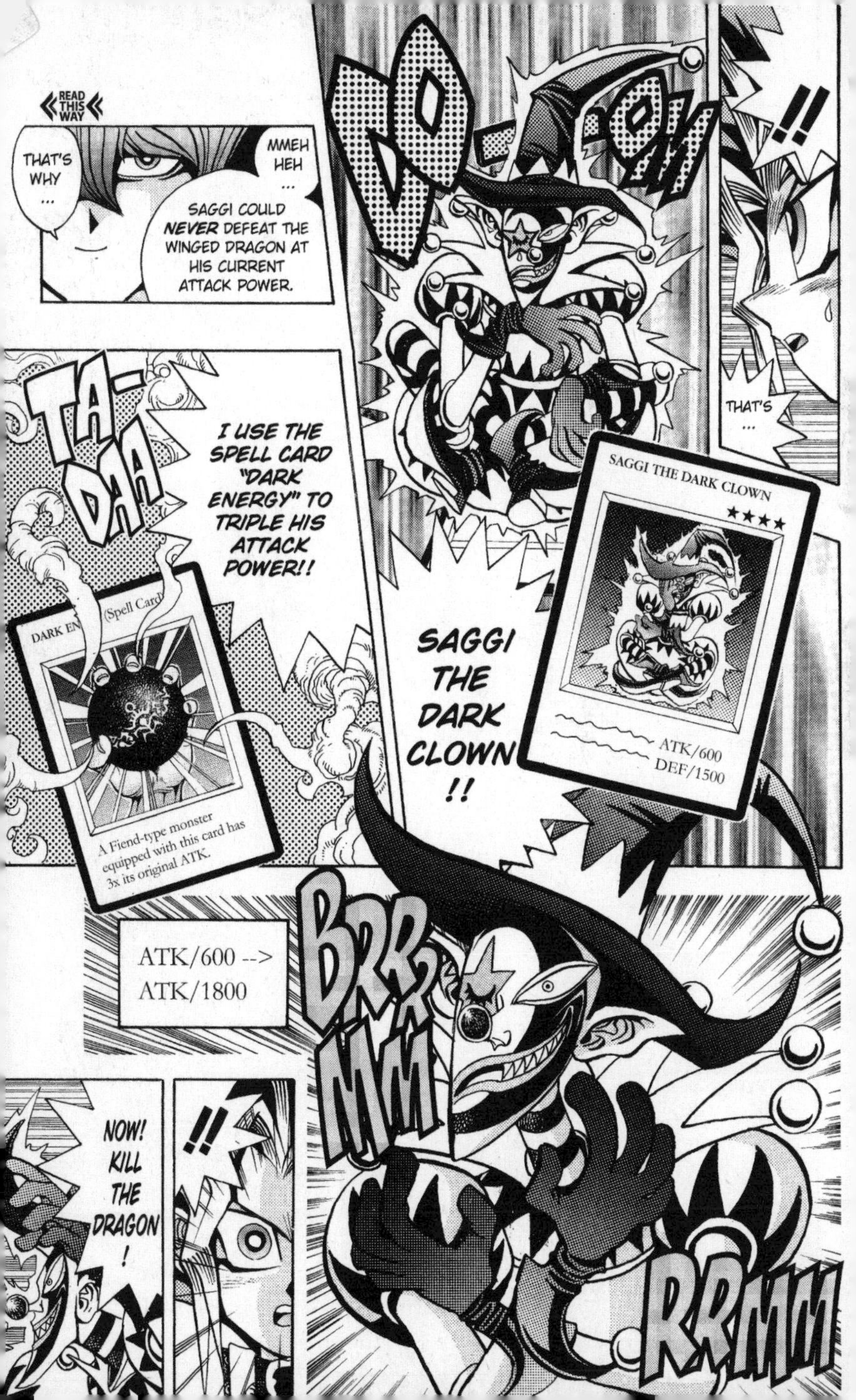
!!
THAT'S ...
ZO-OOM
SAGGI THE DARK CLOWN!!
SAGGI THE DARK CLOWN
ATK/600
DEF/1500
READ THIS WAY
MMEH HEH ...
THAT'S WHY ...
SAGGI COULD NEVER DEFEAT THE WINGED DRAGON AT HIS CURRENT ATTACK POWER.
TA-DAA
I USE THE SPELL CARD "DARK ENERGY" TO TRIPLE HIS ATTACK POWER!!
(Spell Card)
A Fiend-type monster equipped with this card has 3x its original ATK.
BRRMM
RRMM
ATK/600 -->
ATK/1800
!!
NOW! KILL THE DRAGON!

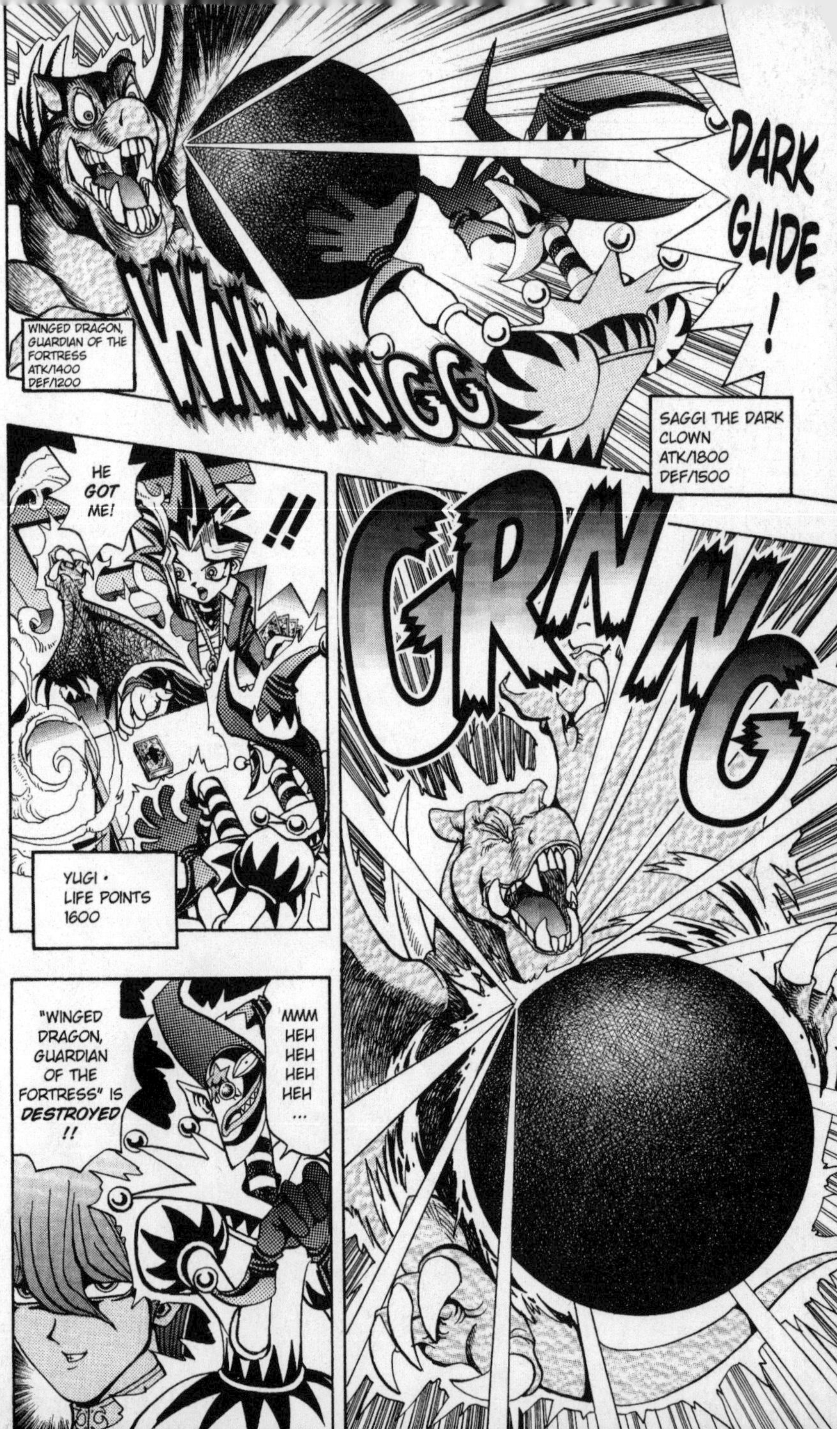
DARK GLIDE !
WNNNGG
WINGED DRAGON, GUARDIAN OF THE FORTRESS ATK/1400 DEF/1200
SAGGI THE DARK CLOWN ATK/1800 DEF/1500
GRNNG
!!
HE GOT ME!
YUGI • LIFE POINTS 1600
MMM HEH HEH HEH HEH ...
"WINGED DRAGON, GUARDIAN OF THE FORTRESS" IS DESTROYED !!

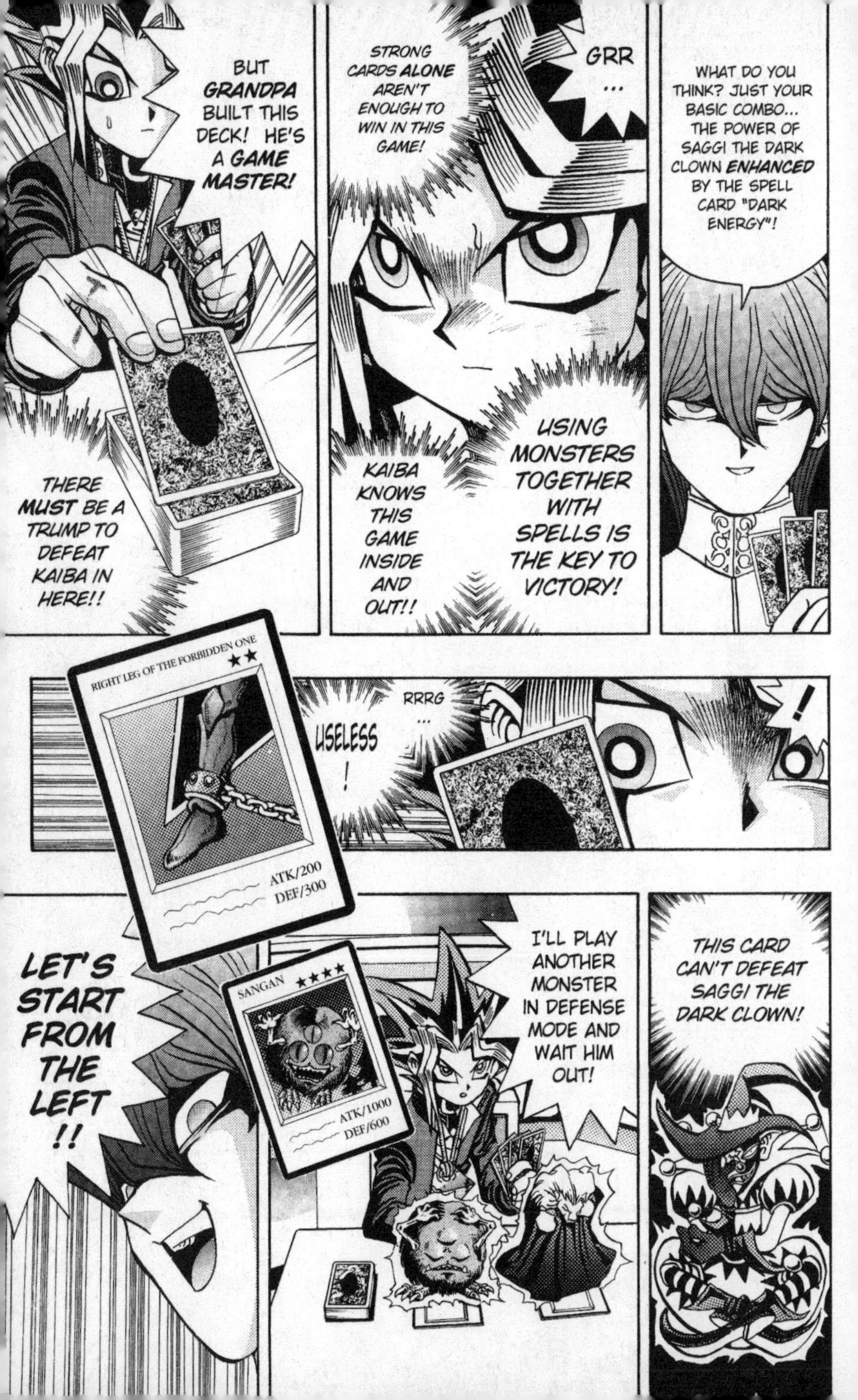
WHAT DO YOU THINK? JUST YOUR BASIC COMBO... THE POWER OF SAGGI THE DARK CLOWN ENHANCED BY THE SPELL CARD "DARK ENERGY"!
GRR ...
STRONG CARDS ALONE AREN'T ENOUGH TO WIN IN THIS GAME!
USING MONSTERS TOGETHER WITH SPELLS IS THE KEY TO VICTORY!
KAIBA KNOWS THIS GAME INSIDE AND OUT!!
BUT GRANDPA BUILT THIS DECK! HE'S A GAME MASTER!
THERE MUST BE A TRUMP TO DEFEAT KAIBA IN HERE!!
!
RRRG ...
USELESS!
RIGHT LEG OF THE FORBIDDEN ONE
ATK/200
DEF/300
THIS CARD CAN'T DEFEAT SAGGI THE DARK CLOWN!
I'LL PLAY ANOTHER MONSTER IN DEFENSE MODE AND WAIT HIM OUT!
SANGAN
ATK/1000
DEF/600
LET'S START FROM THE LEFT!!

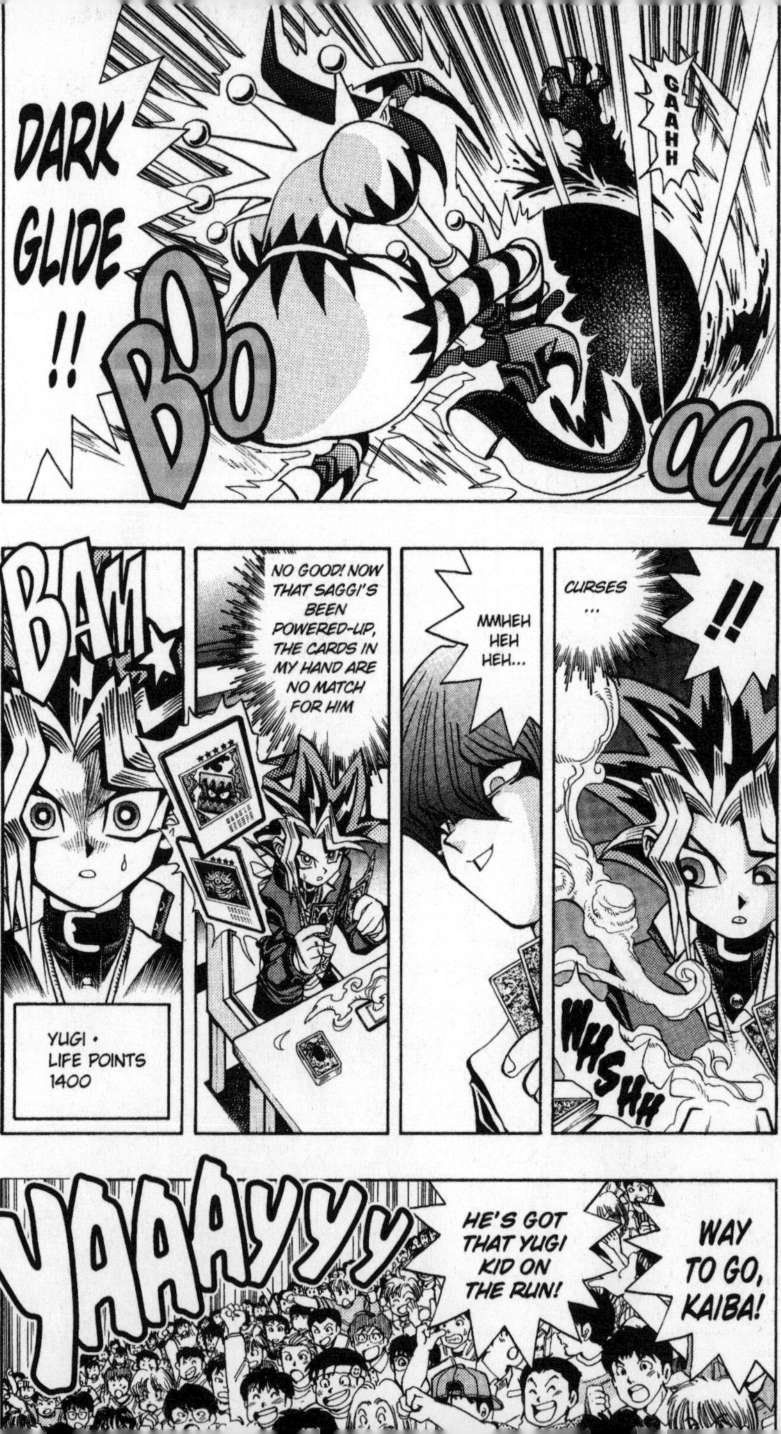
GAAHH
DARK GLIDE !!
BOO
OOM
CURSES ...
!!
WHSHH
MMHEH HEH HEH...
NO GOOD! NOW THAT SAGGI'S BEEN POWERED-UP, THE CARDS IN MY HAND ARE NO MATCH FOR HIM
BAM
YUGI • LIFE POINTS 1400
WAY TO GO, KAIBA!
HE'S GOT THAT YUGI KID ON THE RUN!
YAAAYYY

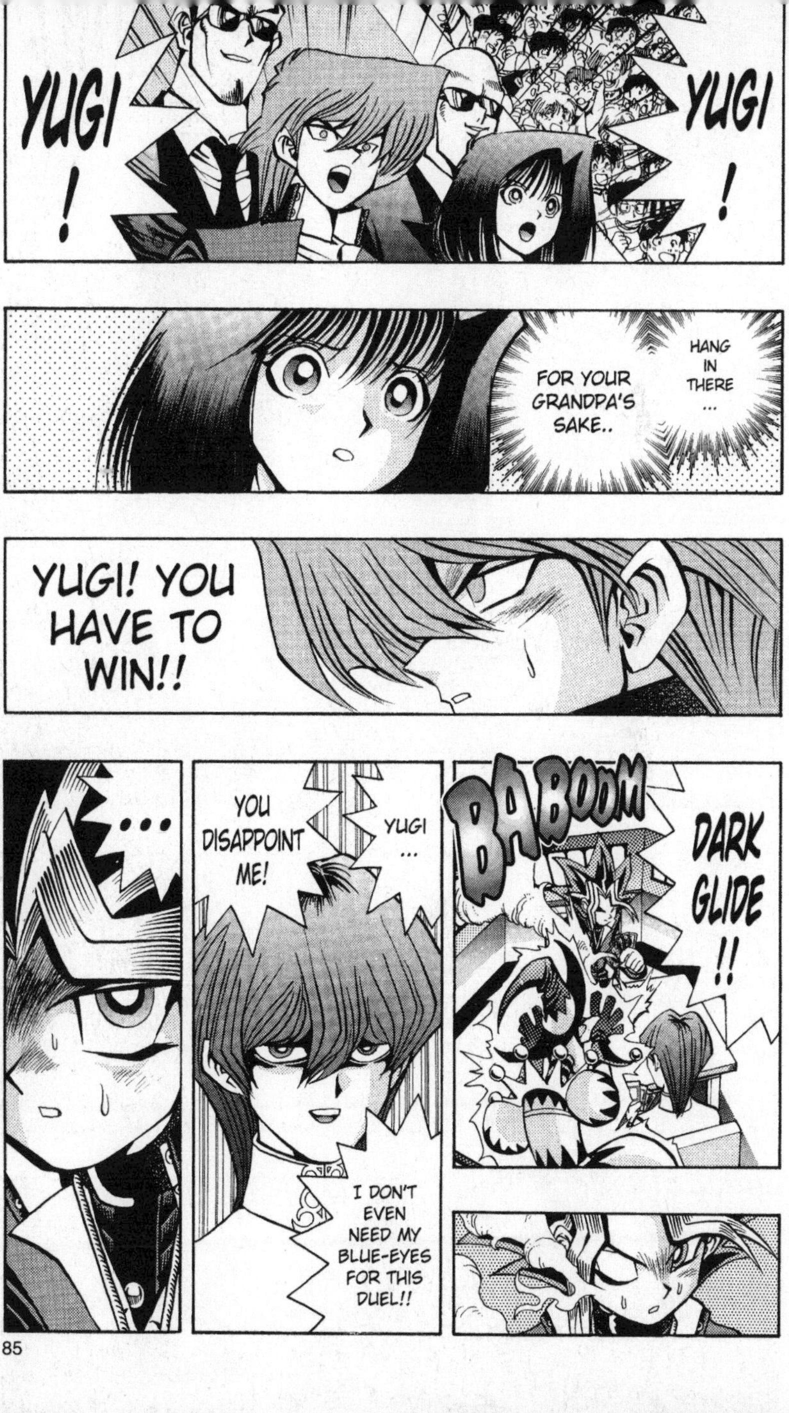
YUGI !
YUGI !
HANG IN THERE ...
FOR YOUR GRANDPA'S SAKE..
YUGI! YOU HAVE TO WIN!!
BA BOOM
DARK GLIDE !!
YUGI ...
YOU DISAPPOINT ME!
I DON'T EVEN NEED MY BLUE-EYES FOR THIS DUEL!!
...

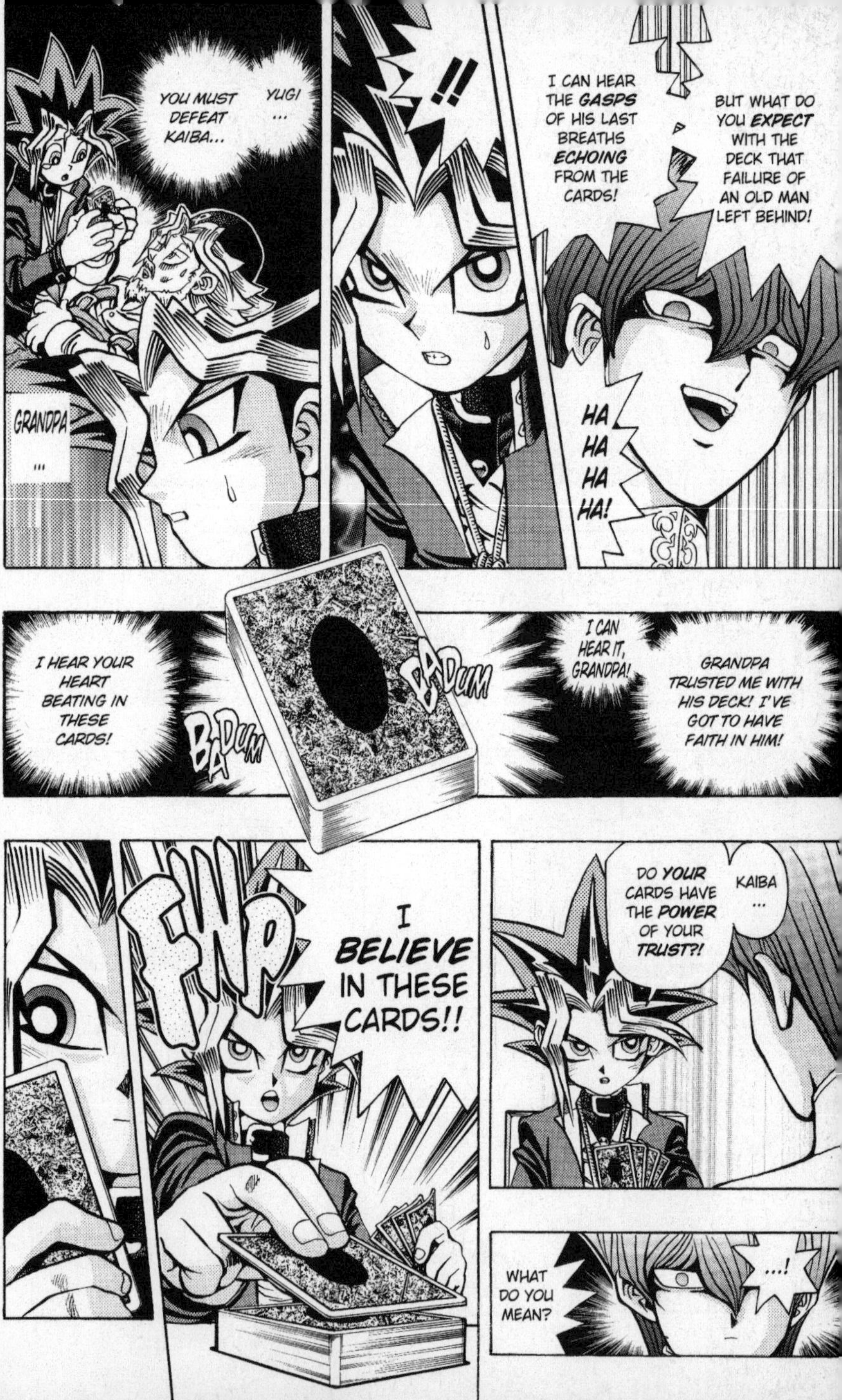
I CAN HEAR THE GASPS OF HIS LAST BREATHS ECHOING FROM THE CARDS!
BUT WHAT DO YOU EXPECT WITH THE DECK THAT FAILURE OF AN OLD MAN LEFT BEHIND!
HA HA HA HA!
!!
YUGI ...
YOU MUST DEFEAT KAIBA...
GRANDPA ...
I CAN HEAR IT, GRANDPA!
GRANDPA TRUSTED ME WITH HIS DECK! I'VE GOT TO HAVE FAITH IN HIM!
BADUM
I HEAR YOUR HEART BEATING IN THESE CARDS!
BADUM
KAIBA ...
DO YOUR CARDS HAVE THE POWER OF YOUR TRUST?!
...!
WHAT DO YOU MEAN?
I BELIEVE IN THESE CARDS!!
FWP

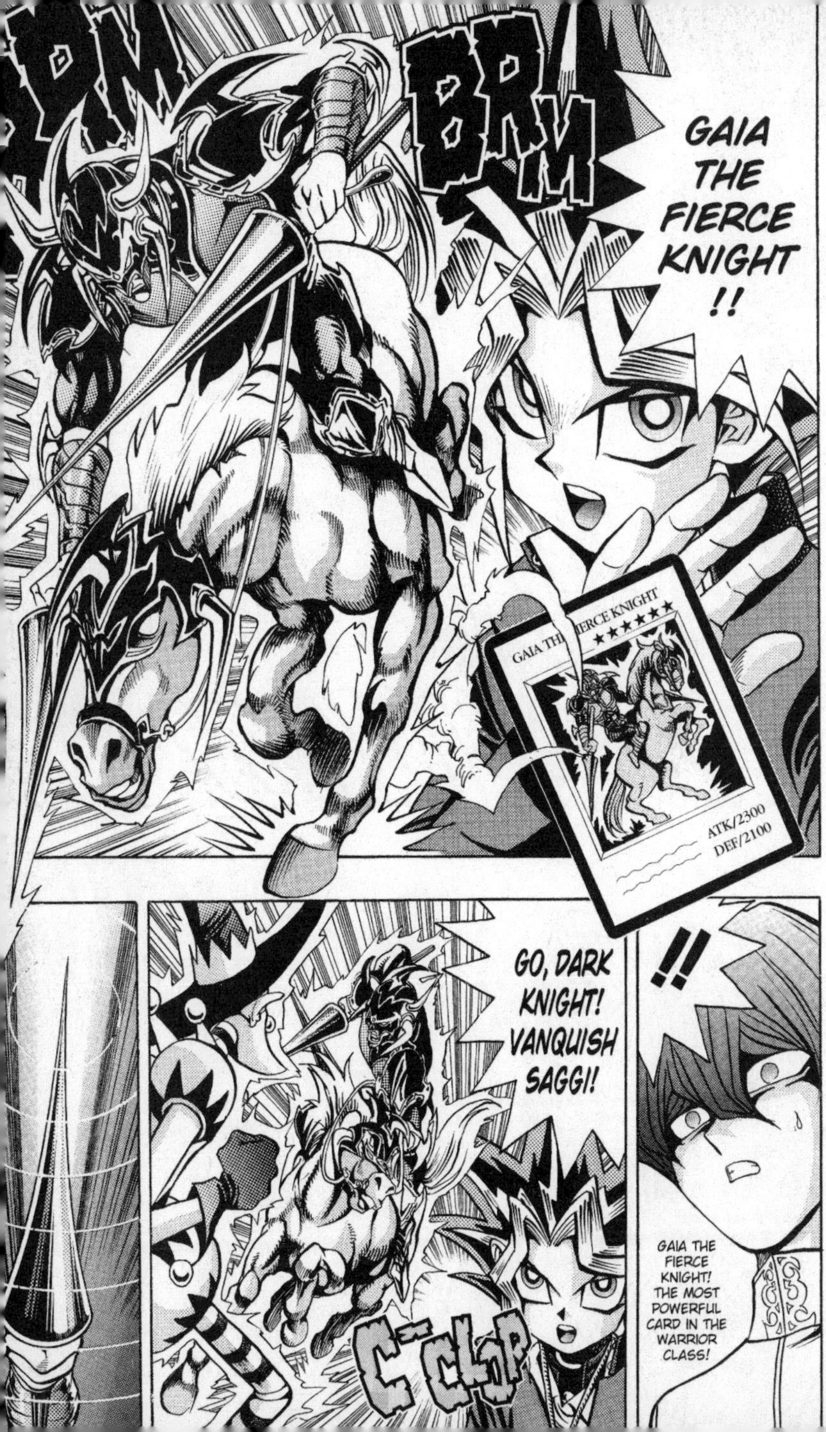
GAIA THE FIERCE KNIGHT !!
BRM
RM
ATK/2300
DEF/2100
!!
GAIA THE FIERCE KNIGHT! THE MOST POWERFUL CARD IN THE WARRIOR CLASS!
GO, DARK KNIGHT! VANQUISH SAGGI!
C-CLOP

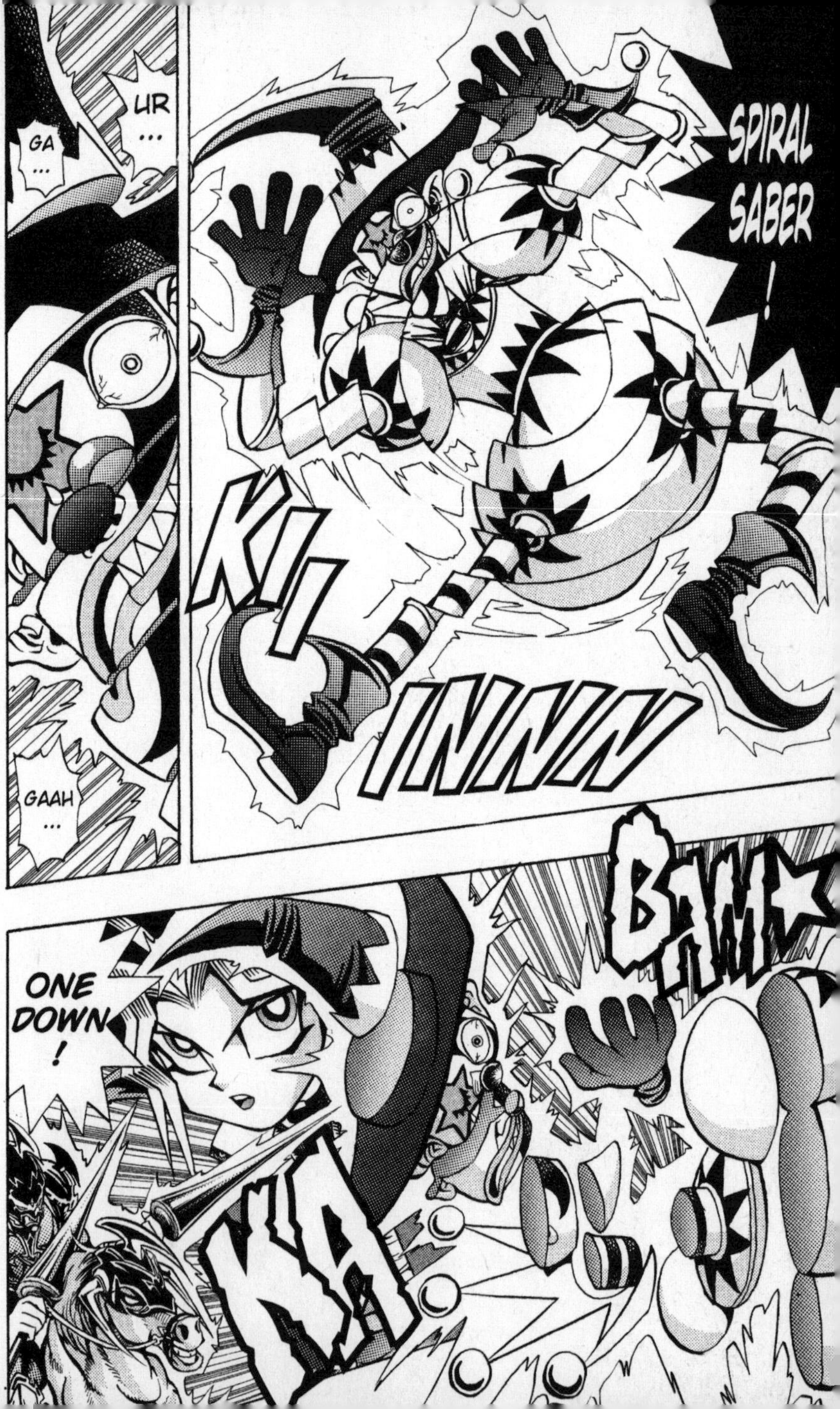
SPIRAL SABER!
KII
INNNN
UR ...
GA ....
GAAH ...
BAM
ONE DOWN!

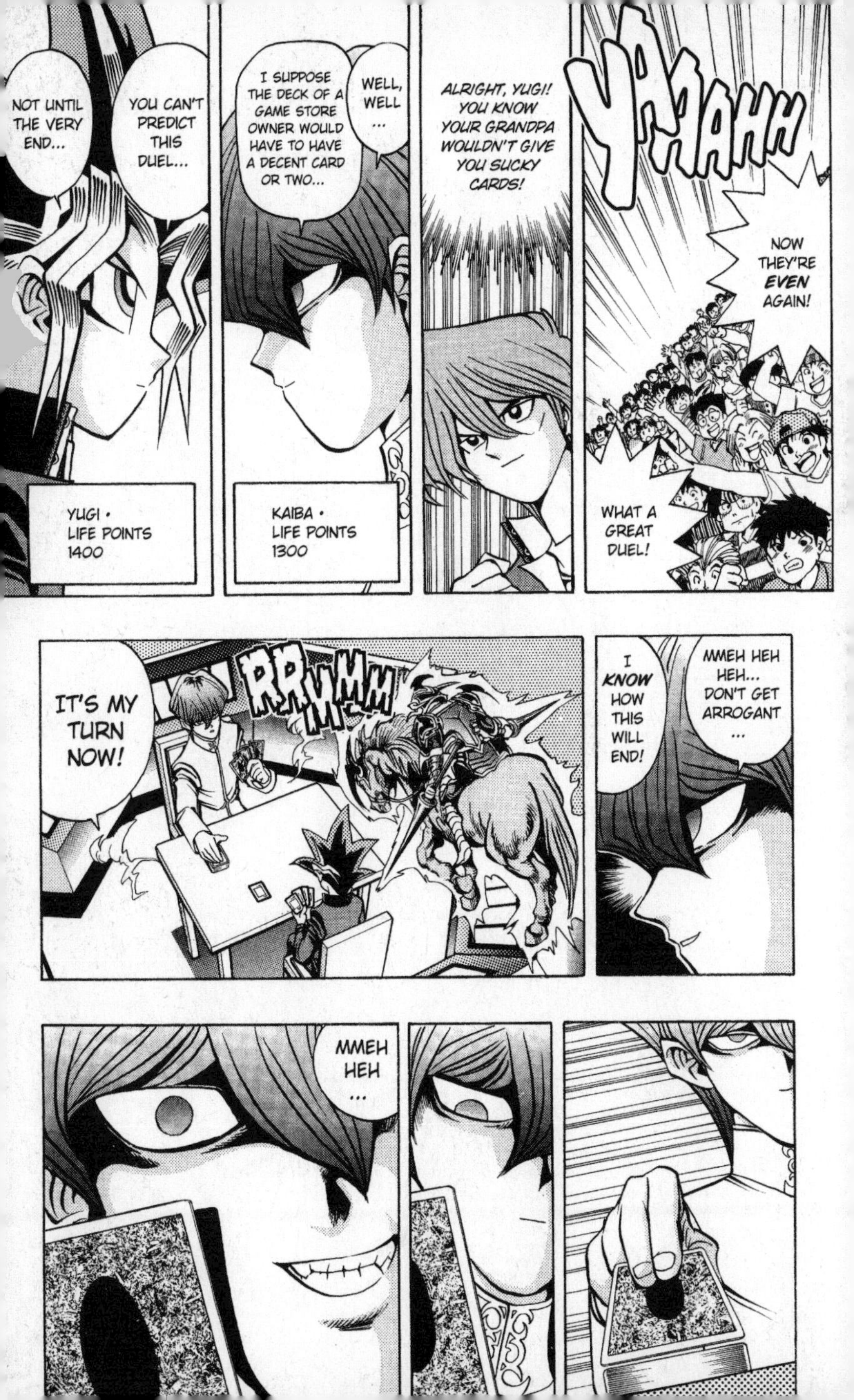
YAAAHH
NOW THEY'RE *EVEN* AGAIN!
WHAT A GREAT DUEL!
ALRIGHT, YUGI! YOU KNOW YOUR GRANDPA WOULDN'T GIVE YOU SUCKY CARDS!
WELL, WELL ...
I SUPPOSE THE DECK OF A GAME STORE OWNER WOULD HAVE TO HAVE A DECENT CARD OR TWO...
KAIBA • LIFE POINTS 1300
YOU CAN'T PREDICT THIS DUEL...
NOT UNTIL THE VERY END...
YUGI • LIFE POINTS 1400
MMEH HEH HEH... DON'T GET ARROGANT ...
I *KNOW* HOW THIS WILL END!
RRUMMM
IT'S MY TURN NOW!
MMEH HEH ...

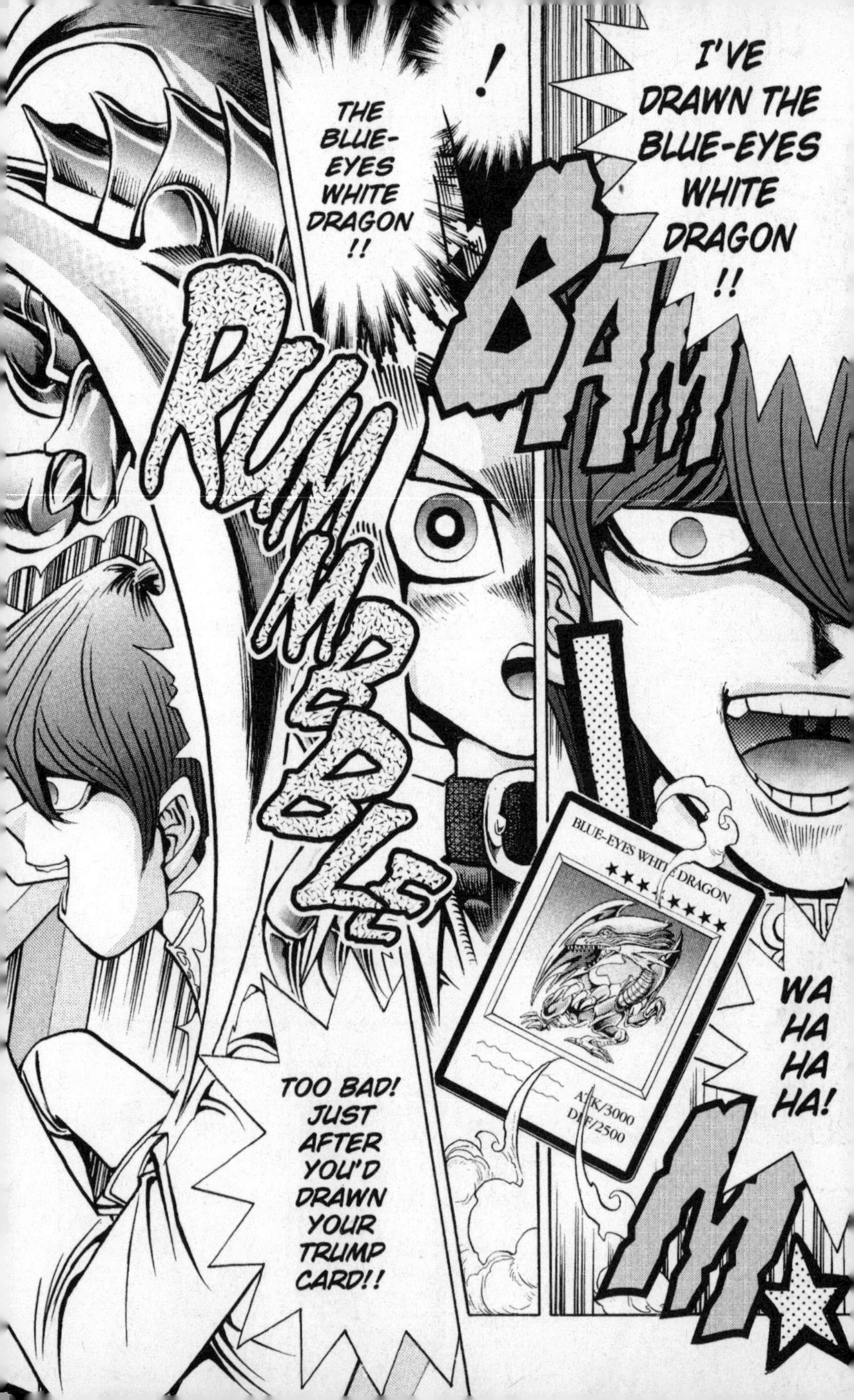
I'VE DRAWN THE BLUE-EYES WHITE DRAGON!!
BAM
BLUE-EYES WHITE DRAGON
WA HA HA HA!
!
THE BLUE-EYES WHITE DRAGON!!
RUMBLE
TOO BAD! JUST AFTER YOU'D DRAWN YOUR TRUMP CARD!!

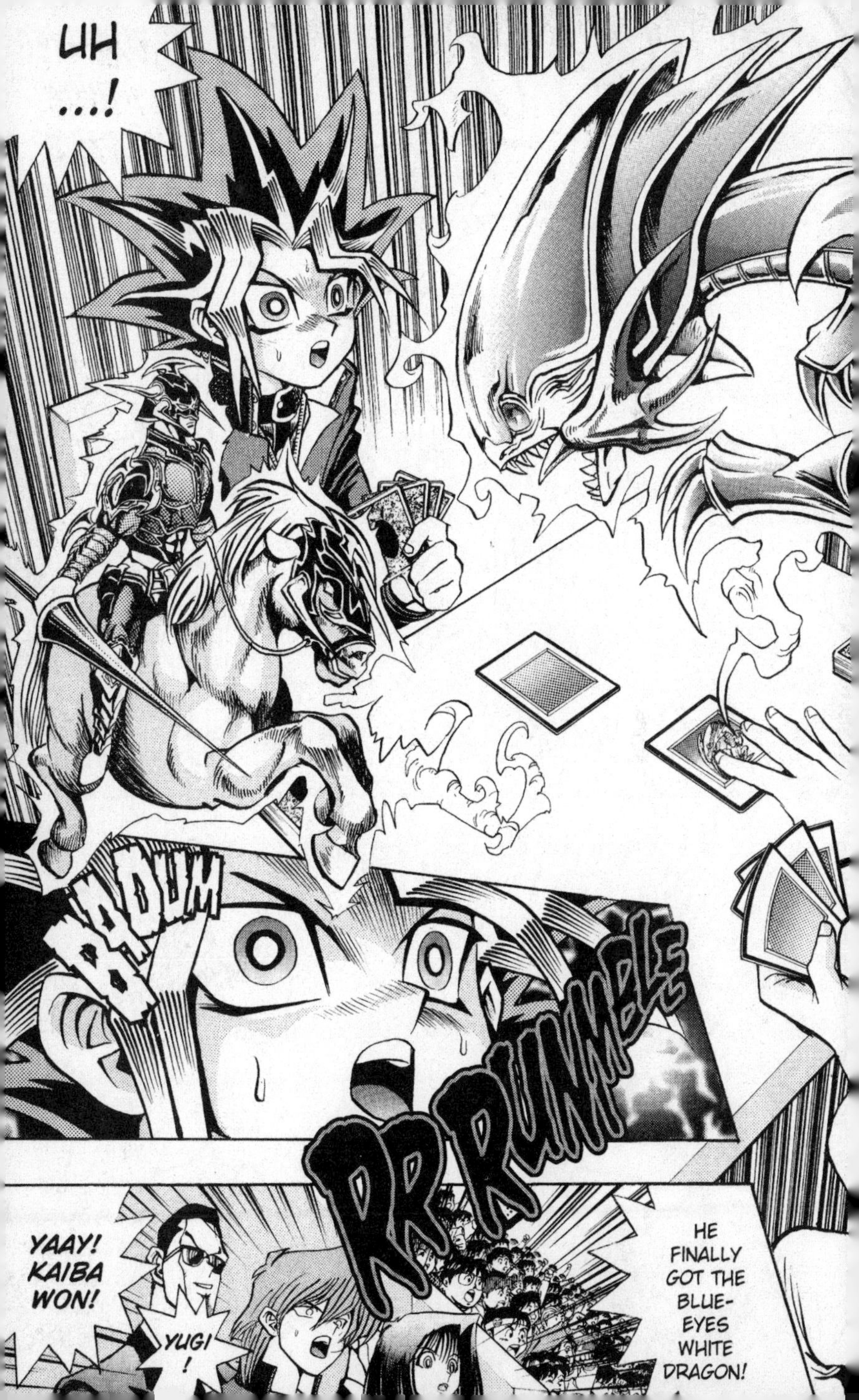
UH ...!
BADUM
RRRUMMBLE
HE FINALLY GOT THE BLUE-EYES WHITE DRAGON!
YAAY! KAIBA WON!
YUGI!

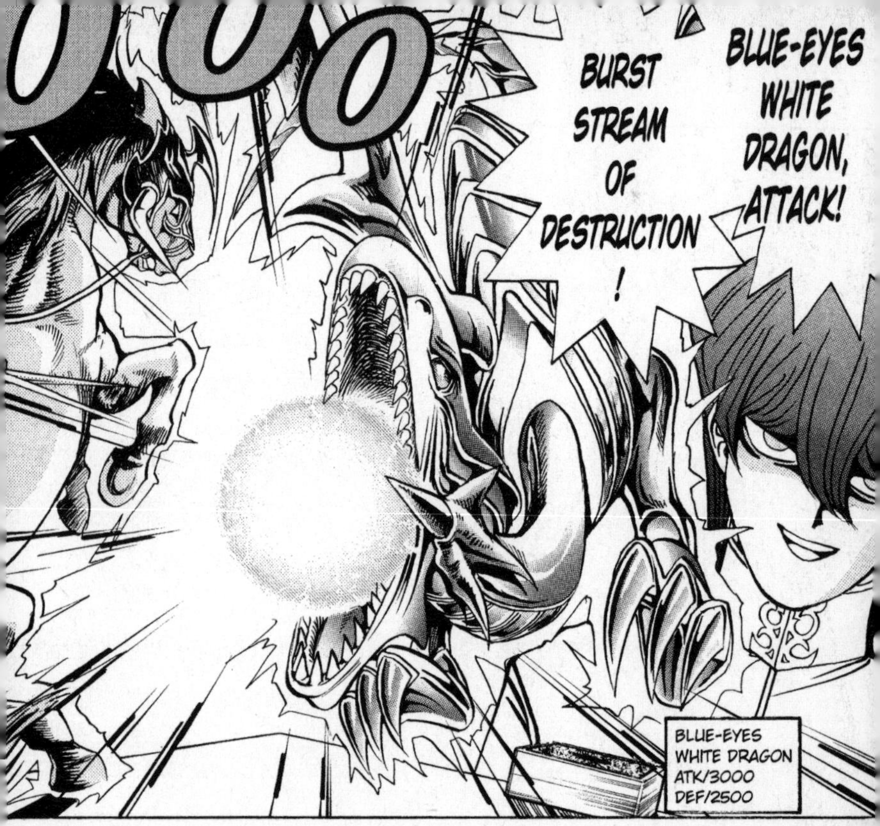
BLUE-EYES WHITE DRAGON, ATTACK!
BURST STREAM OF DESTRUCTION!
OOOO
BLUE-EYES WHITE DRAGON ATK/3000 DEF/2500

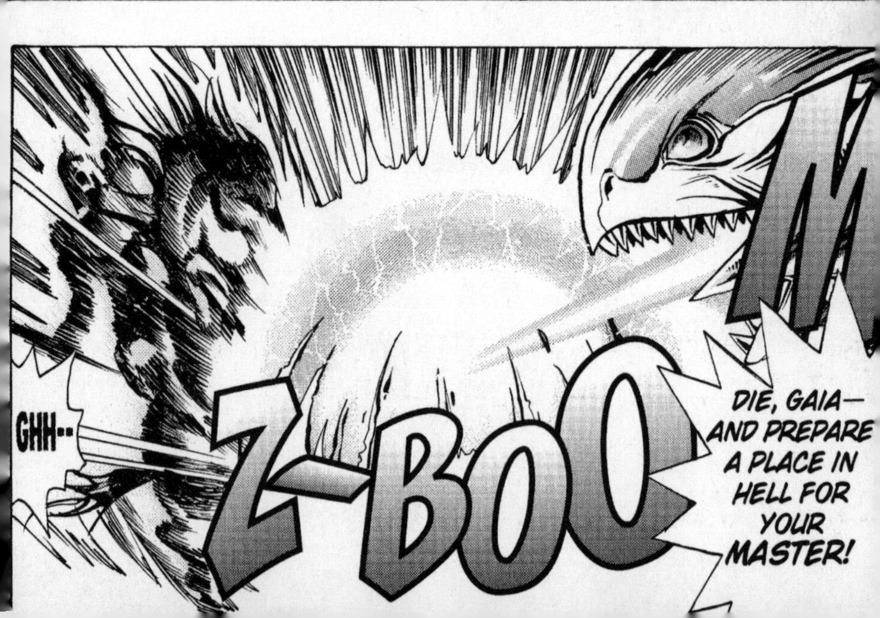
DIE, GAIA— AND PREPARE A PLACE IN HELL FOR YOUR MASTER!
Z-BOOM
GHH--

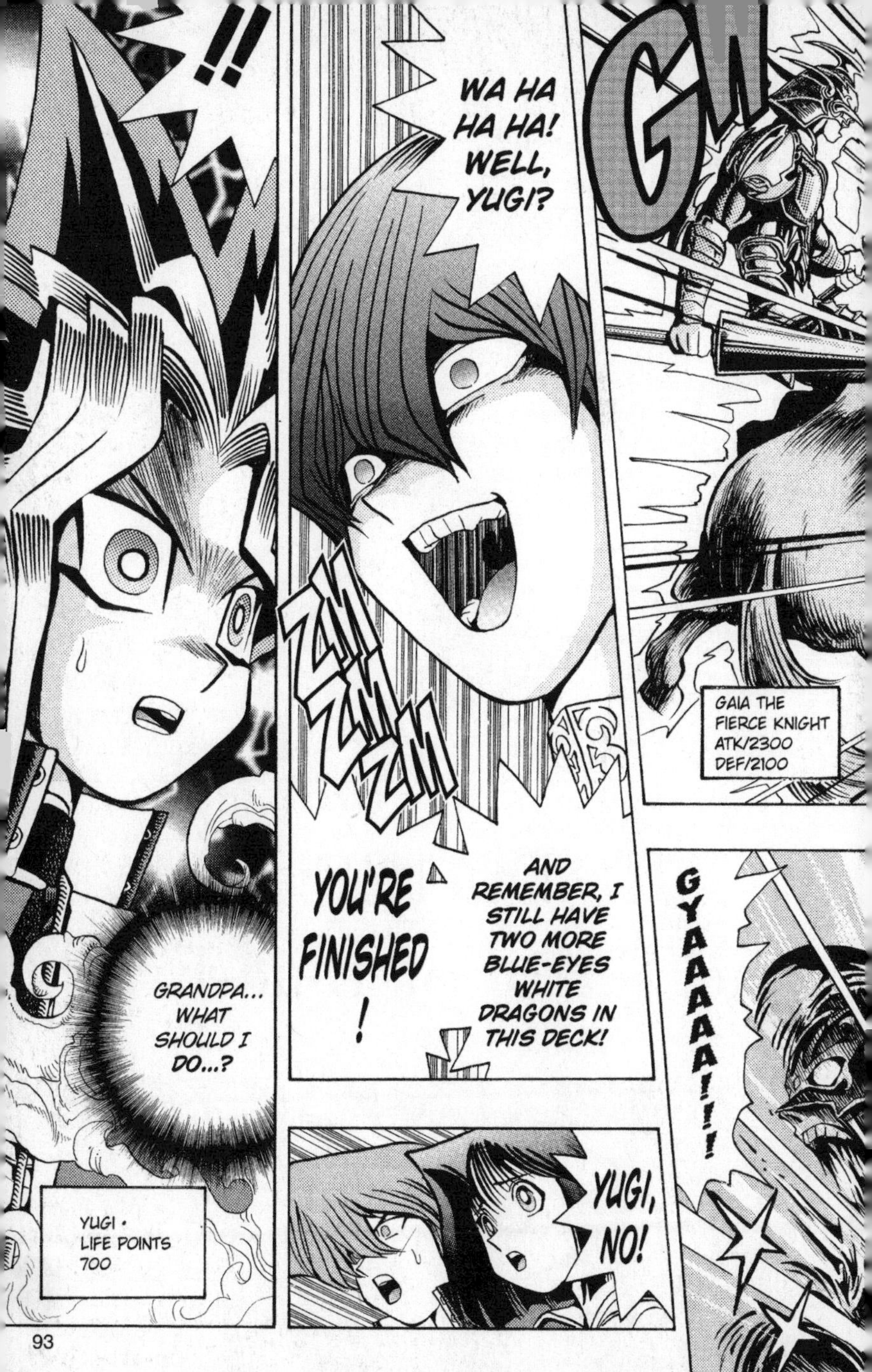
GW
GAIA THE FIERCE KNIGHT ATK/2300 DEF/2100
WA HA HA HA! WELL, YUGI?
ZUM ZUM ZUM
AND REMEMBER, I STILL HAVE TWO MORE BLUE-EYES WHITE DRAGONS IN THIS DECK!
YOU'RE FINISHED!
GYAAAAA!!!!
YUGI, NO!
!!
GRANDPA... WHAT SHOULD I DO...?
YUGI • LIFE POINTS 700

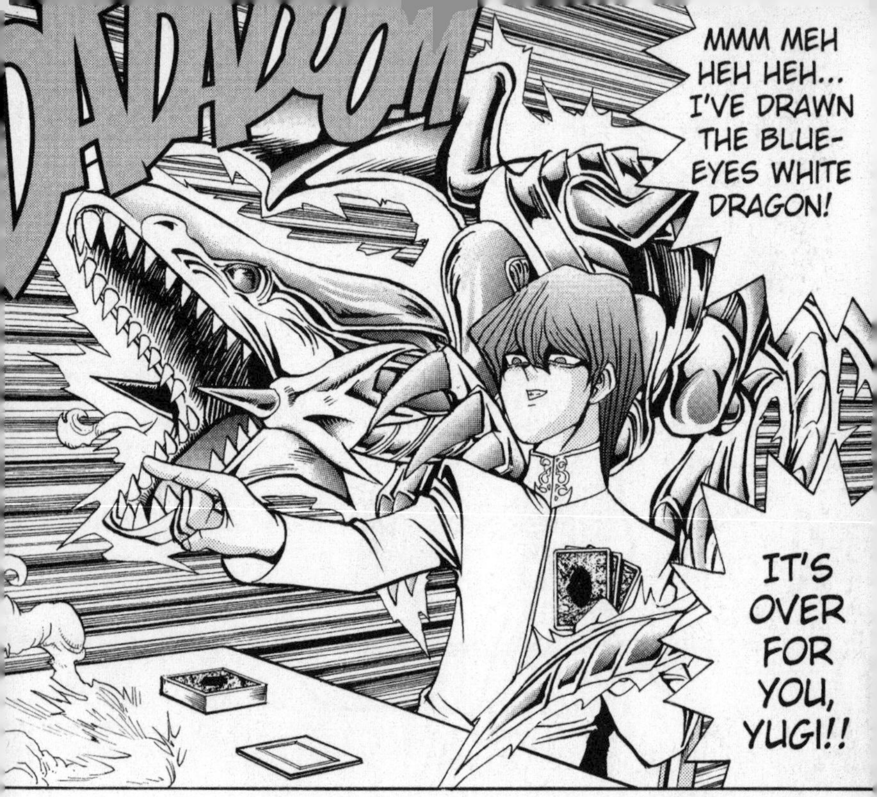
MMM MEH HEH HEH... I'VE DRAWN THE BLUE-EYES WHITE DRAGON!
IT'S OVER FOR YOU, YUGI!!

Duel 38: The Terror of Blue-Eyes!!

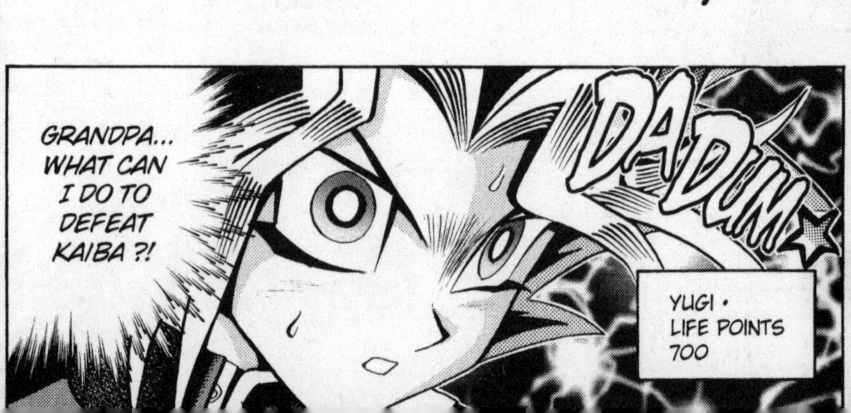
DADUM
YUGI • LIFE POINTS 700
GRANDPA... WHAT CAN I DO TO DEFEAT KAIBA ?!

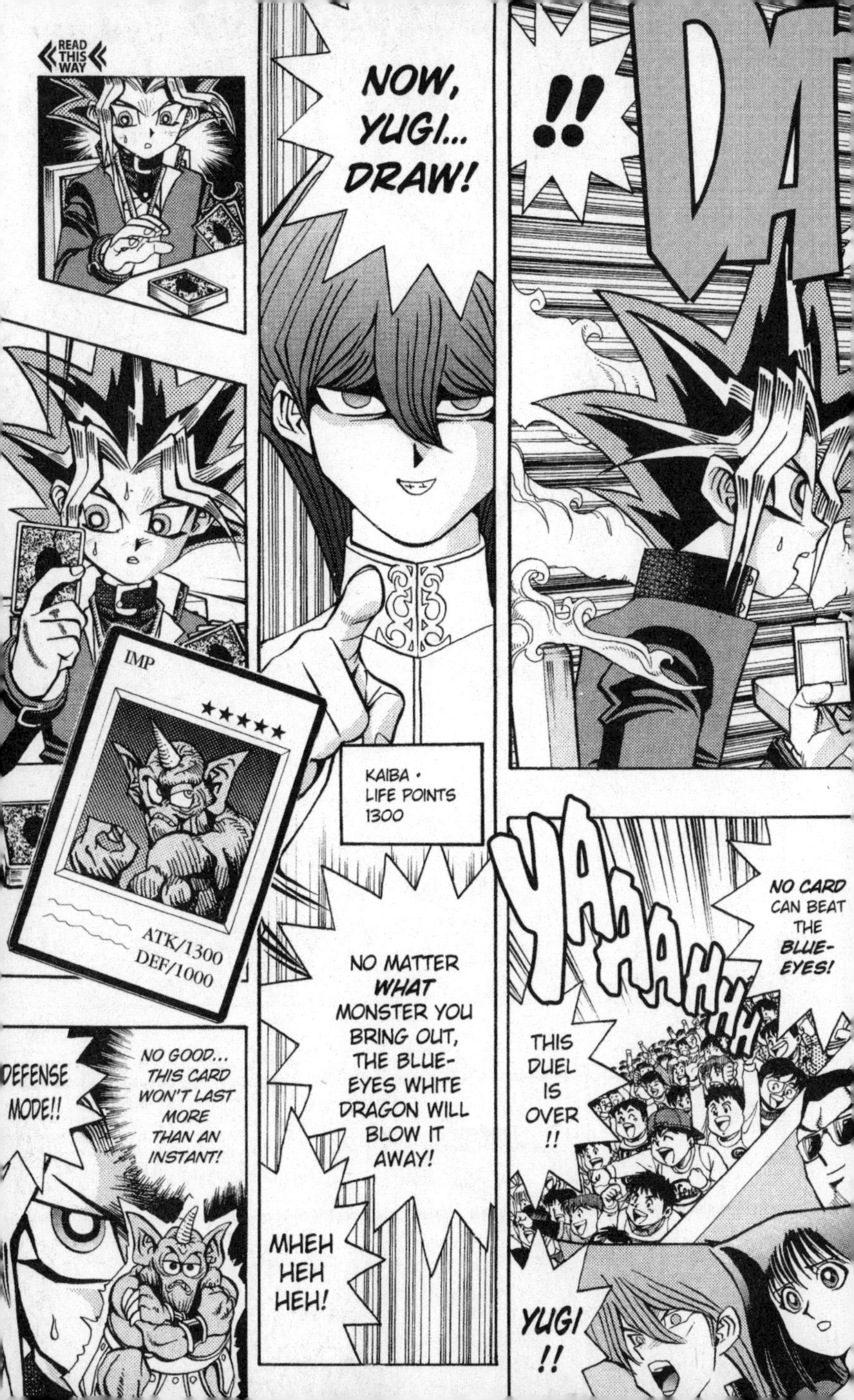

!!
DA
YAAAHHH
NO CARD CAN BEAT THE ***BLUE-EYES!***
THIS DUEL IS OVER !!
YUGI !!
NOW, YUGI... DRAW!
KAIBA • LIFE POINTS 1300
NO MATTER ***WHAT*** MONSTER YOU BRING OUT, THE BLUE-EYES WHITE DRAGON WILL BLOW IT AWAY!
MHEH HEH HEH!
READ THIS WAY
IMP
ATK/1300 DEF/1000
DEFENSE MODE!!
NO GOOD... THIS CARD WON'T LAST MORE THAN AN INSTANT!

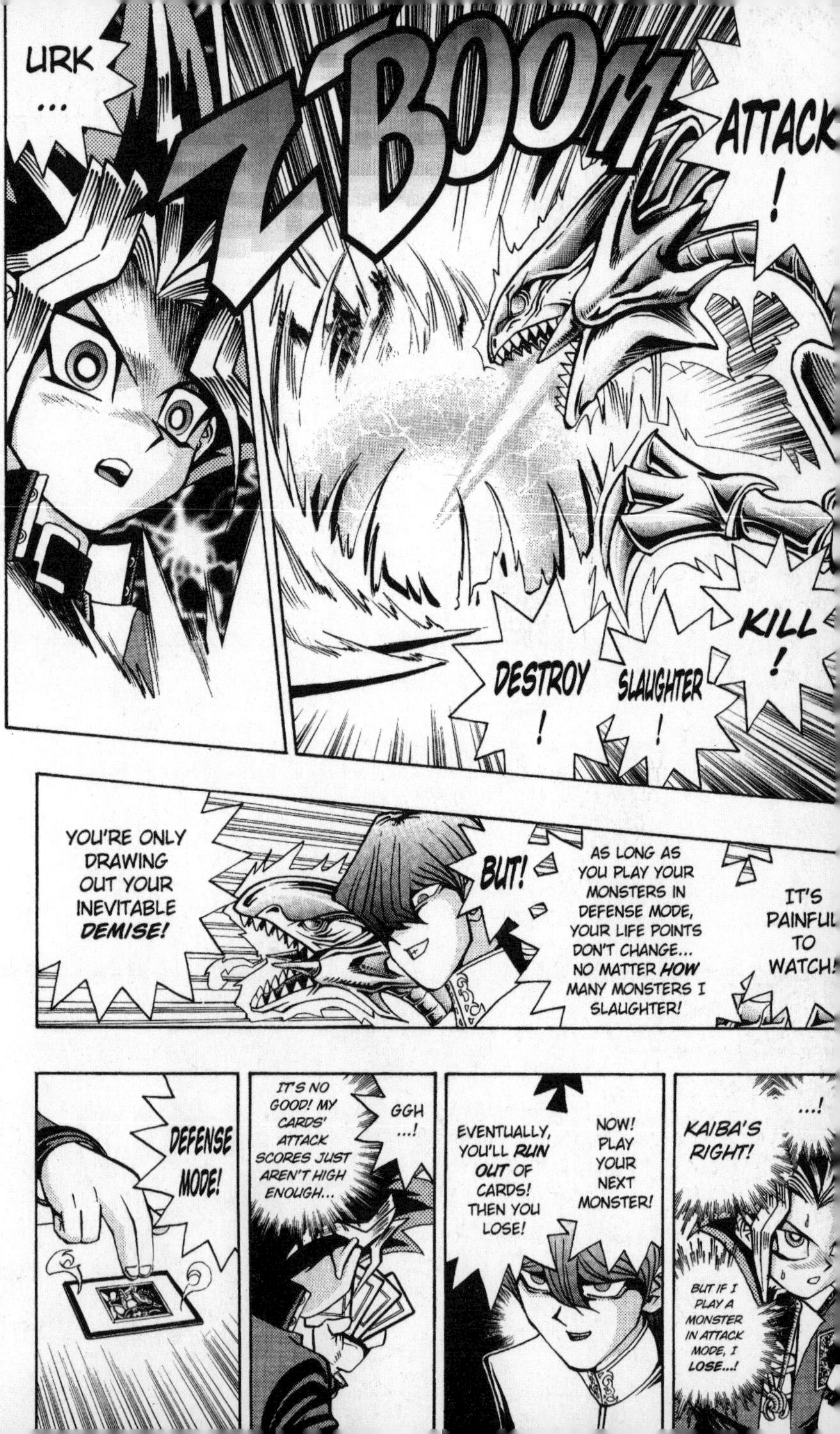
ATTACK!
KILL!
SLAUGHTER!
DESTROY!
ZBOOM
URK...
IT'S PAINFUL TO WATCH!
AS LONG AS YOU PLAY YOUR MONSTERS IN DEFENSE MODE, YOUR LIFE POINTS DON'T CHANGE... NO MATTER HOW MANY MONSTERS I SLAUGHTER!
BUT!
YOU'RE ONLY DRAWING OUT YOUR INEVITABLE DEMISE!
...!
KAIBA'S RIGHT!
BUT IF I PLAY A MONSTER IN ATTACK MODE, I LOSE...!
NOW! PLAY YOUR NEXT MONSTER!
EVENTUALLY, YOU'LL RUN OUT OF CARDS! THEN YOU LOSE!
GGH ...!
IT'S NO GOOD! MY CARDS' ATTACK SCORES JUST AREN'T HIGH ENOUGH...
DEFENSE MODE!

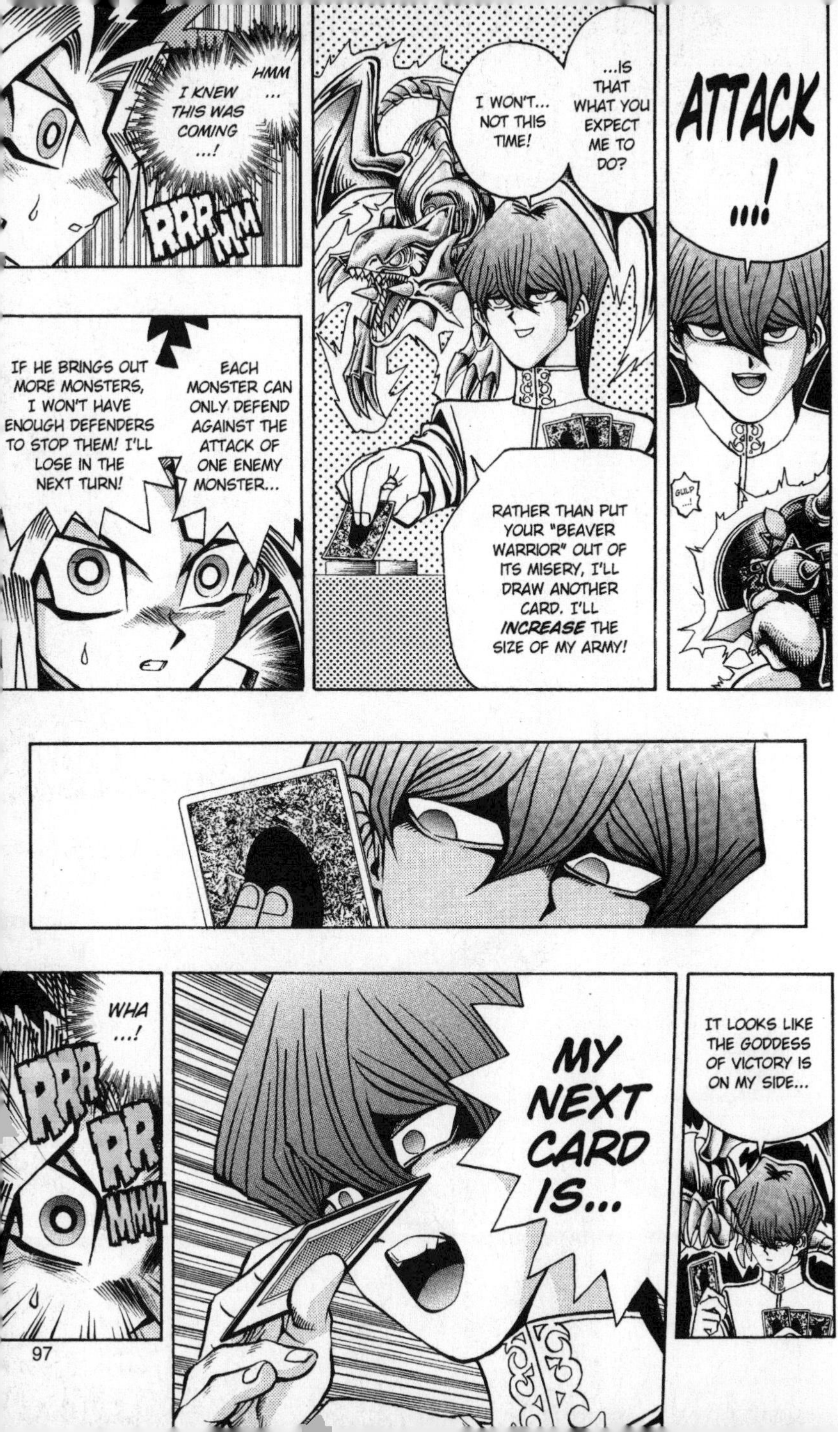
ATTACK ...!
GULP ...!
...IS THAT WHAT YOU EXPECT ME TO DO?
I WON'T... NOT THIS TIME!
RATHER THAN PUT YOUR "BEAVER WARRIOR" OUT OF ITS MISERY, I'LL DRAW ANOTHER CARD. I'LL INCREASE THE SIZE OF MY ARMY!
HMM ...
I KNEW THIS WAS COMING ...!
RRRMMM
EACH MONSTER CAN ONLY DEFEND AGAINST THE ATTACK OF ONE ENEMY MONSTER...
IF HE BRINGS OUT MORE MONSTERS, I WON'T HAVE ENOUGH DEFENDERS TO STOP THEM! I'LL LOSE IN THE NEXT TURN!
IT LOOKS LIKE THE GODDESS OF VICTORY IS ON MY SIDE...
MY NEXT CARD IS...
WHA ...!
RRRRRMMM

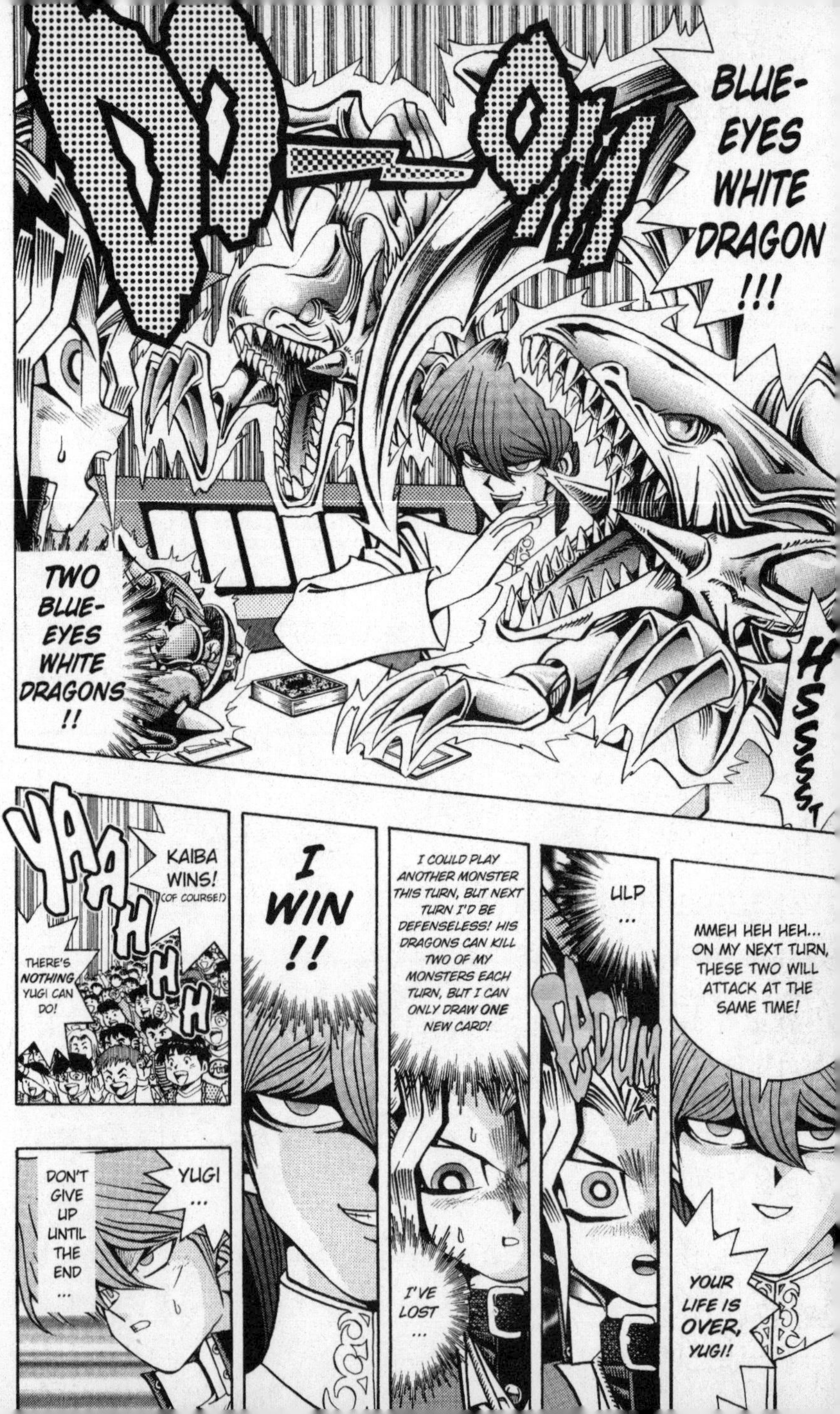

BLUE-EYES WHITE DRAGON !!!
HSSSSS
TWO BLUE-EYES WHITE DRAGONS !!
MMEH HEH HEH... ON MY NEXT TURN, THESE TWO WILL ATTACK AT THE SAME TIME!
YOUR LIFE IS OVER, YUGI!
ULP ...
BADUM
I COULD PLAY ANOTHER MONSTER THIS TURN, BUT NEXT TURN I'D BE DEFENSELESS! HIS DRAGONS CAN KILL TWO OF MY MONSTERS EACH TURN, BUT I CAN ONLY DRAW ONE NEW CARD!
I'VE LOST ...
I WIN !!
YAAHHHH
KAIBA WINS! (OF COURSE!)
THERE'S NOTHING YUGI CAN DO!
YUGI ...
DON'T GIVE UP UNTIL THE END ...

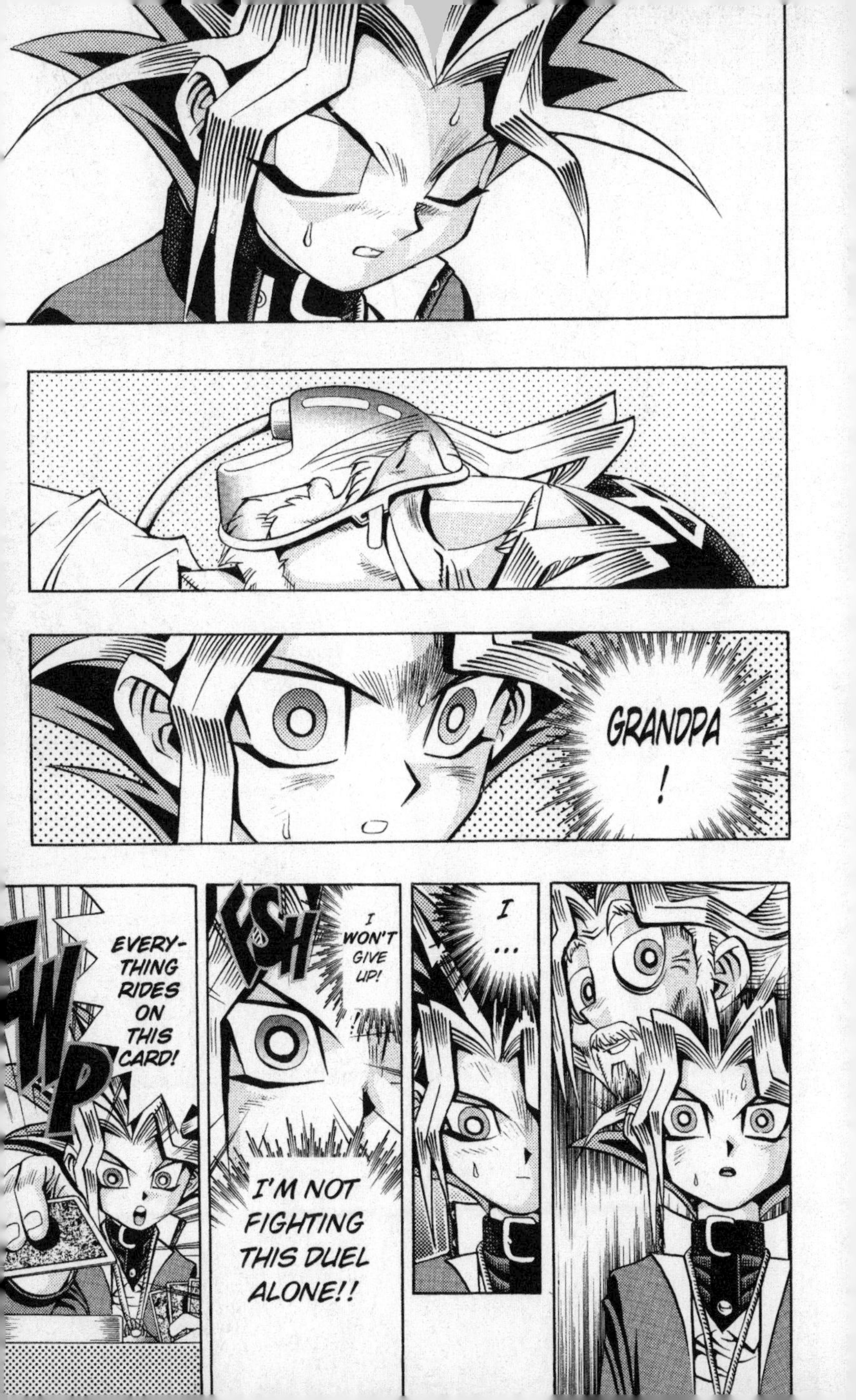
GRANDPA !
I ...
I WON'T GIVE UP!
I'M NOT FIGHTING THIS DUEL ALONE!!
EVERY-THING RIDES ON THIS CARD!

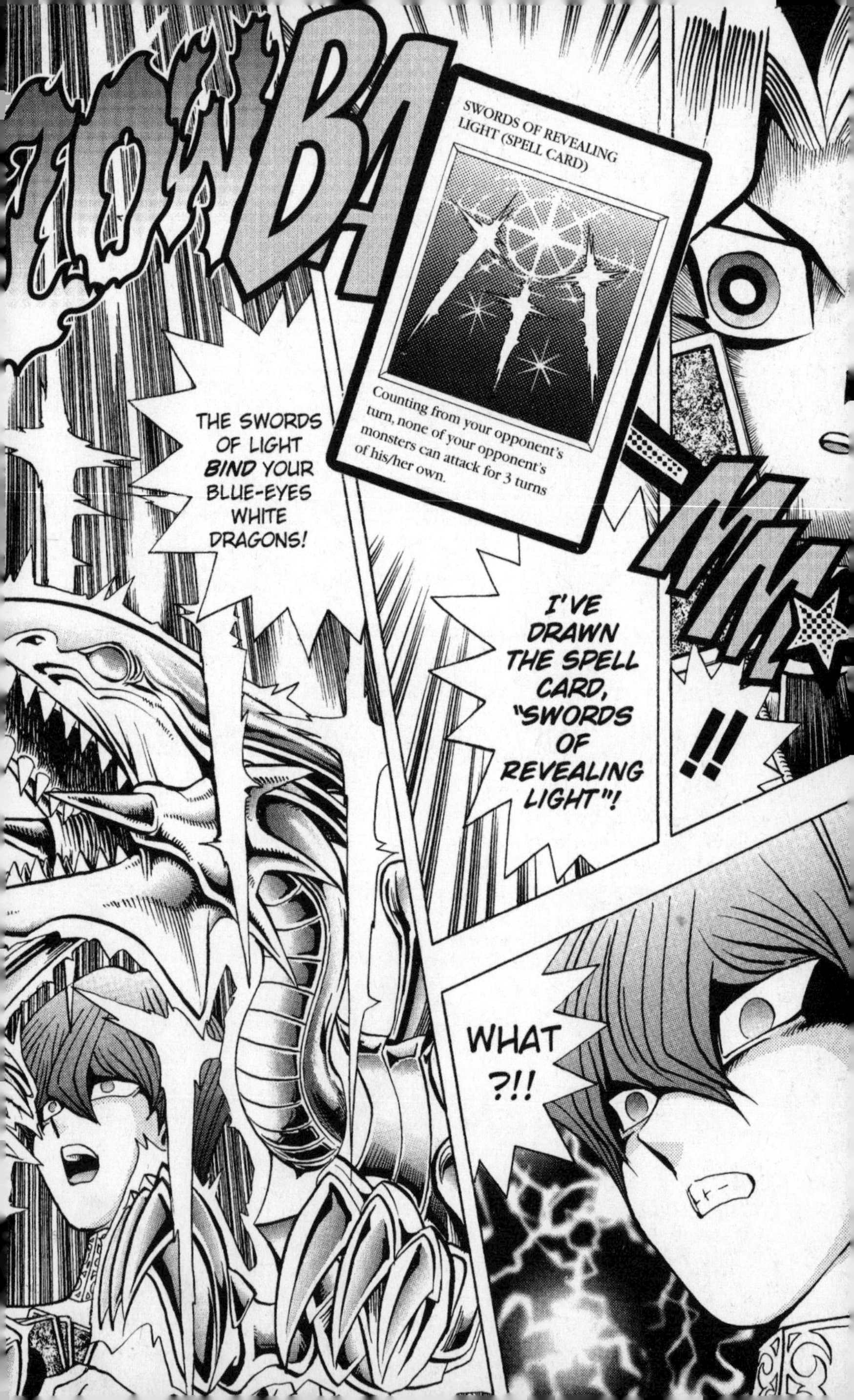
!!
I'VE DRAWN THE SPELL CARD, "SWORDS OF REVEALING LIGHT"!
SWORDS OF REVEALING LIGHT (SPELL CARD)
Counting from your opponent's turn, none of your opponent's monsters can attack for 3 turns of his/her own.
THE SWORDS OF LIGHT BIND YOUR BLUE-EYES WHITE DRAGONS!
WHAT ?!!

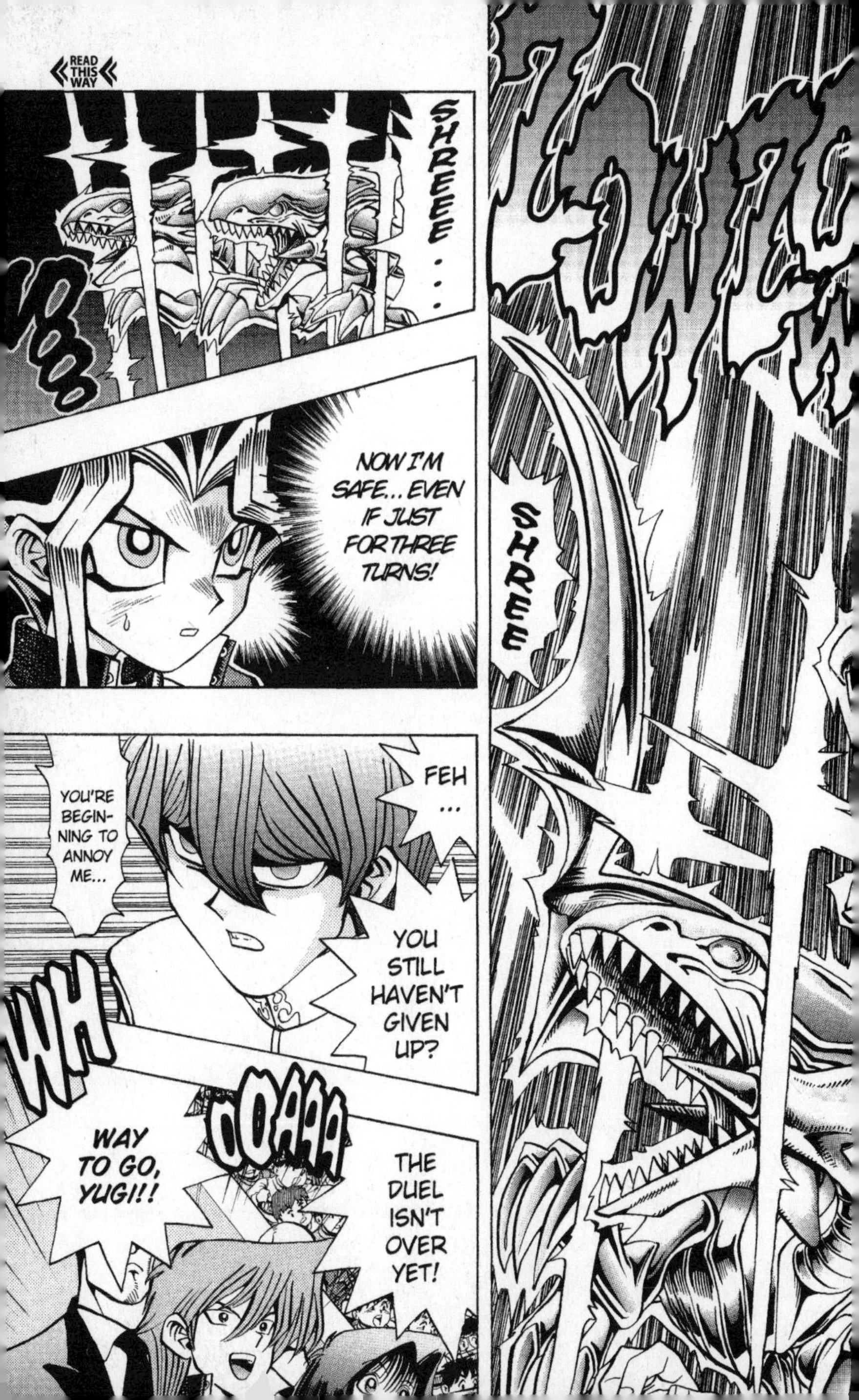
READ THIS WAY
SHREE
SHREEE...
NOW I'M SAFE... EVEN IF JUST FOR THREE TURNS!
FEH...
YOU STILL HAVEN'T GIVEN UP?
YOU'RE BEGIN-NING TO ANNOY ME...
THE DUEL ISN'T OVER YET!
WAY TO GO, YUGI!!

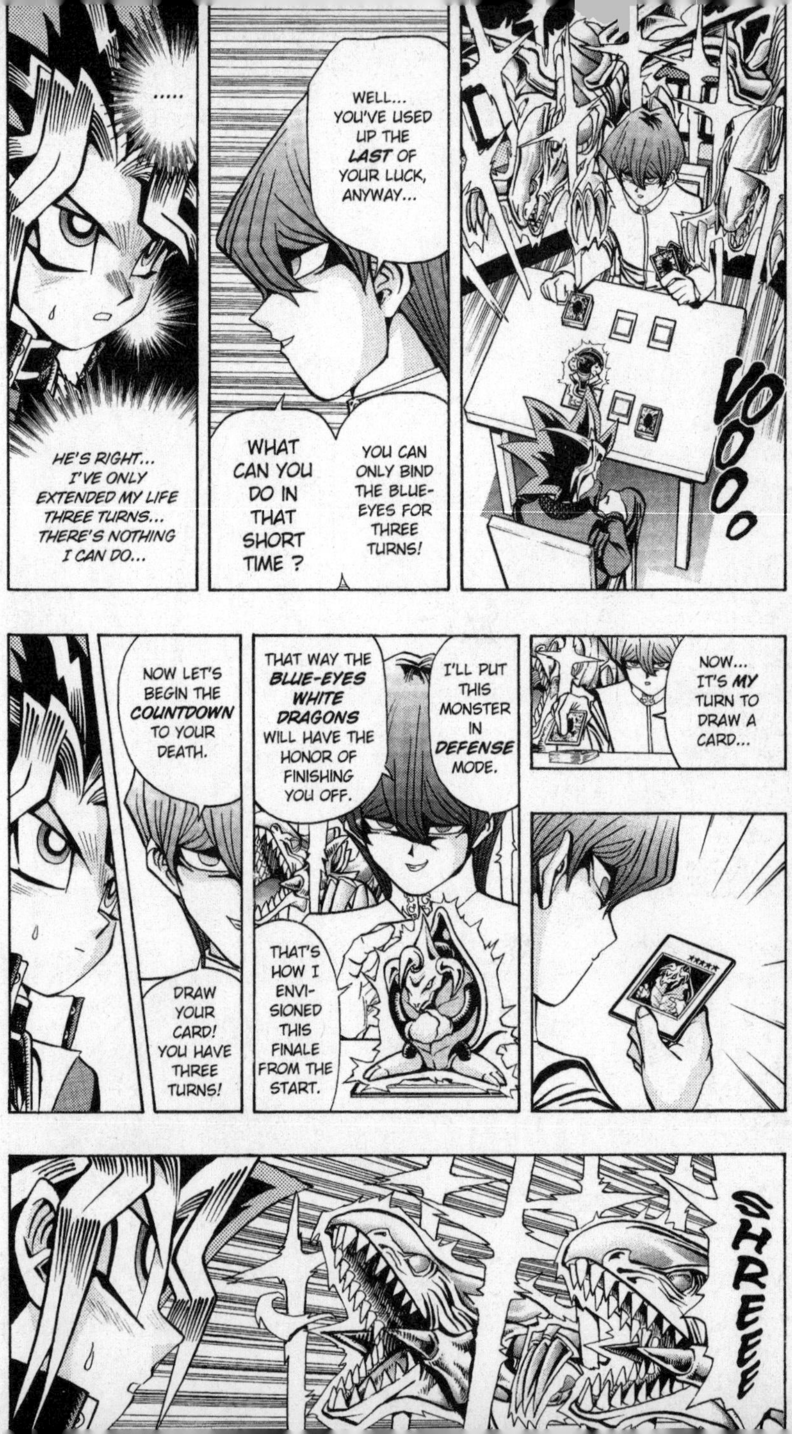
VOOOO
WELL... YOU'VE USED UP THE LAST OF YOUR LUCK, ANYWAY...
YOU CAN ONLY BIND THE BLUE-EYES FOR THREE TURNS!
WHAT CAN YOU DO IN THAT SHORT TIME?
.....
HE'S RIGHT... I'VE ONLY EXTENDED MY LIFE THREE TURNS... THERE'S NOTHING I CAN DO...
NOW... IT'S MY TURN TO DRAW A CARD...
I'LL PUT THIS MONSTER IN DEFENSE MODE.
THAT WAY THE BLUE-EYES WHITE DRAGONS WILL HAVE THE HONOR OF FINISHING YOU OFF.
THAT'S HOW I ENVISIONED THIS FINALE FROM THE START.
NOW LET'S BEGIN THE COUNTDOWN TO YOUR DEATH.
DRAW YOUR CARD! YOU HAVE THREE TURNS!
SHREEE

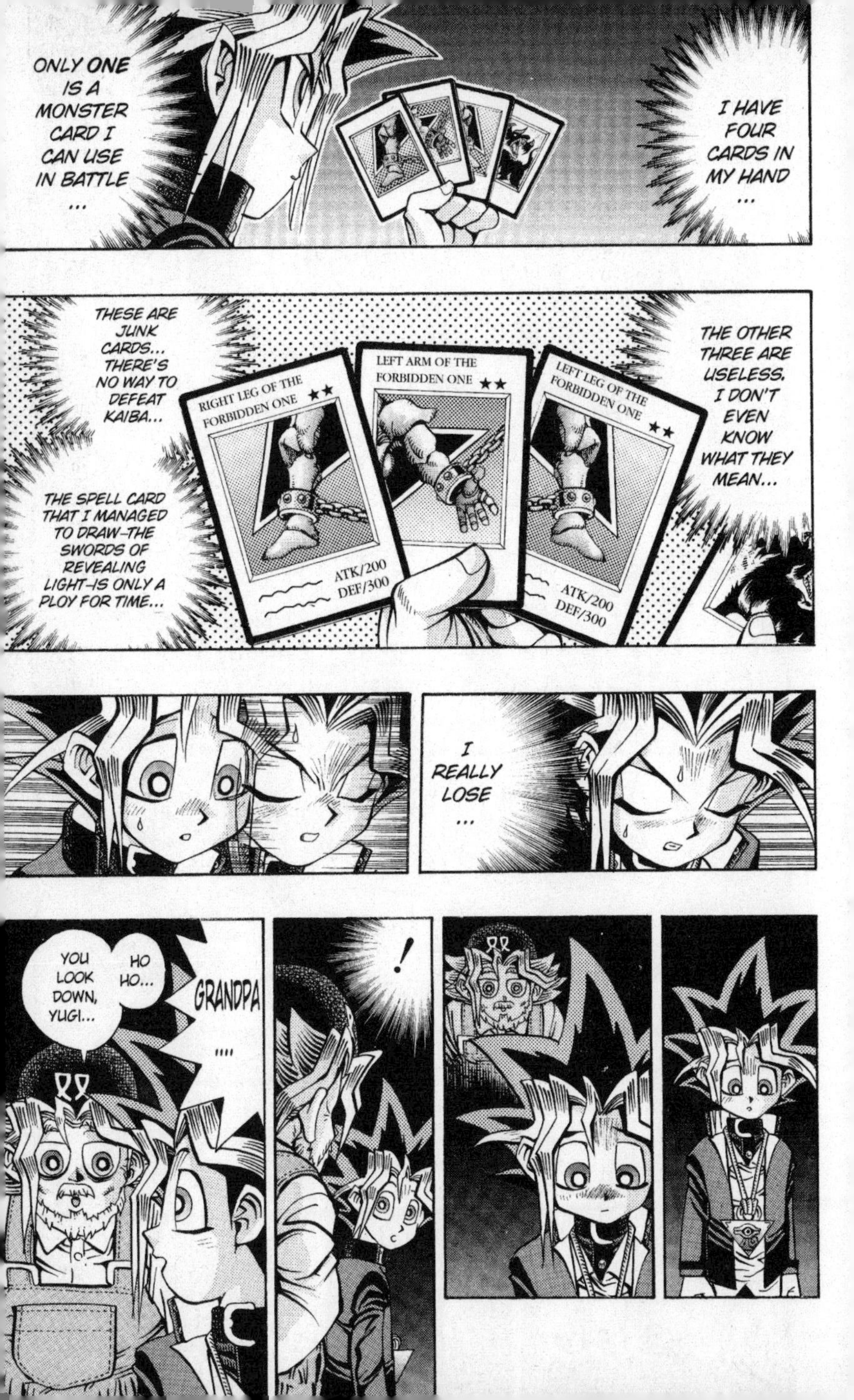
I HAVE FOUR CARDS IN MY HAND ...
ONLY ONE IS A MONSTER CARD I CAN USE IN BATTLE ...
THE OTHER THREE ARE USELESS. I DON'T EVEN KNOW WHAT THEY MEAN...
LEFT LEG OF THE FORBIDDEN ONE
ATK/200 DEF/300
LEFT ARM OF THE FORBIDDEN ONE
THESE ARE JUNK CARDS... THERE'S NO WAY TO DEFEAT KAIBA...
RIGHT LEG OF THE FORBIDDEN ONE
ATK/200 DEF/300
THE SPELL CARD THAT I MANAGED TO DRAW–THE SWORDS OF REVEALING LIGHT–IS ONLY A PLOY FOR TIME...
I REALLY LOSE ...
!
HO HO...
YOU LOOK DOWN, YUGI...
GRANDPA ....

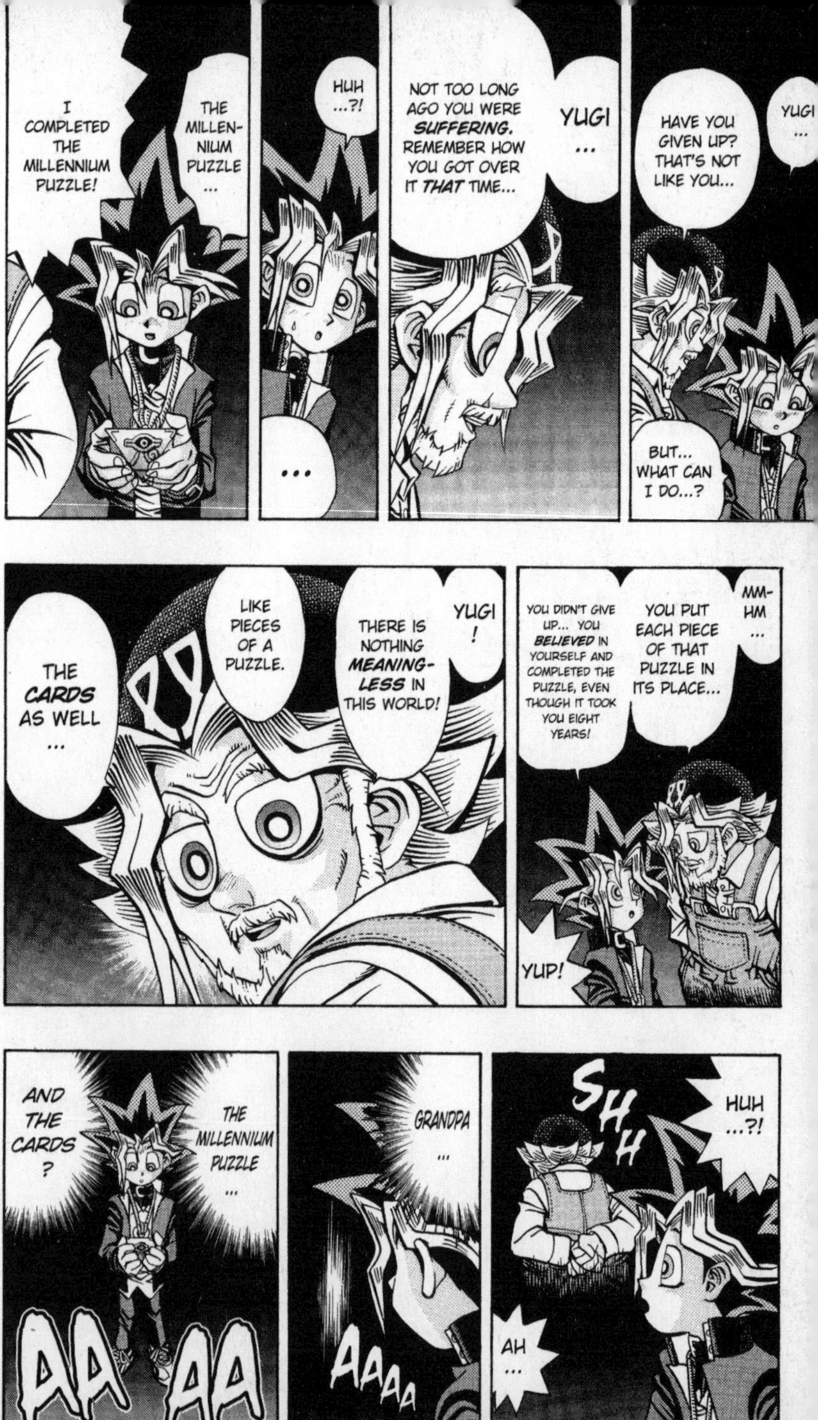
YUGI ...
HAVE YOU GIVEN UP? THAT'S NOT LIKE YOU...
BUT... WHAT CAN I DO...?
YUGI ...
NOT TOO LONG AGO YOU WERE SUFFERING. REMEMBER HOW YOU GOT OVER IT THAT TIME...
HUH ...?!
...
THE MILLEN-NIUM PUZZLE ...
I COMPLETED THE MILLENNIUM PUZZLE!
MM-HM ...
YOU PUT EACH PIECE OF THAT PUZZLE IN ITS PLACE...
YOU DIDN'T GIVE UP... YOU BELIEVED IN YOURSELF AND COMPLETED THE PUZZLE, EVEN THOUGH IT TOOK YOU EIGHT YEARS!
YUP!
YUGI !
THERE IS NOTHING MEANING-LESS IN THIS WORLD!
LIKE PIECES OF A PUZZLE.
THE CARDS AS WELL ...
HUH ...?!
SHH
AH ...
GRANDPA ...
AAAA
THE MILLENNIUM PUZZLE ...
AND THE CARDS ?
AAAA

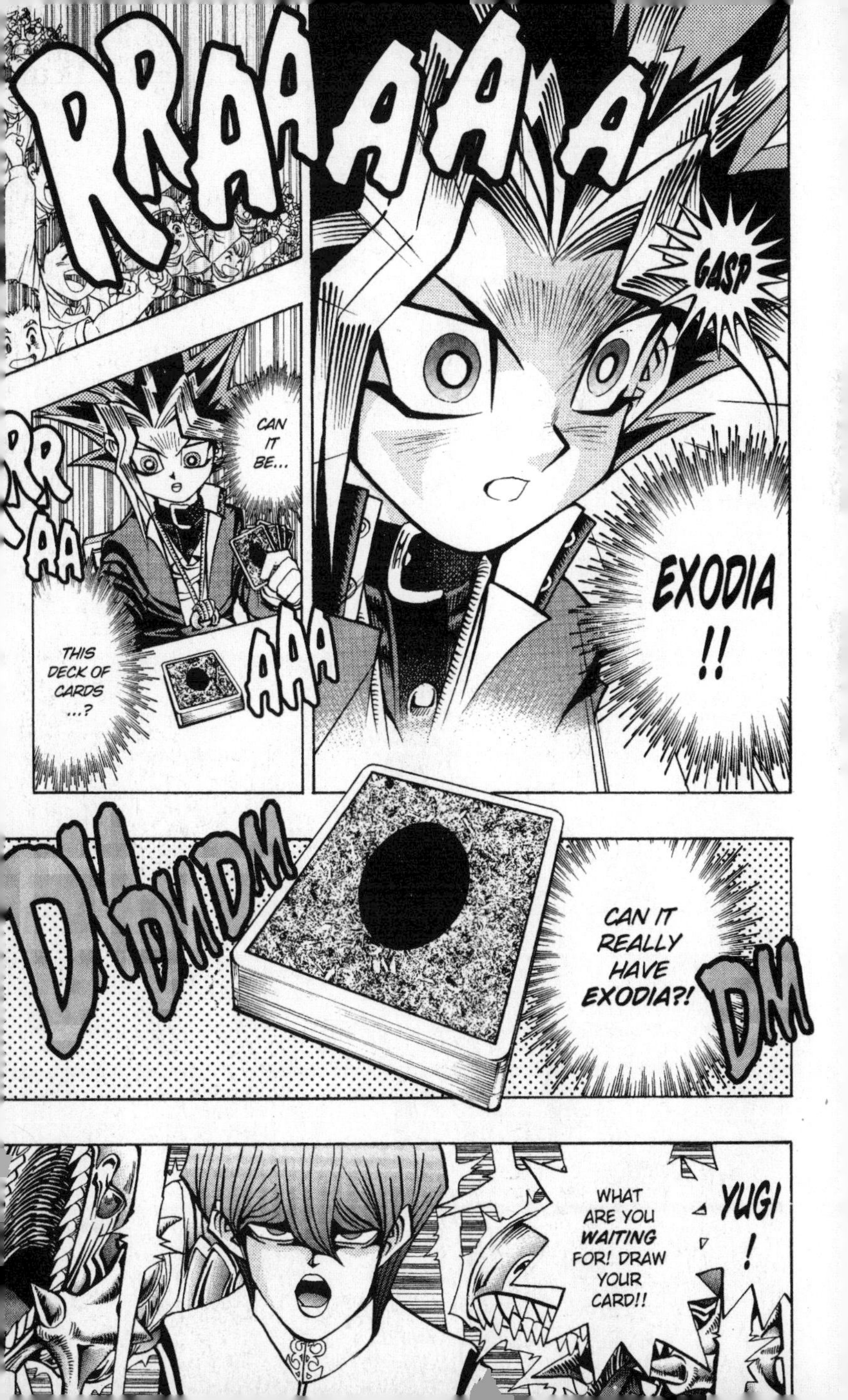
RRAAAAAA
GASP
EXODIA !!
RR
AA
CAN IT BE...
THIS DECK OF CARDS ...?
AAA
CAN IT REALLY HAVE EXODIA?!
DM
DMDMDM
YUGI !
WHAT ARE YOU WAITING FOR! DRAW YOUR CARD!!

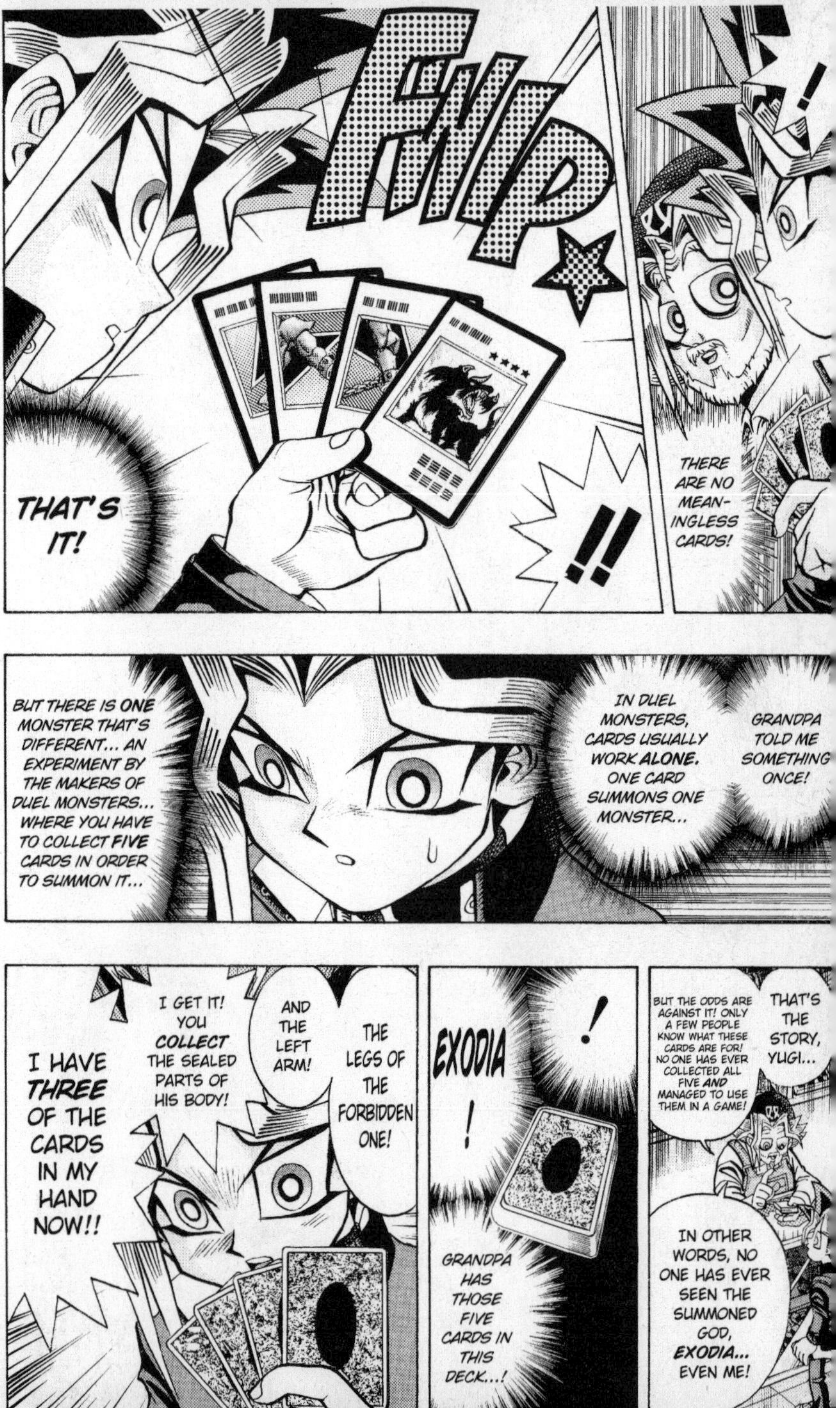
!
THERE ARE NO MEAN-INGLESS CARDS!
FLIP
THAT'S IT!
!!
GRANDPA TOLD ME SOMETHING ONCE!
IN DUEL MONSTERS, CARDS USUALLY WORK ALONE. ONE CARD SUMMONS ONE MONSTER...
BUT THERE IS ONE MONSTER THAT'S DIFFERENT... AN EXPERIMENT BY THE MAKERS OF DUEL MONSTERS... WHERE YOU HAVE TO COLLECT FIVE CARDS IN ORDER TO SUMMON IT...
THAT'S THE STORY, YUGI...
BUT THE ODDS ARE AGAINST IT! ONLY A FEW PEOPLE KNOW WHAT THESE CARDS ARE FOR! NO ONE HAS EVER COLLECTED ALL FIVE AND MANAGED TO USE THEM IN A GAME!
IN OTHER WORDS, NO ONE HAS EVER SEEN THE SUMMONED GOD, EXODIA... EVEN ME!
!
EXODIA !
GRANDPA HAS THOSE FIVE CARDS IN THIS DECK...!
THE LEGS OF THE FORBIDDEN ONE!
AND THE LEFT ARM!
I GET IT! YOU COLLECT THE SEALED PARTS OF HIS BODY!
I HAVE THREE OF THE CARDS IN MY HAND NOW!!

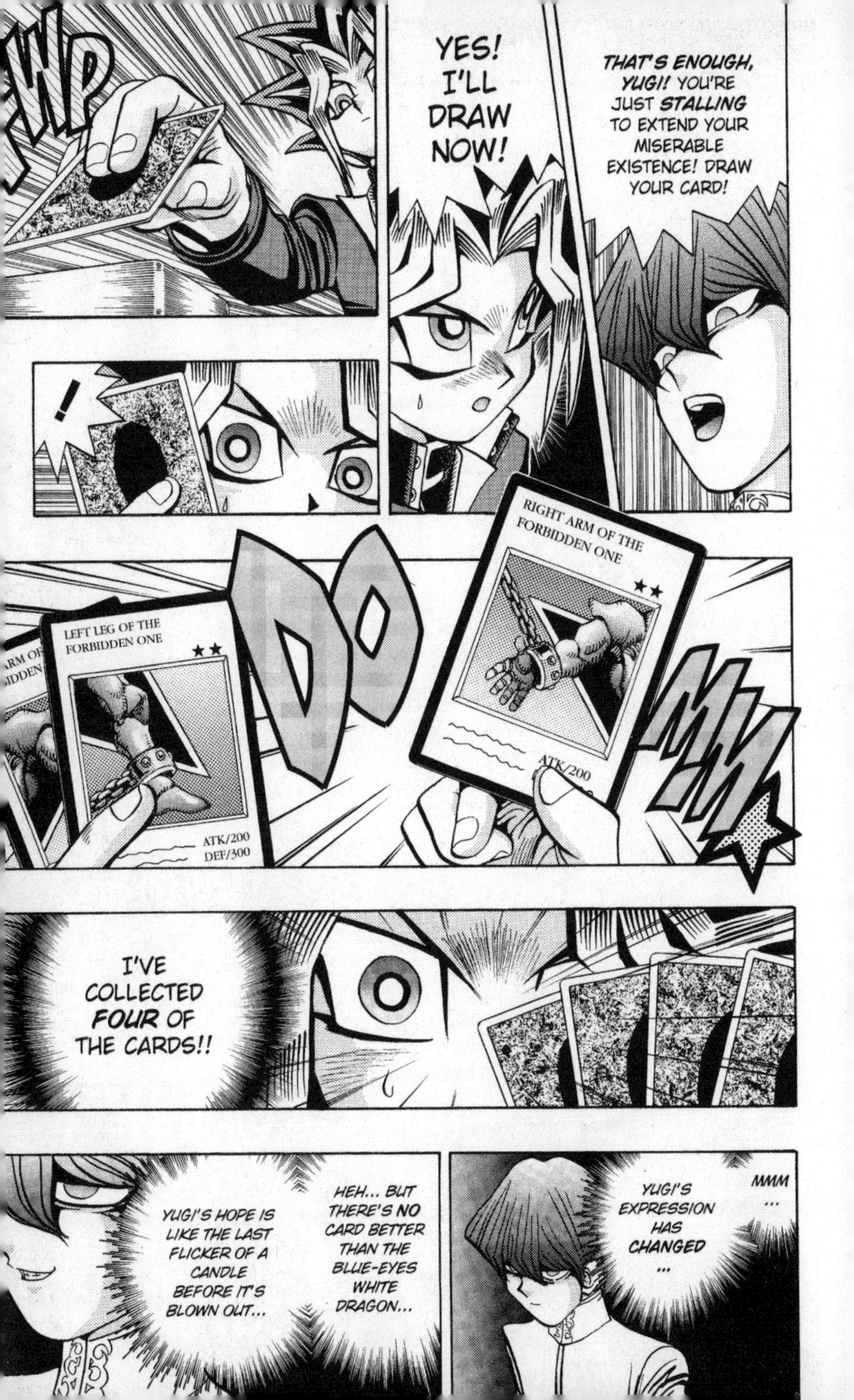
THAT'S ENOUGH, YUGI! YOU'RE JUST STALLING TO EXTEND YOUR MISERABLE EXISTENCE! DRAW YOUR CARD!
YES! I'LL DRAW NOW!
!
RIGHT ARM OF THE FORBIDDEN ONE
ATK/200
LEFT LEG OF THE FORBIDDEN ONE
ATK/200
DEF/300
I'VE COLLECTED FOUR OF THE CARDS!!
MMM ...
YUGI'S EXPRESSION HAS CHANGED ...
HEH... BUT THERE'S NO CARD BETTER THAN THE BLUE-EYES WHITE DRAGON...
YUGI'S HOPE IS LIKE THE LAST FLICKER OF A CANDLE BEFORE IT'S BLOWN OUT...

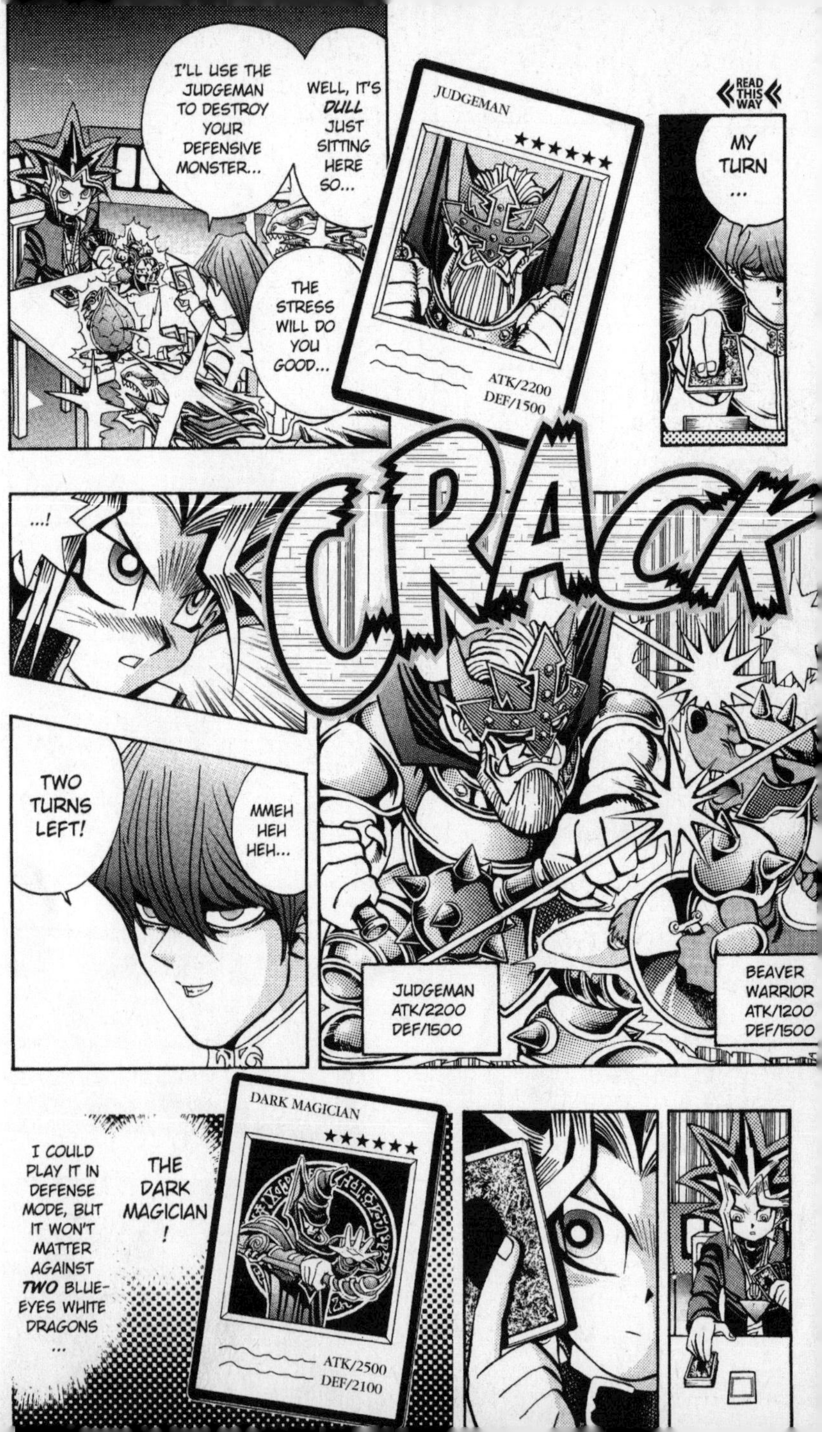
READ THIS WAY
MY TURN ...
JUDGEMAN
ATK/2200
DEF/1500
WELL, IT'S DULL JUST SITTING HERE SO...
I'LL USE THE JUDGEMAN TO DESTROY YOUR DEFENSIVE MONSTER...
THE STRESS WILL DO YOU GOOD...
CRACK
BEAVER WARRIOR ATK/1200 DEF/1500
JUDGEMAN ATK/2200 DEF/1500
...!
MMEH HEH HEH...
TWO TURNS LEFT!
DARK MAGICIAN
ATK/2500
DEF/2100
THE DARK MAGICIAN!
I COULD PLAY IT IN DEFENSE MODE, BUT IT WON'T MATTER AGAINST TWO BLUE-EYES WHITE DRAGONS ...

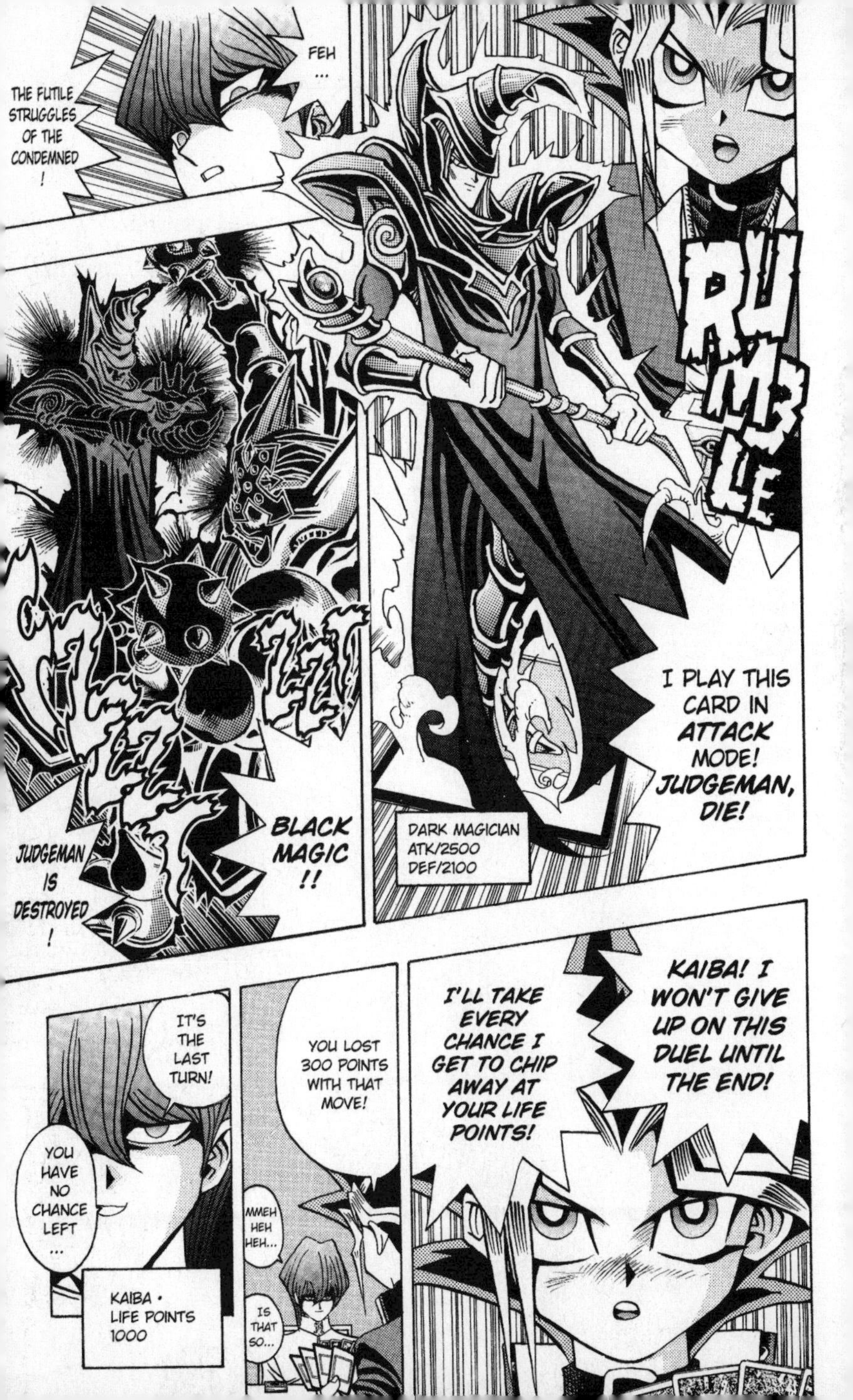
RUMBLE
I PLAY THIS CARD IN **ATTACK** MODE! JUDGEMAN, DIE!
DARK MAGICIAN ATK/2500 DEF/2100
FEH ...
THE FUTILE STRUGGLES OF THE CONDEMNED!
BLACK MAGIC!!
JUDGEMAN IS DESTROYED!
KAIBA! I WON'T GIVE UP ON THIS DUEL UNTIL THE END!
I'LL TAKE EVERY CHANCE I GET TO CHIP AWAY AT YOUR LIFE POINTS!
YOU LOST 300 POINTS WITH THAT MOVE!
MMEH HEH HEH...
IS THAT SO...
IT'S THE LAST TURN!
YOU HAVE NO CHANCE LEFT ...
KAIBA • LIFE POINTS 1000

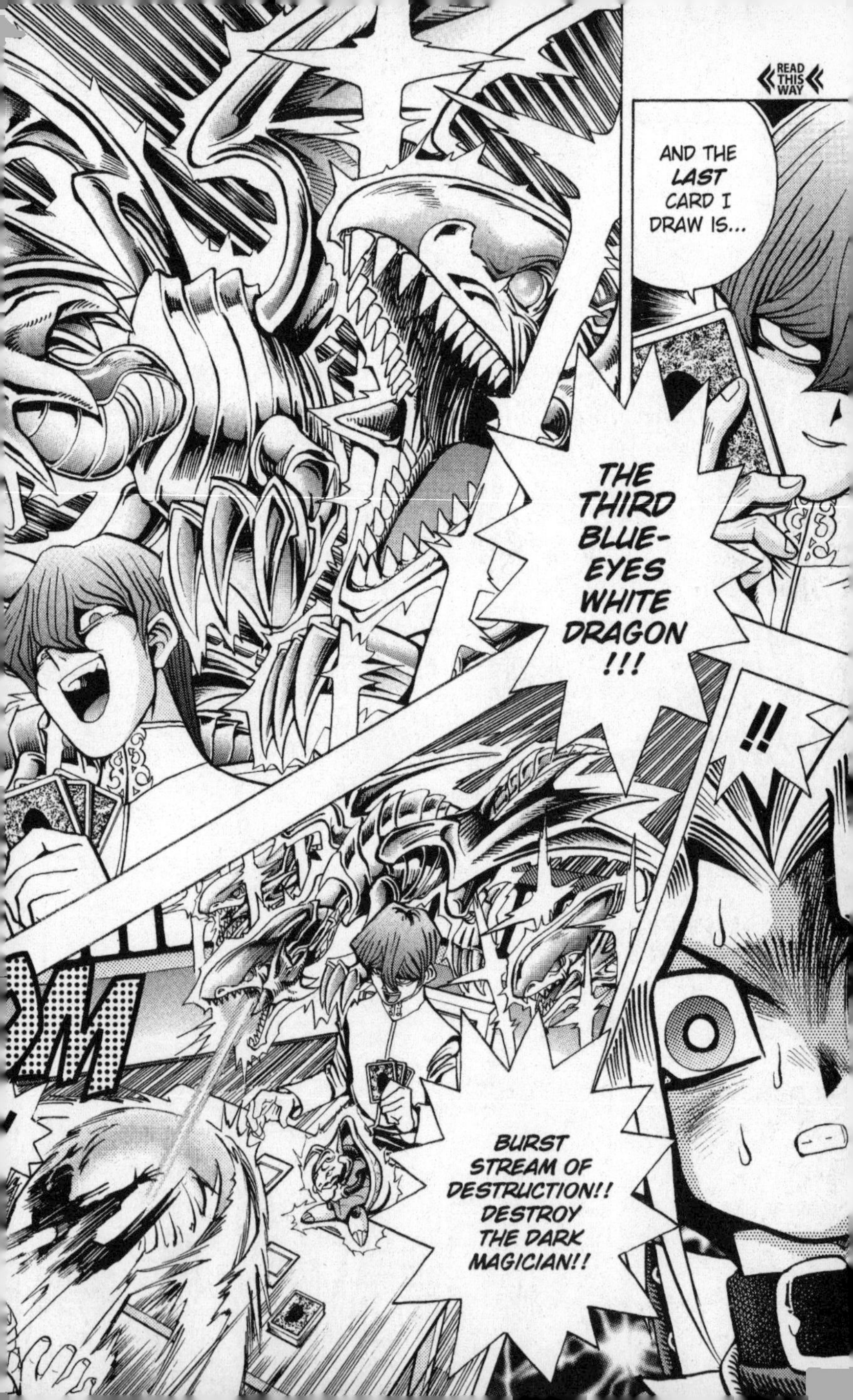
READ THIS WAY
AND THE LAST CARD I DRAW IS...
THE THIRD BLUE-EYES WHITE DRAGON !!!
!!
BURST STREAM OF DESTRUCTION!! DESTROY THE DARK MAGICIAN!!

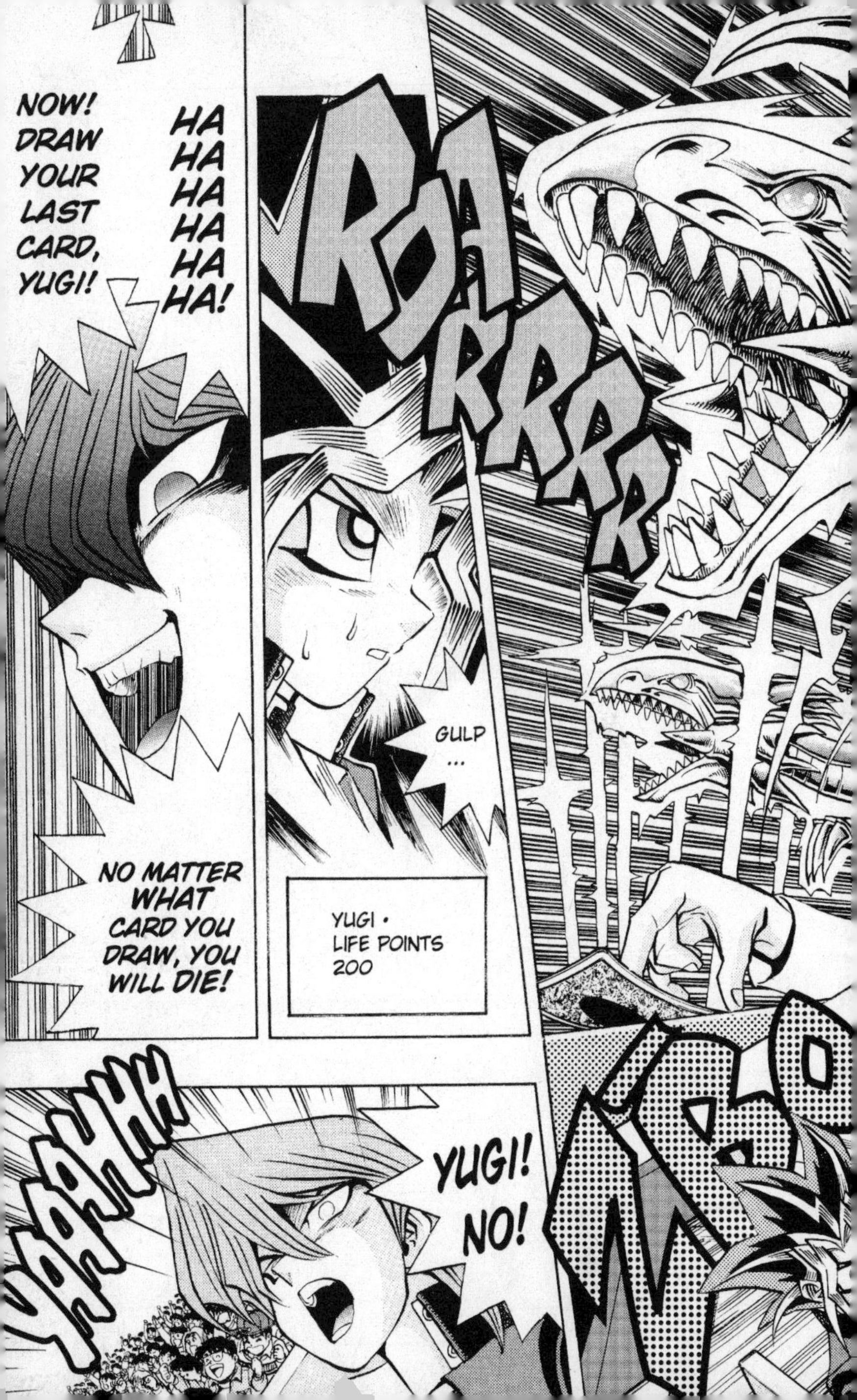
GULP ...
YUGI • LIFE POINTS 200
NOW! DRAW YOUR LAST CARD, YUGI!
HA HA HA HA HA HA!
NO MATTER WHAT CARD YOU DRAW, YOU WILL DIE!
YUGI! NO!

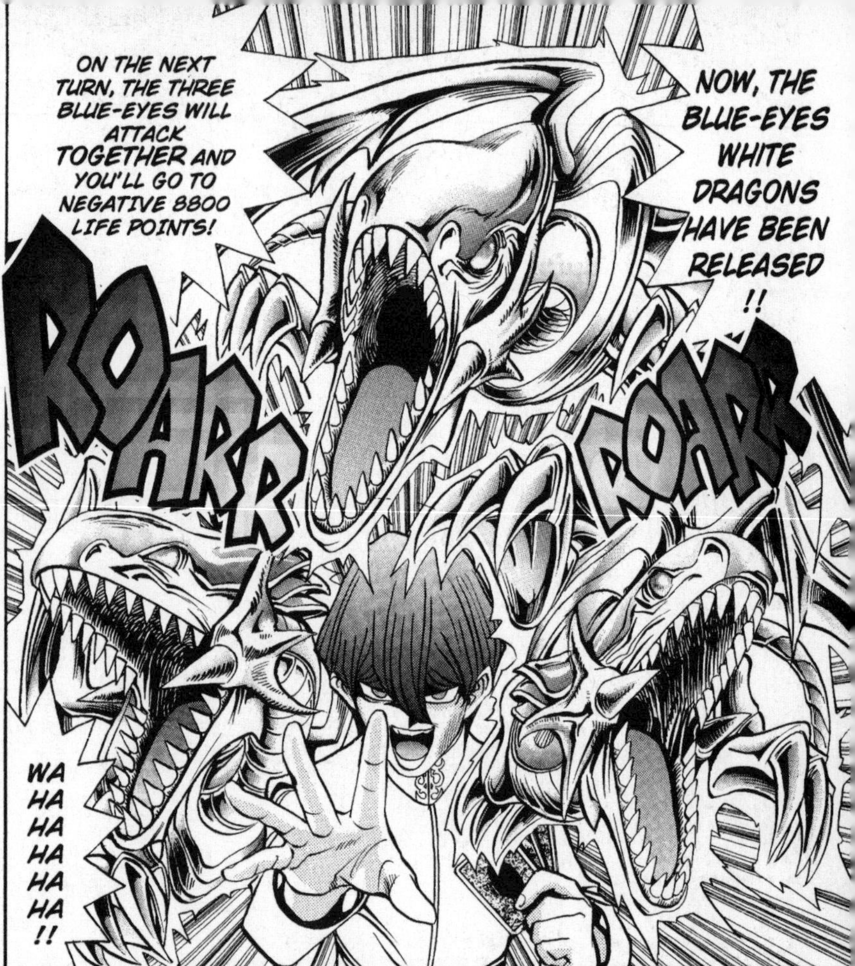
NOW, THE BLUE-EYES WHITE DRAGONS HAVE BEEN RELEASED!!
ON THE NEXT TURN, THE THREE BLUE-EYES WILL ATTACK TOGETHER AND YOU'LL GO TO NEGATIVE 8800 LIFE POINTS!
ROARR
ROARR
ROARR
WA HA HA HA HA HA!!

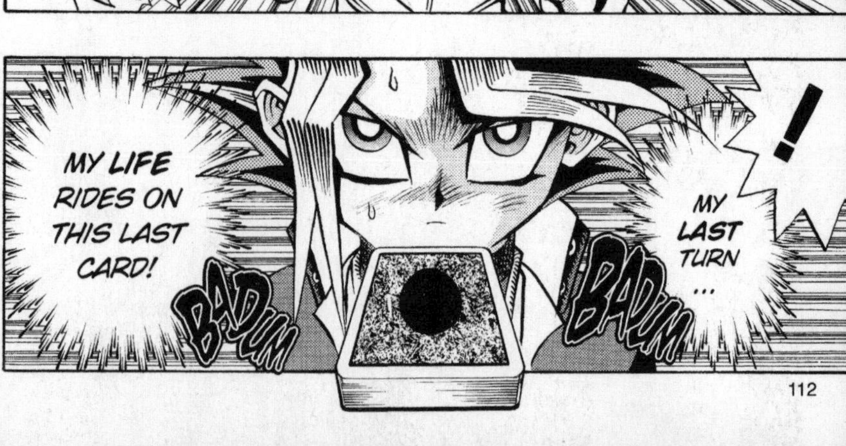
!
MY LAST TURN...
BADUM
MY LIFE RIDES ON THIS LAST CARD!
BADUM

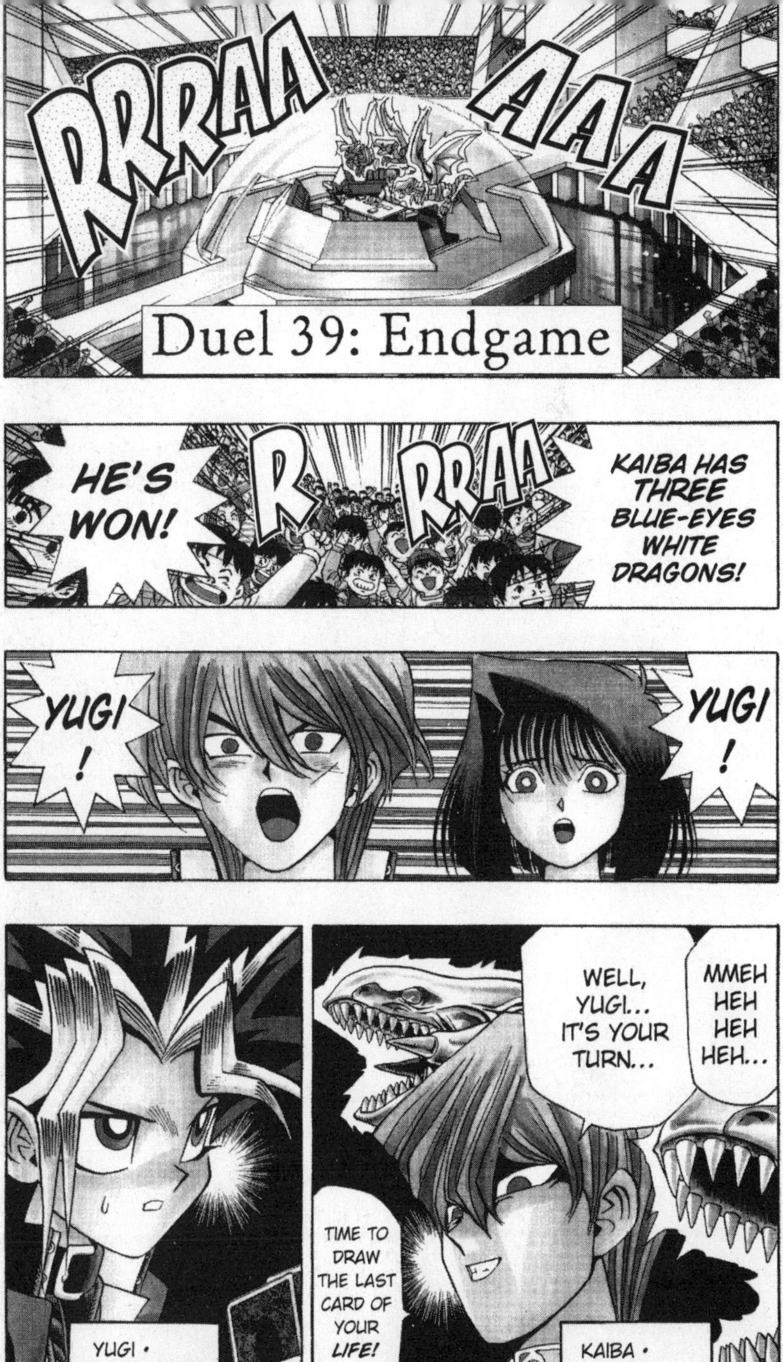
RRRAAAAAA
Duel 39: Endgame
KAIBA HAS THREE BLUE-EYES WHITE DRAGONS!
RRRAA
HE'S WON!
YUGI!
YUGI!
MMEH HEH HEH HEH...
WELL, YUGI... IT'S YOUR TURN...
TIME TO DRAW THE LAST CARD OF YOUR *LIFE!*
KAIBA • LIFE POINTS 1000
YUGI • LIFE POINTS 200

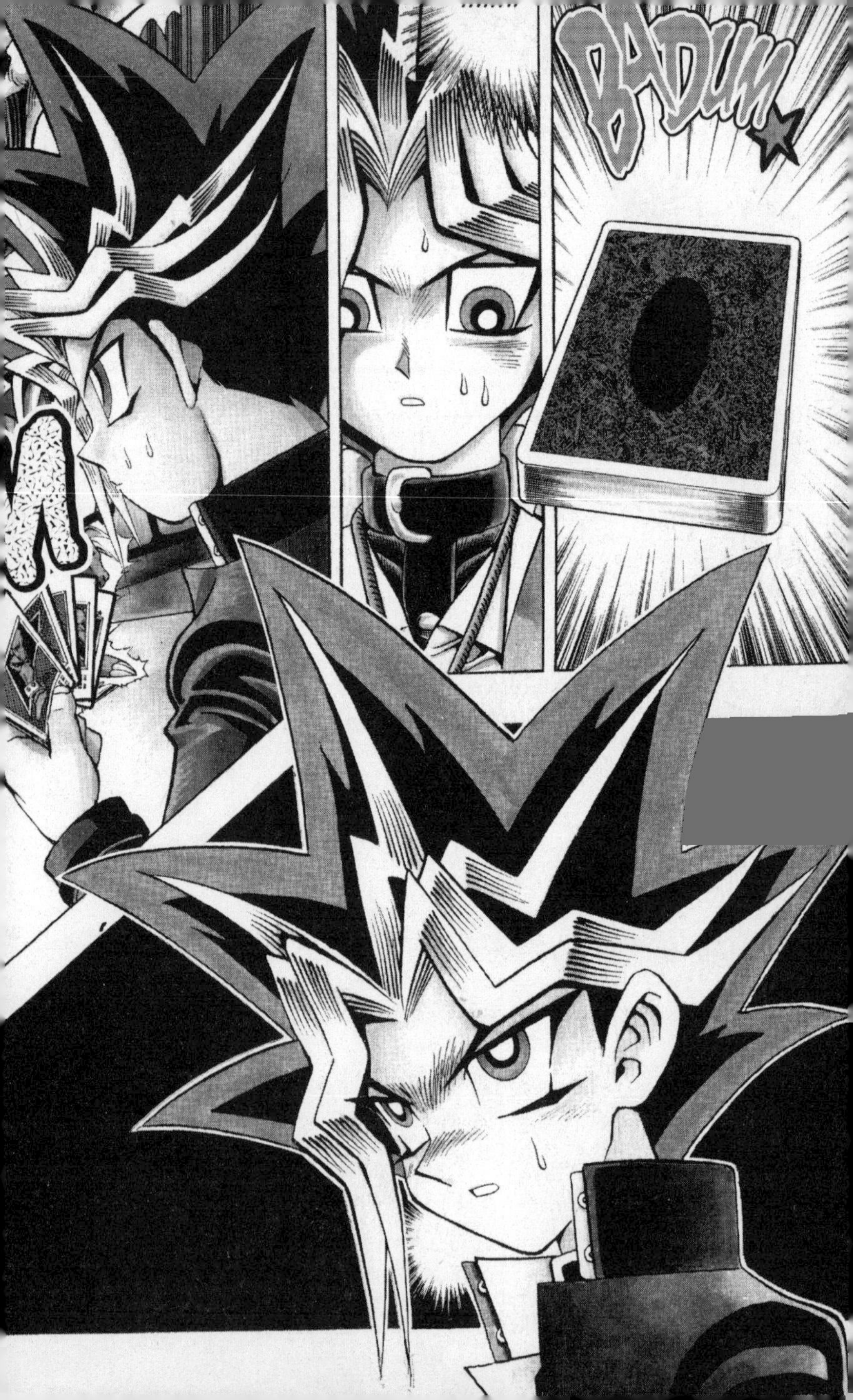
BADUM

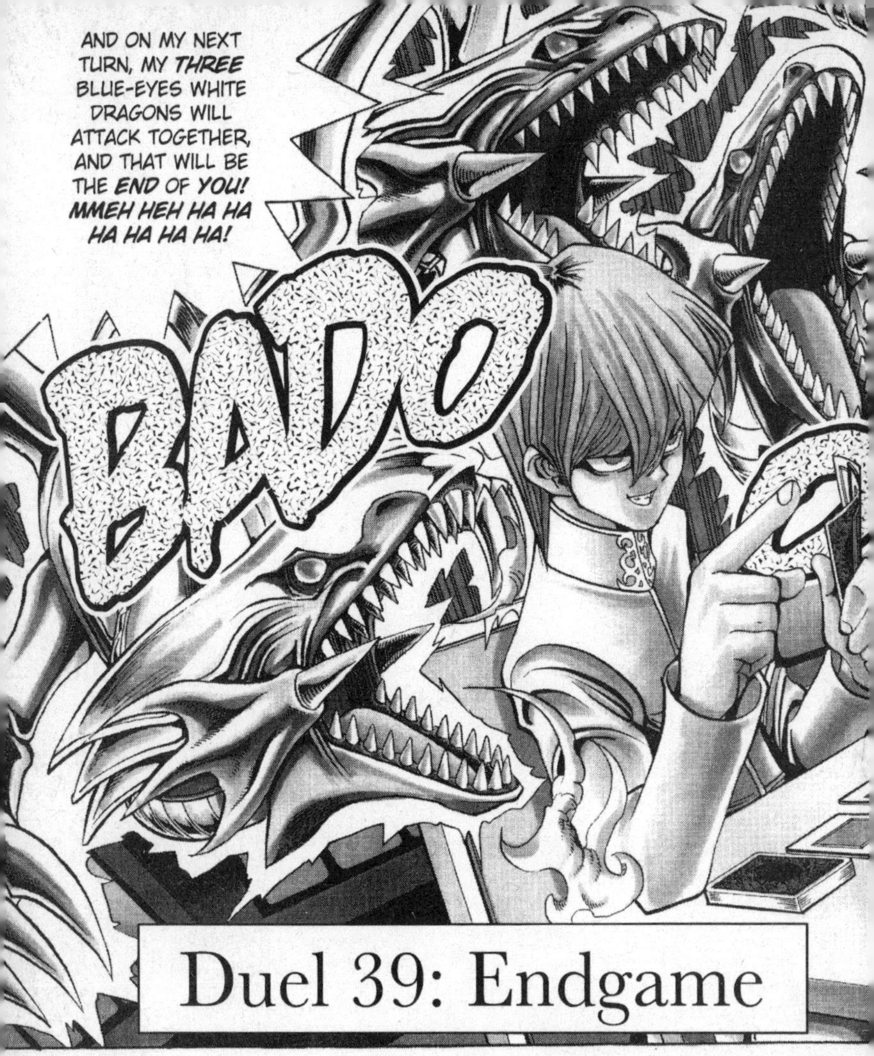
AND ON MY NEXT TURN, MY THREE BLUE-EYES WHITE DRAGONS WILL ATTACK TOGETHER, AND THAT WILL BE THE END OF YOU! MMEH HEH HA HA HA HA HA HA!
BADO

Duel 39: Endgame

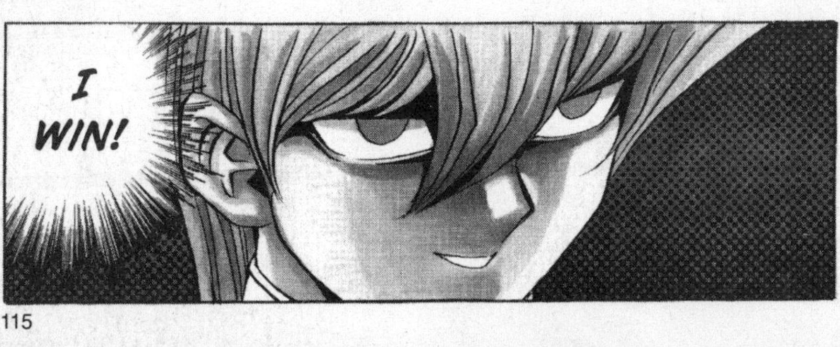
I WIN!

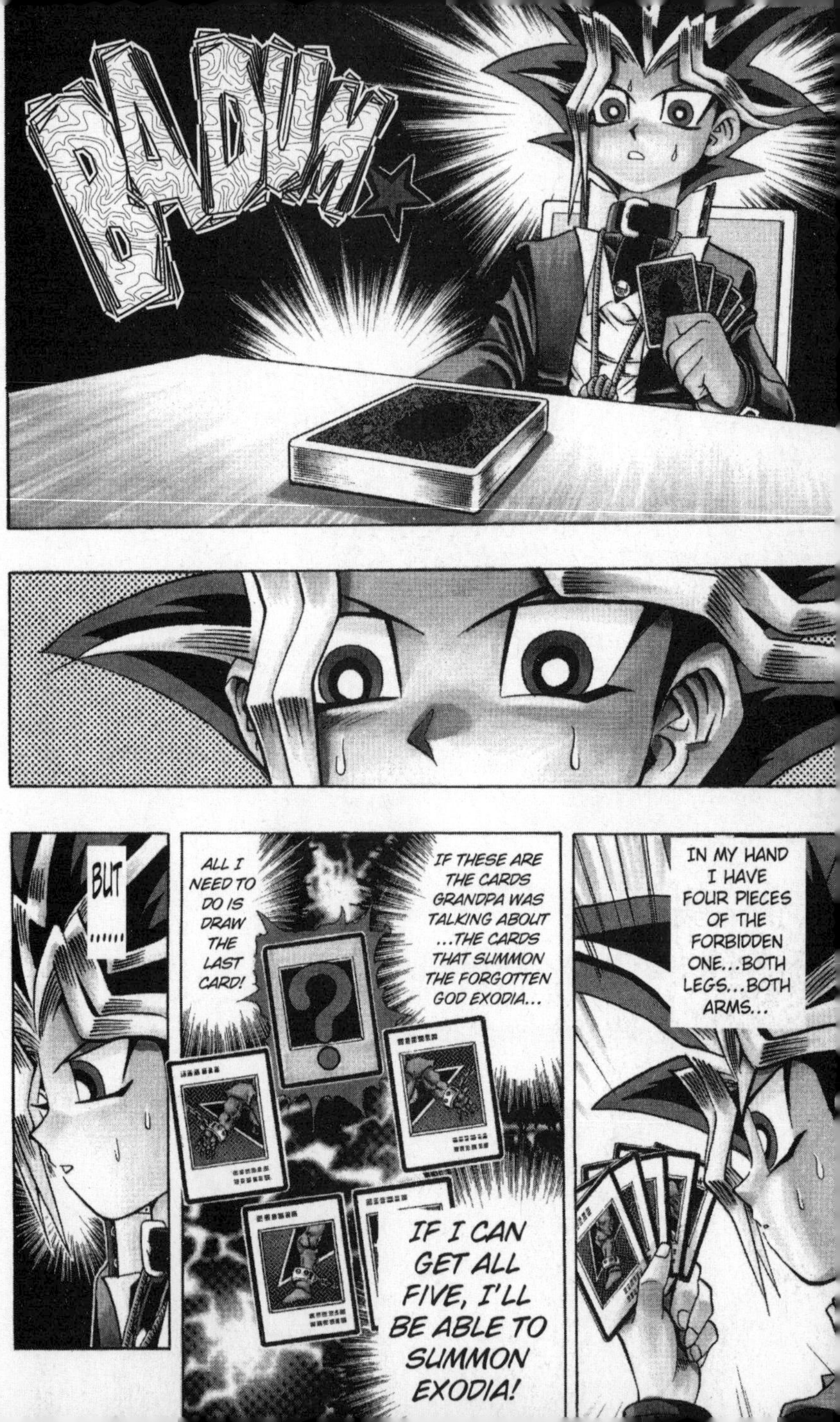
BADUM
IN MY HAND I HAVE FOUR PIECES OF THE FORBIDDEN ONE...BOTH LEGS...BOTH ARMS...
IF THESE ARE THE CARDS GRANDPA WAS TALKING ABOUT ...THE CARDS THAT SUMMON THE FORGOTTEN GOD EXODIA...
ALL I NEED TO DO IS DRAW THE LAST CARD!
IF I CAN GET ALL FIVE, I'LL BE ABLE TO SUMMON EXODIA!
BUT ......

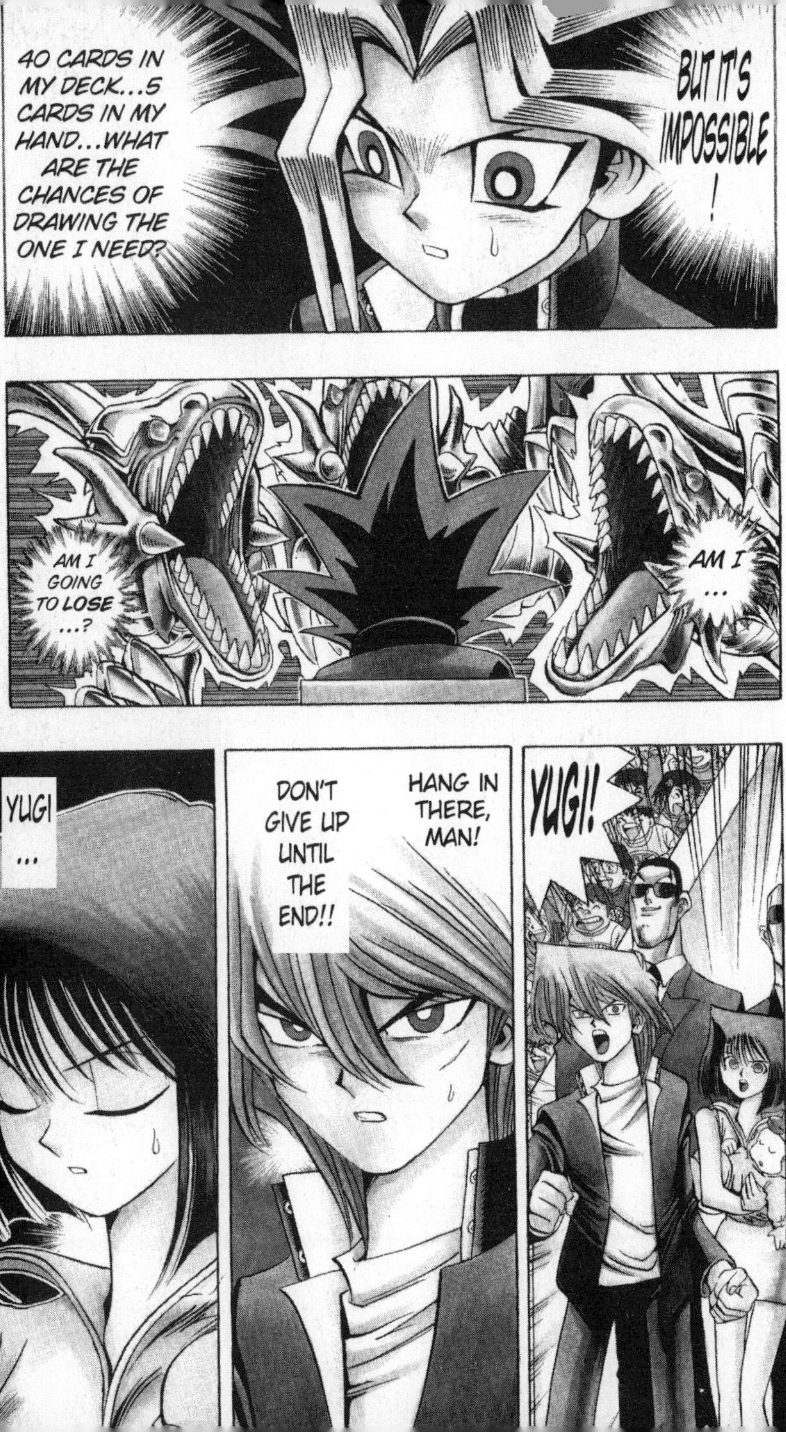
BUT IT'S IMPOSSIBLE!
40 CARDS IN MY DECK...5 CARDS IN MY HAND...WHAT ARE THE CHANCES OF DRAWING THE ONE I NEED?
AM I ...
AM I GOING TO LOSE ...?
YUGI!
HANG IN THERE, MAN!
DON'T GIVE UP UNTIL THE END!!
YUGI ...

READ THIS WAY

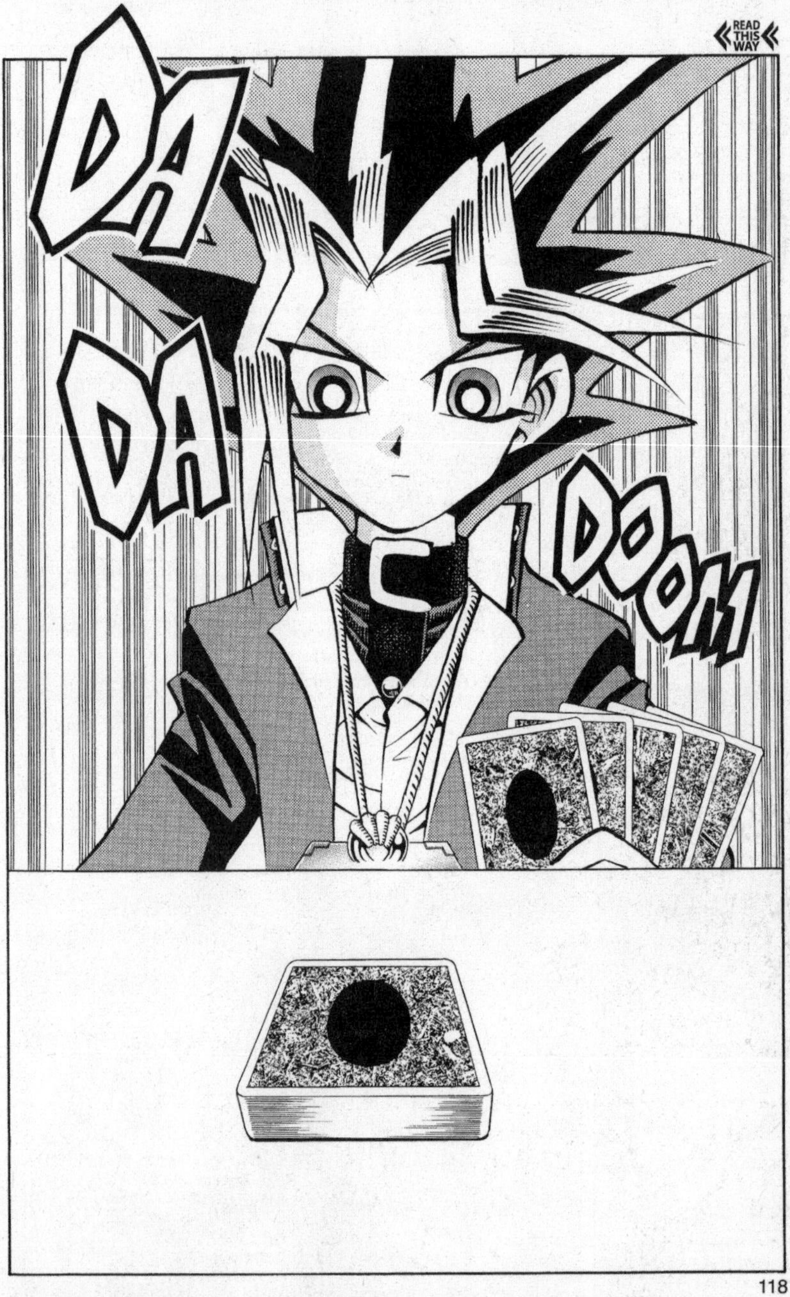
DA
DA
DOOM

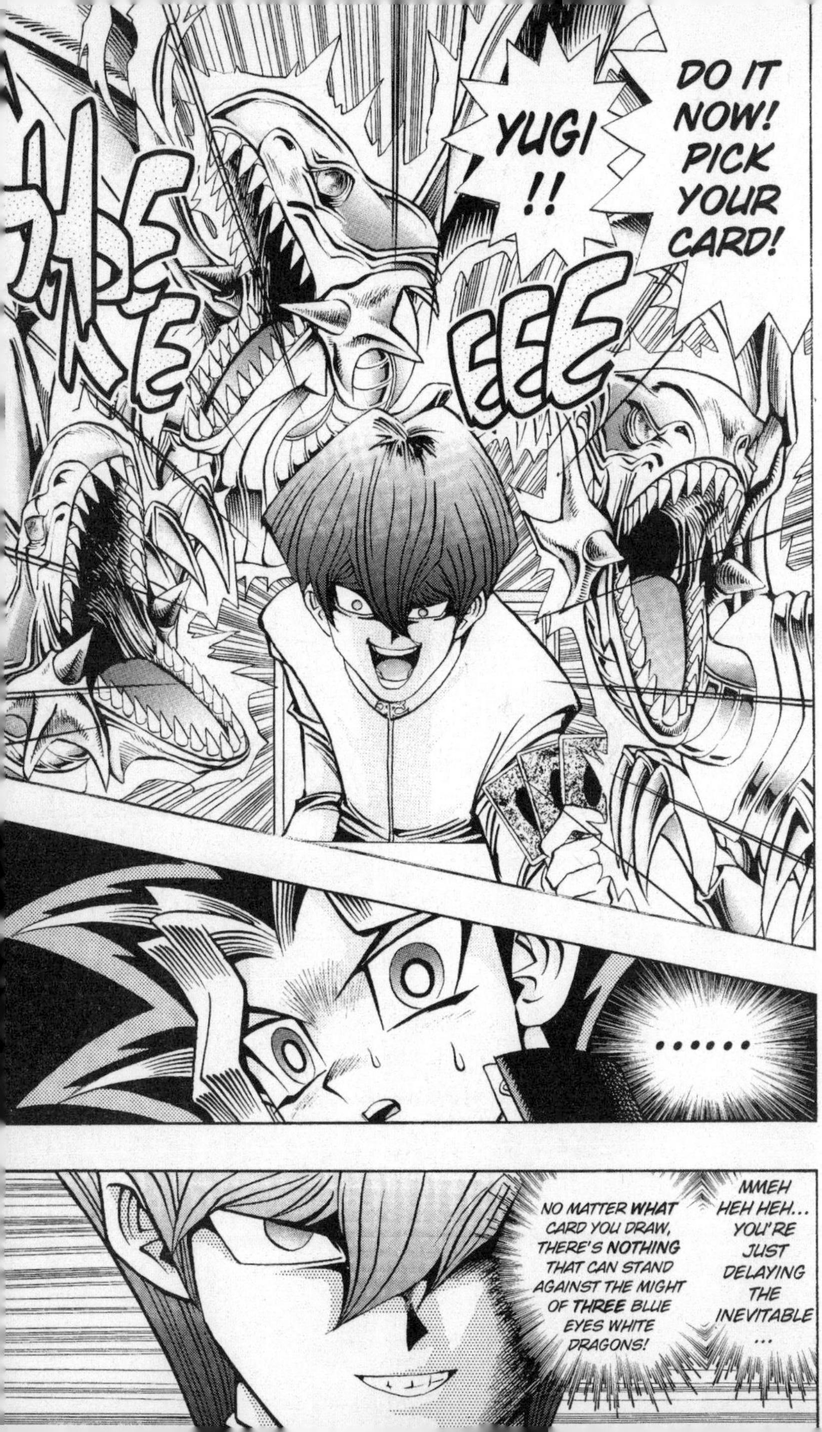
DO IT NOW! PICK YOUR CARD!
YUGI !!
......
MMEH HEH HEH... YOU'RE JUST DELAYING THE INEVITABLE...
NO MATTER WHAT CARD YOU DRAW, THERE'S NOTHING THAT CAN STAND AGAINST THE MIGHT OF THREE BLUE EYES WHITE DRAGONS!

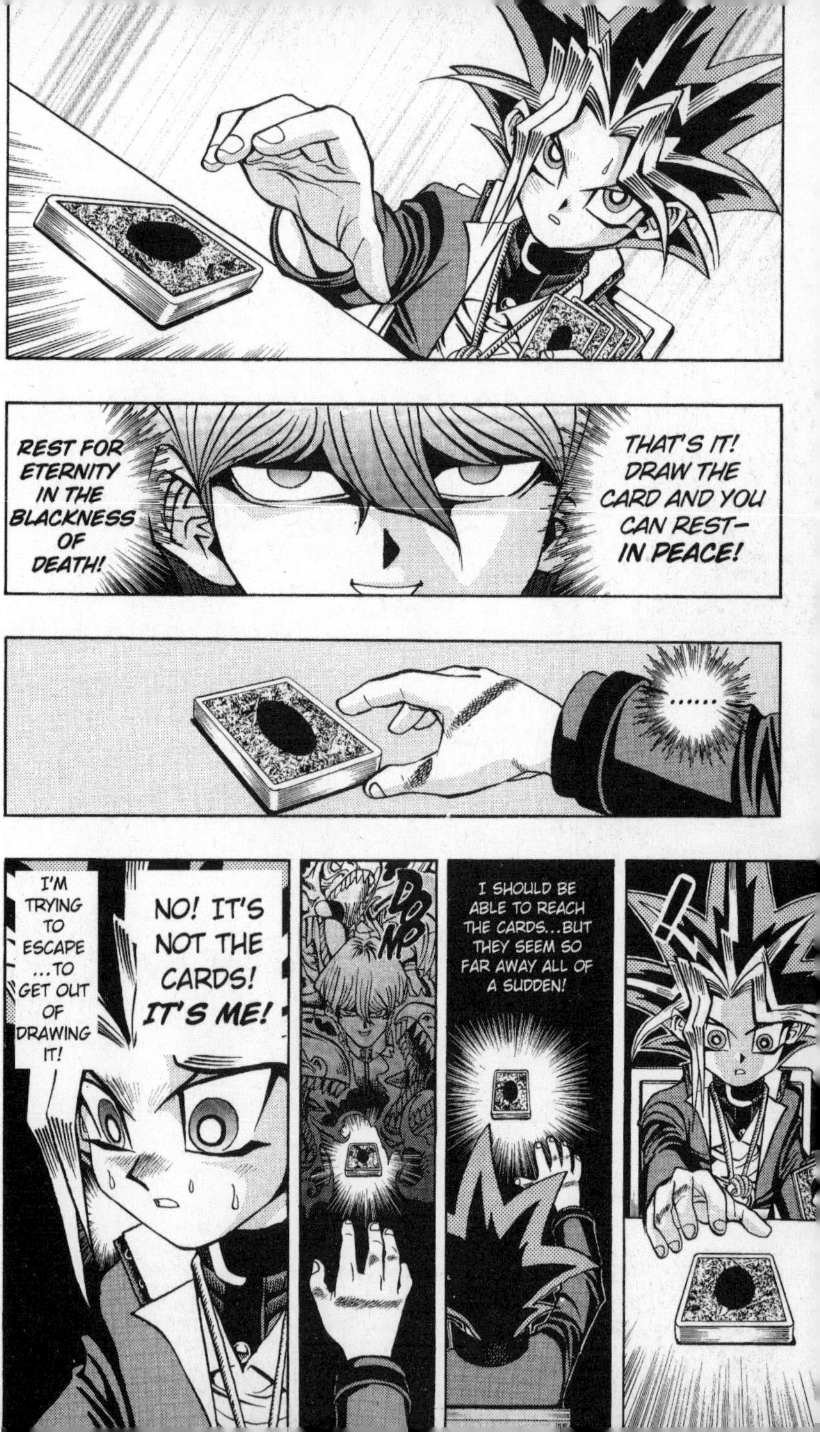
THAT'S IT! DRAW THE CARD AND YOU CAN REST— IN PEACE!
REST FOR ETERNITY IN THE BLACKNESS OF DEATH!
......
!
I SHOULD BE ABLE TO REACH THE CARDS...BUT THEY SEEM SO FAR AWAY ALL OF A SUDDEN!
DOOM
NO! IT'S NOT THE CARDS! IT'S ME!
I'M TRYING TO ESCAPE ...TO GET OUT OF DRAWING IT!

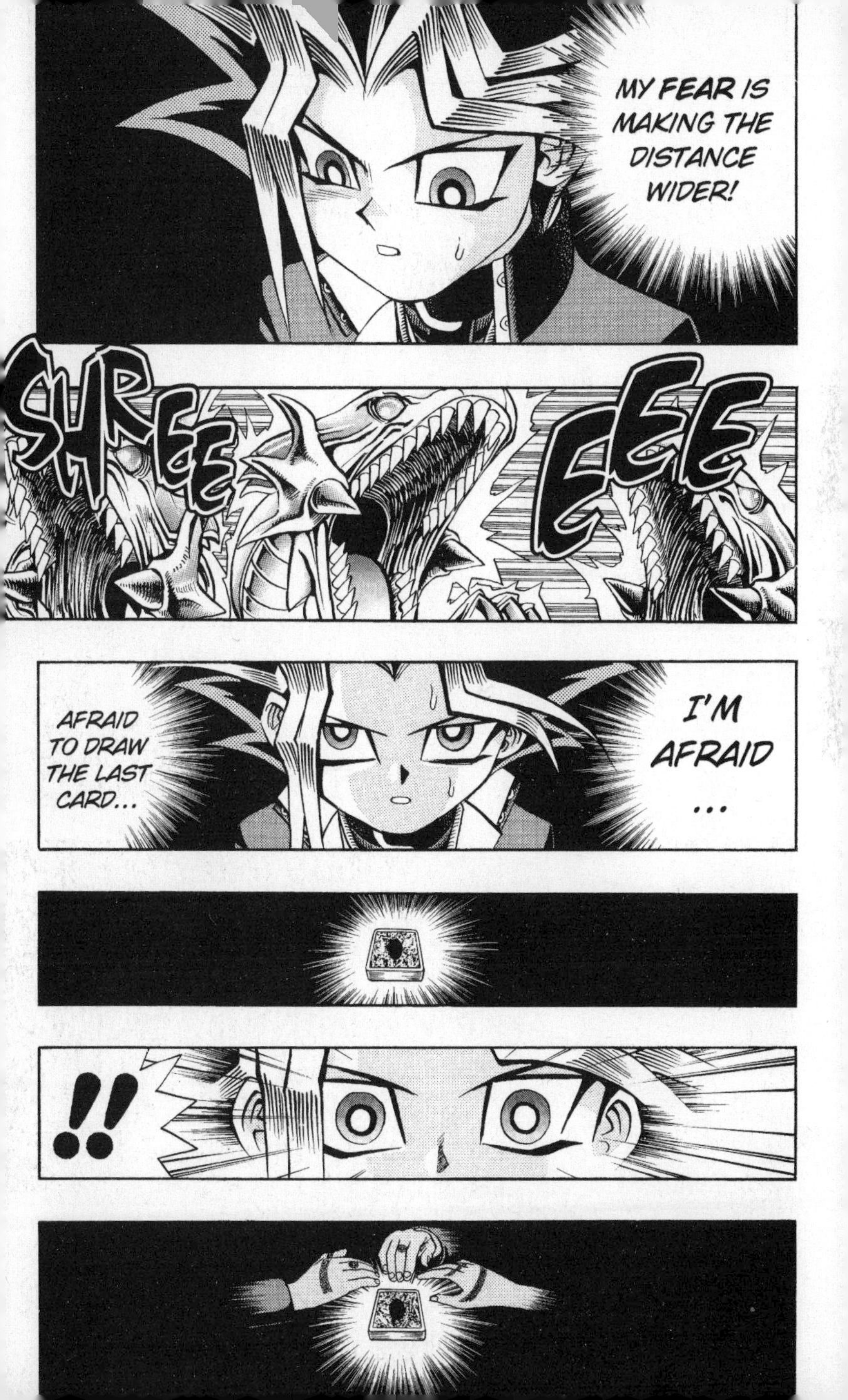
MY FEAR IS MAKING THE DISTANCE WIDER!
SHREE
EEE
I'M AFRAID ...
AFRAID TO DRAW THE LAST CARD...
!!

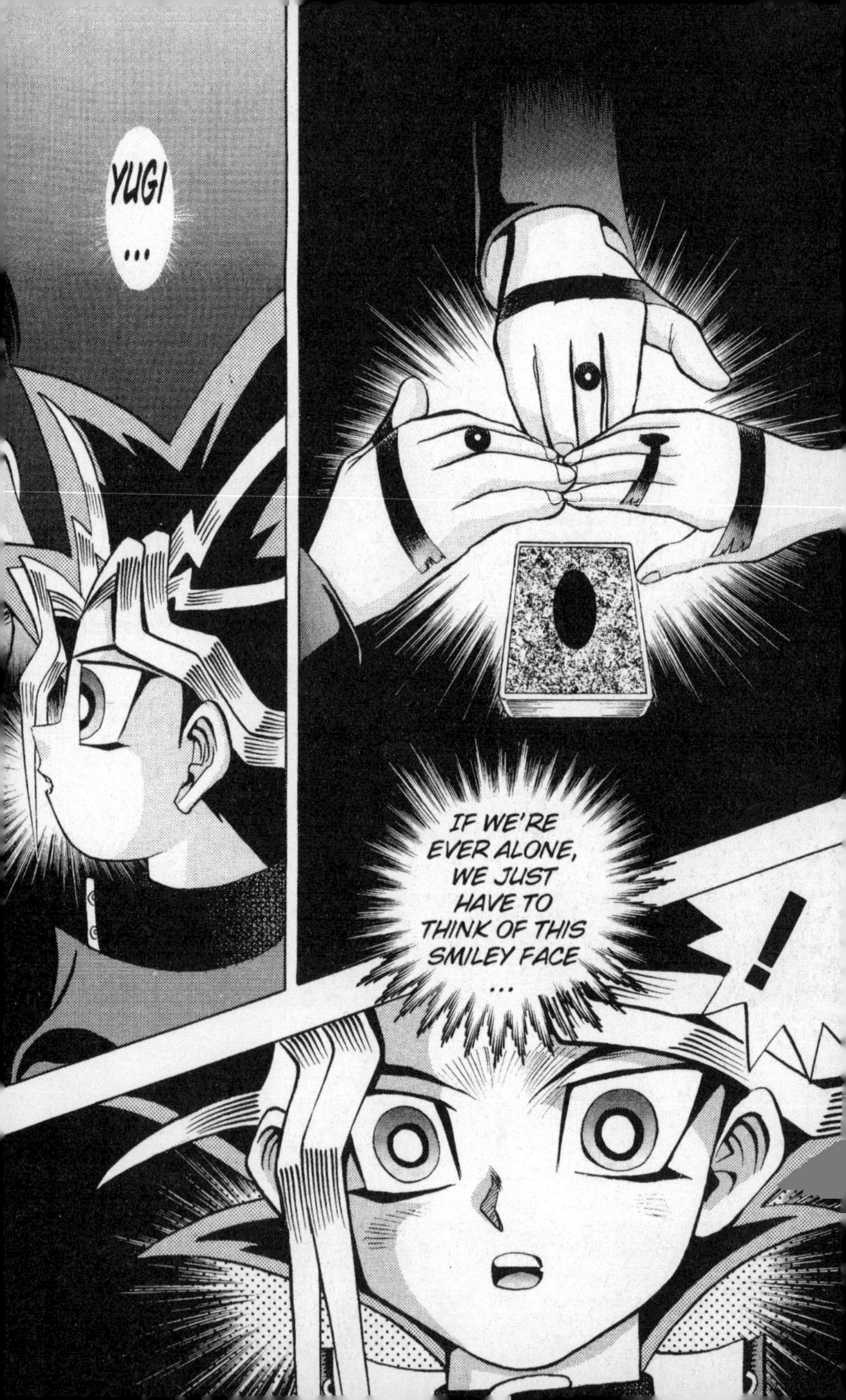
YUGI …
IF WE'RE EVER ALONE, WE JUST HAVE TO THINK OF THIS SMILEY FACE …
!

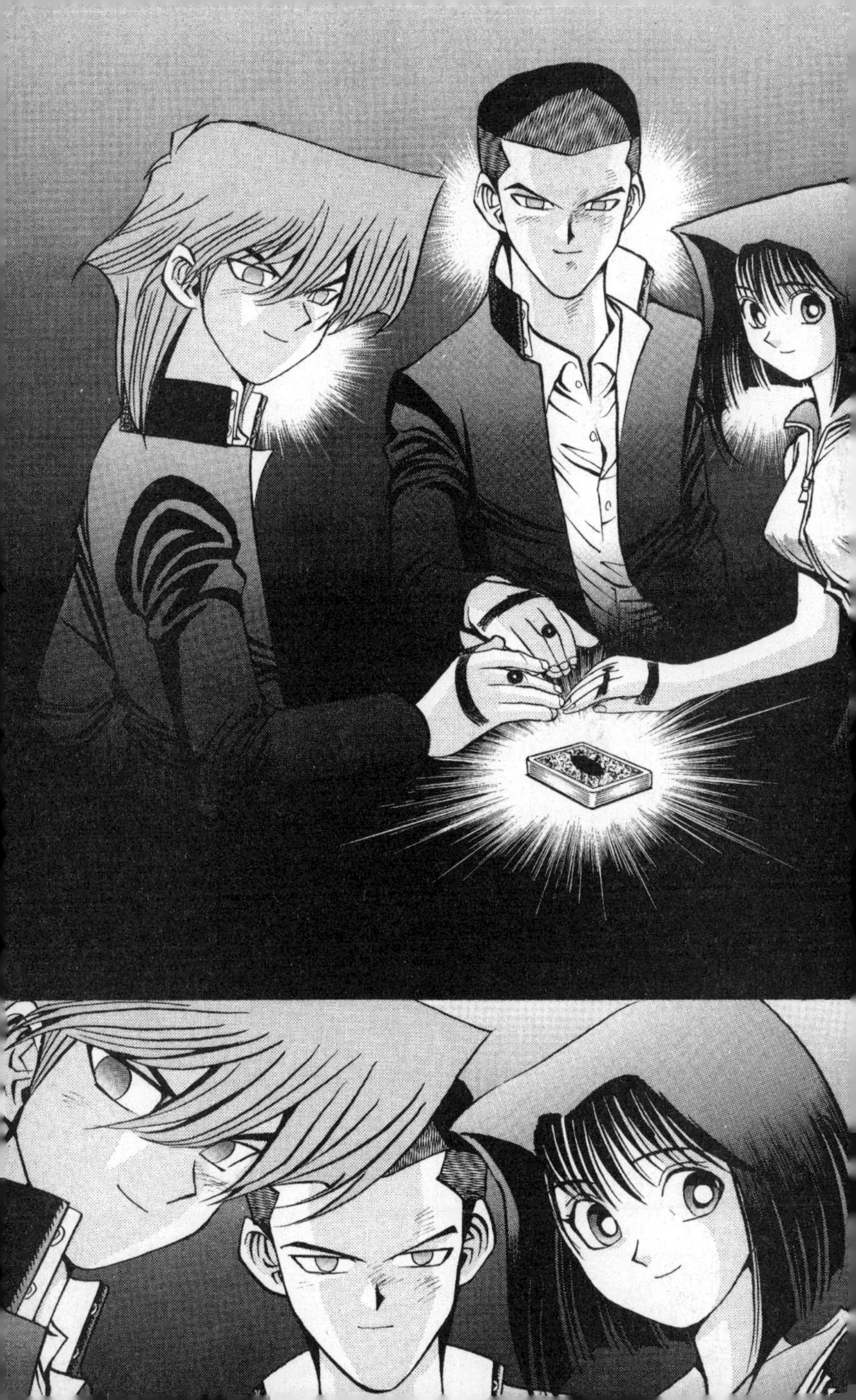

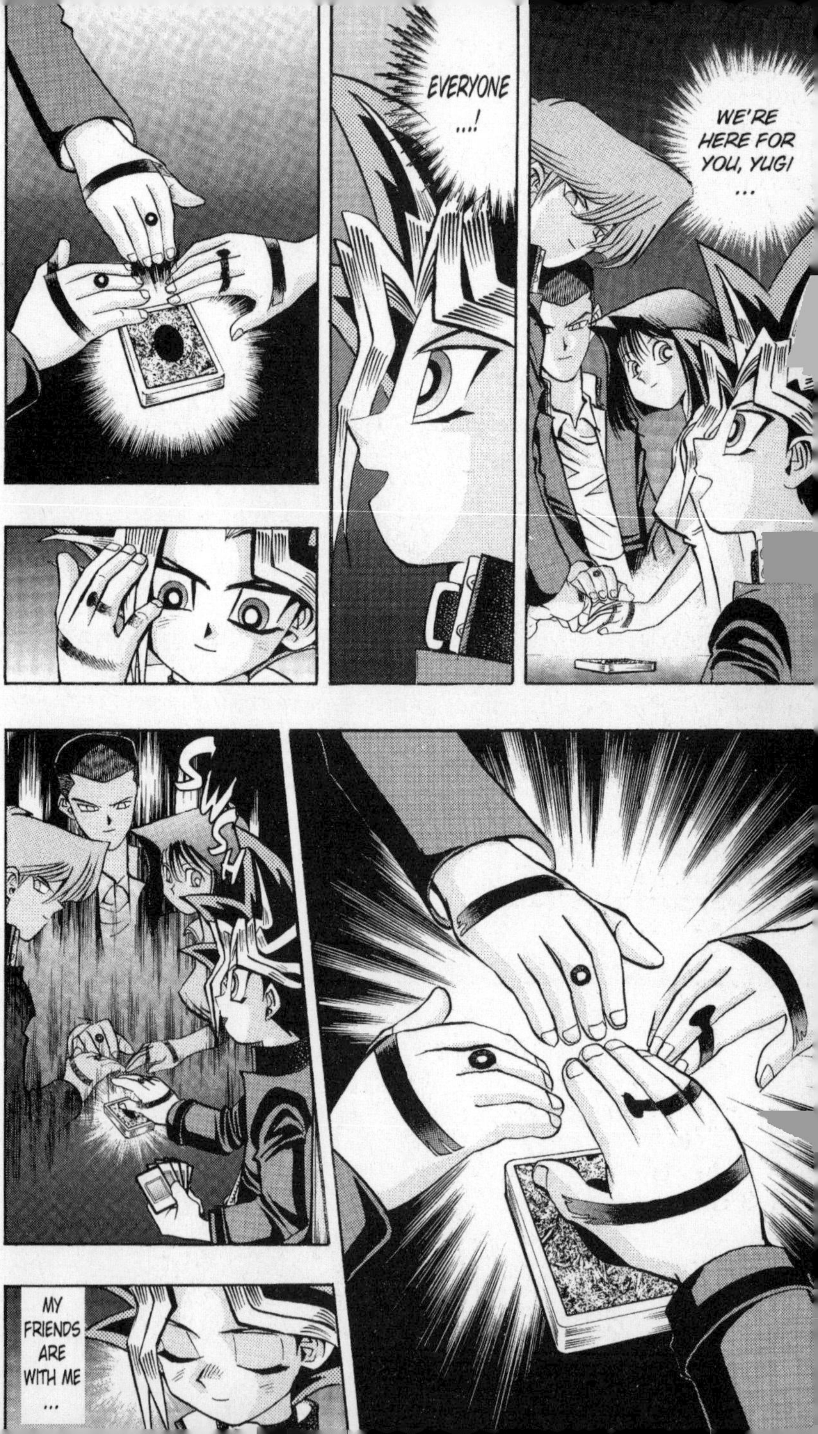
WE'RE HERE FOR YOU, YUGI ...
EVERYONE ...!
SWISH
MY FRIENDS ARE WITH ME ...

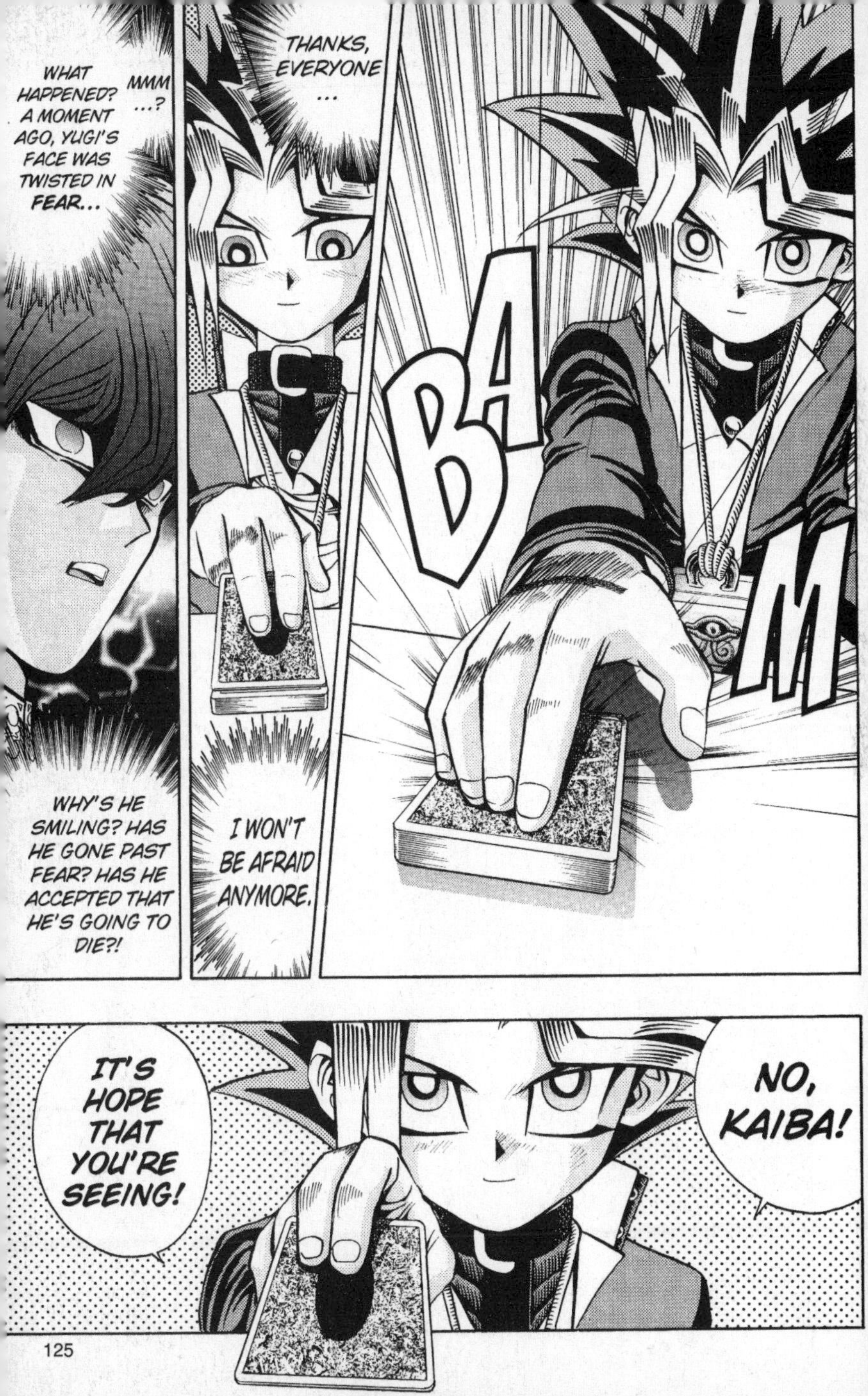
BAM
THANKS, EVERYONE ...
I WON'T BE AFRAID ANYMORE.
MMM ...?
WHAT HAPPENED? A MOMENT AGO, YUGI'S FACE WAS TWISTED IN FEAR...
WHY'S HE SMILING? HAS HE GONE PAST FEAR? HAS HE ACCEPTED THAT HE'S GOING TO DIE?!
NO, KAIBA!
IT'S HOPE THAT YOU'RE SEEING!

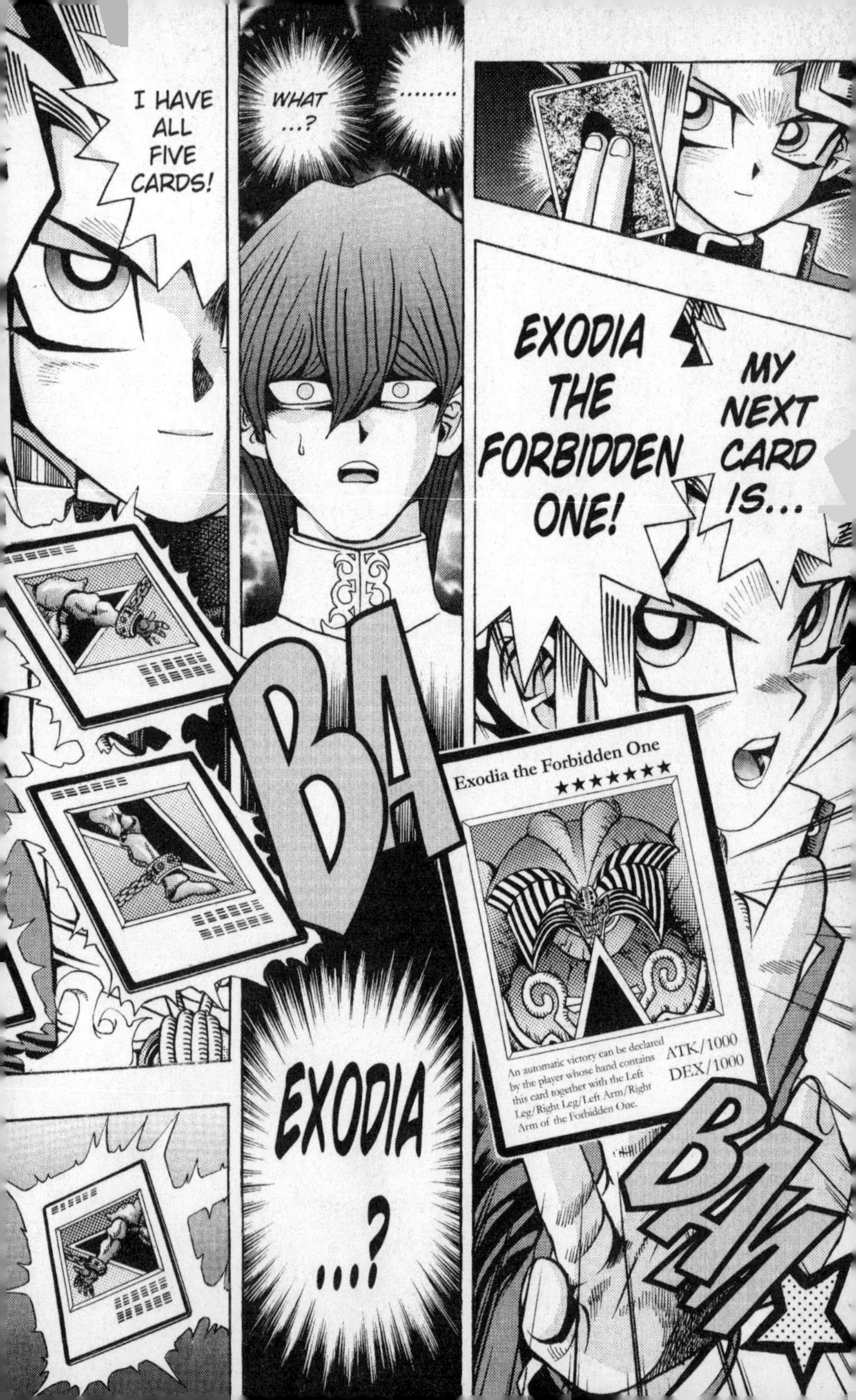
MY NEXT CARD IS...
EXODIA THE FORBIDDEN ONE!
Exodia the Forbidden One
ATK/1000
DEX/1000
An automatic victory can be declared by the player whose hand contains this card together with the Left Leg/Right Leg/Left Arm/Right Arm of the Forbidden One.
BA
BA
....
WHAT ...?
EXODIA ...?
I HAVE ALL FIVE CARDS!

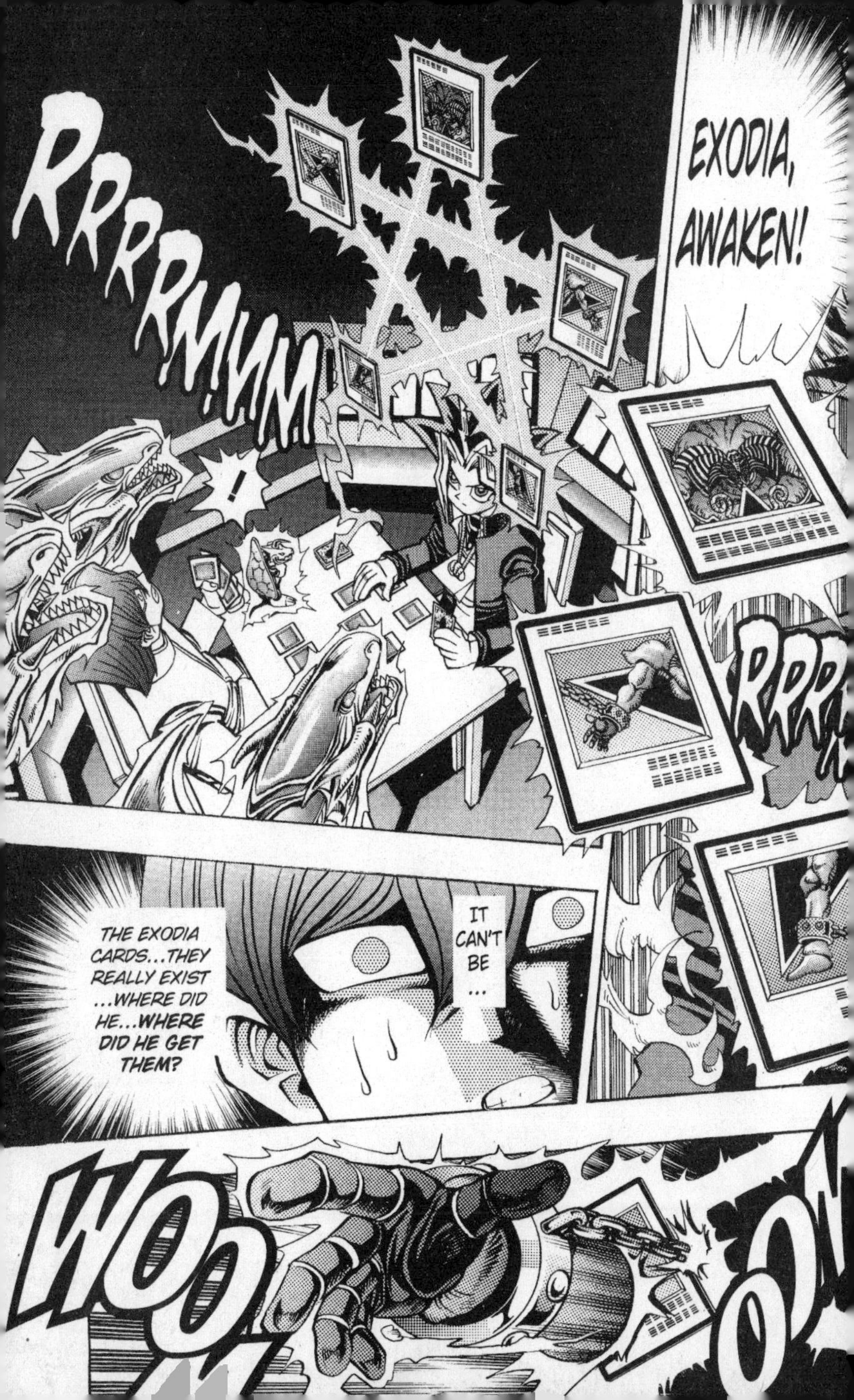
EXODIA, AWAKEN!
RRRRMMM
!
RRRR
IT CAN'T BE ...
THE EXODIA CARDS...THEY REALLY EXIST ...WHERE DID HE...WHERE DID HE GET THEM?
WHOOOO!

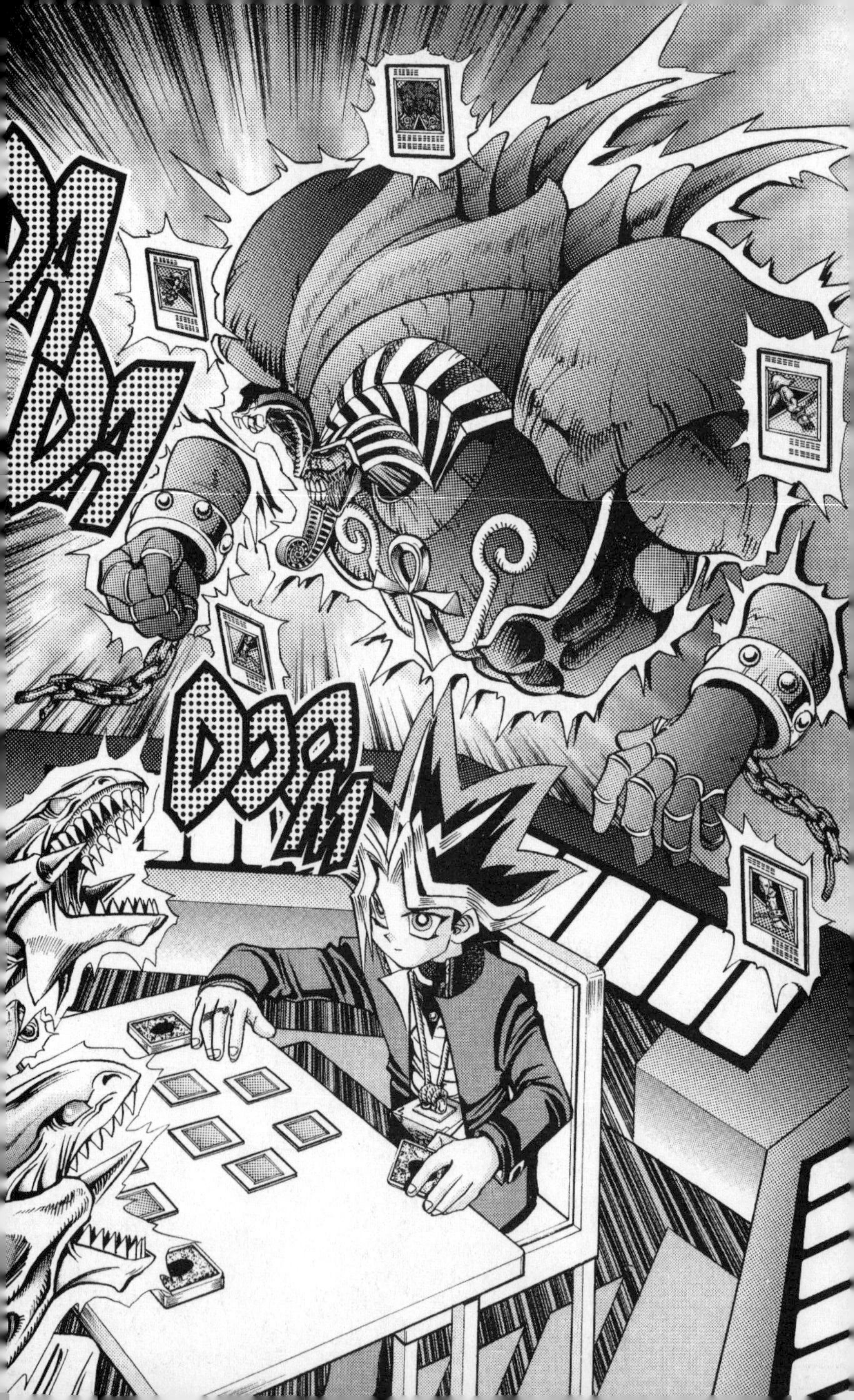
DA DA DA
DORM

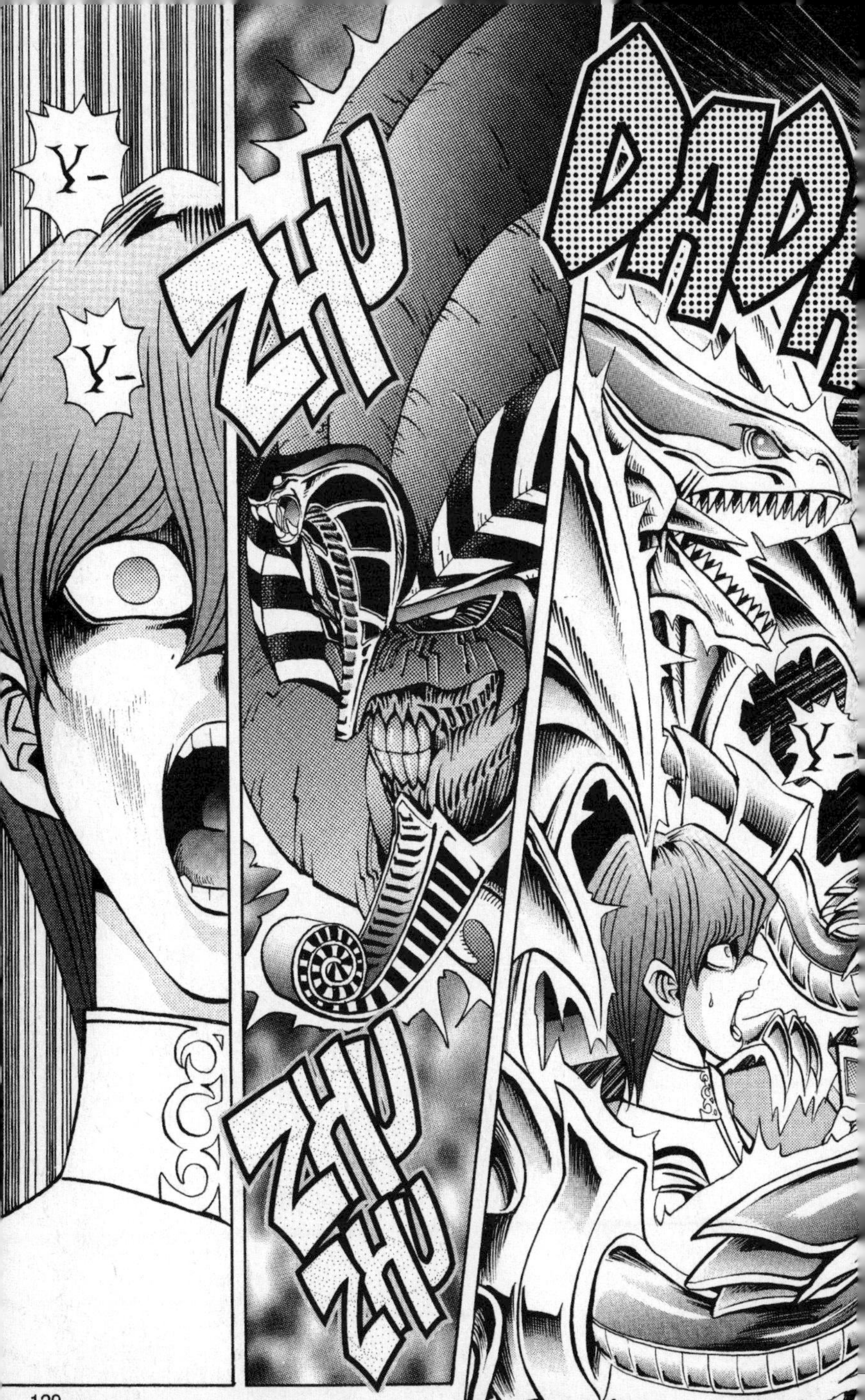
DAD
Y-
ZHU
ZHU
ZHU
Y-
Y-

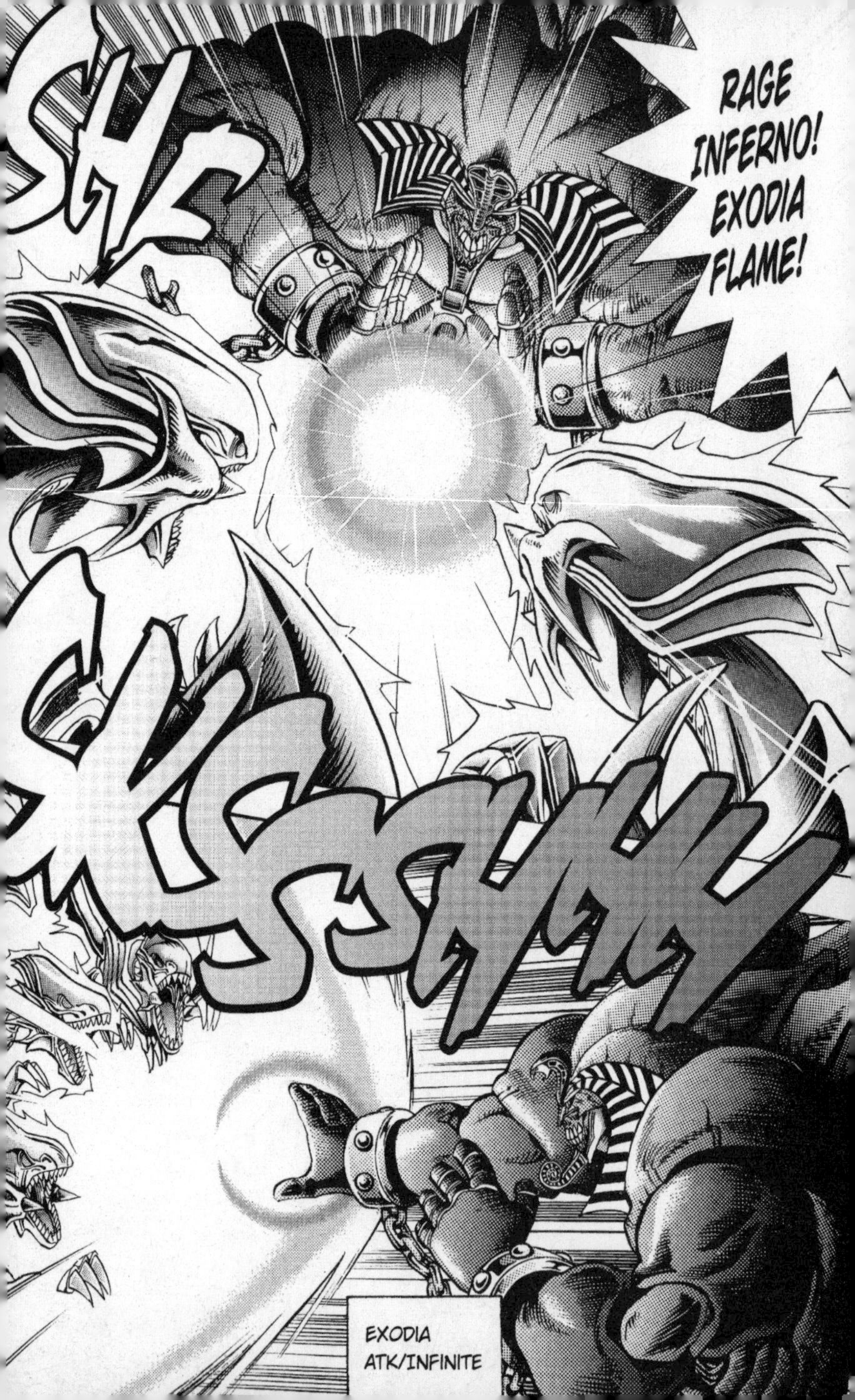
RAGE INFERNO! EXODIA FLAME!
SH
SHSSHHH
EXODIA ATK/INFINITE

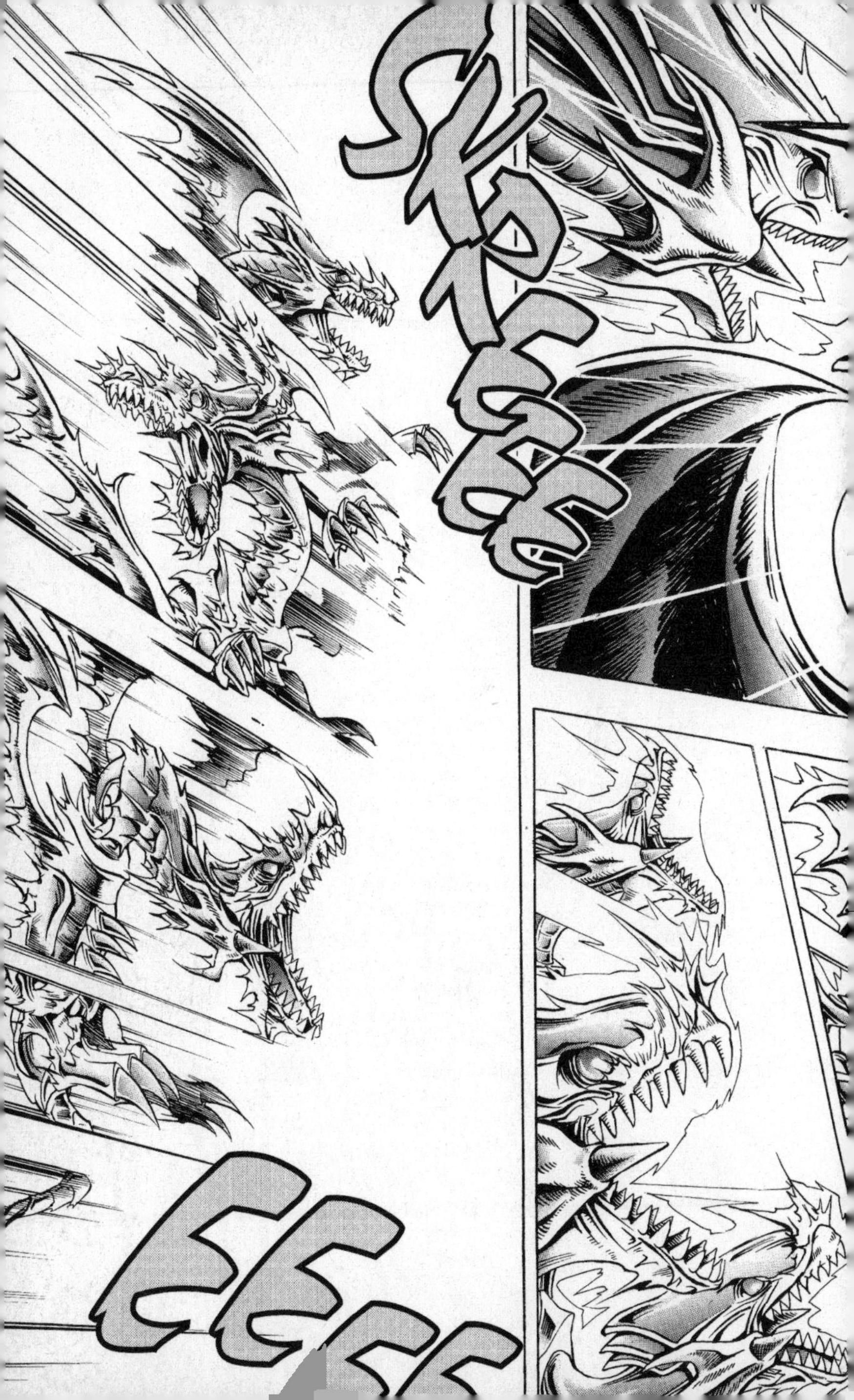
SKREEEE
EEEE

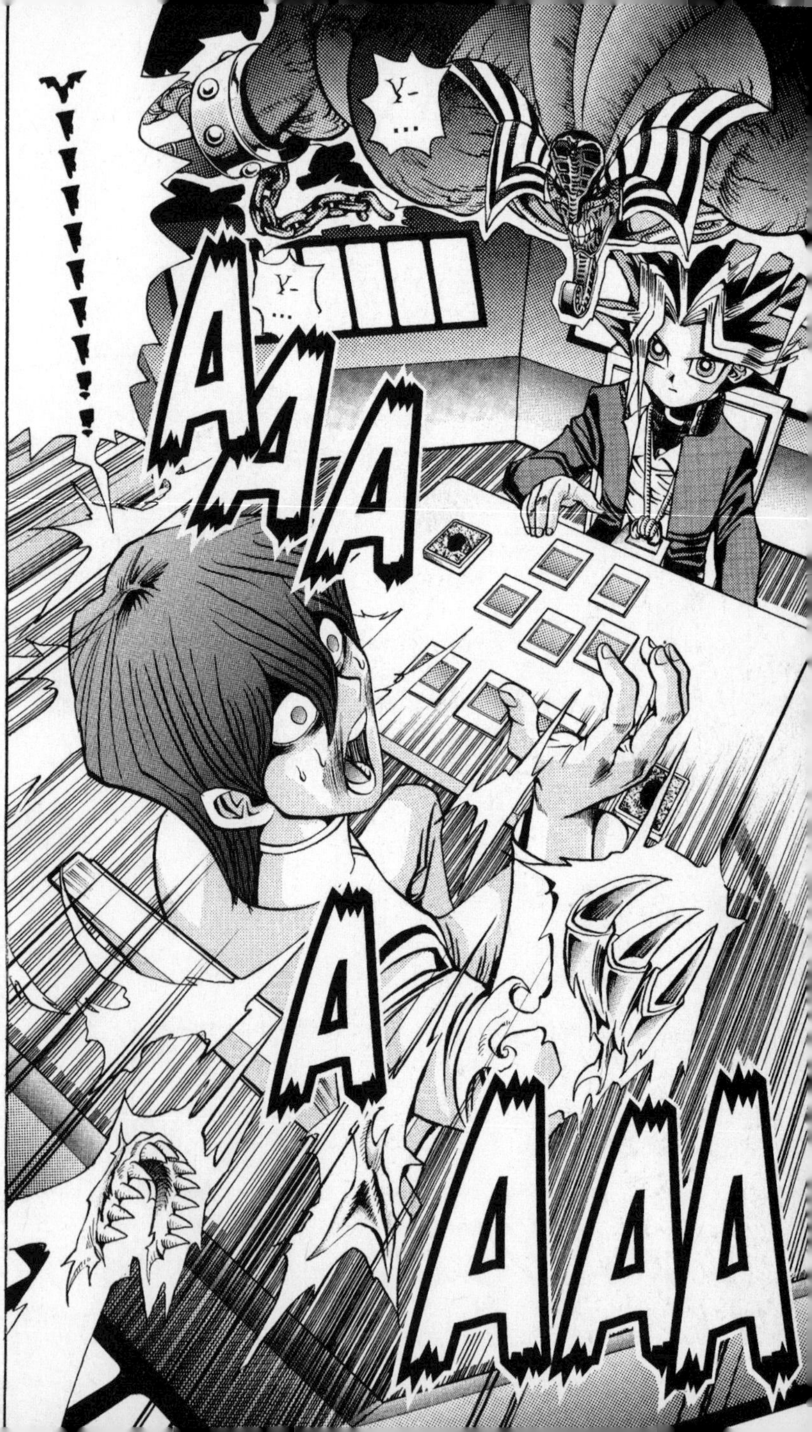
Y-...
Y-...
AAAA
AAAA

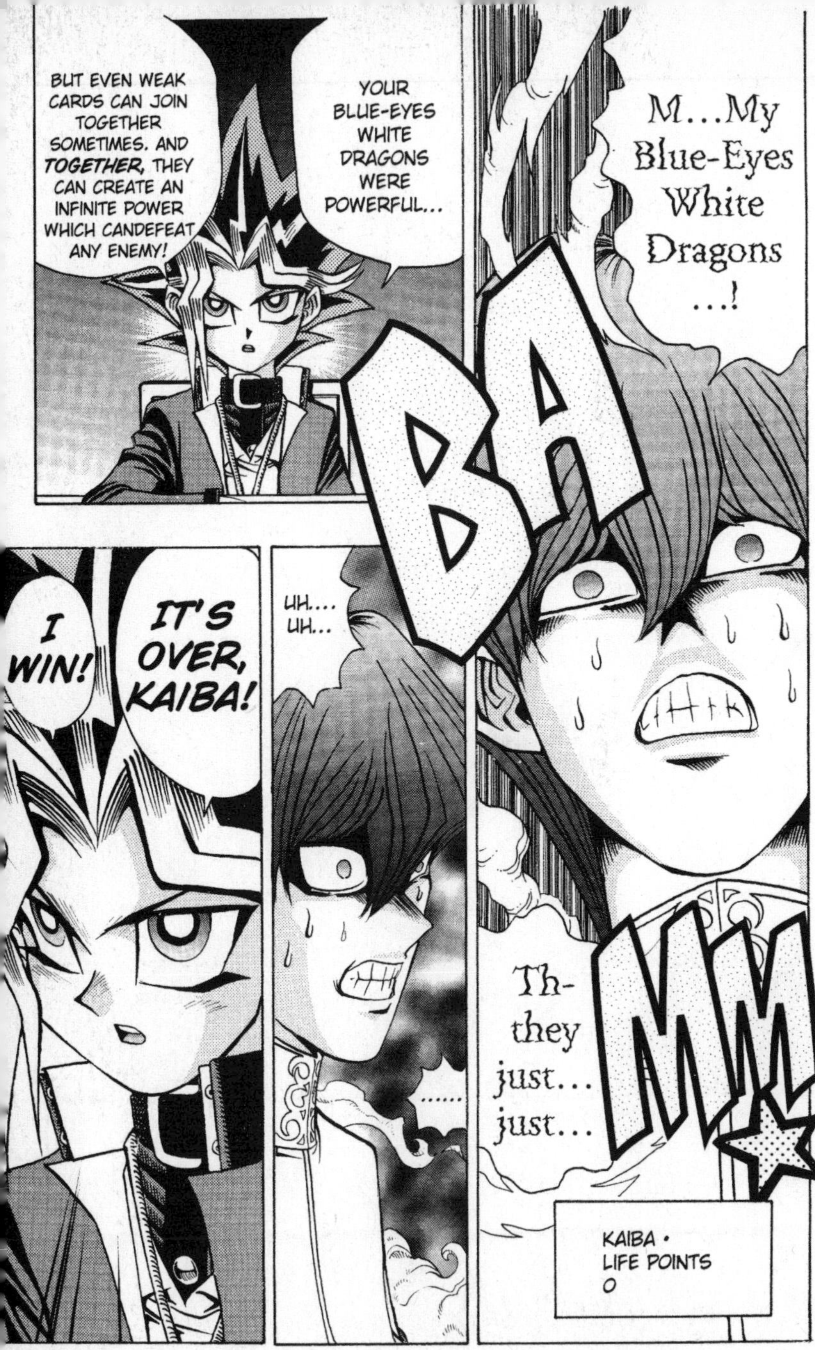
M...My Blue-Eyes White Dragons ...!
BAMM
Th-they just... just...
KAIBA • LIFE POINTS 0
YOUR BLUE-EYES WHITE DRAGONS WERE POWERFUL...
BUT EVEN WEAK CARDS CAN JOIN TOGETHER SOMETIMES. AND *TOGETHER*, THEY CAN CREATE AN INFINITE POWER WHICH CANDEFEAT ANY ENEMY!
UH.... UH...
......
IT'S OVER, KAIBA!
I WIN!

Duel 40: A Piece of His Heart

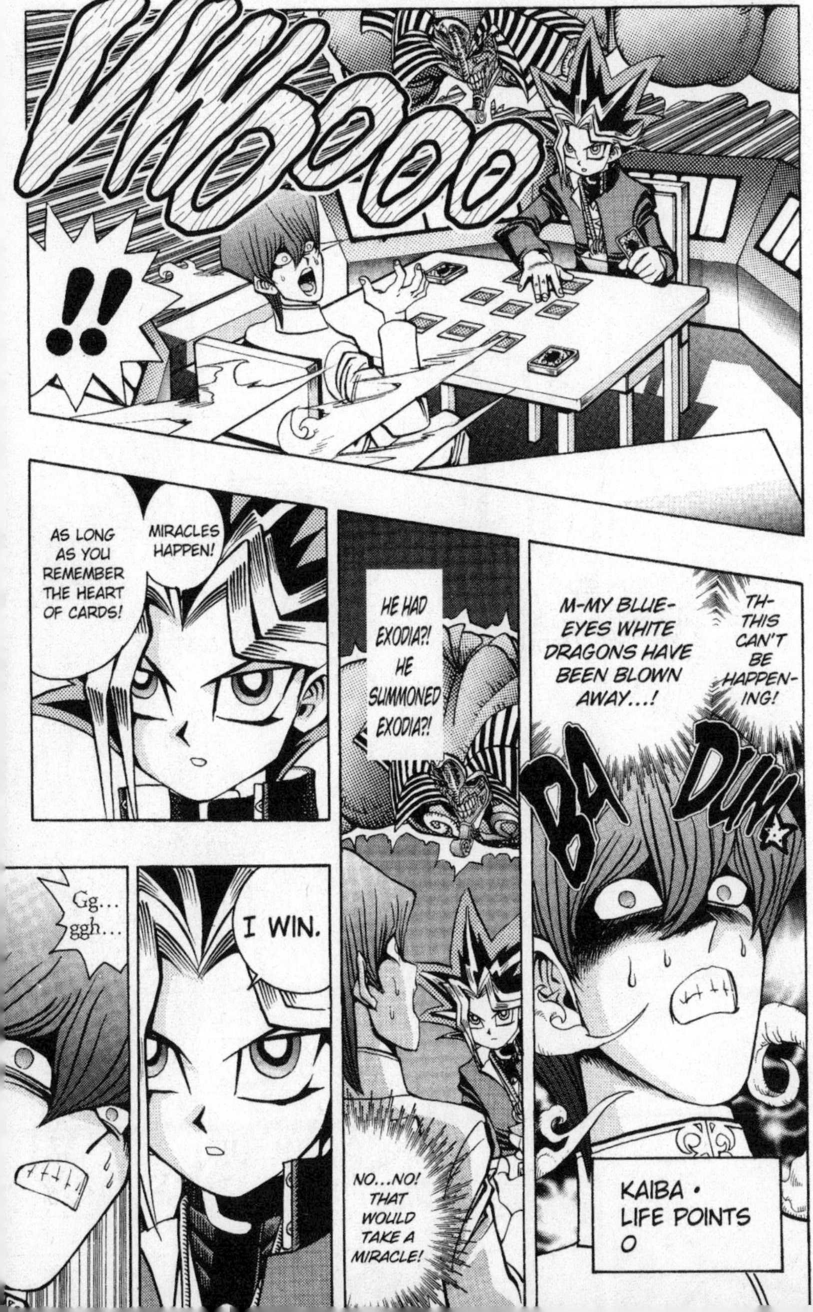
WHOOOO
!!
TH-THIS CAN'T BE HAPPENING!
M-MY BLUE-EYES WHITE DRAGONS HAVE BEEN BLOWN AWAY...!
BA DUM
KAIBA • LIFE POINTS 0
HE HAD EXODIA?! HE SUMMONED EXODIA?!
NO...NO! THAT WOULD TAKE A MIRACLE!
MIRACLES HAPPEN!
AS LONG AS YOU REMEMBER THE HEART OF CARDS!
I WIN.
Gg... ggh...

Duel 40: A Piece of His Heart

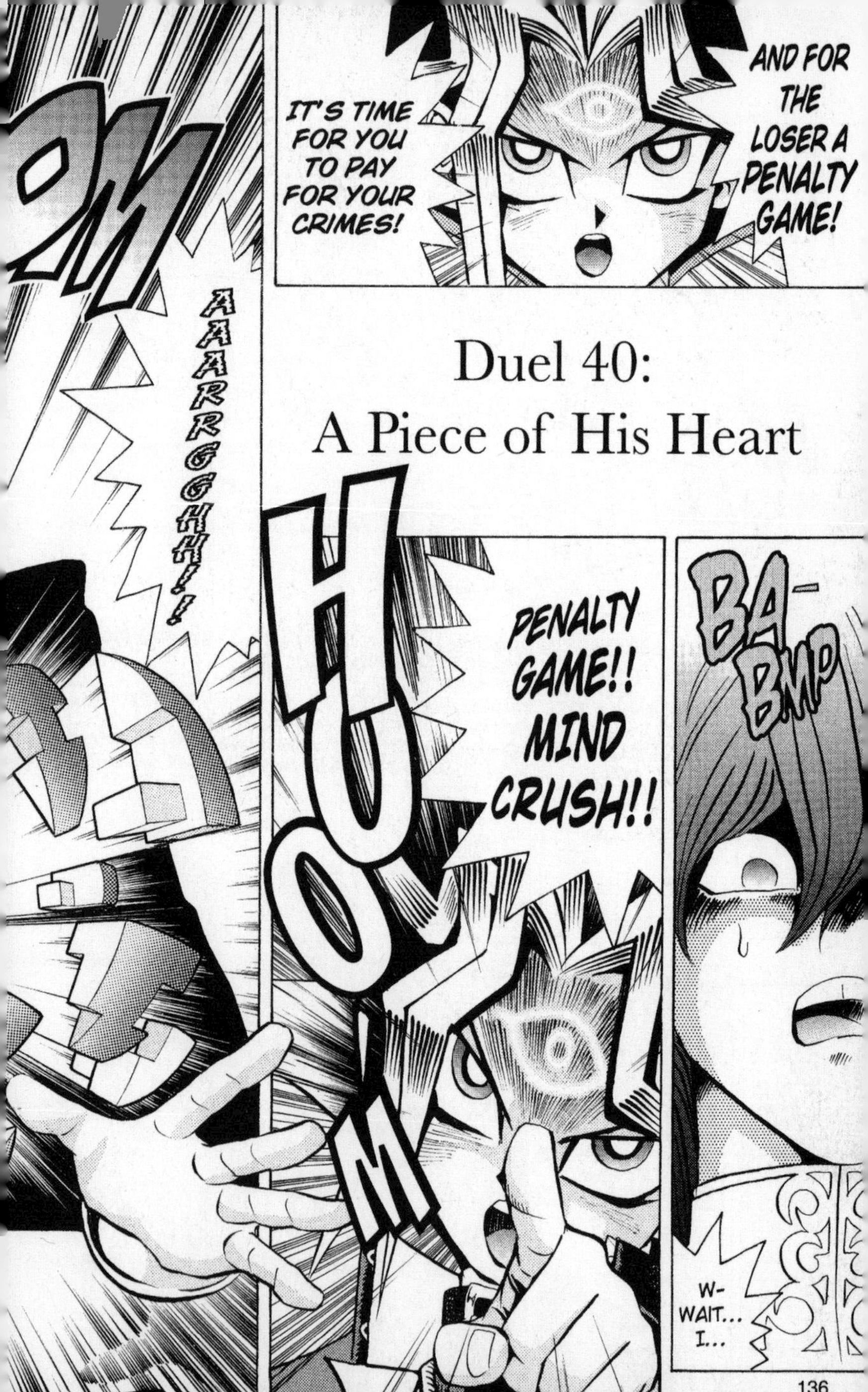
AND FOR THE LOSER A PENALTY GAME!
IT'S TIME FOR YOU TO PAY FOR YOUR CRIMES!
BA-BMP
W-WAIT... I...
PENALTY GAME!! MIND CRUSH!!
AAARRGHH!!

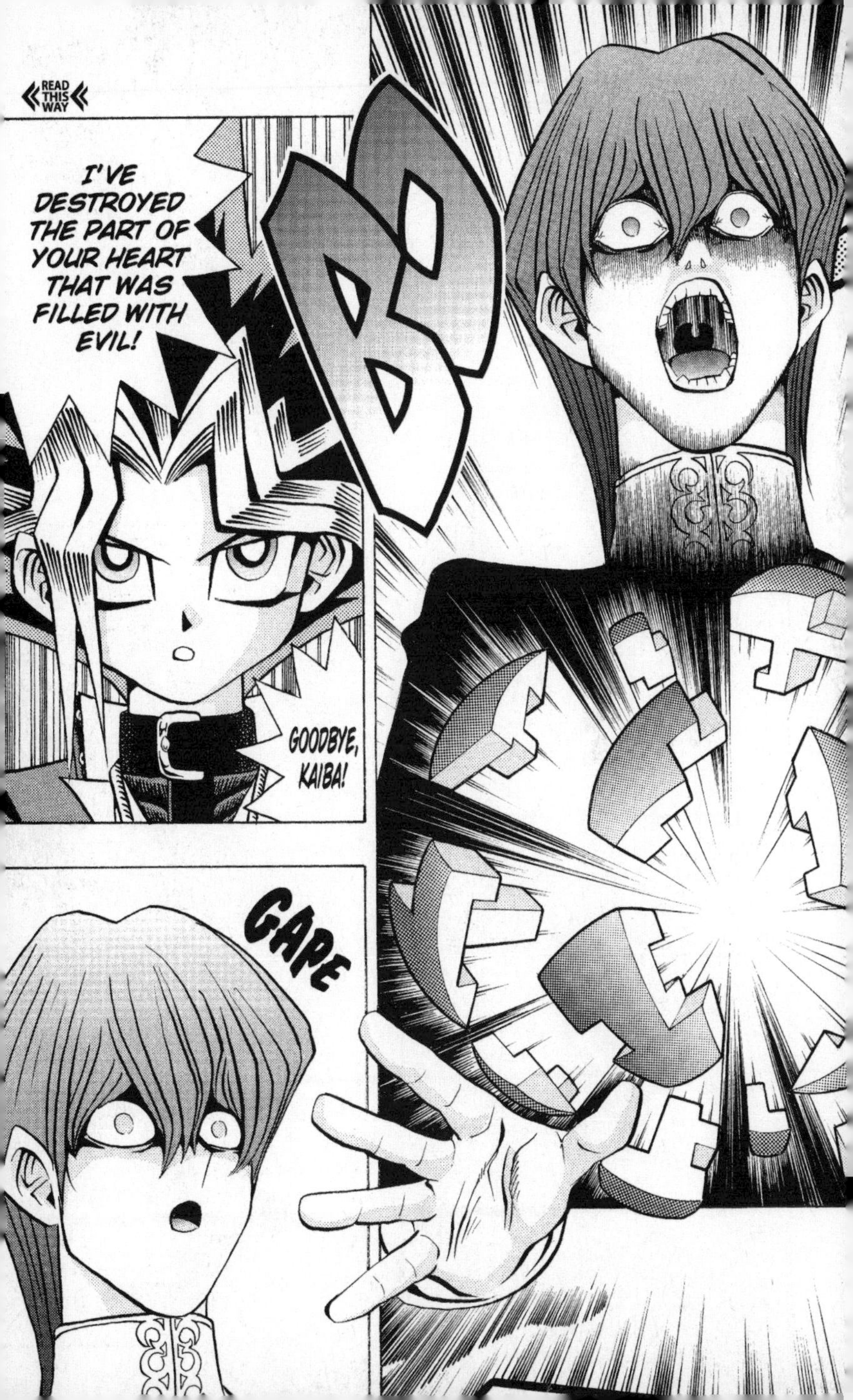
READ THIS WAY
I'VE DESTROYED THE PART OF YOUR HEART THAT WAS FILLED WITH EVIL!
GOODBYE, KAIBA!
GAPE

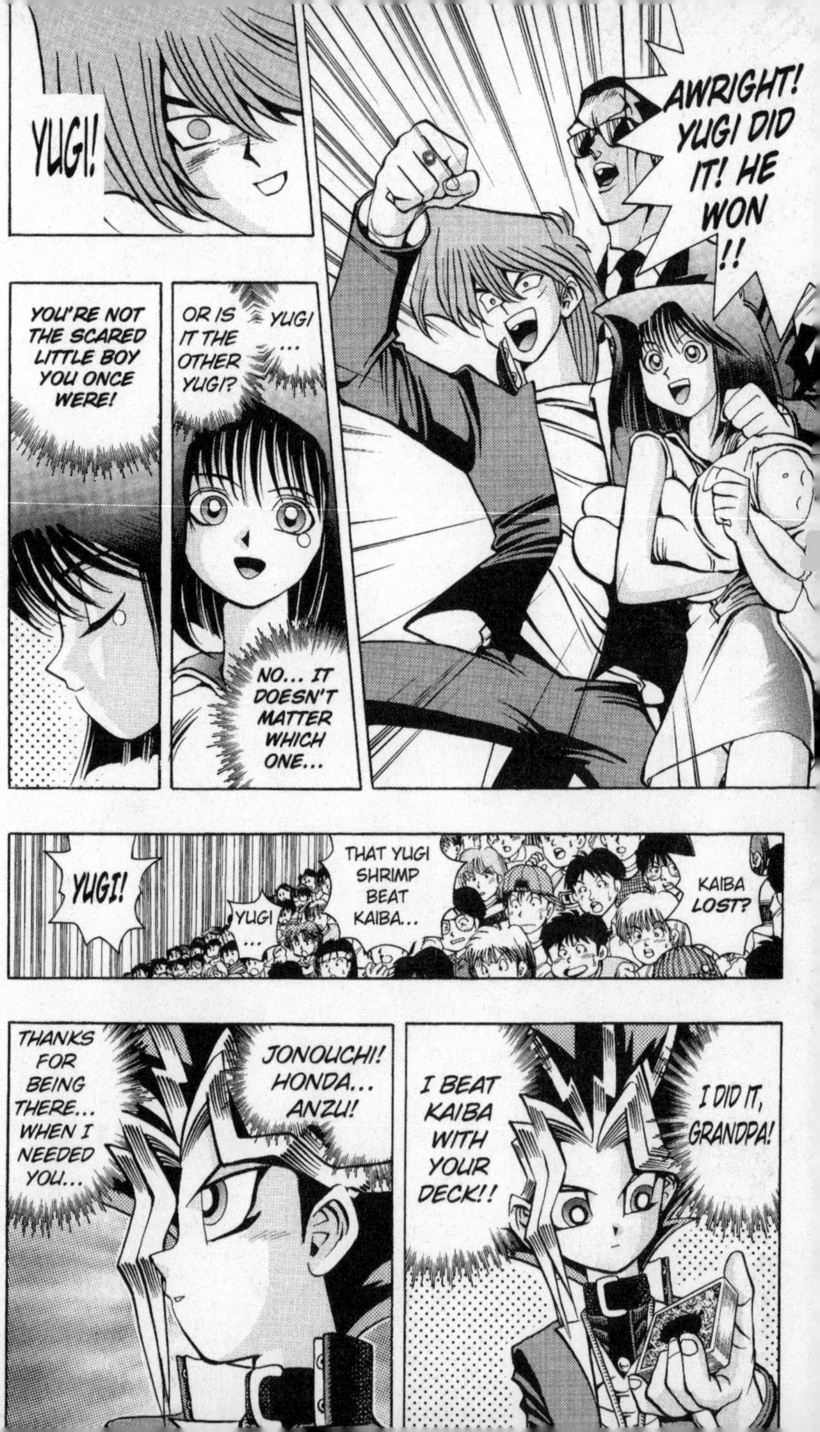
AWRIGHT! YUGI DID IT! HE WON!!
YUGI!
YUGI...
OR IS IT THE OTHER YUGI?
NO... IT DOESN'T MATTER WHICH ONE...
YOU'RE NOT THE SCARED LITTLE BOY YOU ONCE WERE!
KAIBA LOST?
THAT YUGI SHRIMP BEAT KAIBA...
YUGI...
YUGI!
I DID IT, GRANDPA!
I BEAT KAIBA WITH YOUR DECK!!
JONOUCHI! HONDA... ANZU!
THANKS FOR BEING THERE... WHEN I NEEDED YOU...

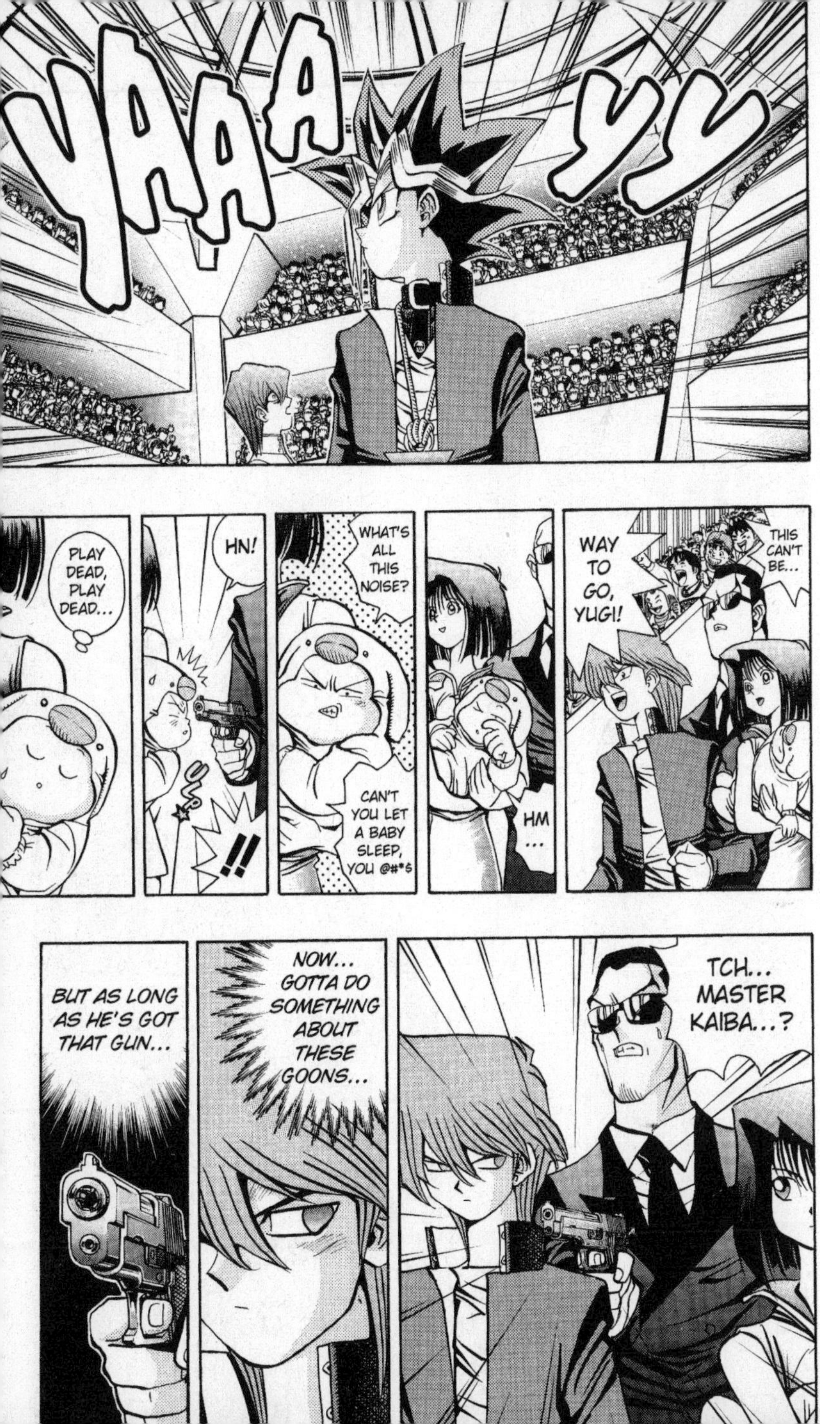
YAAAYY
THIS CAN'T BE...
WAY TO GO, YUGI!
HM ...
WHAT'S ALL THIS NOISE?
CAN'T YOU LET A BABY SLEEP, YOU @#*$
HN!
ULP
!!
PLAY DEAD, PLAY DEAD...
TCH... MASTER KAIBA...?
NOW... GOTTA DO SOMETHING ABOUT THESE GOONS...
BUT AS LONG AS HE'S GOT THAT GUN...

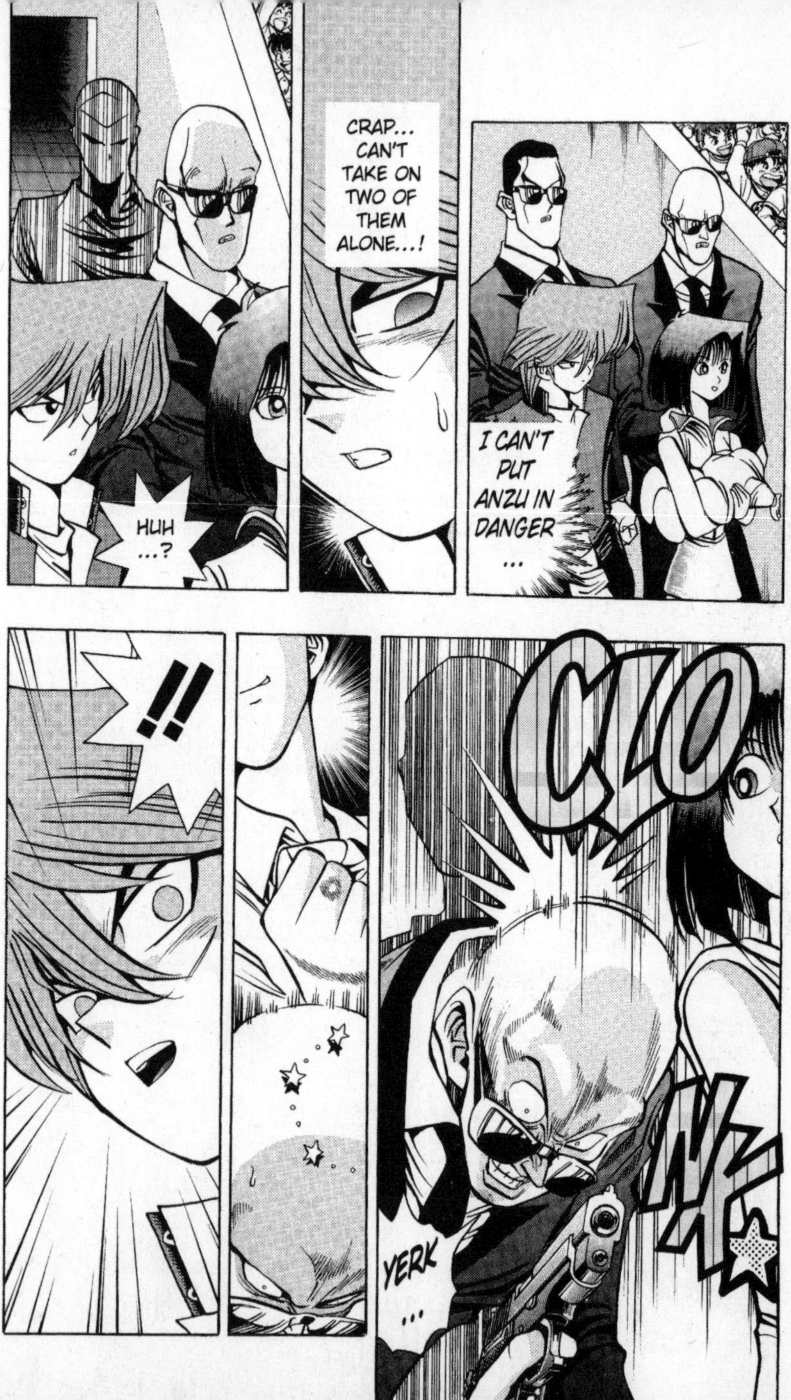

I CAN'T PUT ANZU IN DANGER ...
CRAP... CAN'T TAKE ON TWO OF THEM ALONE...!
HUH ...?
CLO
NK
YERK ...
!!

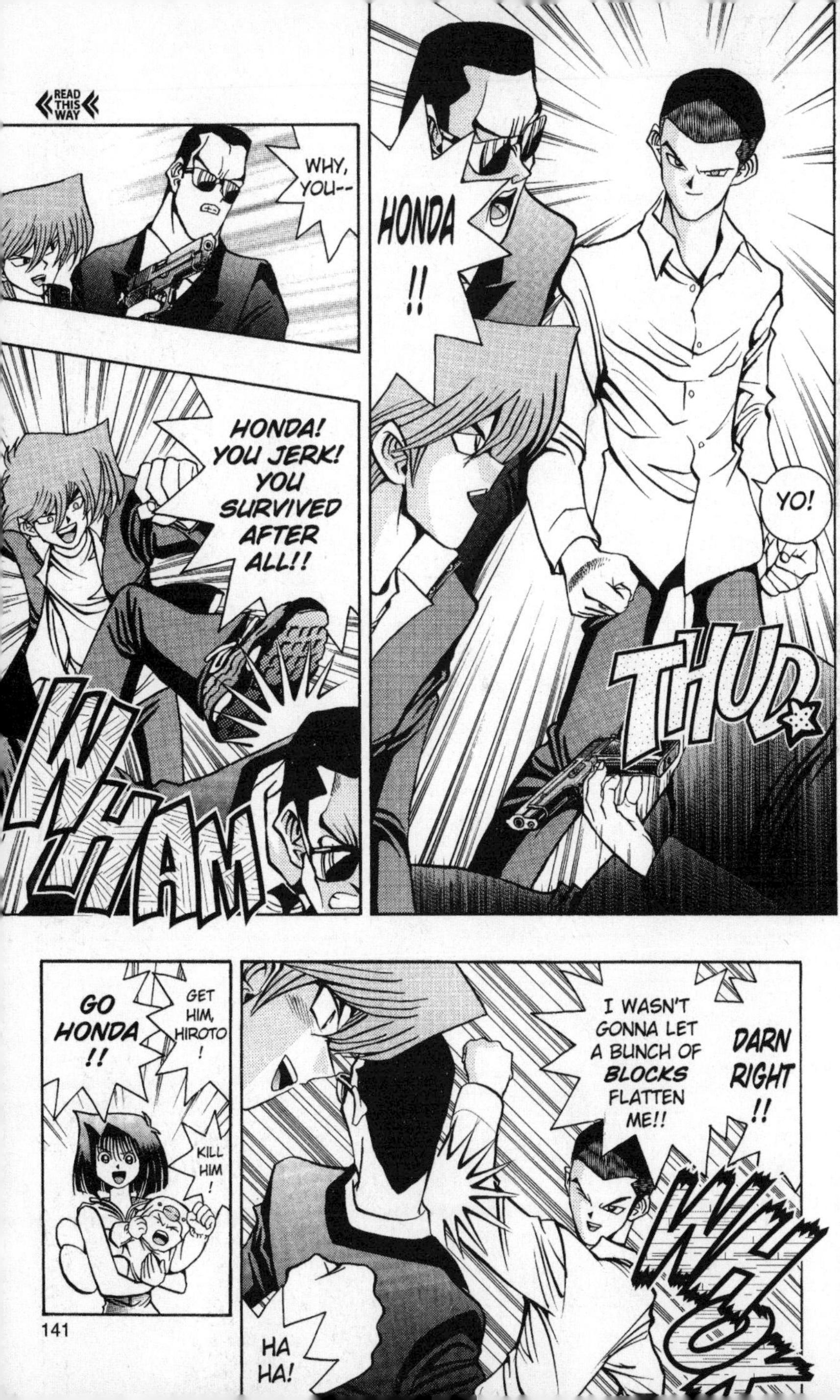
READ THIS WAY
HONDA !!
YO!
THUD
WHY, YOU--
HONDA! YOU JERK! YOU SURVIVED AFTER ALL!!
WHAM
I WASN'T GONNA LET A BUNCH OF BLOCKS FLATTEN ME!!
DARN RIGHT !!
HA HA!
GO HONDA !!
GET HIM, HIROTO !
KILL HIM !

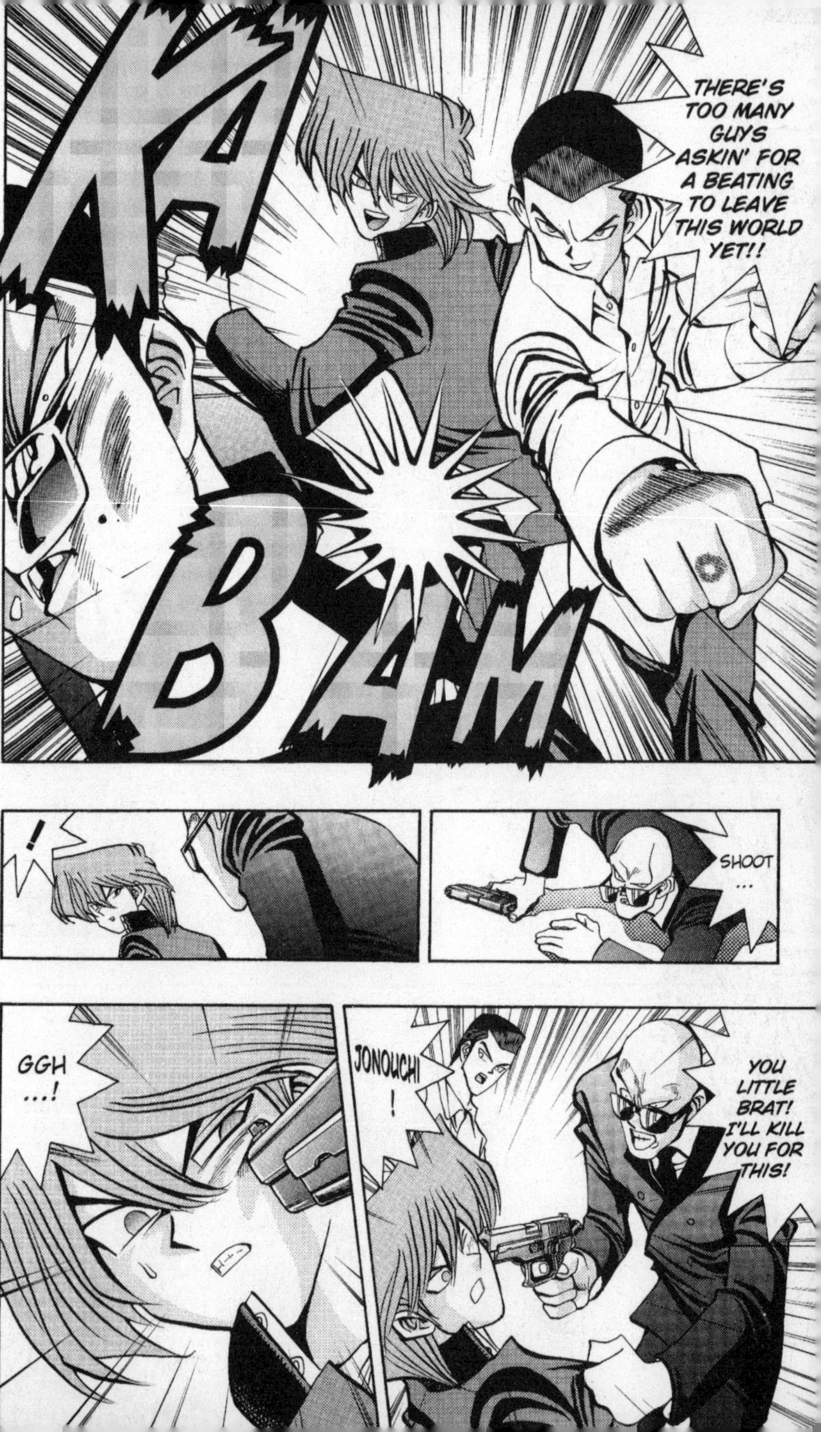
THERE'S TOO MANY GUYS ASKIN' FOR A BEATING TO LEAVE THIS WORLD YET!!
KA
BAM
SHOOT ...
!
YOU LITTLE BRAT! I'LL KILL YOU FOR THIS!
JONOUCHI !
GGH ...!

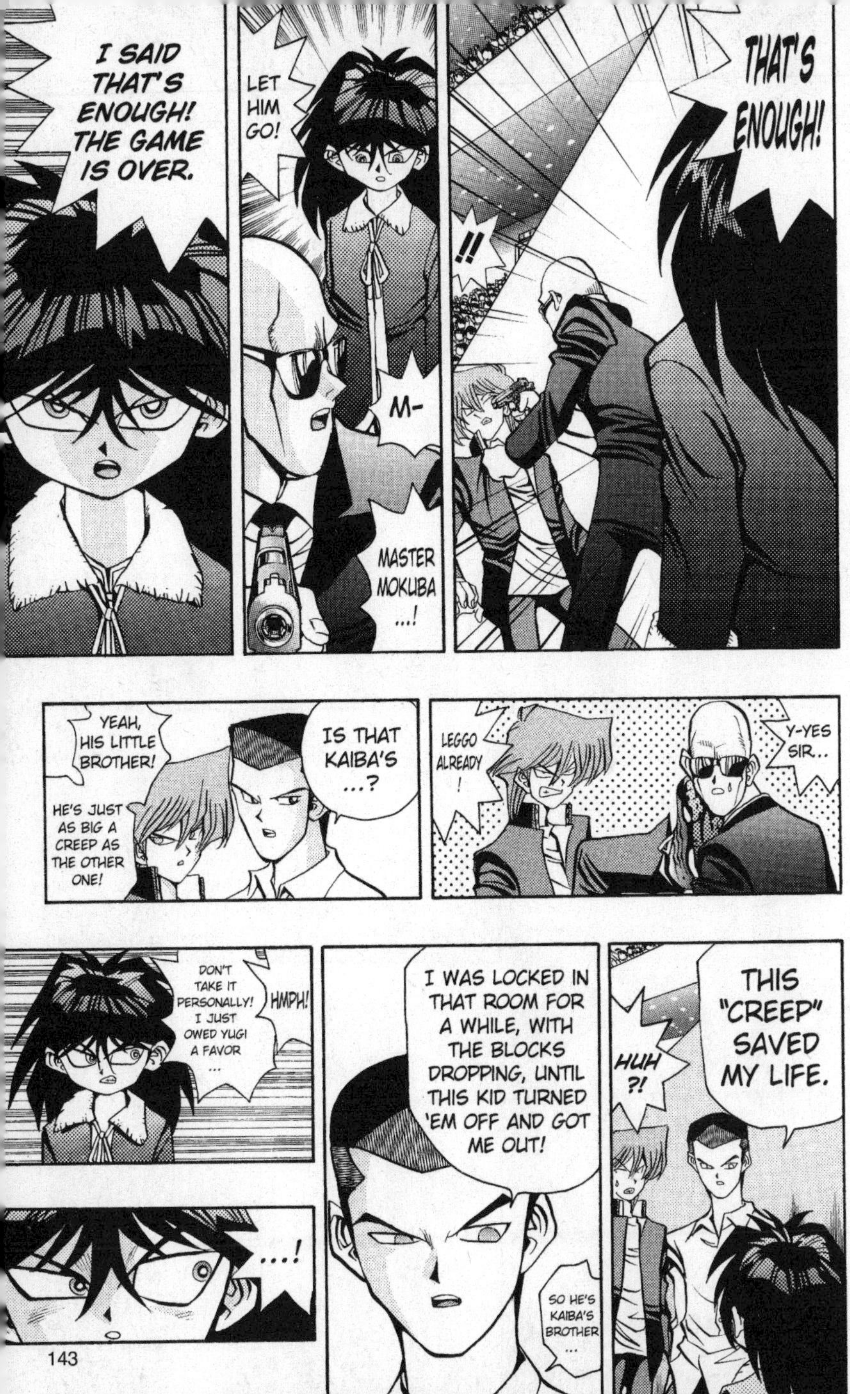
THAT'S ENOUGH!
!!
LET HIM GO!
M-
MASTER MOKUBA ...!
I SAID THAT'S ENOUGH! THE GAME IS OVER.
Y-YES SIR...
LEGGO ALREADY!
IS THAT KAIBA'S ...?
YEAH, HIS LITTLE BROTHER!
HE'S JUST AS BIG A CREEP AS THE OTHER ONE!
THIS "CREEP" SAVED MY LIFE.
HUH ?!
I WAS LOCKED IN THAT ROOM FOR A WHILE, WITH THE BLOCKS DROPPING, UNTIL THIS KID TURNED 'EM OFF AND GOT ME OUT!
SO HE'S KAIBA'S BROTHER ...
HMPH!
DON'T TAKE IT PERSONALLY! I JUST OWED YUGI A FAVOR ...
...!

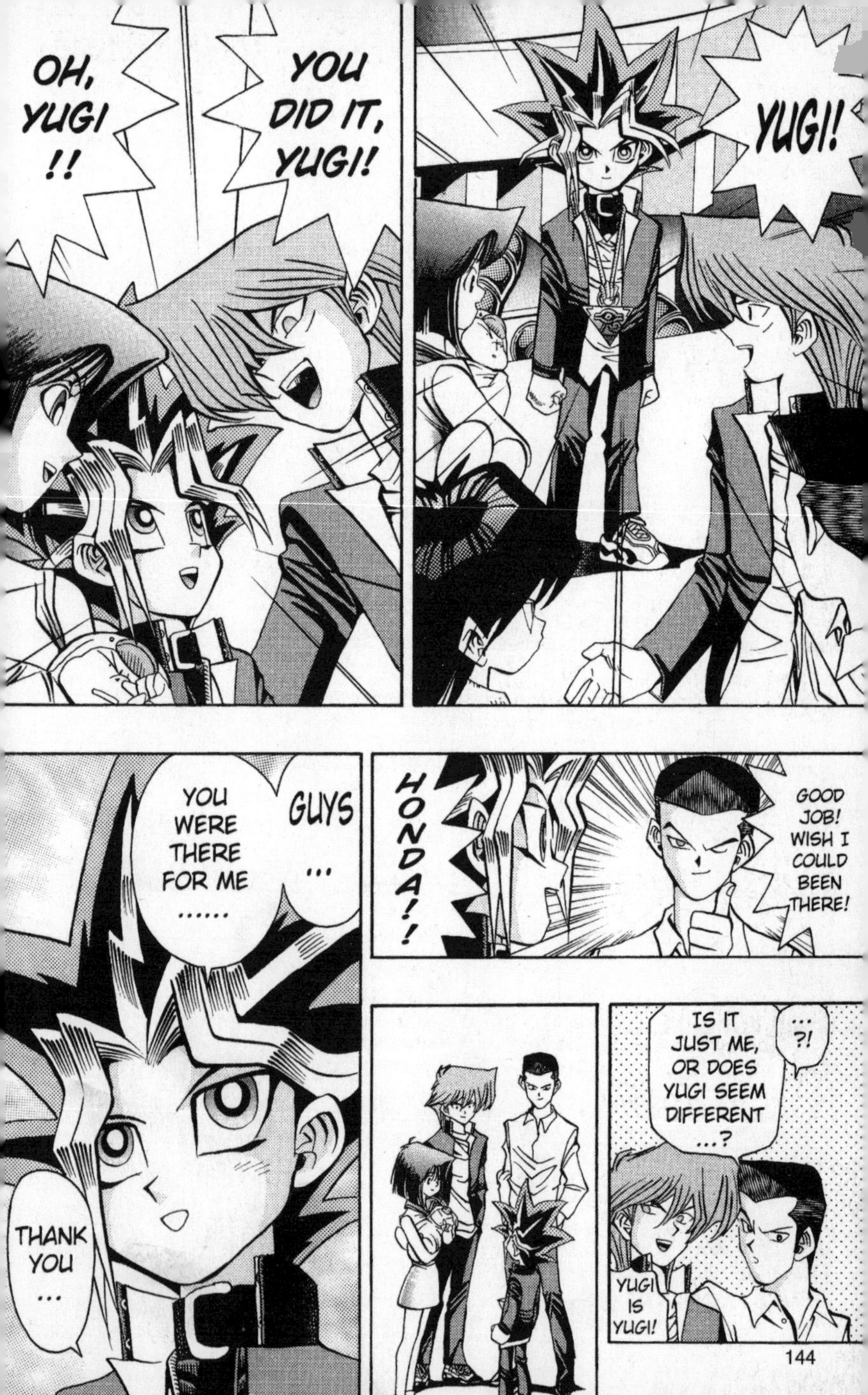
YUGI!
YOU DID IT, YUGI!
OH, YUGI !!
GOOD JOB! WISH I COULD BEEN THERE!
HONDA!!
...?!
IS IT JUST ME, OR DOES YUGI SEEM DIFFERENT ...?
YUGI IS YUGI!
GUYS ...
YOU WERE THERE FOR ME ......
THANK YOU ...

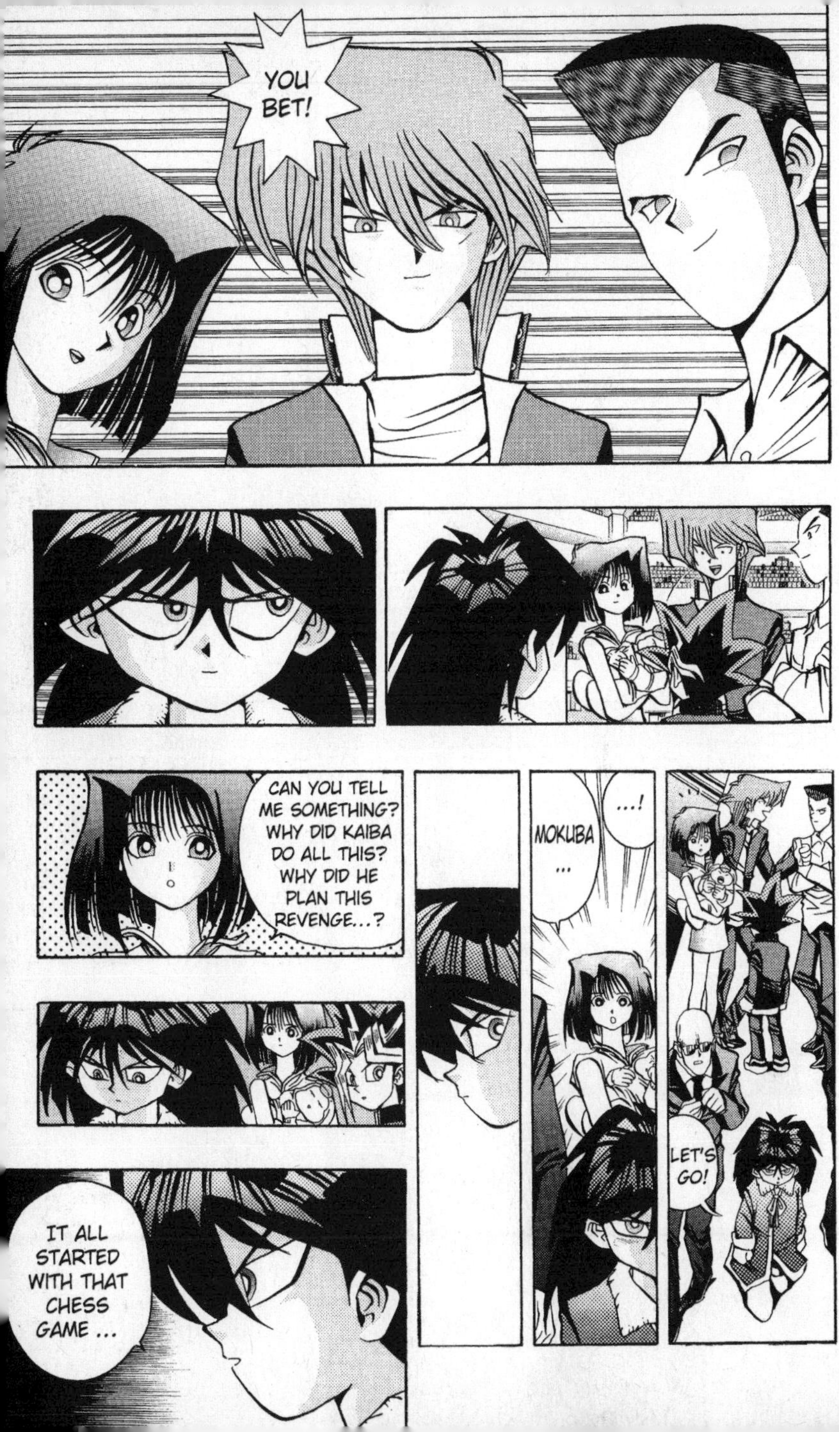
YOU BET!
LET'S GO!
...!
MOKUBA ...
CAN YOU TELL ME SOMETHING? WHY DID KAIBA DO ALL THIS? WHY DID HE PLAN THIS REVENGE...?
IT ALL STARTED WITH THAT CHESS GAME ...

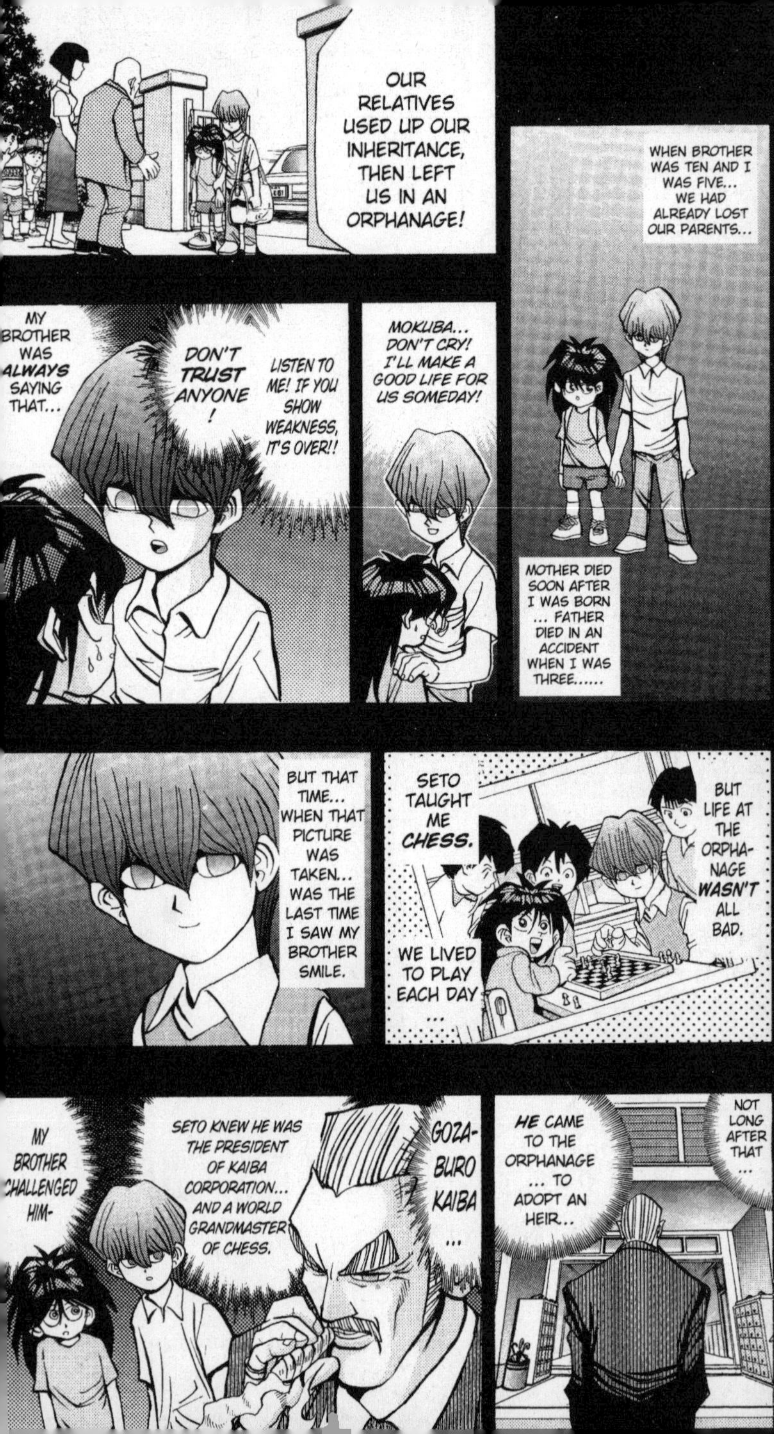
WHEN BROTHER WAS TEN AND I WAS FIVE... WE HAD ALREADY LOST OUR PARENTS...
MOTHER DIED SOON AFTER I WAS BORN ... FATHER DIED IN AN ACCIDENT WHEN I WAS THREE......
OUR RELATIVES USED UP OUR INHERITANCE, THEN LEFT US IN AN ORPHANAGE!
MOKUBA... DON'T CRY! I'LL MAKE A GOOD LIFE FOR US SOMEDAY!
LISTEN TO ME! IF YOU SHOW WEAKNESS, IT'S OVER!!
DON'T TRUST ANYONE!
MY BROTHER WAS ALWAYS SAYING THAT...
BUT LIFE AT THE ORPHA-NAGE WASN'T ALL BAD.
SETO TAUGHT ME CHESS.
WE LIVED TO PLAY EACH DAY ...
BUT THAT TIME... WHEN THAT PICTURE WAS TAKEN... WAS THE LAST TIME I SAW MY BROTHER SMILE.
NOT LONG AFTER THAT ...
HE CAME TO THE ORPHANAGE ... TO ADOPT AN HEIR...
GOZA-BURO KAIBA ...
SETO KNEW HE WAS THE PRESIDENT OF KAIBA CORPORATION... AND A WORLD GRANDMASTER OF CHESS.
MY BROTHER CHALLENGED HIM-

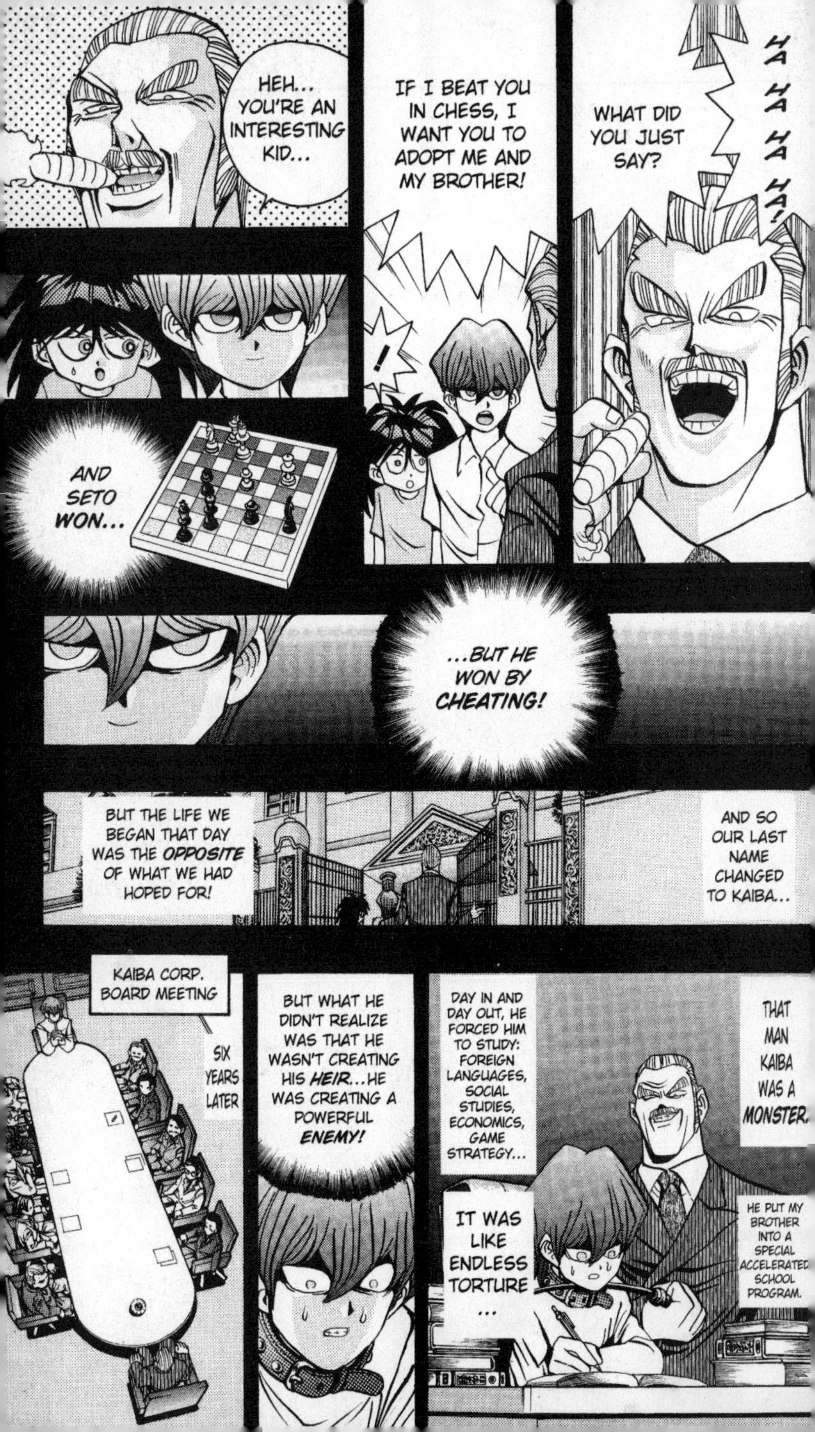

WHAT DID YOU JUST SAY?
HA HA HA HA!
IF I BEAT YOU IN CHESS, I WANT YOU TO ADOPT ME AND MY BROTHER!
!
HEH... YOU'RE AN INTERESTING KID...
AND SETO WON...
...BUT HE WON BY CHEATING!
AND SO OUR LAST NAME CHANGED TO KAIBA...
BUT THE LIFE WE BEGAN THAT DAY WAS THE OPPOSITE OF WHAT WE HAD HOPED FOR!
THAT MAN KAIBA WAS A MONSTER.
DAY IN AND DAY OUT, HE FORCED HIM TO STUDY: FOREIGN LANGUAGES, SOCIAL STUDIES, ECONOMICS, GAME STRATEGY...
HE PUT MY BROTHER INTO A SPECIAL ACCELERATED SCHOOL PROGRAM.
IT WAS LIKE ENDLESS TORTURE...
BUT WHAT HE DIDN'T REALIZE WAS THAT HE WASN'T CREATING HIS HEIR...HE WAS CREATING A POWERFUL ENEMY!
KAIBA CORP. BOARD MEETING
SIX YEARS LATER

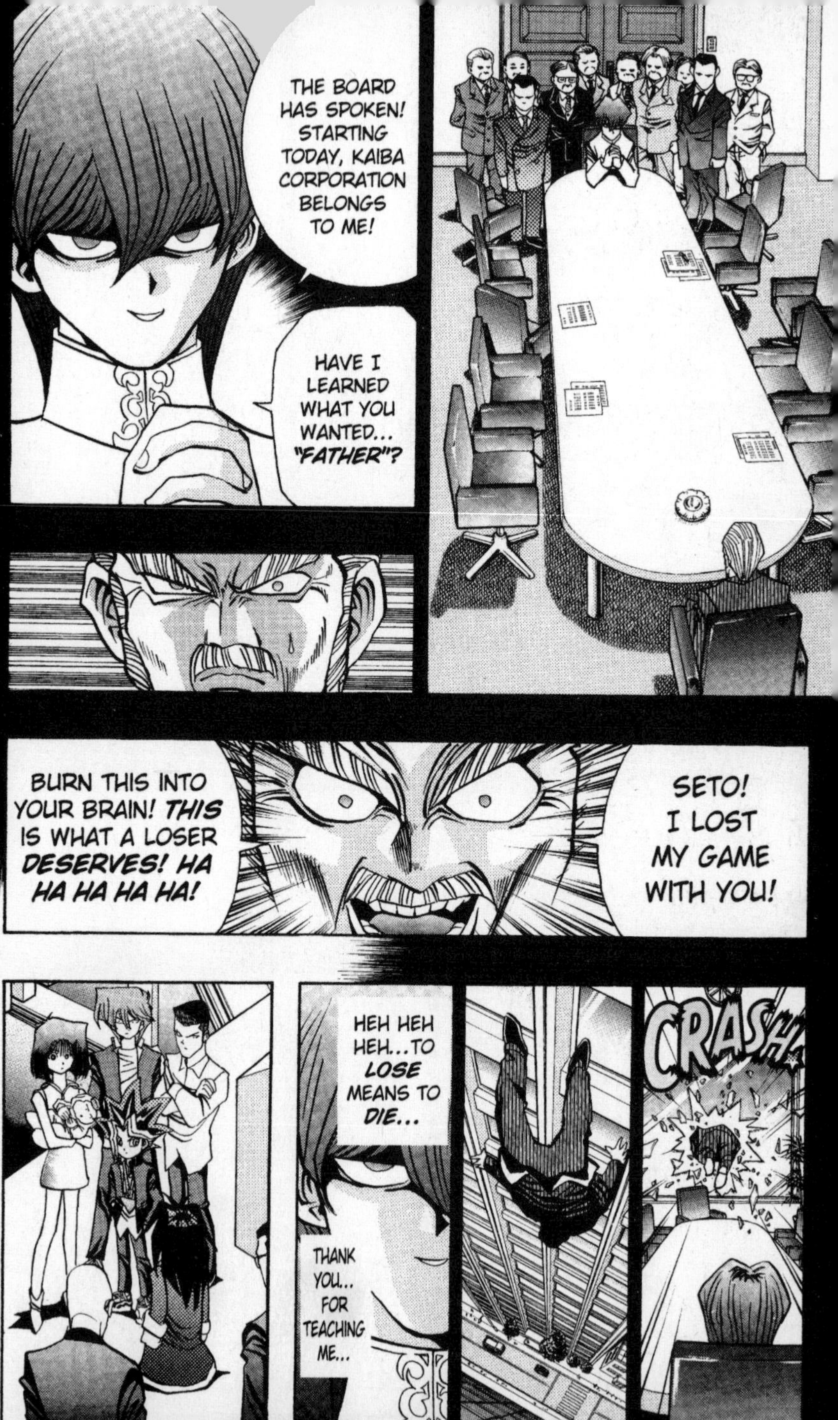
THE BOARD HAS SPOKEN! STARTING TODAY, KAIBA CORPORATION BELONGS TO ME!
HAVE I LEARNED WHAT YOU WANTED... "FATHER"?
SETO! I LOST MY GAME WITH YOU!
BURN THIS INTO YOUR BRAIN! THIS IS WHAT A LOSER DESERVES! HA HA HA HA HA!
CRASH
HEH HEH HEH...TO LOSE MEANS TO DIE...
THANK YOU... FOR TEACHING ME...

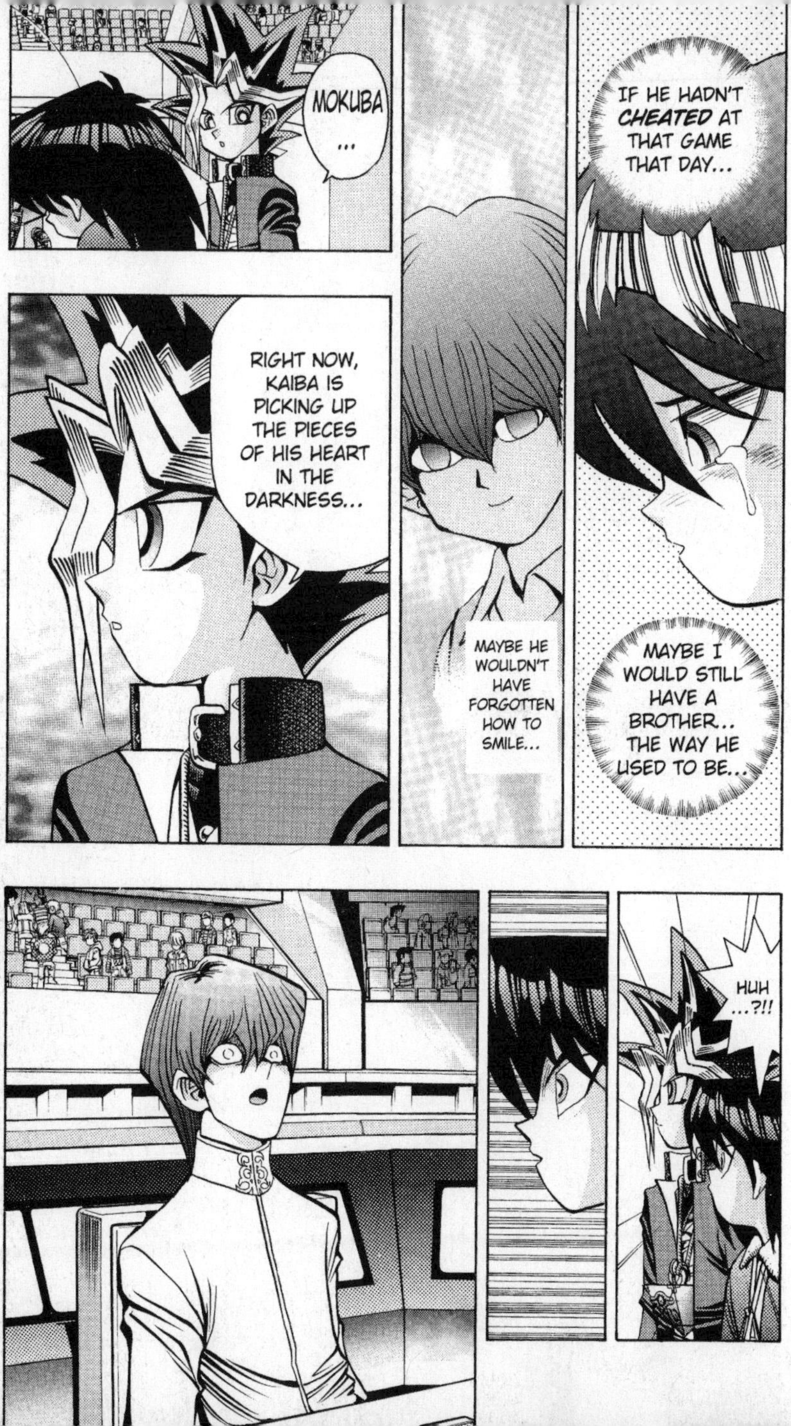
IF HE HADN'T *CHEATED* AT THAT GAME THAT DAY...
MAYBE I WOULD STILL HAVE A BROTHER... THE WAY HE USED TO BE...
MAYBE HE WOULDN'T HAVE FORGOTTEN HOW TO SMILE...
MOKUBA ...
RIGHT NOW, KAIBA IS PICKING UP THE PIECES OF HIS HEART IN THE DARKNESS...
HUH ...?!!

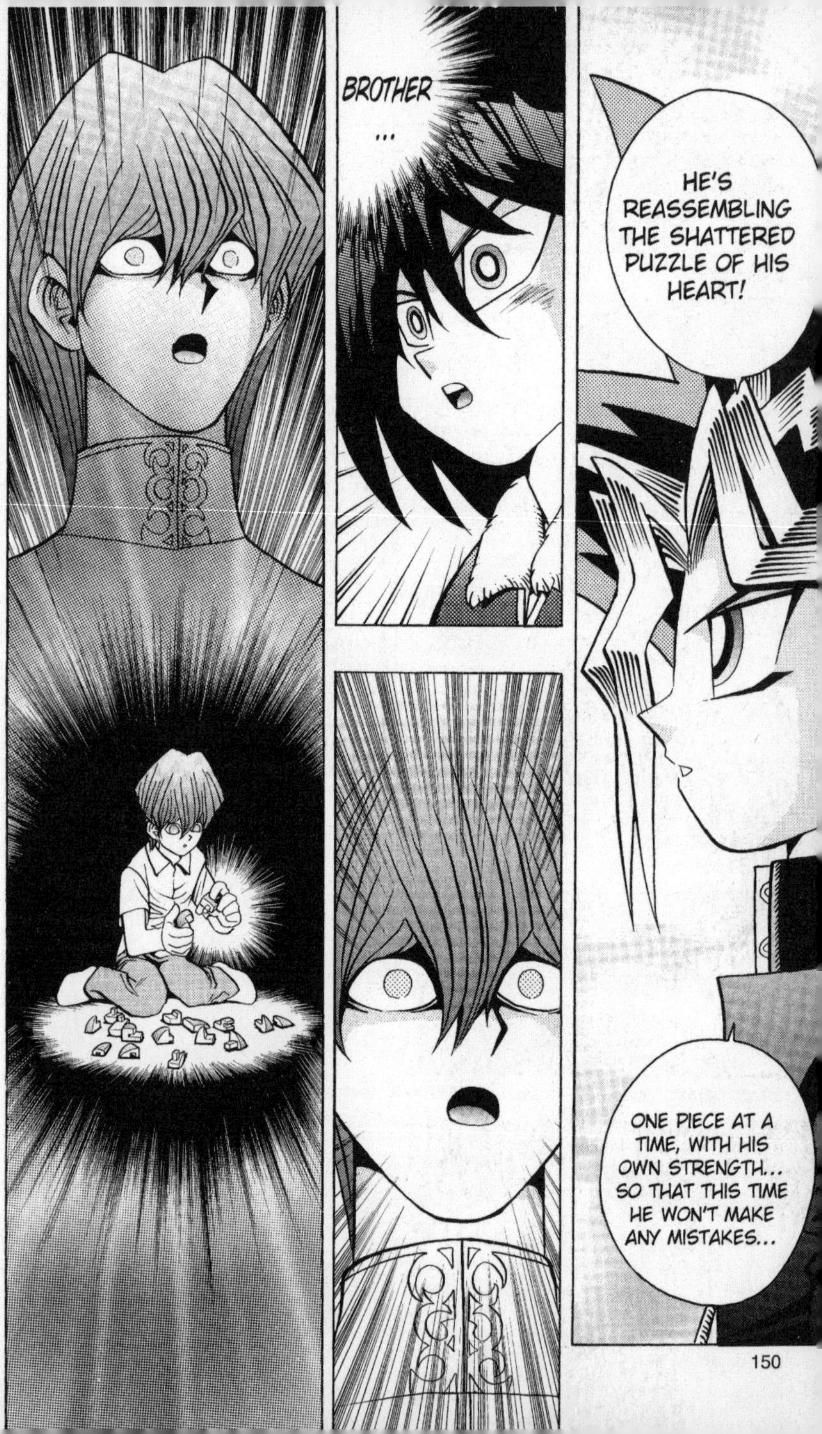
HE'S REASSEMBLING THE SHATTERED PUZZLE OF HIS HEART!
ONE PIECE AT A TIME, WITH HIS OWN STRENGTH... SO THAT THIS TIME HE WON'T MAKE ANY MISTAKES...
BROTHER ...

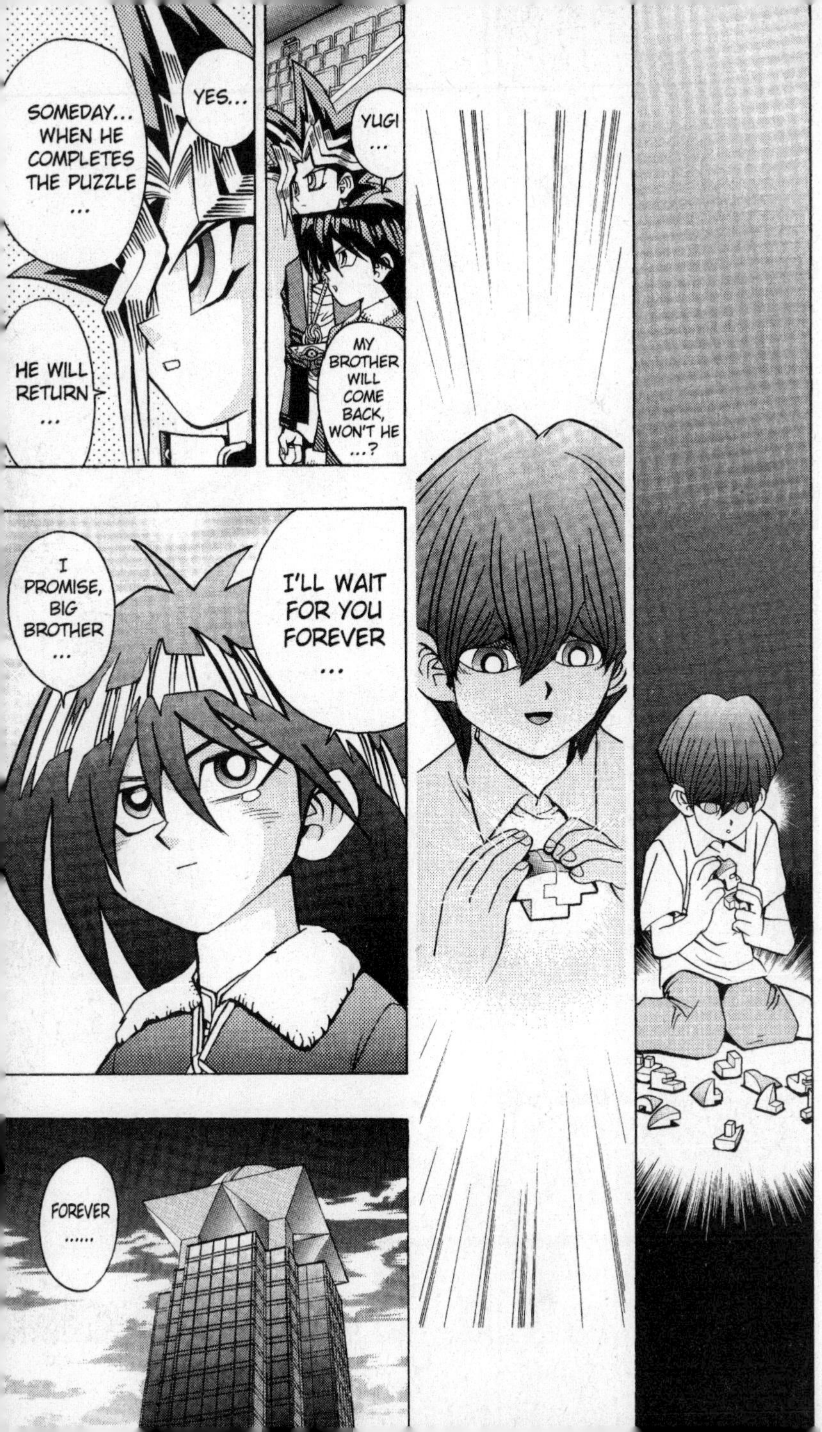
YUGI ...
MY BROTHER WILL COME BACK, WON'T HE ...?
YES...
SOMEDAY... WHEN HE COMPLETES THE PUZZLE ...
HE WILL RETURN ...
I'LL WAIT FOR YOU FOREVER ...
I PROMISE, BIG BROTHER ...
FOREVER ......

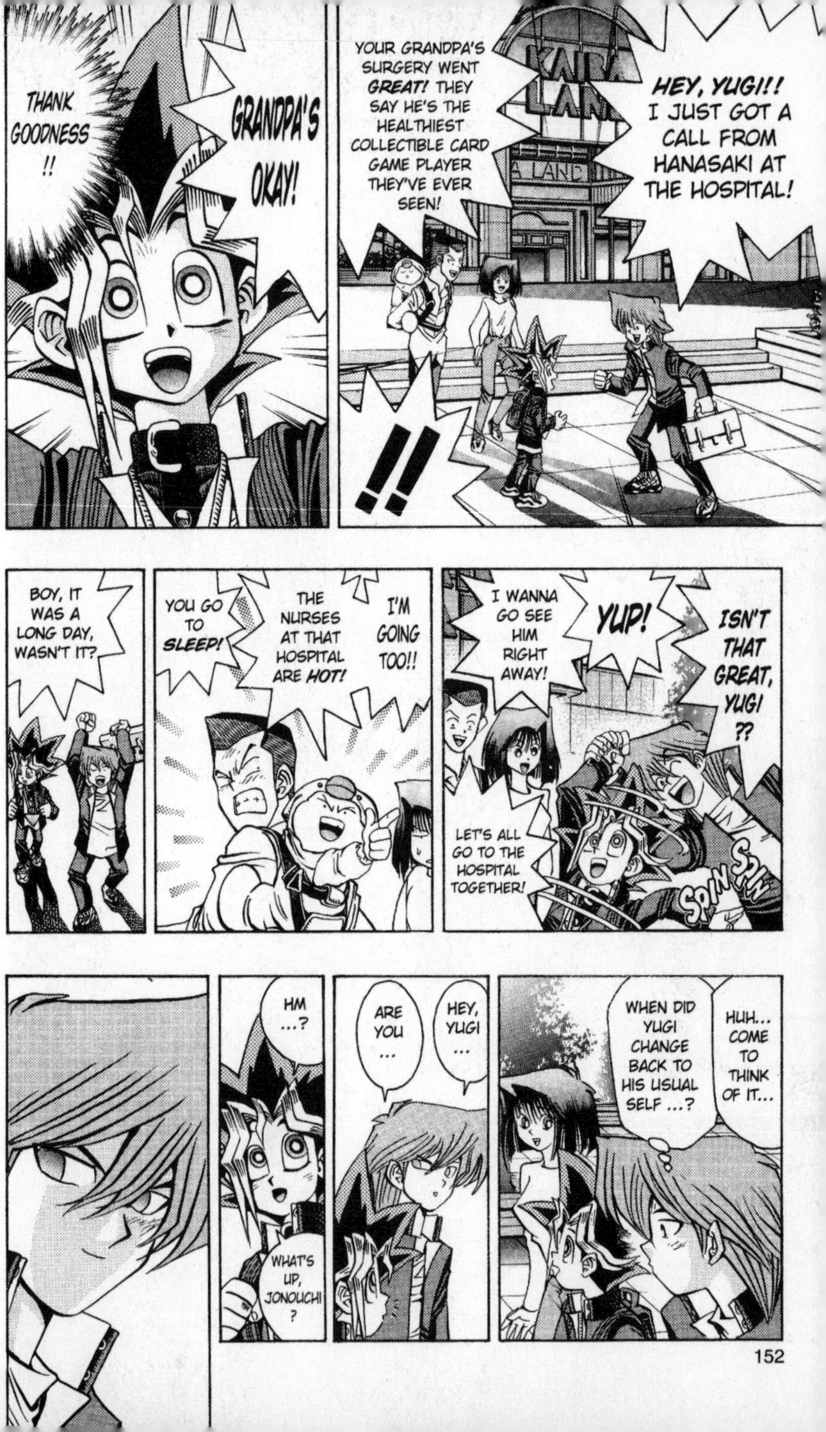
HEY, YUGI!! I JUST GOT A CALL FROM HANASAKI AT THE HOSPITAL!
YOUR GRANDPA'S SURGERY WENT GREAT! THEY SAY HE'S THE HEALTHIEST COLLECTIBLE CARD GAME PLAYER THEY'VE EVER SEEN!
!!
GRANDPA'S OKAY!
THANK GOODNESS !!
ISN'T THAT GREAT, YUGI ??
YUP!
I WANNA GO SEE HIM RIGHT AWAY!
LET'S ALL GO TO THE HOSPITAL TOGETHER!
SPIN SPIN
I'M GOING TOO!!
THE NURSES AT THAT HOSPITAL ARE HOT!
YOU GO TO SLEEP!
BOY, IT WAS A LONG DAY, WASN'T IT?
HUH... COME TO THINK OF IT...
WHEN DID YUGI CHANGE BACK TO HIS USUAL SELF ...?
HEY, YUGI ...
ARE YOU ...
HM ...?
WHAT'S UP, JONOUCHI ?

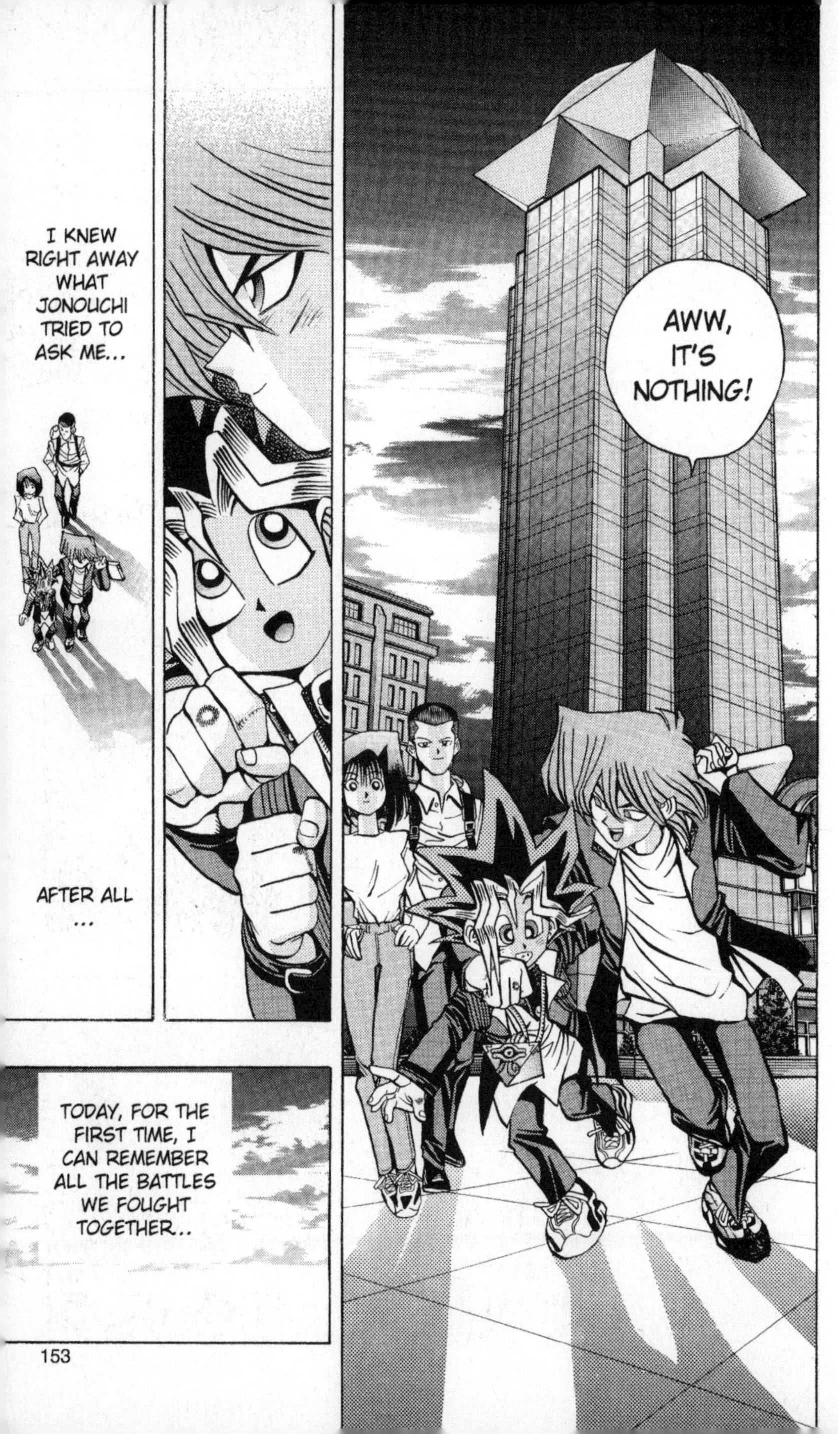
AWW, IT'S NOTHING!
I KNEW RIGHT AWAY WHAT JONOUCHI TRIED TO ASK ME...
AFTER ALL ...
TODAY, FOR THE FIRST TIME, I CAN REMEMBER ALL THE BATTLES WE FOUGHT TOGETHER...

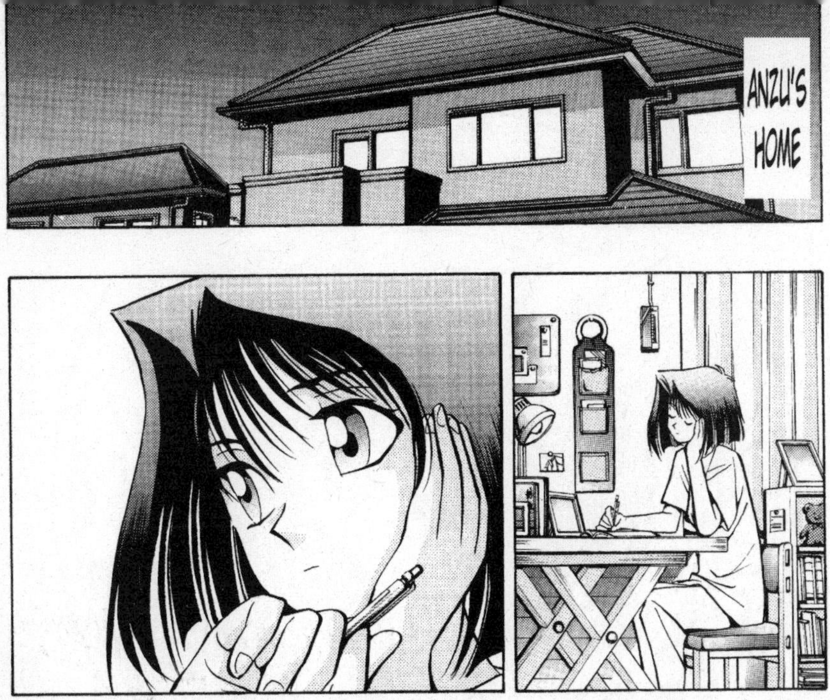
ANZU'S HOME

Duel 41: Let's Find "Love"!

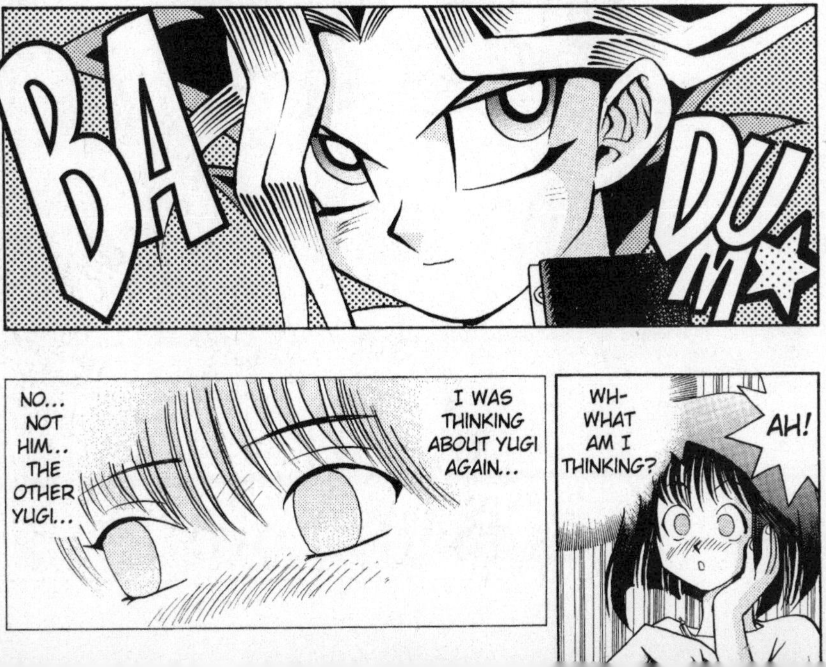
BA DUM
AH!
WH- WHAT AM I THINKING?
I WAS THINKING ABOUT YUGI AGAIN...
NO... NOT HIM.. THE OTHER YUGI...

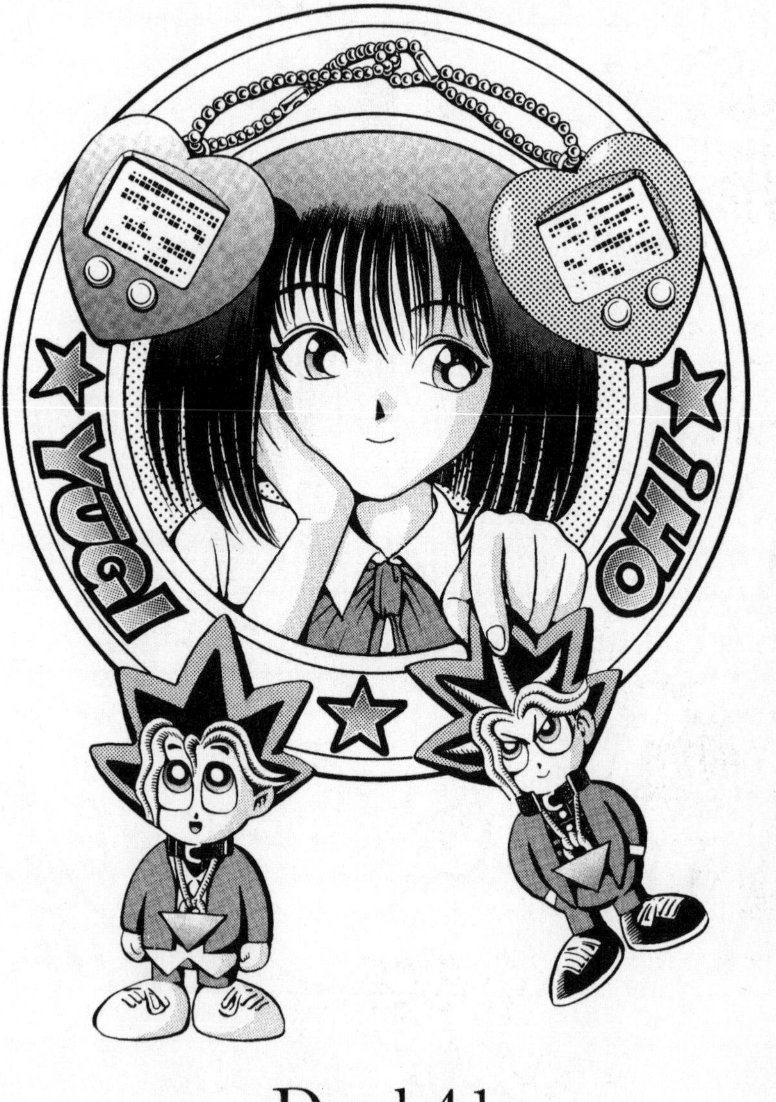
YUGI OH!

Duel 41: Let's Find "Love"!

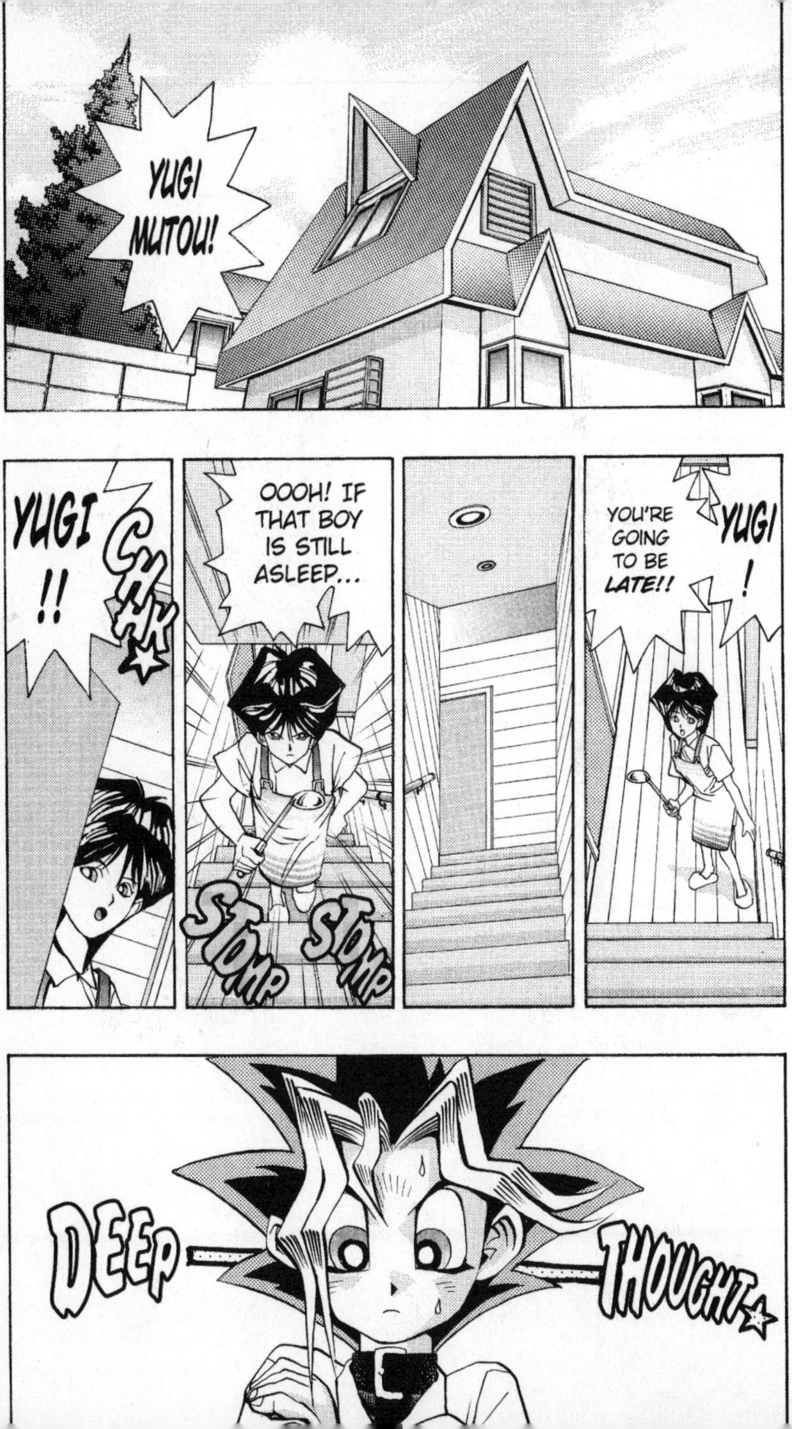

YUGI MUTOU!
YUGI!
YOU'RE GOING TO BE *LATE!!*
OOOH! IF THAT BOY IS STILL ASLEEP...
STOMP
STOMP
YUGI!!
CHK★
DEEP THOUGHT★

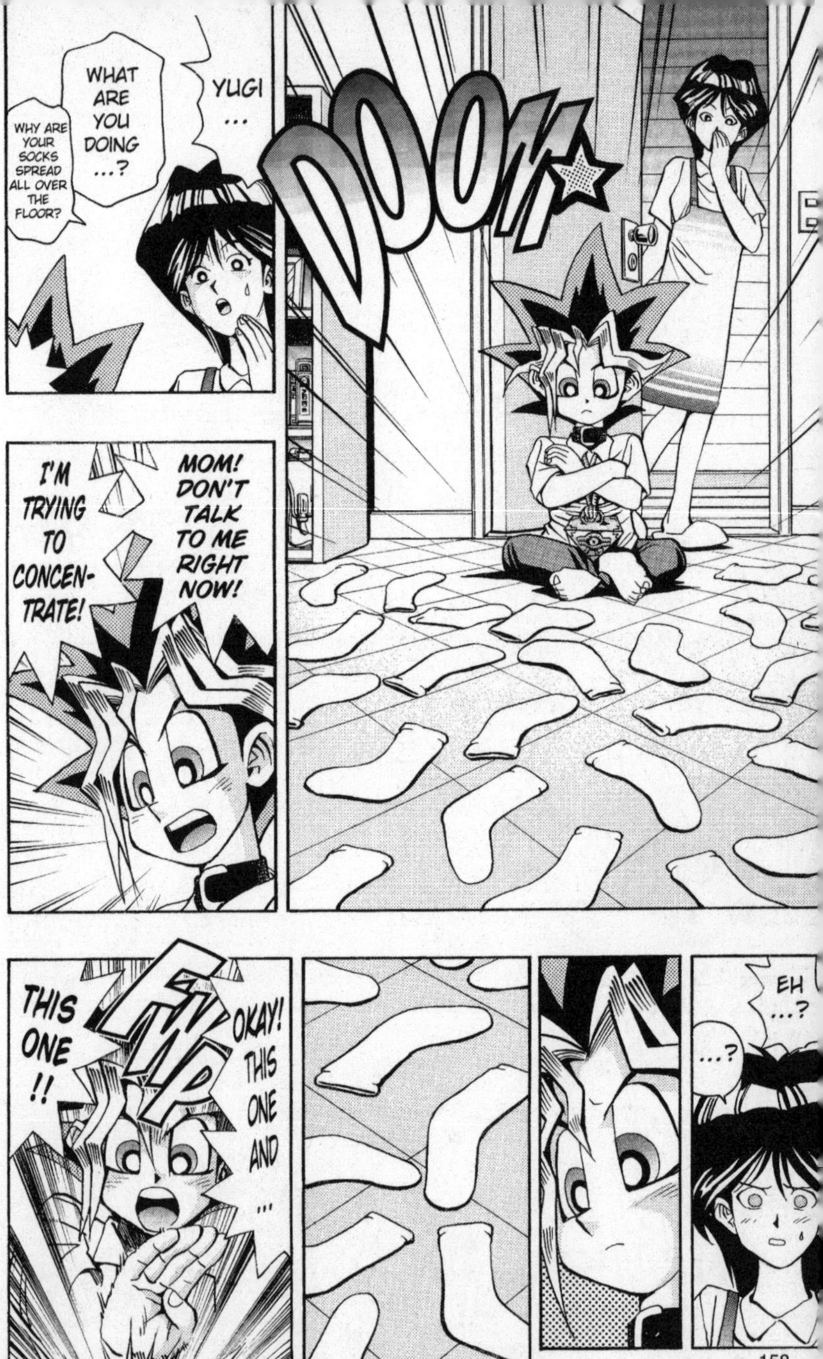
DOOM
YUGI ...
WHAT ARE YOU DOING ...?
WHY ARE YOUR SOCKS SPREAD ALL OVER THE FLOOR?
MOM! DON'T TALK TO ME RIGHT NOW!
I'M TRYING TO CONCENTRATE!
EH ...?
...?
OKAY! THIS ONE AND ...
THIS ONE !!

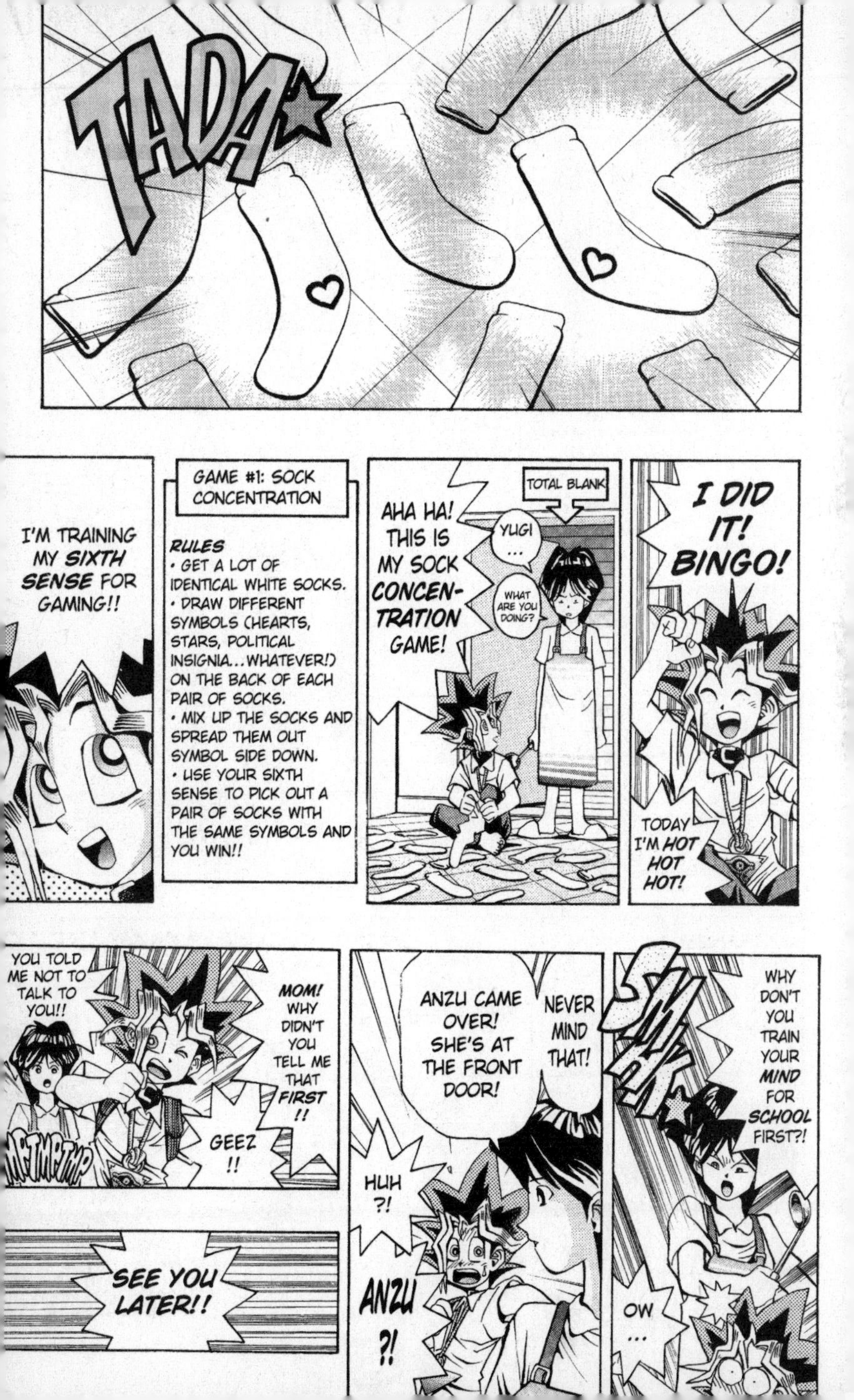
TADA★
I DID IT! BINGO!
TODAY I'M HOT HOT HOT!
TOTAL BLANK
AHA HA! THIS IS MY SOCK CONCENTRATION GAME!
YUGI …
WHAT ARE YOU DOING?
GAME #1: SOCK CONCENTRATION
RULES
• GET A LOT OF IDENTICAL WHITE SOCKS.
• DRAW DIFFERENT SYMBOLS (HEARTS, STARS, POLITICAL INSIGNIA…WHATEVER!) ON THE BACK OF EACH PAIR OF SOCKS.
• MIX UP THE SOCKS AND SPREAD THEM OUT SYMBOL SIDE DOWN.
• USE YOUR SIXTH SENSE TO PICK OUT A PAIR OF SOCKS WITH THE SAME SYMBOLS AND YOU WIN!!
I'M TRAINING MY SIXTH SENSE FOR GAMING!!
WHY DON'T YOU TRAIN YOUR MIND FOR SCHOOL FIRST?!
OW …
NEVER MIND THAT!
ANZU CAME OVER! SHE'S AT THE FRONT DOOR!
HUH ?!
ANZU ?!
MOM! WHY DIDN'T YOU TELL ME THAT FIRST !!
YOU TOLD ME NOT TO TALK TO YOU!!
GEEZ !!
SEE YOU LATER!!

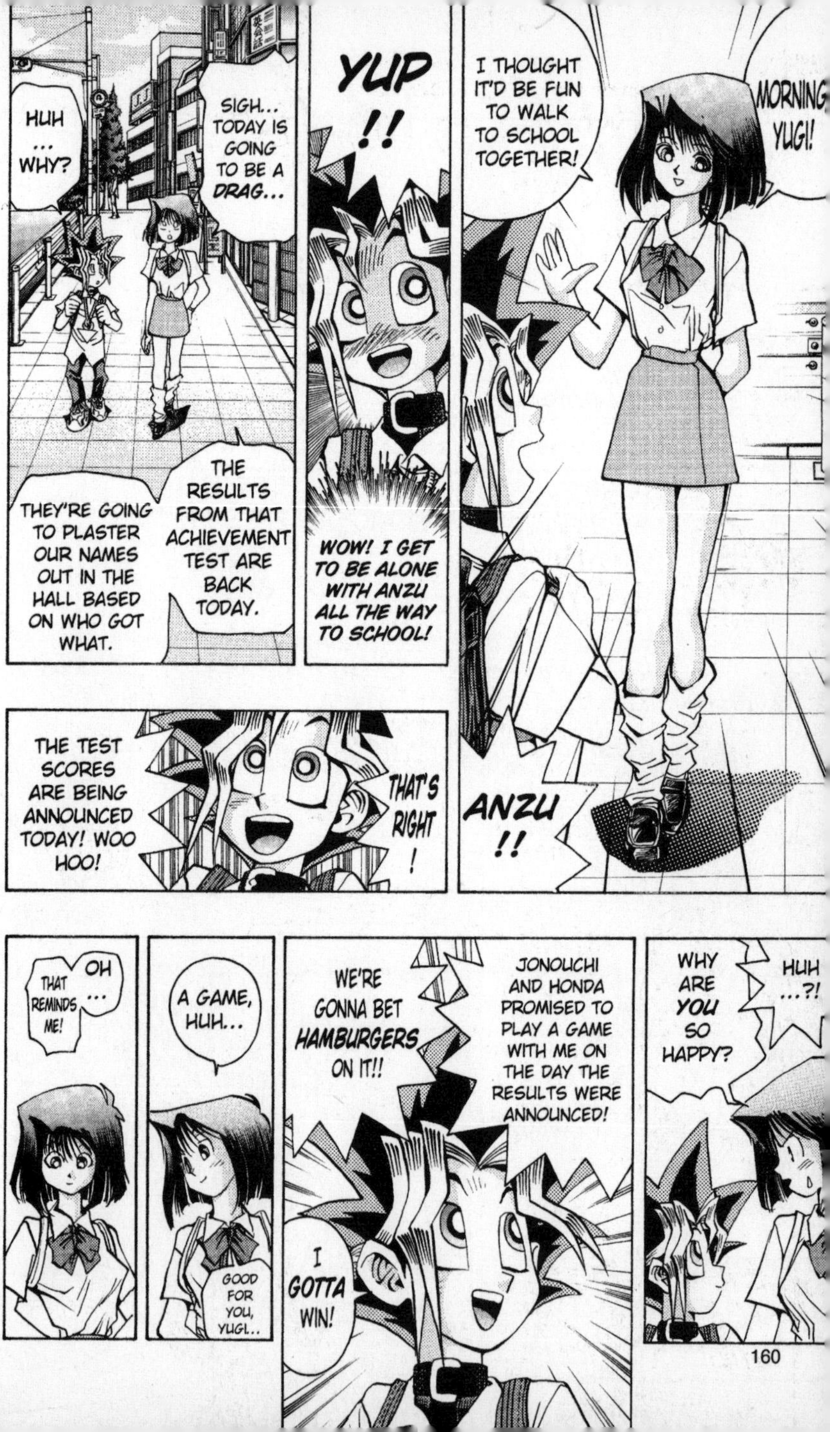
MORNING, YUGI!
I THOUGHT IT'D BE FUN TO WALK TO SCHOOL TOGETHER!
ANZU!!
YUP!!
WOW! I GET TO BE ALONE WITH ANZU ALL THE WAY TO SCHOOL!
SIGH... TODAY IS GOING TO BE A DRAG...
HUH ... WHY?
THE RESULTS FROM THAT ACHIEVEMENT TEST ARE BACK TODAY.
THEY'RE GOING TO PLASTER OUR NAMES OUT IN THE HALL BASED ON WHO GOT WHAT.
THAT'S RIGHT!
THE TEST SCORES ARE BEING ANNOUNCED TODAY! WOO HOO!
HUH ...?!
WHY ARE YOU SO HAPPY?
JONOUCHI AND HONDA PROMISED TO PLAY A GAME WITH ME ON THE DAY THE RESULTS WERE ANNOUNCED!
WE'RE GONNA BET HAMBURGERS ON IT!!
I GOTTA WIN!
A GAME, HUH...
GOOD FOR YOU, YUGI...
OH ...
THAT REMINDS ME!

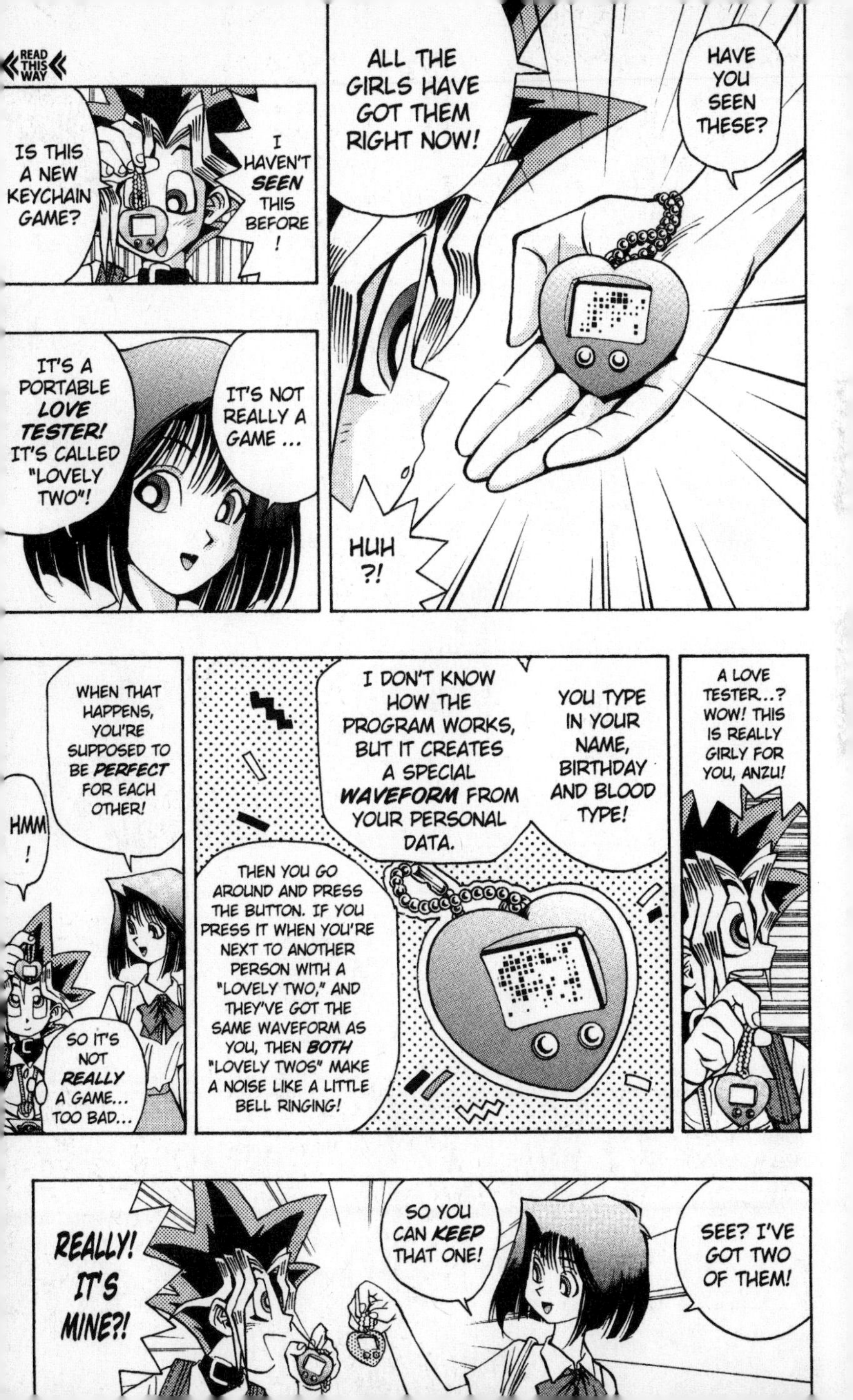
READ THIS WAY
HAVE YOU SEEN THESE?
ALL THE GIRLS HAVE GOT THEM RIGHT NOW!
HUH?!
I HAVEN'T SEEN THIS BEFORE!
IS THIS A NEW KEYCHAIN GAME?
IT'S NOT REALLY A GAME...
IT'S A PORTABLE LOVE TESTER! IT'S CALLED "LOVELY TWO"!
A LOVE TESTER...? WOW! THIS IS REALLY GIRLY FOR YOU, ANZU!
YOU TYPE IN YOUR NAME, BIRTHDAY AND BLOOD TYPE!
I DON'T KNOW HOW THE PROGRAM WORKS, BUT IT CREATES A SPECIAL WAVEFORM FROM YOUR PERSONAL DATA.
THEN YOU GO AROUND AND PRESS THE BUTTON. IF YOU PRESS IT WHEN YOU'RE NEXT TO ANOTHER PERSON WITH A "LOVELY TWO," AND THEY'VE GOT THE SAME WAVEFORM AS YOU, THEN BOTH "LOVELY TWOS" MAKE A NOISE LIKE A LITTLE BELL RINGING!
WHEN THAT HAPPENS, YOU'RE SUPPOSED TO BE PERFECT FOR EACH OTHER!
HMM!
SO IT'S NOT REALLY A GAME... TOO BAD...
SEE? I'VE GOT TWO OF THEM!
SO YOU CAN KEEP THAT ONE!
REALLY! IT'S MINE?!

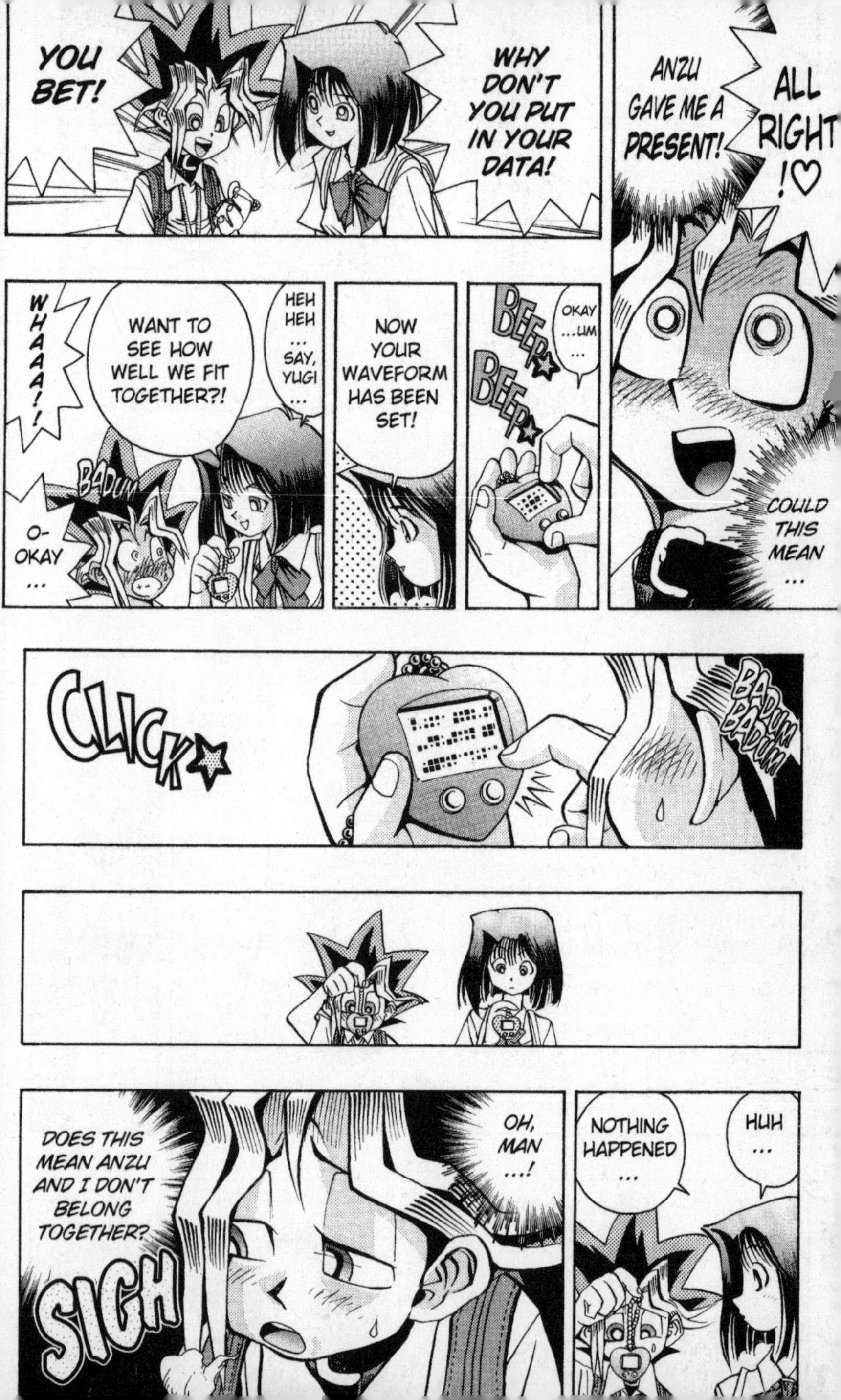
ANZU GAVE ME A PRESENT!
ALL RIGHT !♡
COULD THIS MEAN ...
WHY DON'T YOU PUT IN YOUR DATA!
YOU BET!
OKAY ...UM ...
BEEP☆ BEEP☆
NOW YOUR WAVEFORM HAS BEEN SET!
HEH HEH ... SAY, YUGI ...
WANT TO SEE HOW WELL WE FIT TOGETHER?!
WHAAAA!!
BADUM
O-OKAY ...
BADUM BADUM
CLICK☆
HUH ...
NOTHING HAPPENED ...
OH, MAN ...!
DOES THIS MEAN ANZU AND I DON'T BELONG TOGETHER?
SIGH

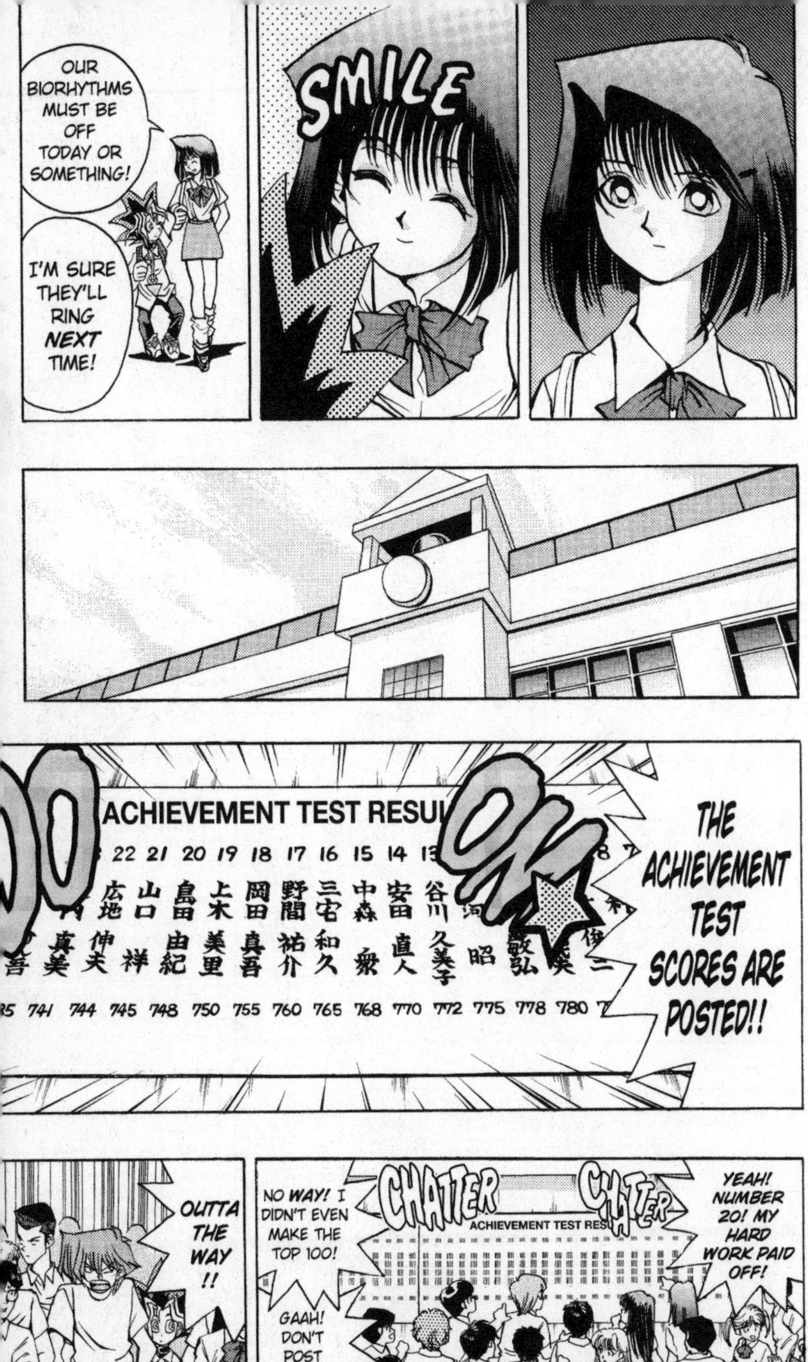
SMILE
OUR BIORHYTHMS MUST BE OFF TODAY OR SOMETHING!
I'M SURE THEY'LL RING NEXT TIME!
THE ACHIEVEMENT TEST SCORES ARE POSTED!!
CHATTER
CHATTER
YEAH! NUMBER 20! MY HARD WORK PAID OFF!
NO WAY! I DIDN'T EVEN MAKE THE TOP 100!
GAAH! DON'T POST THOSE NUMBERS!
OUTTA THE WAY!!

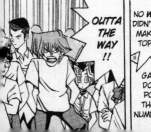

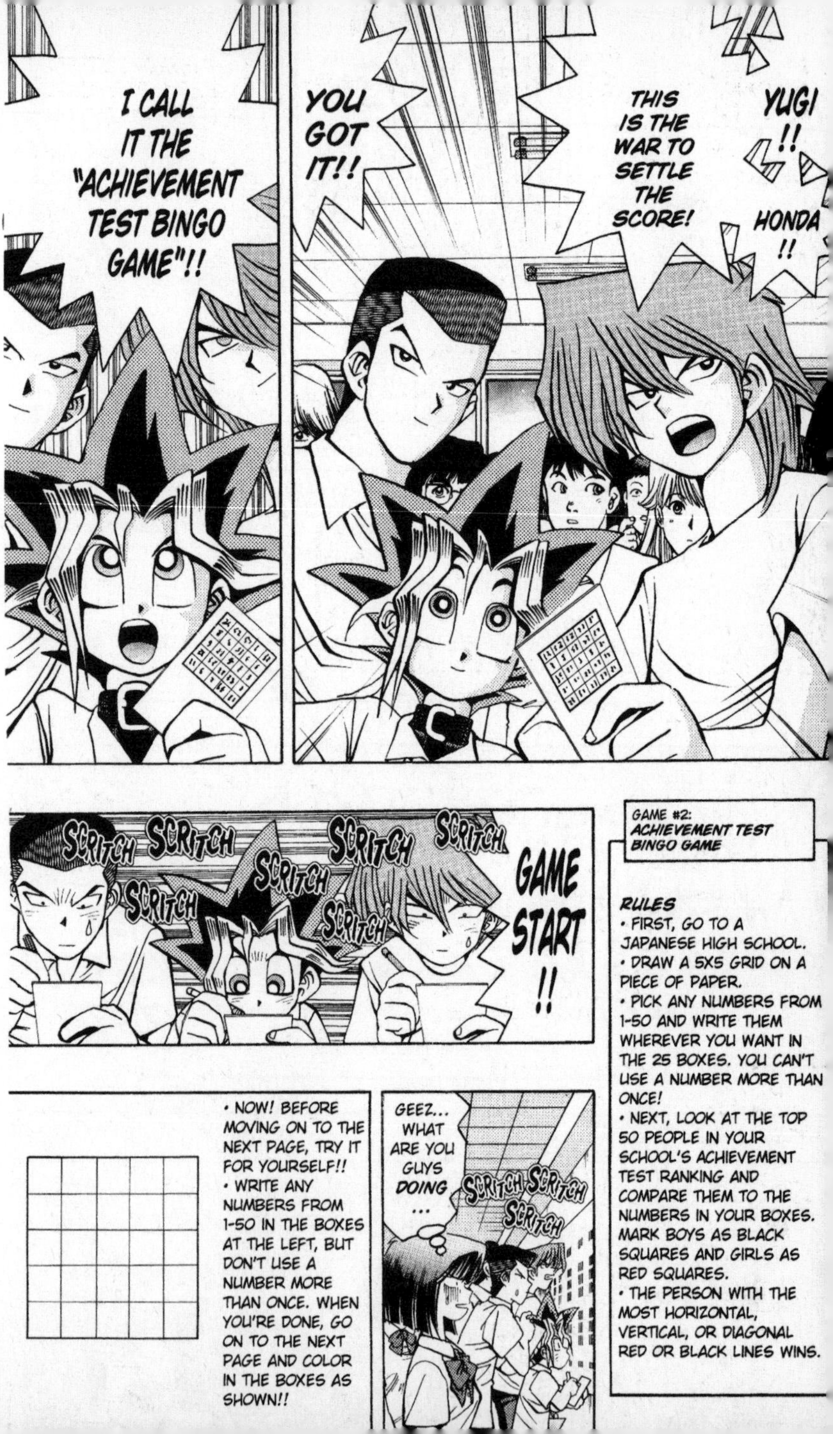
YUGI!!
HONDA!!
THIS IS THE WAR TO SETTLE THE SCORE!
YOU GOT IT!!
I CALL IT THE "ACHIEVEMENT TEST BINGO GAME"!!
GAME #2: ACHIEVEMENT TEST BINGO GAME
RULES
• FIRST, GO TO A JAPANESE HIGH SCHOOL.
• DRAW A 5X5 GRID ON A PIECE OF PAPER.
• PICK ANY NUMBERS FROM 1-50 AND WRITE THEM WHEREVER YOU WANT IN THE 25 BOXES. YOU CAN'T USE A NUMBER MORE THAN ONCE!
• NEXT, LOOK AT THE TOP 50 PEOPLE IN YOUR SCHOOL'S ACHIEVEMENT TEST RANKING AND COMPARE THEM TO THE NUMBERS IN YOUR BOXES. MARK BOYS AS BLACK SQUARES AND GIRLS AS RED SQUARES.
• THE PERSON WITH THE MOST HORIZONTAL, VERTICAL, OR DIAGONAL RED OR BLACK LINES WINS.
GAME START!!
SCRITCH SCRITCH SCRITCH SCRITCH SCRITCH SCRITCH SCRITCH
GEEZ... WHAT ARE YOU GUYS DOING...
SCRITCH SCRITCH SCRITCH
• NOW! BEFORE MOVING ON TO THE NEXT PAGE, TRY IT FOR YOURSELF!!
• WRITE ANY NUMBERS FROM 1-50 IN THE BOXES AT THE LEFT, BUT DON'T USE A NUMBER MORE THAN ONCE. WHEN YOU'RE DONE, GO ON TO THE NEXT PAGE AND COLOR IN THE BOXES AS SHOWN!!

NAMES NOT SHOWN TO PROTECT THE INNOCENT

1 RED	26 BLACK
2 RED	27 RED
3 BLACK	28 RED
4 BLACK	29 RED
5 RED	30 BLACK
6 BLACK	31 BLACK
7 RED	32 BLACK
8 BLACK	33 RED
9 RED	34 BLACK
10 BLACK	35 RED
11 RED	36 BLACK
12 BLACK	37 RED
13 BLACK	38 RED
14 BLACK	39 BLACK
15 RED	40 BLACK
16 BLACK	41 RED
17 RED	42 BLACK
18 BLACK	43 RED
19 BLACK	44 RED
20 BLACK	45 BLACK
21 RED	46 BLACK
22 RED	47 RED
23 RED	48 RED
24 BLACK	49 BLACK
25 RED	50 RED

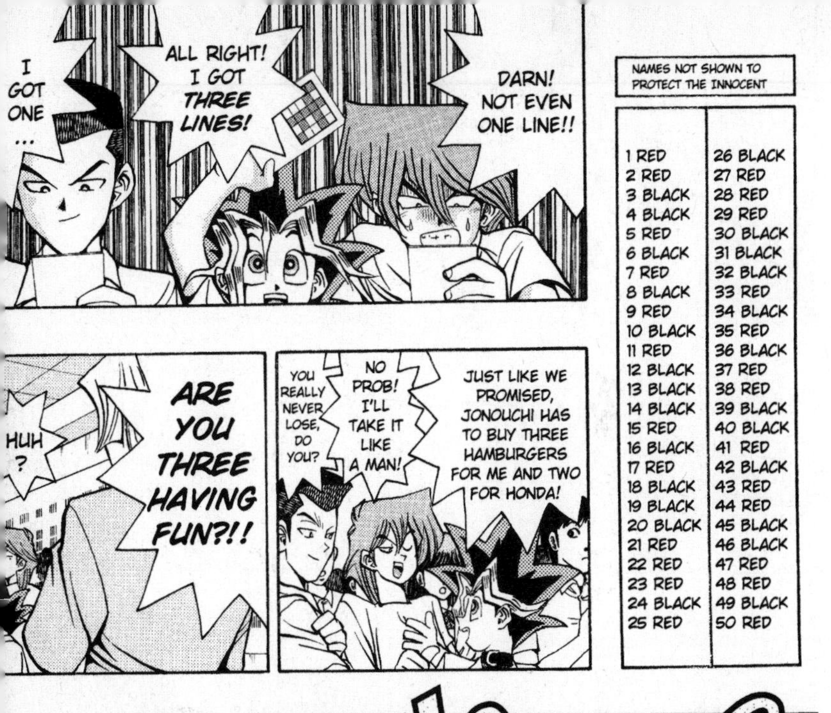
DARN! NOT EVEN ONE LINE!!
ALL RIGHT! I GOT THREE LINES!
I GOT ONE ...
JUST LIKE WE PROMISED, JONOUCHI HAS TO BUY THREE HAMBURGERS FOR ME AND TWO FOR HONDA!
NO PROB! I'LL TAKE IT LIKE A MAN!
YOU REALLY NEVER LOSE, DO YOU?
ARE YOU THREE HAVING FUN?!!
HUH ?

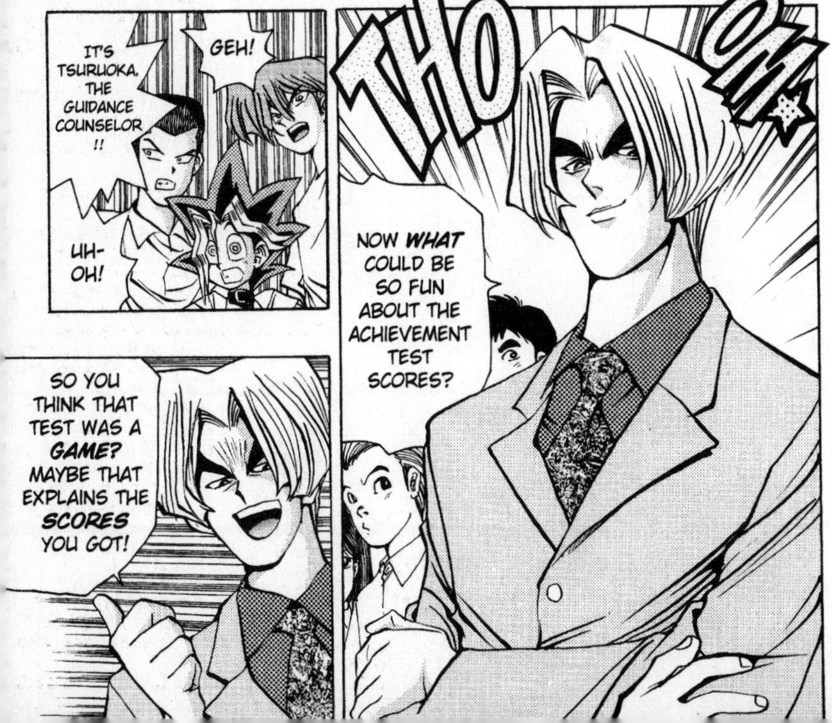
THOOM
NOW WHAT COULD BE SO FUN ABOUT THE ACHIEVEMENT TEST SCORES?
GEH!
IT'S TSURUOKA, THE GUIDANCE COUNSELOR !!
UH-OH!
SO YOU THINK THAT TEST WAS A GAME? MAYBE THAT EXPLAINS THE SCORES YOU GOT!

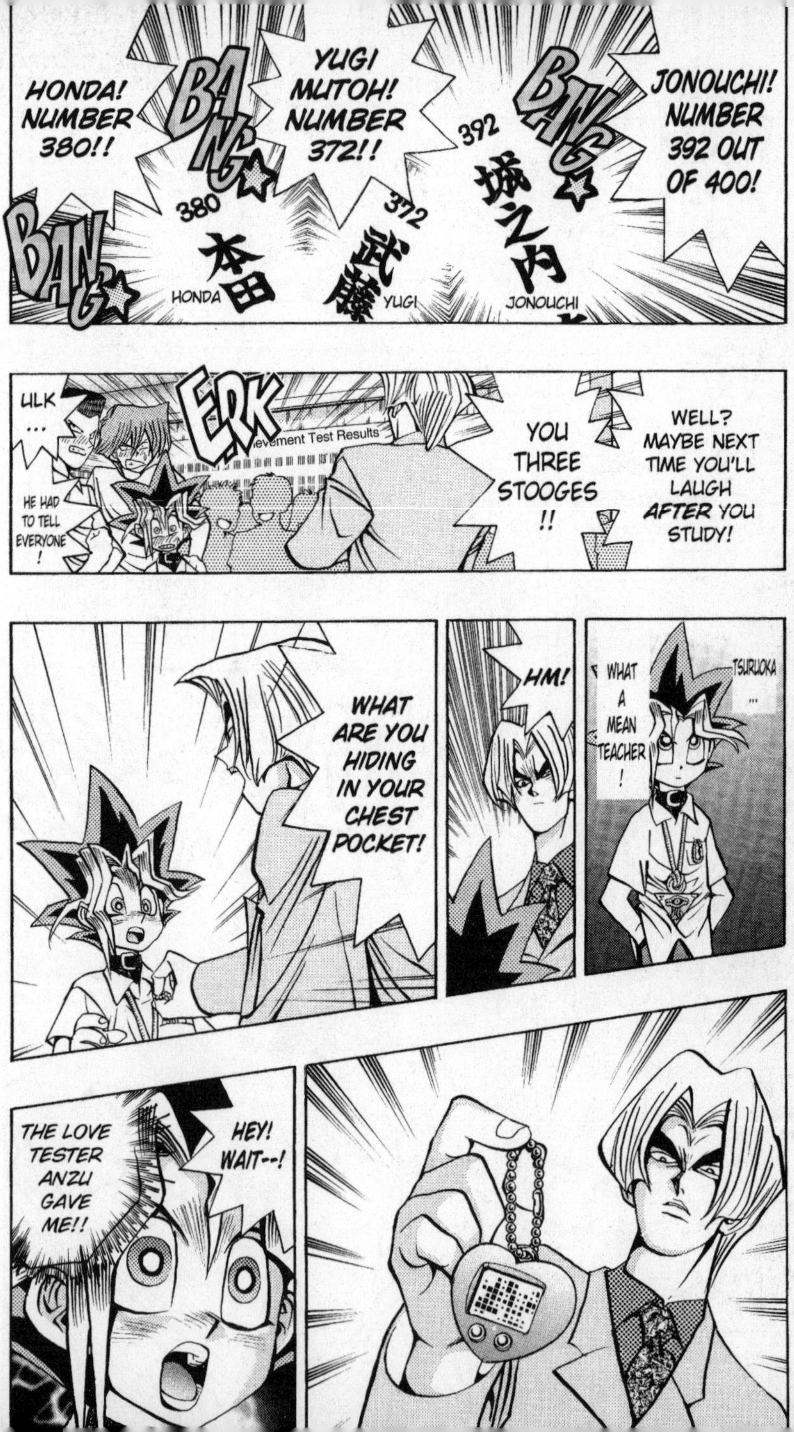
JONOUCHI! NUMBER 392 OUT OF 400!
BANG
392
城之内
JONOUCHI
YUGI MUTOH! NUMBER 372!!
372
武藤
YUGI
BANG
HONDA! NUMBER 380!!
380
本田
HONDA
BANG
WELL? MAYBE NEXT TIME YOU'LL LAUGH AFTER YOU STUDY!
YOU THREE STOOGES !!
ERK
ievement Test Results
ULK ...
HE HAD TO TELL EVERYONE !
TSURUOKA ...
WHAT A MEAN TEACHER !
HM!
WHAT ARE YOU HIDING IN YOUR CHEST POCKET!
HEY! WAIT--!
THE LOVE TESTER ANZU GAVE ME!!

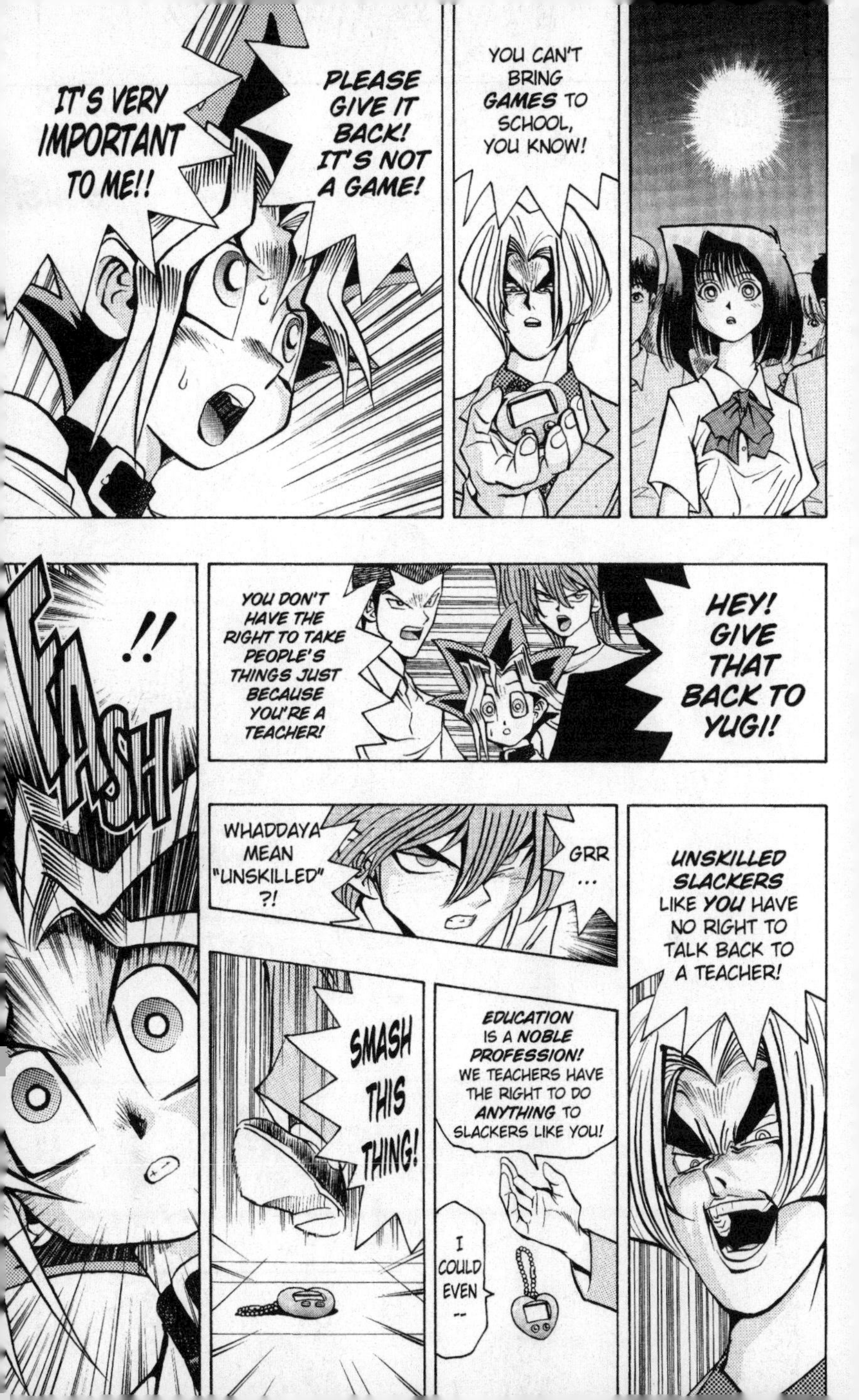
YOU CAN'T BRING GAMES TO SCHOOL, YOU KNOW!
PLEASE GIVE IT BACK! IT'S NOT A GAME!
IT'S VERY IMPORTANT TO ME!!
HEY! GIVE THAT BACK TO YUGI!
YOU DON'T HAVE THE RIGHT TO TAKE PEOPLE'S THINGS JUST BECAUSE YOU'RE A TEACHER!
UNSKILLED SLACKERS LIKE YOU HAVE NO RIGHT TO TALK BACK TO A TEACHER!
GRR ...
WHADDAYA MEAN "UNSKILLED" ?!
EDUCATION IS A NOBLE PROFESSION! WE TEACHERS HAVE THE RIGHT TO DO ANYTHING TO SLACKERS LIKE YOU!
I COULD EVEN --
SMASH THIS THING!
!!
FLASH

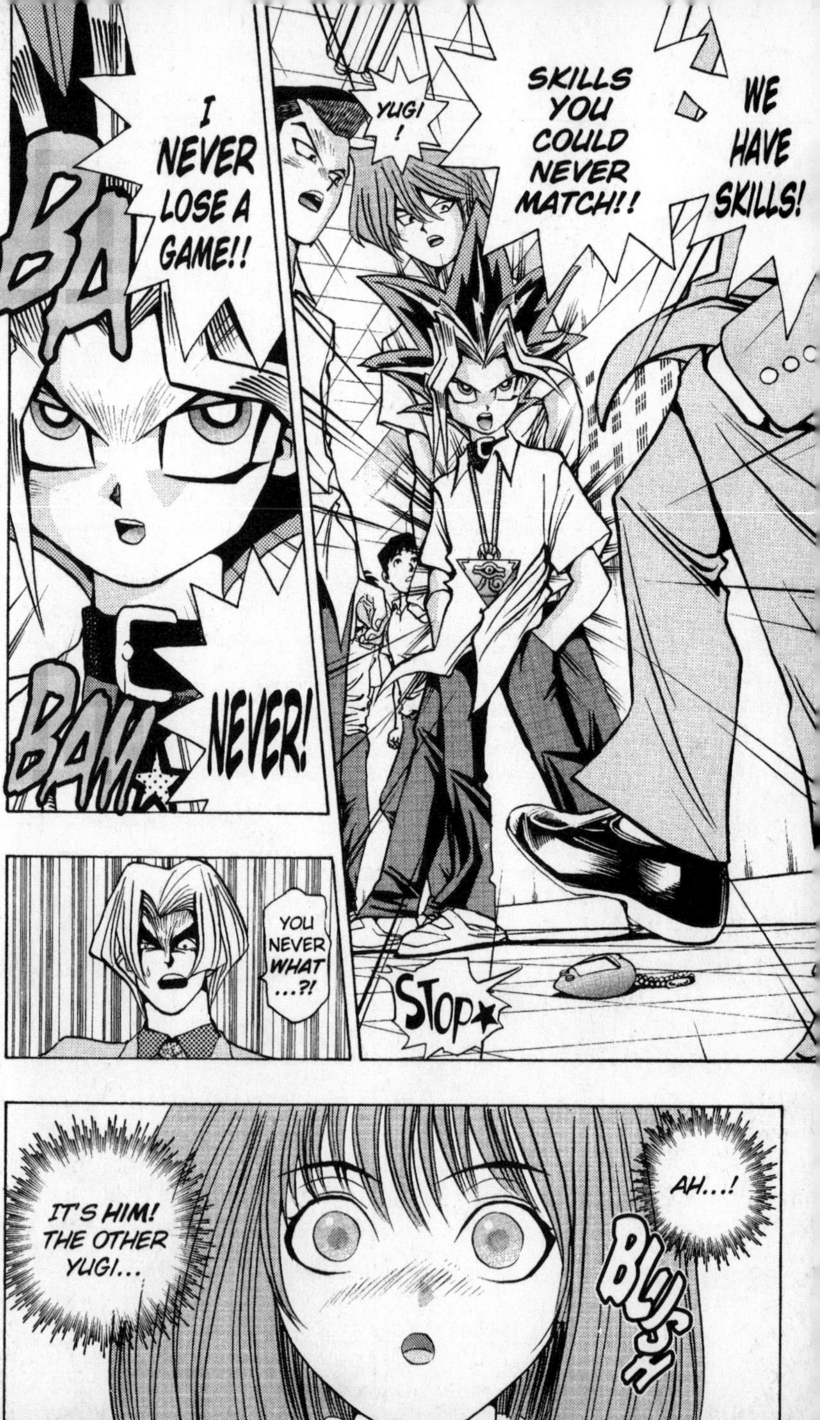

WE HAVE SKILLS!
SKILLS YOU COULD NEVER MATCH!!
YUGI!
STOP
BA
I NEVER LOSE A GAME!!
BAM
NEVER!
YOU NEVER WHAT ...?!
AH...!
BLUSH
IT'S HIM! THE OTHER YUGI...

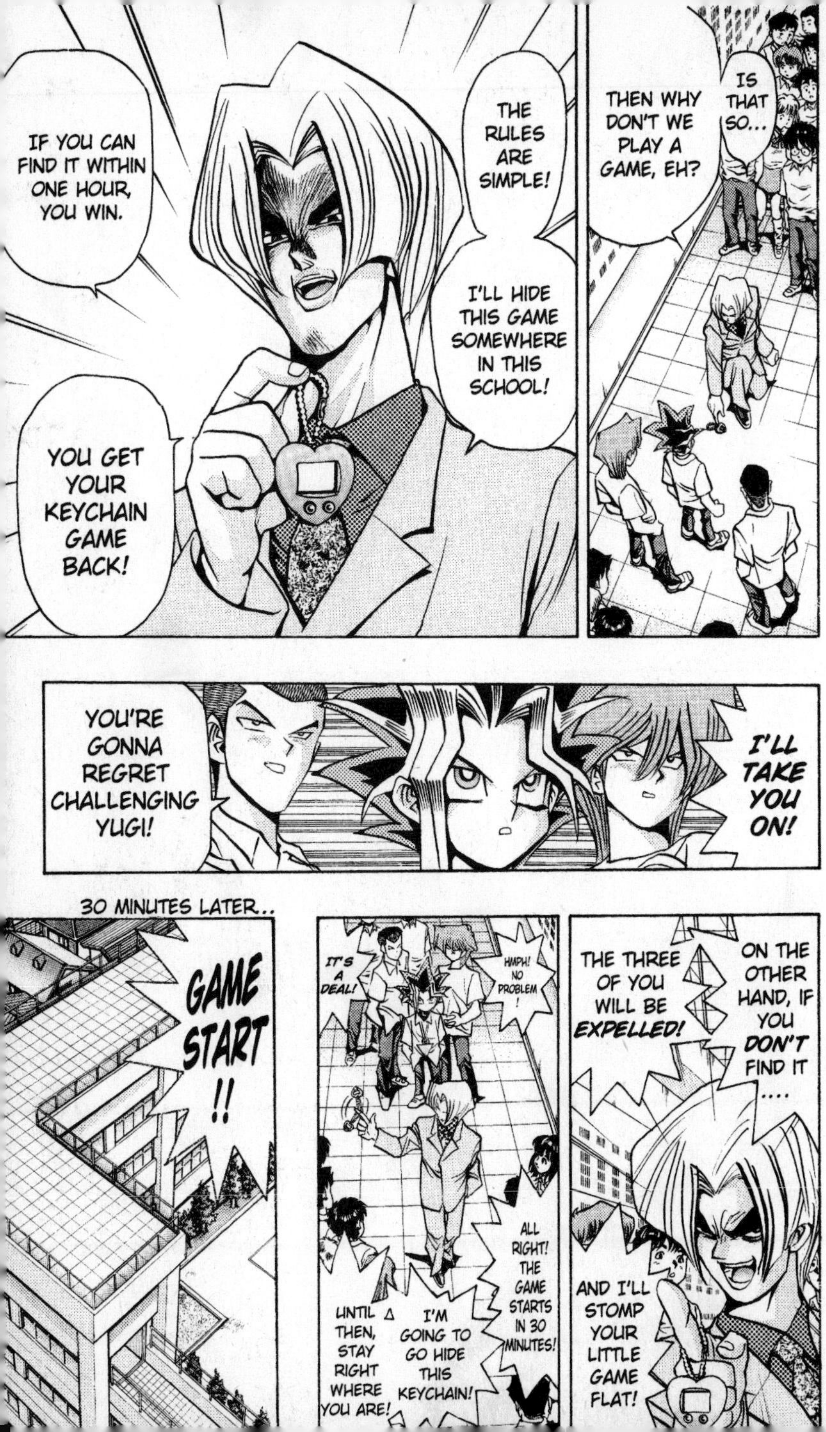
IS THAT SO...
THEN WHY DON'T WE PLAY A GAME, EH?
THE RULES ARE SIMPLE!
I'LL HIDE THIS GAME SOMEWHERE IN THIS SCHOOL!
IF YOU CAN FIND IT WITHIN ONE HOUR, YOU WIN.
YOU GET YOUR KEYCHAIN GAME BACK!
I'LL TAKE YOU ON!
YOU'RE GONNA REGRET CHALLENGING YUGI!
ON THE OTHER HAND, IF YOU DON'T FIND IT....
THE THREE OF YOU WILL BE EXPELLED!
AND I'LL STOMP YOUR LITTLE GAME FLAT!
HMPH! NO PROBLEM!
IT'S A DEAL!
ALL RIGHT! THE GAME STARTS IN 30 MINUTES!
I'M GOING TO GO HIDE THIS KEYCHAIN!
UNTIL THEN, STAY RIGHT WHERE YOU ARE!
30 MINUTES LATER...
GAME START!!

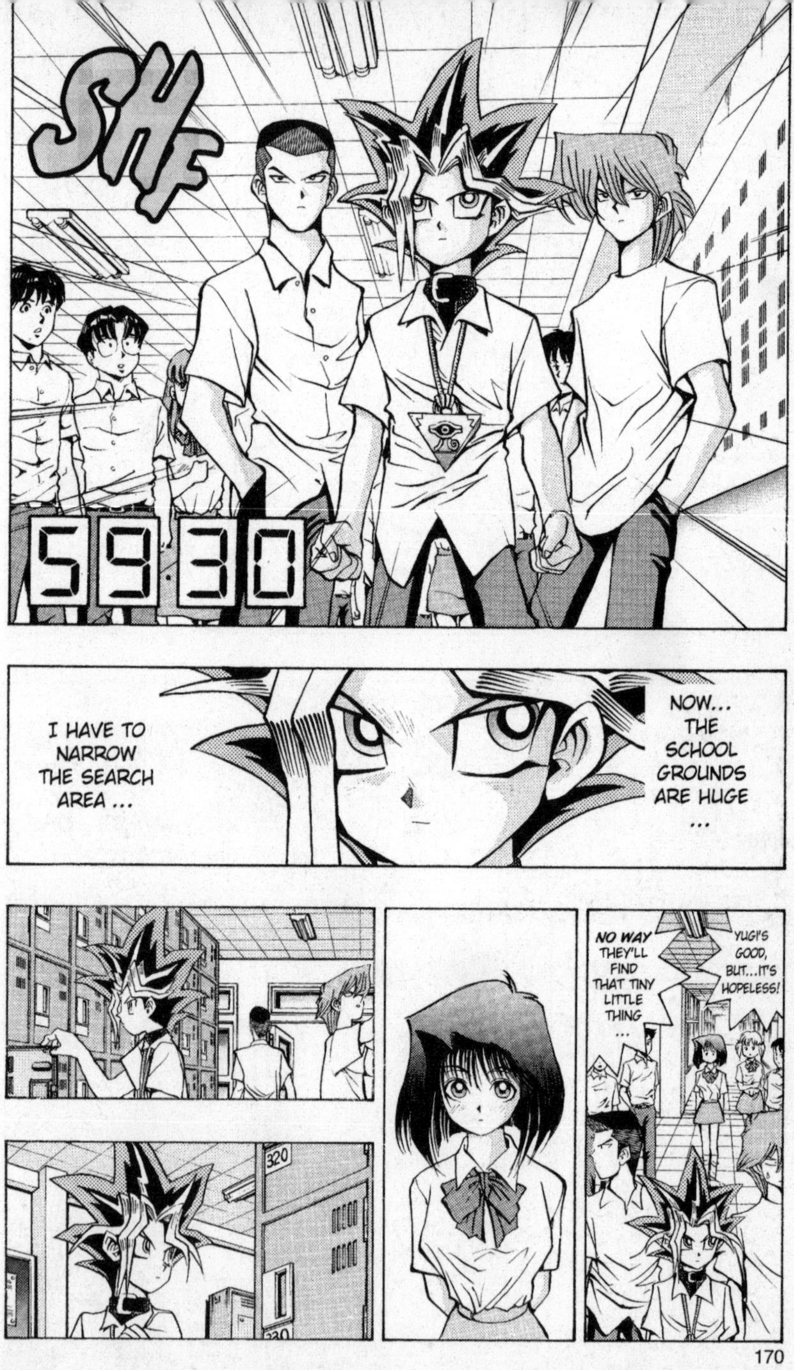
SHF
59:30
NOW... THE SCHOOL GROUNDS ARE HUGE ...
I HAVE TO NARROW THE SEARCH AREA ...
YUGI'S GOOD, BUT...IT'S HOPELESS!
NO WAY THEY'LL FIND THAT TINY LITTLE THING ...
320

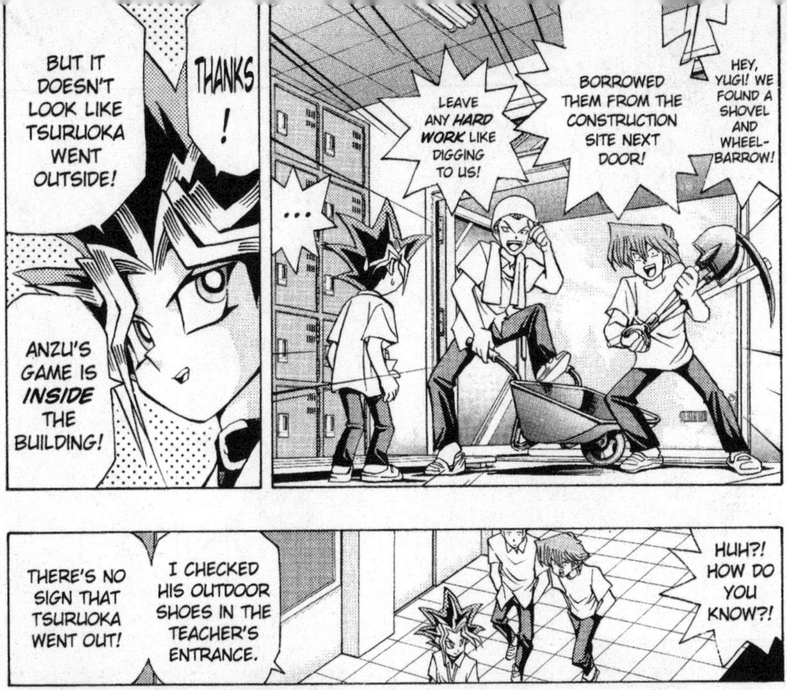
HEY, YUGI! WE FOUND A SHOVEL AND WHEEL-BARROW!
BORROWED THEM FROM THE CONSTRUCTION SITE NEXT DOOR!
LEAVE ANY HARD WORK LIKE DIGGING TO US!
...
THANKS!
BUT IT DOESN'T LOOK LIKE TSURUOKA WENT OUTSIDE!
ANZU'S GAME IS INSIDE THE BUILDING!
HUH?! HOW DO YOU KNOW?!
I CHECKED HIS OUTDOOR SHOES IN THE TEACHER'S ENTRANCE.
THERE'S NO SIGN THAT TSURUOKA WENT OUT!

* LIKE MOST JAPANESE BUILDINGS, YOU'RE SUPPOSED TO CHANGE YOUR SHOES WHEN YOU ENTER A JAPANESE SCHOOL.

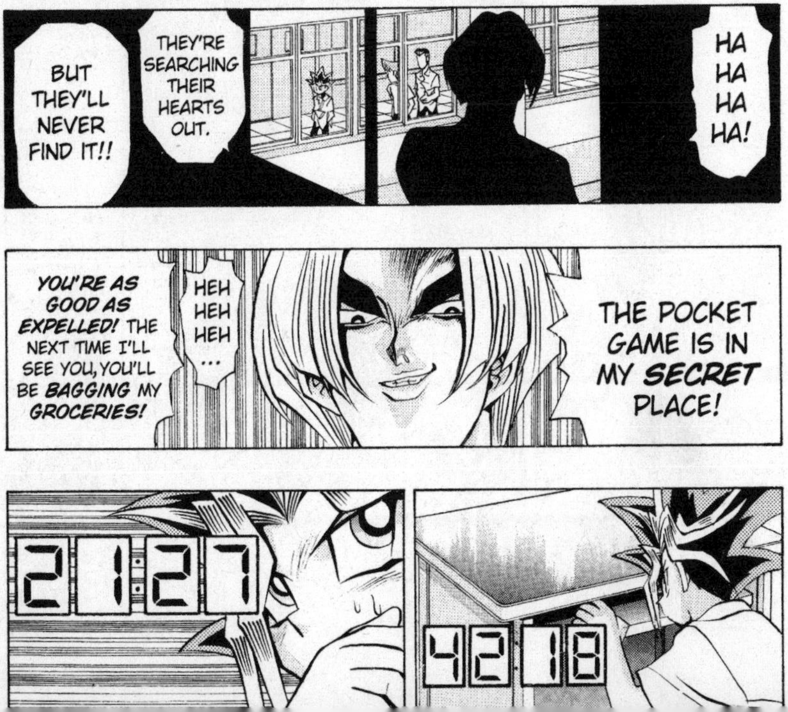
HA HA HA HA!
THEY'RE SEARCHING THEIR HEARTS OUT.
BUT THEY'LL NEVER FIND IT!!
THE POCKET GAME IS IN MY SECRET PLACE!
HEH HEH HEH ...
YOU'RE AS GOOD AS EXPELLED! THE NEXT TIME I'LL SEE YOU, YOU'LL BE BAGGING MY GROCERIES!
4218
2127

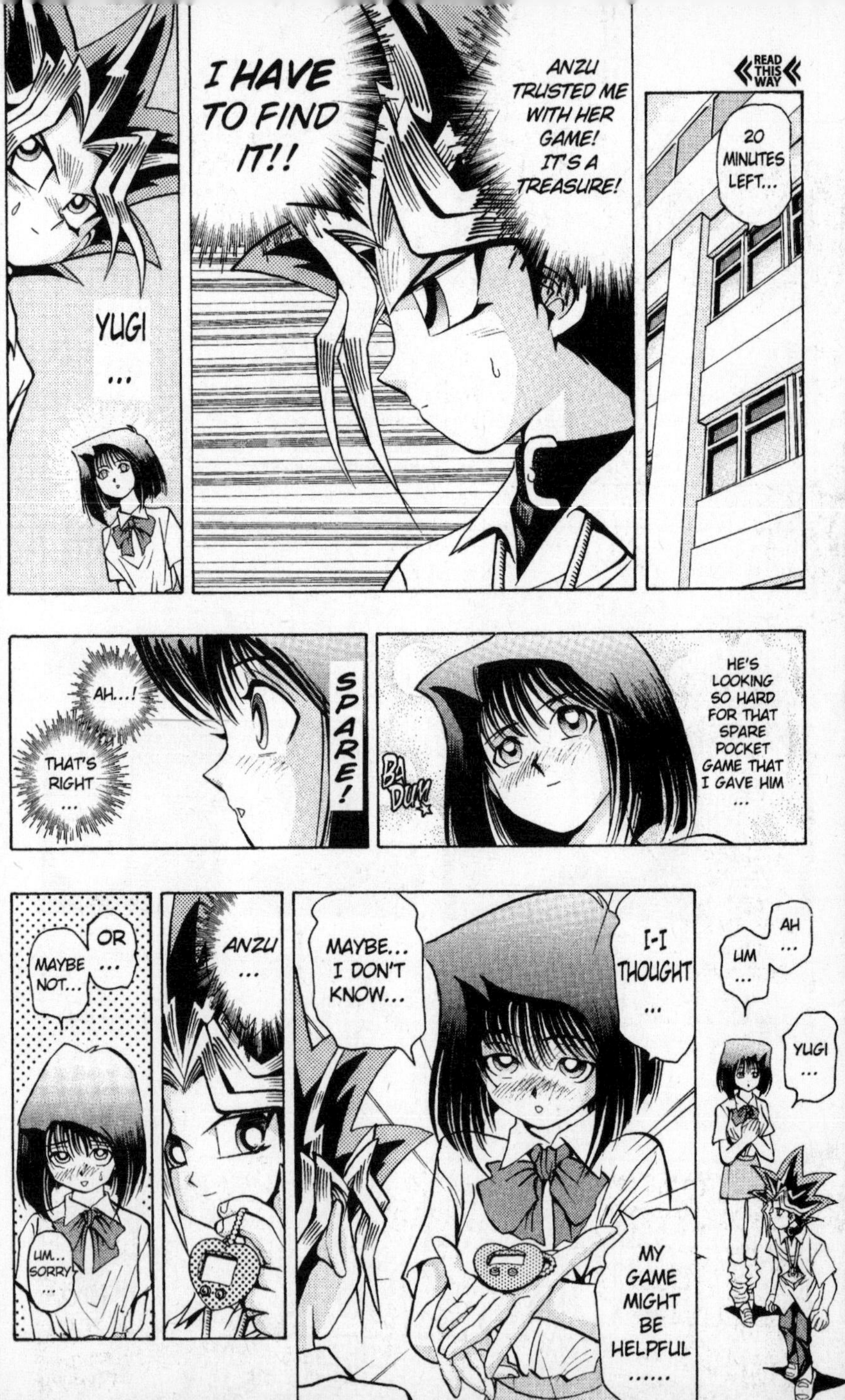
READ THIS WAY
20 MINUTES LEFT...
ANZU TRUSTED ME WITH HER GAME! IT'S A TREASURE!
I HAVE TO FIND IT!!
YUGI ...
HE'S LOOKING SO HARD FOR THAT SPARE POCKET GAME THAT I GAVE HIM ...
BA DUM
SPARE!
AH...!
THAT'S RIGHT ...
AH ...
UM ...
YUGI ...
[-I THOUGHT ...
MY GAME MIGHT BE HELPFUL ......
MAYBE... I DON'T KNOW...
ANZU ...
OR ...
MAYBE NOT...
UM.. SORRY ...

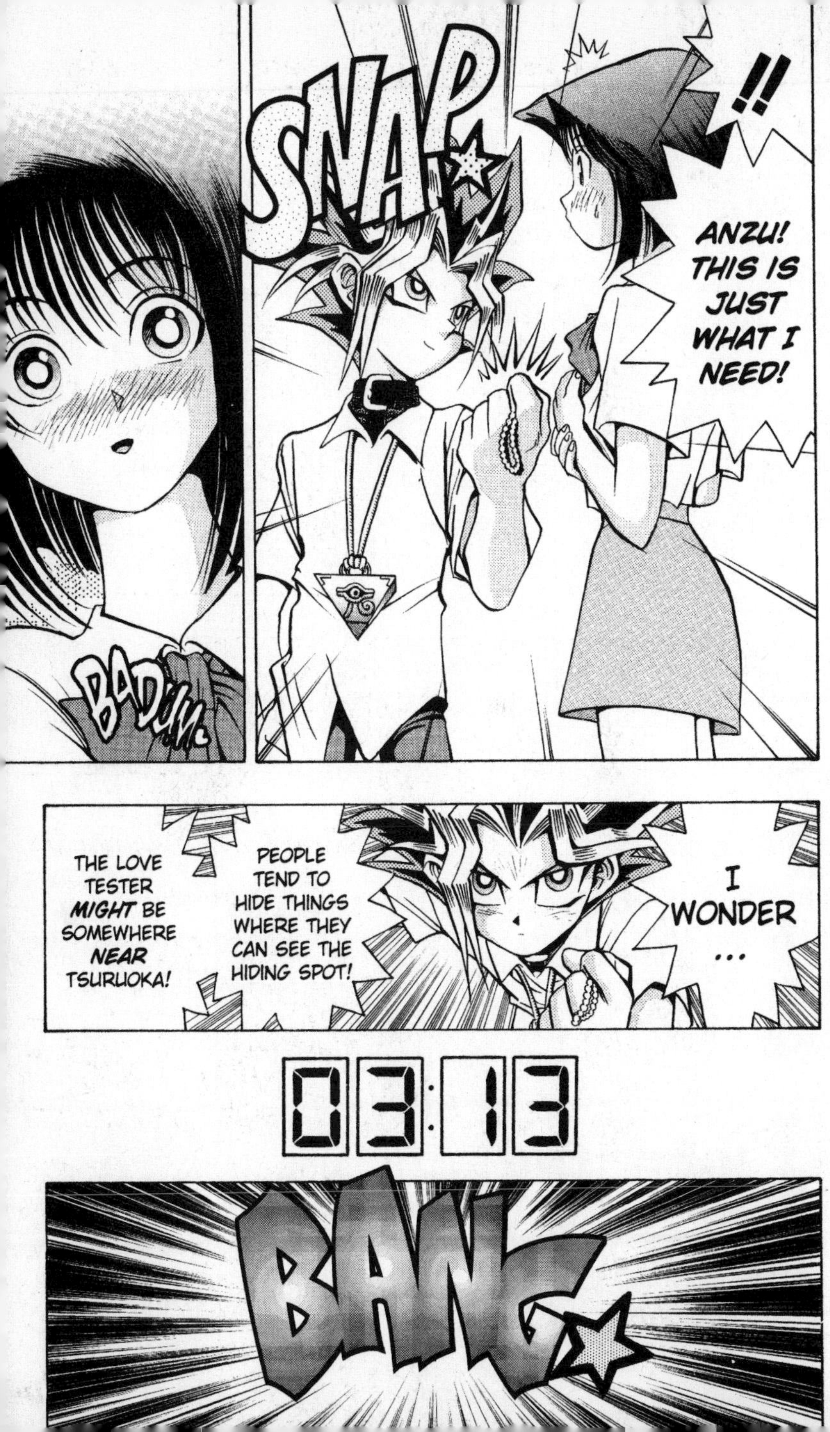
SNAP☆
!!
ANZU! THIS IS JUST WHAT I NEED!
BADUM
I WONDER ...
PEOPLE TEND TO HIDE THINGS WHERE THEY CAN SEE THE HIDING SPOT!
THE LOVE TESTER *MIGHT* BE SOMEWHERE *NEAR* TSURUOKA!
03:13
BANG☆

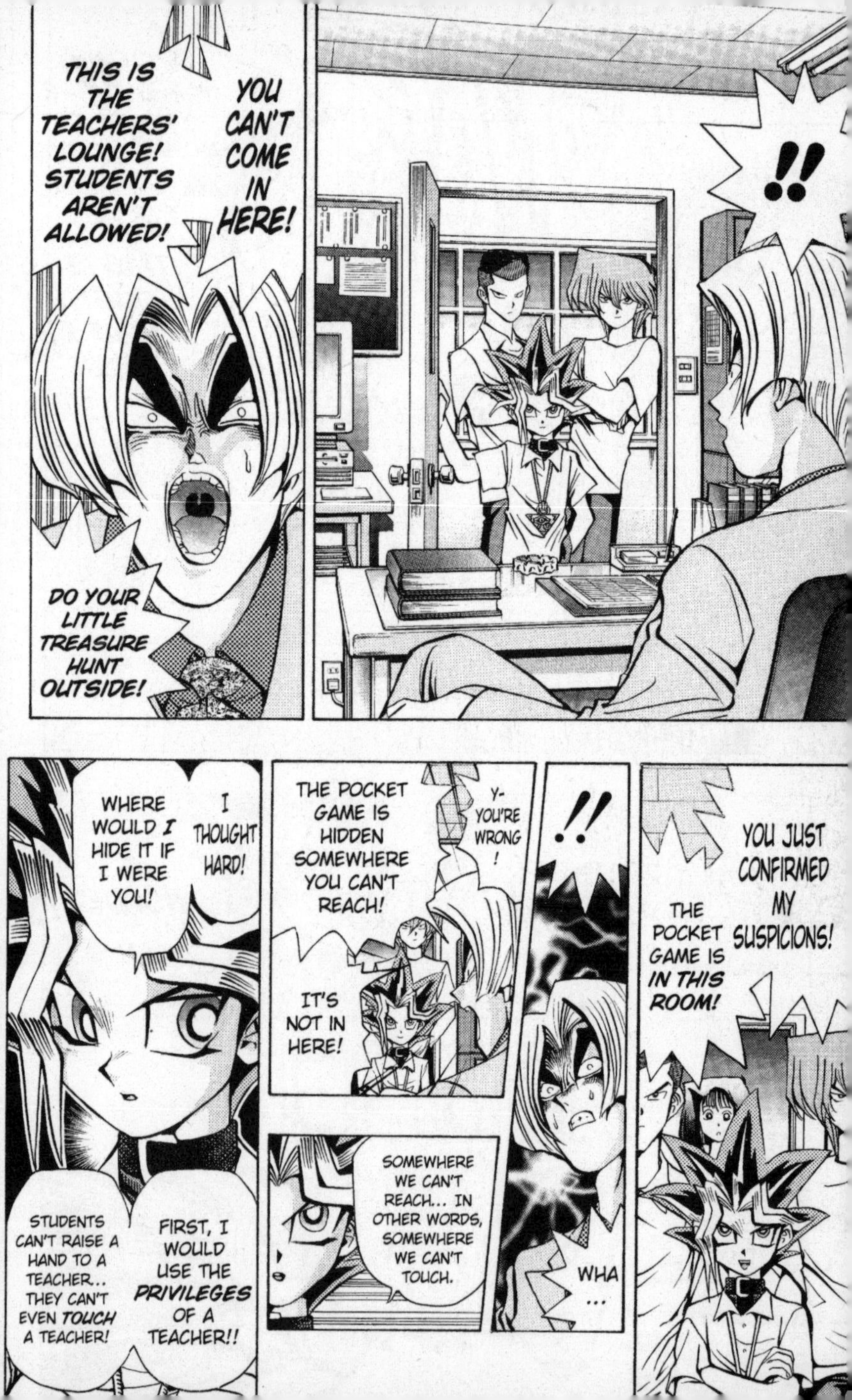
!!
YOU CAN'T COME IN HERE!
THIS IS THE TEACHERS' LOUNGE! STUDENTS AREN'T ALLOWED!
DO YOUR LITTLE TREASURE HUNT OUTSIDE!
YOU JUST CONFIRMED MY SUSPICIONS!
THE POCKET GAME IS IN THIS ROOM!
!!
WHA...
Y- YOU'RE WRONG!
IT'S NOT IN HERE!
THE POCKET GAME IS HIDDEN SOMEWHERE YOU CAN'T REACH!
SOMEWHERE WE CAN'T REACH... IN OTHER WORDS, SOMEWHERE WE CAN'T TOUCH.
I THOUGHT HARD!
WHERE WOULD I HIDE IT IF I WERE YOU!
FIRST, I WOULD USE THE PRIVILEGES OF A TEACHER!!
STUDENTS CAN'T RAISE A HAND TO A TEACHER... THEY CAN'T EVEN TOUCH A TEACHER!

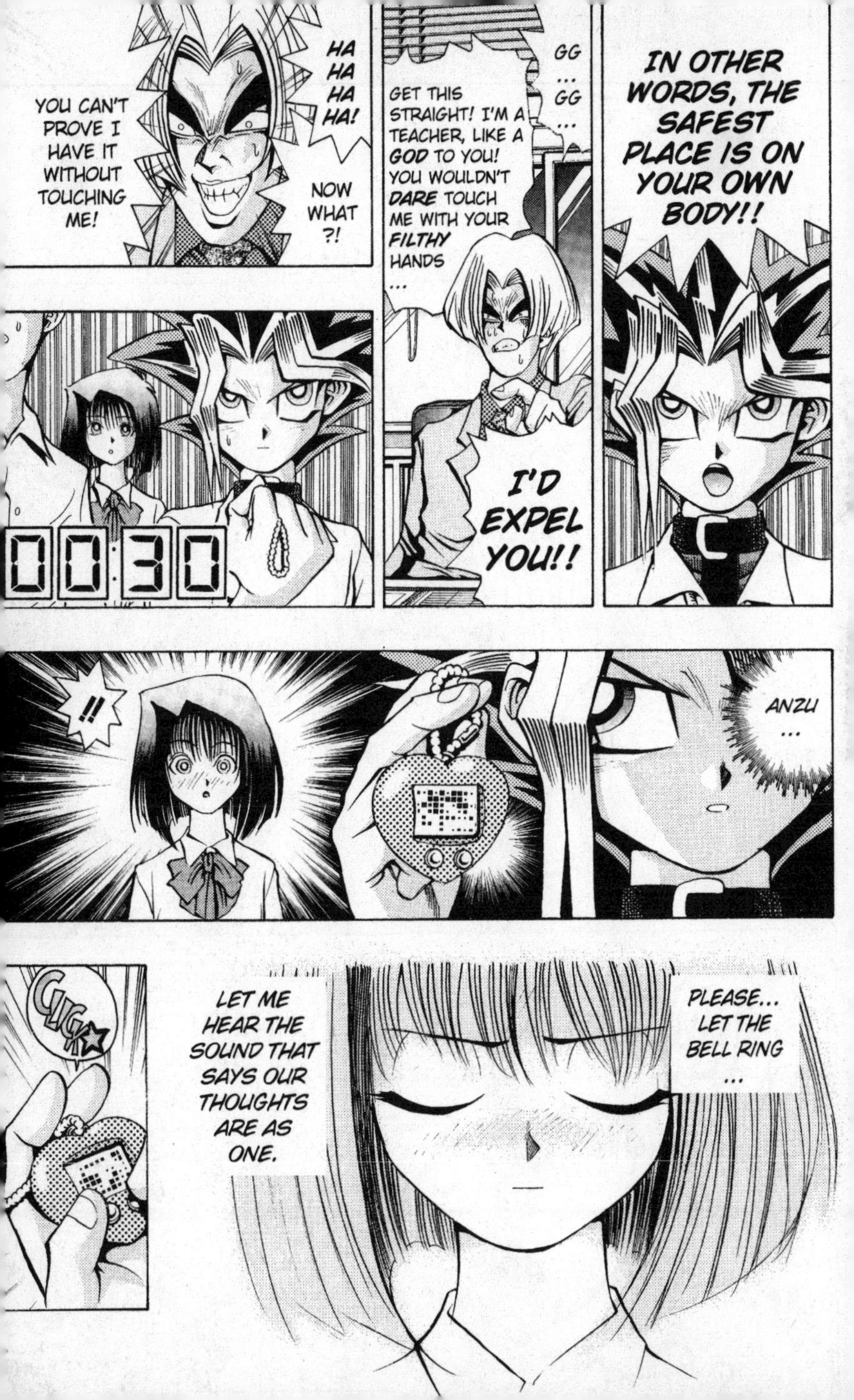
IN OTHER WORDS, THE SAFEST PLACE IS ON YOUR OWN BODY!!
GG ... GG ...
GET THIS STRAIGHT! I'M A TEACHER, LIKE A GOD TO YOU! YOU WOULDN'T DARE TOUCH ME WITH YOUR FILTHY HANDS ...
I'D EXPEL YOU!!
HA HA HA HA!
NOW WHAT ?!
YOU CAN'T PROVE I HAVE IT WITHOUT TOUCHING ME!
00:30
ANZU ...
!!
PLEASE... LET THE BELL RING ...
LET ME HEAR THE SOUND THAT SAYS OUR THOUGHTS ARE AS ONE.
CLICK☆

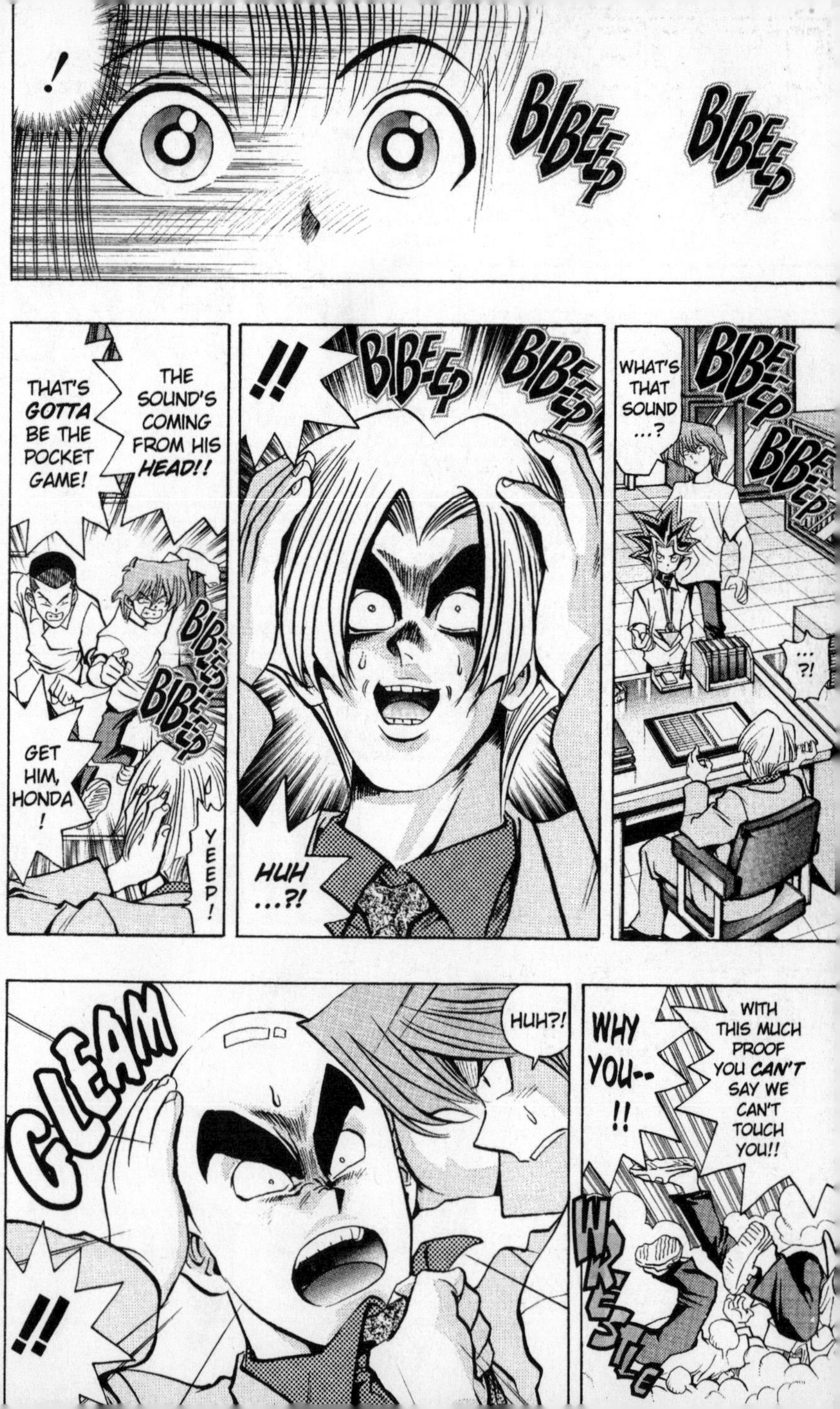
!
BIBEEP
BIBEEP
WHAT'S THAT SOUND ...?
BIBEEP
BIBEEP
...?!
!!
BIBEEP
BIBEEP
HUH ...?!
THE SOUND'S COMING FROM HIS HEAD!!
THAT'S GOTTA BE THE POCKET GAME!
BIBEEP
BIBEEP
GET HIM, HONDA!
YEEP!
WITH THIS MUCH PROOF YOU CAN'T SAY WE CAN'T TOUCH YOU!!
WHY YOU--!!
HUH?!
GLEAM
!!

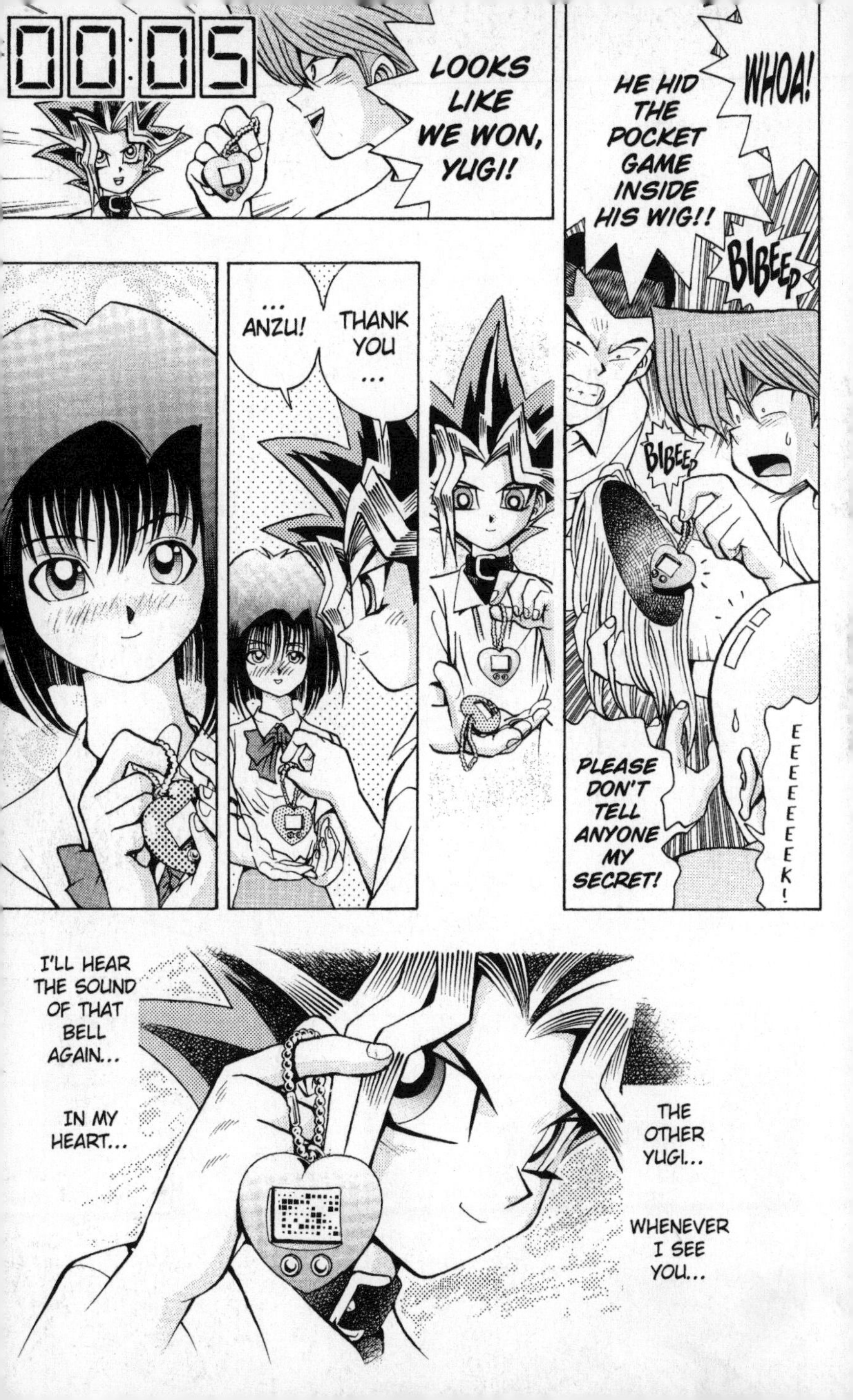
WHOA!
HE HID THE POCKET GAME INSIDE HIS WIG!!
BIBEEP
BIBEEP
PLEASE DON'T TELL ANYONE MY SECRET!
EEEEEEEEEEK!
00:05
LOOKS LIKE WE WON, YUGI!
THANK YOU...
...ANZU!
THE OTHER YUGI...
WHENEVER I SEE YOU...
I'LL HEAR THE SOUND OF THAT BELL AGAIN...
IN MY HEART...

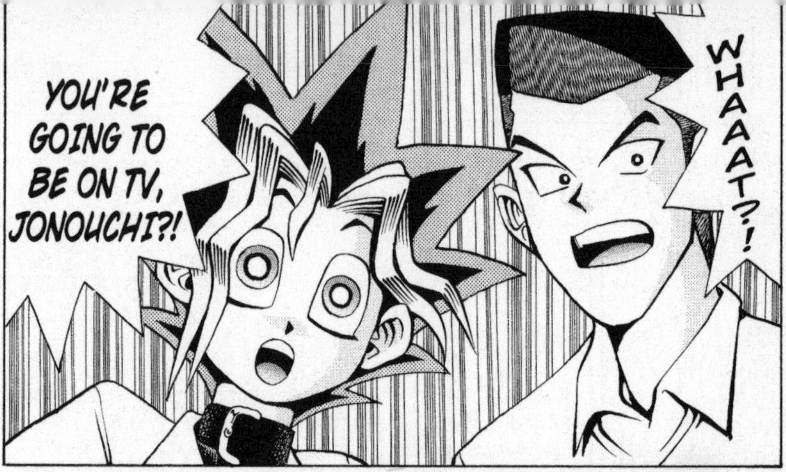
WHAAAT?!
YOU'RE GOING TO BE ON TV, JONOUCHI?!

Duel 42: Get the Million!!

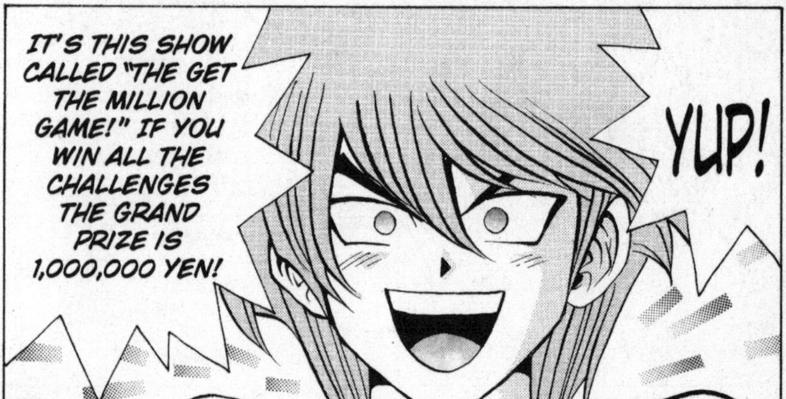
YUP!
IT'S THIS SHOW CALLED "THE GET THE MILLION GAME!" IF YOU WIN ALL THE CHALLENGES THE GRAND PRIZE IS 1,000,000 YEN!

* ABOUT $10,000 U.S.

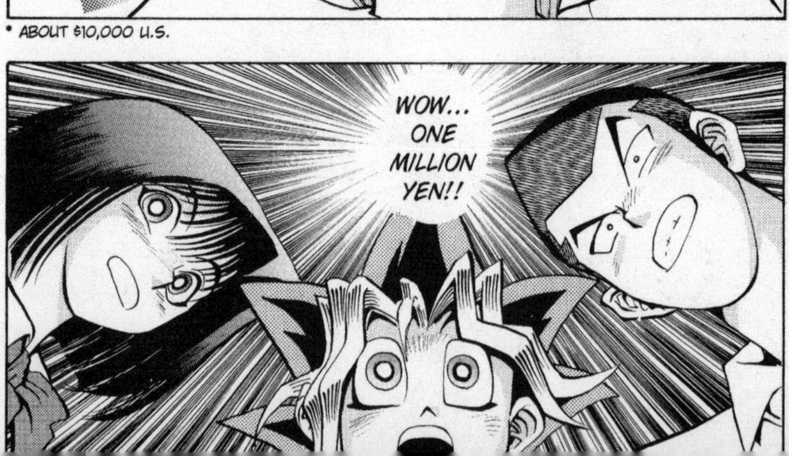
WOW... ONE MILLION YEN!!

READ THIS WAY

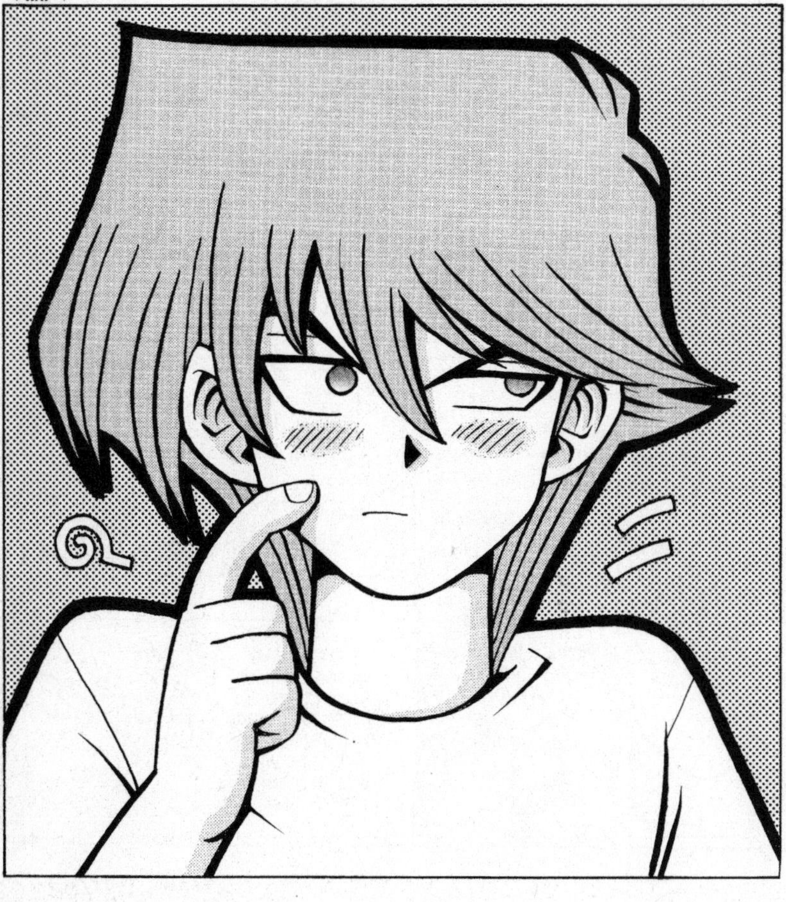

Duel 42:

Get the Million!!

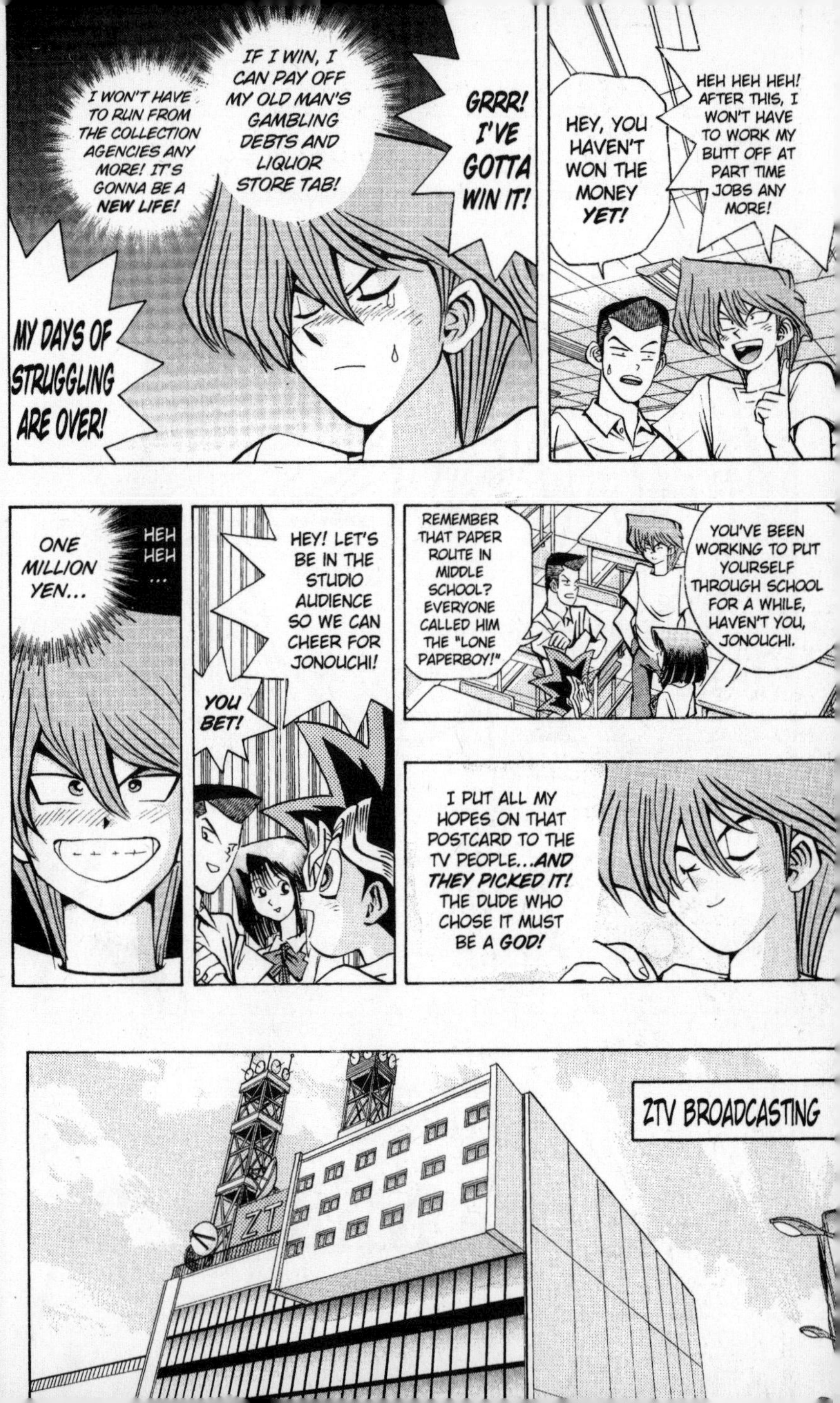
HEH HEH HEH! AFTER THIS, I WON'T HAVE TO WORK MY BUTT OFF AT PART TIME JOBS ANY MORE!
HEY, YOU HAVEN'T WON THE MONEY YET!
GRRR! I'VE GOTTA WIN IT!
IF I WIN, I CAN PAY OFF MY OLD MAN'S GAMBLING DEBTS AND LIQUOR STORE TAB!
I WON'T HAVE TO RUN FROM THE COLLECTION AGENCIES ANY MORE! IT'S GONNA BE A NEW LIFE!
MY DAYS OF STRUGGLING ARE OVER!
YOU'VE BEEN WORKING TO PUT YOURSELF THROUGH SCHOOL FOR A WHILE, HAVEN'T YOU, JONOUCHI.
REMEMBER THAT PAPER ROUTE IN MIDDLE SCHOOL? EVERYONE CALLED HIM THE "LONE PAPERBOY!"
I PUT ALL MY HOPES ON THAT POSTCARD TO THE TV PEOPLE...AND THEY PICKED IT! THE DUDE WHO CHOSE IT MUST BE A GOD!
HEY! LET'S BE IN THE STUDIO AUDIENCE SO WE CAN CHEER FOR JONOUCHI!
YOU BET!
HEH HEH ...
ONE MILLION YEN...
ZTV BROADCASTING

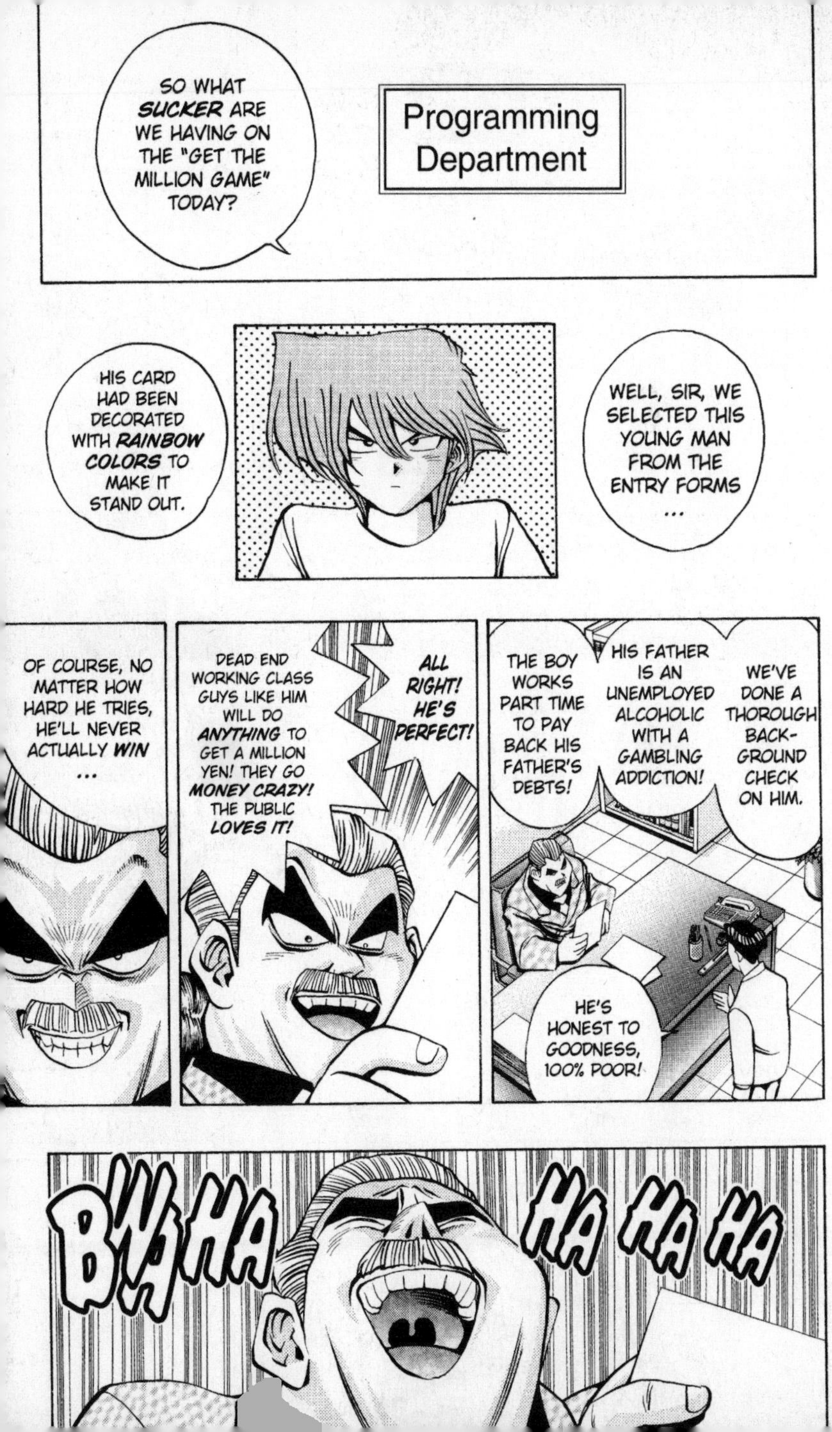
Programming Department
SO WHAT SUCKER ARE WE HAVING ON THE "GET THE MILLION GAME" TODAY?
WELL, SIR, WE SELECTED THIS YOUNG MAN FROM THE ENTRY FORMS ...
HIS CARD HAD BEEN DECORATED WITH RAINBOW COLORS TO MAKE IT STAND OUT.
WE'VE DONE A THOROUGH BACK-GROUND CHECK ON HIM.
HIS FATHER IS AN UNEMPLOYED ALCOHOLIC WITH A GAMBLING ADDICTION!
THE BOY WORKS PART TIME TO PAY BACK HIS FATHER'S DEBTS!
HE'S HONEST TO GOODNESS, 100% POOR!
ALL RIGHT! HE'S PERFECT!
DEAD END WORKING CLASS GUYS LIKE HIM WILL DO ANYTHING TO GET A MILLION YEN! THEY GO MONEY CRAZY! THE PUBLIC LOVES IT!
OF COURSE, NO MATTER HOW HARD HE TRIES, HE'LL NEVER ACTUALLY WIN ...
BWAHA HA HA HA

On Air

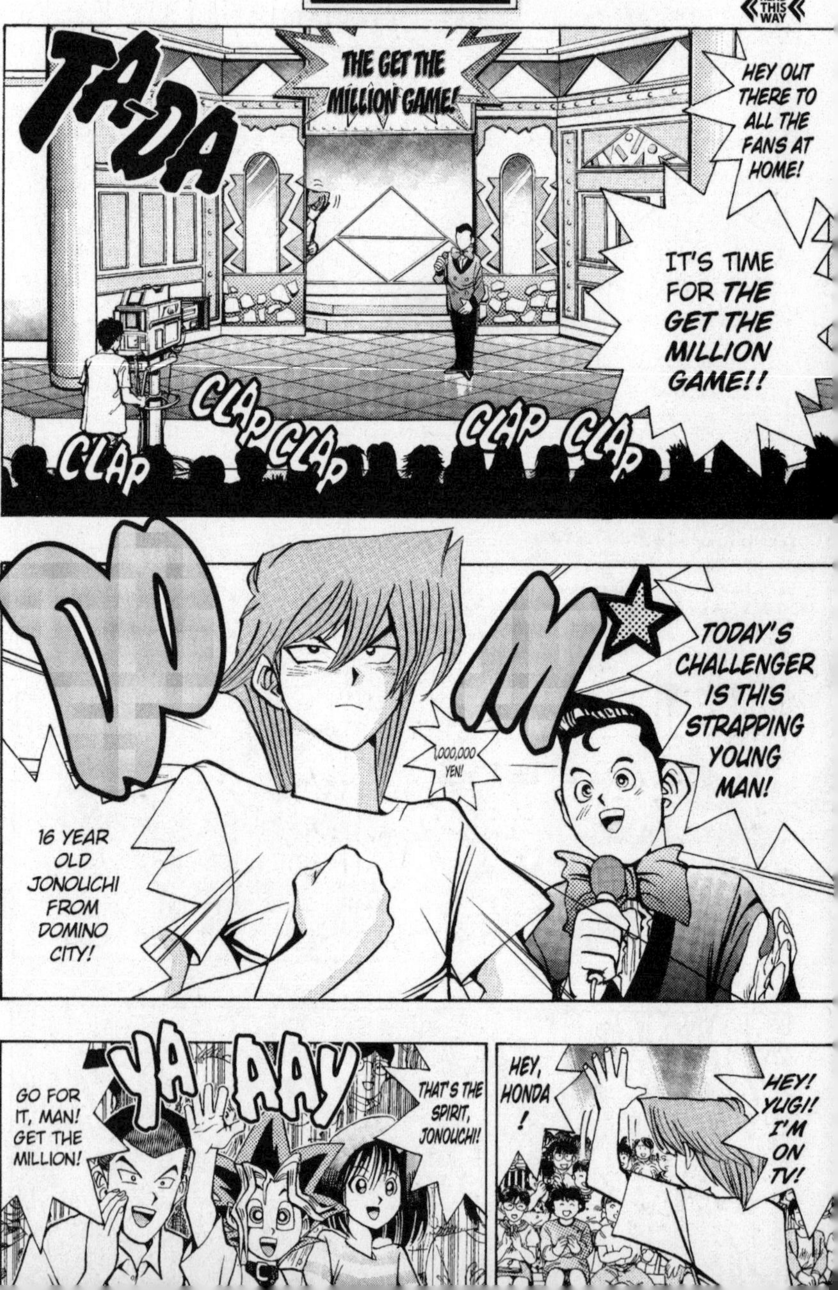
READ THIS WAY
HEY OUT THERE TO ALL THE FANS AT HOME!
IT'S TIME FOR THE GET THE MILLION GAME!!
THE GET THE MILLION GAME!
TA-DA
CLAP CLAP
CLAP CLAP
CLAP
TODAY'S CHALLENGER IS THIS STRAPPING YOUNG MAN!
1,000,000 YEN!
DOM
16 YEAR OLD JONOUCHI FROM DOMINO CITY!
HEY! YUGI! I'M ON TV!
HEY, HONDA!
THAT'S THE SPIRIT, JONOUCHI!
YAAAY
GO FOR IT, MAN! GET THE MILLION!

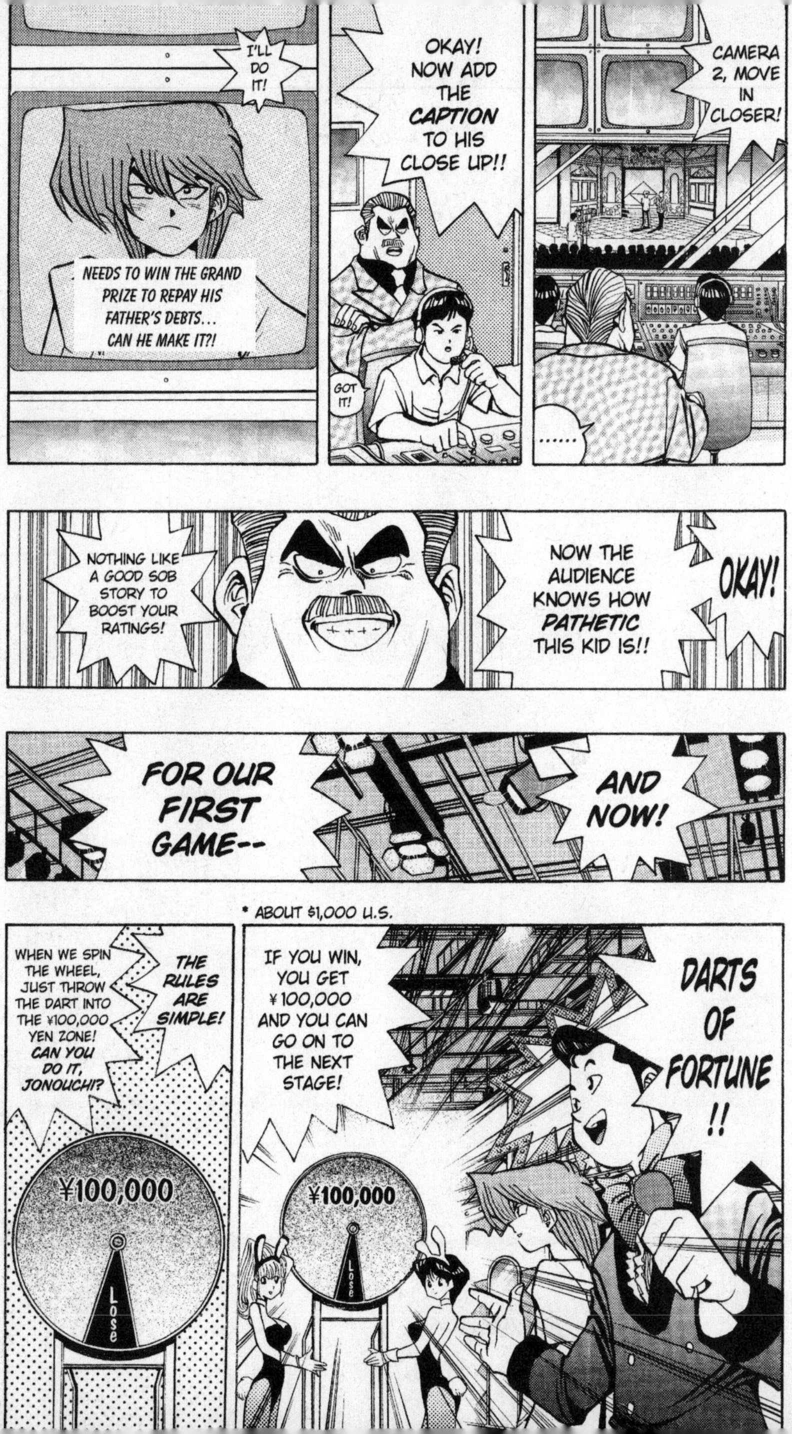
CAMERA 2, MOVE IN CLOSER!
......
OKAY! NOW ADD THE CAPTION TO HIS CLOSE UP!!
GOT IT!
I'LL DO IT!
NEEDS TO WIN THE GRAND PRIZE TO REPAY HIS FATHER'S DEBTS... CAN HE MAKE IT?!
OKAY!
NOW THE AUDIENCE KNOWS HOW PATHETIC THIS KID IS!!
NOTHING LIKE A GOOD SOB STORY TO BOOST YOUR RATINGS!
AND NOW!
FOR OUR FIRST GAME--
DARTS OF FORTUNE!!
IF YOU WIN, YOU GET ¥100,000 AND YOU CAN GO ON TO THE NEXT STAGE!
¥100,000
Lose
THE RULES ARE SIMPLE!
WHEN WE SPIN THE WHEEL, JUST THROW THE DART INTO THE ¥100,000 YEN ZONE! CAN YOU DO IT, JONOUCHI?
¥100,000
Lose

* ABOUT $1,000 U.S.

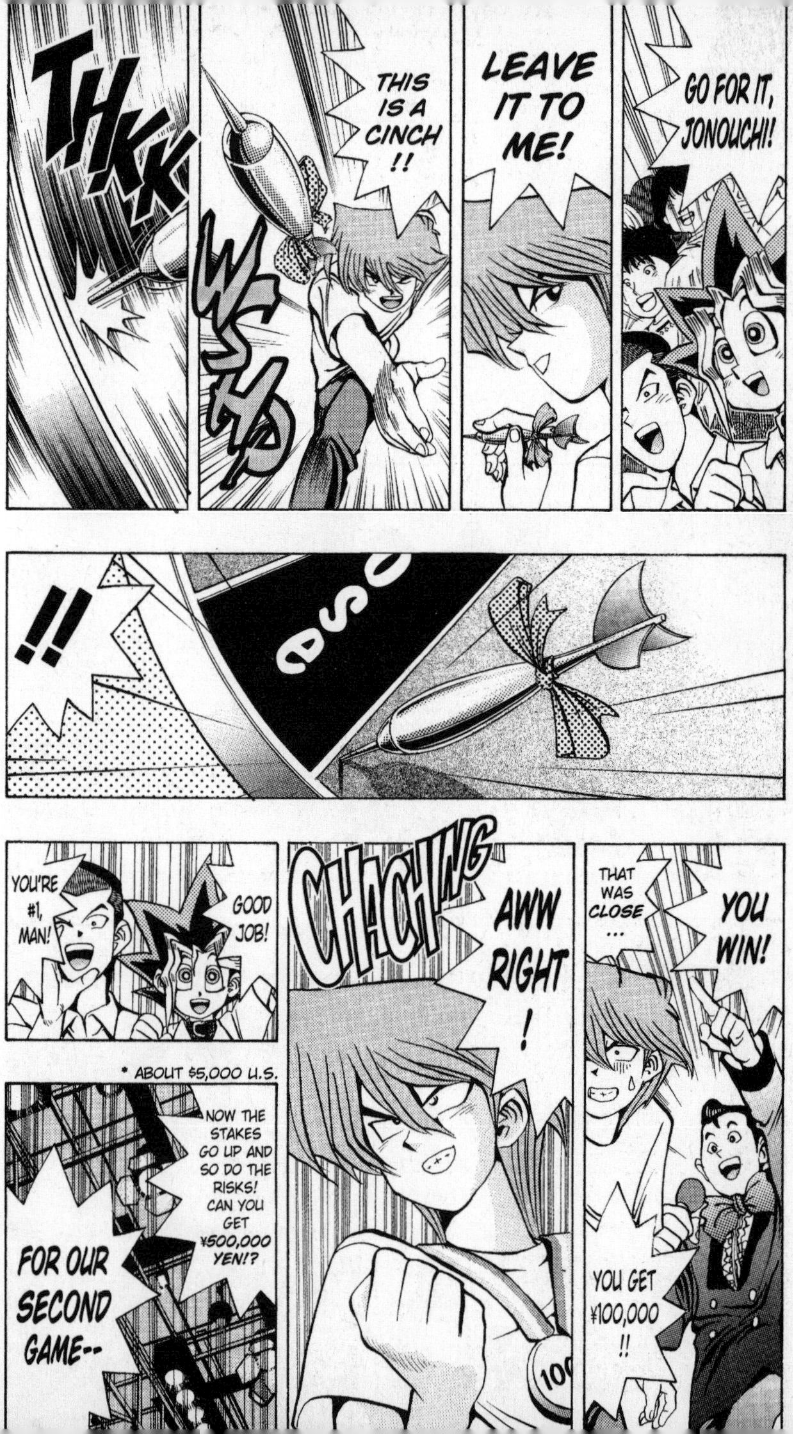
GO FOR IT, JONOUCHI!
LEAVE IT TO ME!
THIS IS A CINCH !!
THKK
!!
YOU WIN!
THAT WAS CLOSE ...
YOU GET ¥100,000 !!
CHACHING
AWW RIGHT !
GOOD JOB!
YOU'RE #1, MAN!
* ABOUT $5,000 U.S.
NOW THE STAKES GO UP AND SO DO THE RISKS! CAN YOU GET ¥500,000 YEN!?
FOR OUR SECOND GAME--

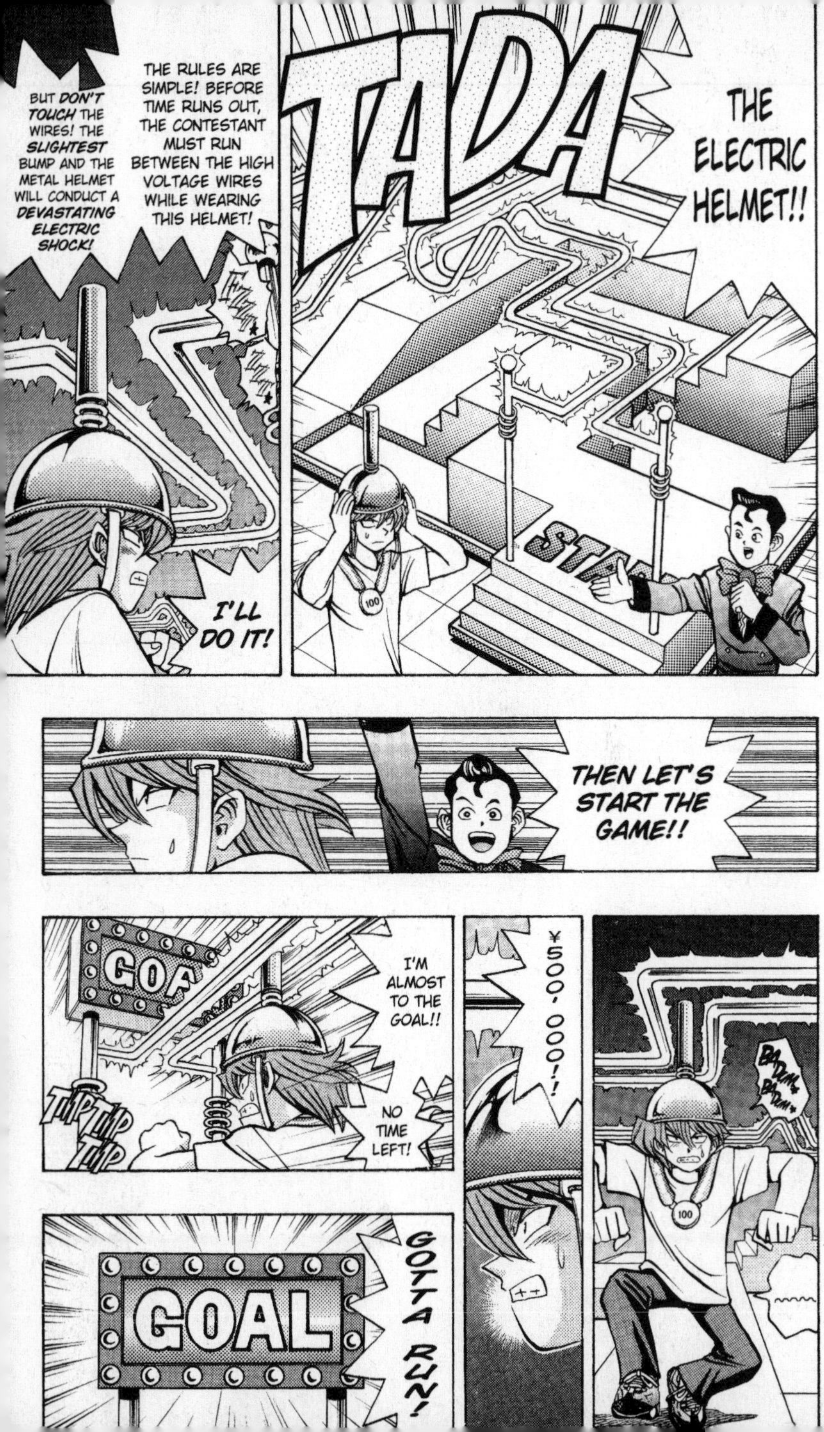
TADA
THE ELECTRIC HELMET!!
THE RULES ARE SIMPLE! BEFORE TIME RUNS OUT, THE CONTESTANT MUST RUN BETWEEN THE HIGH VOLTAGE WIRES WHILE WEARING THIS HELMET!
BUT DON'T TOUCH THE WIRES! THE SLIGHTEST BUMP AND THE METAL HELMET WILL CONDUCT A DEVASTATING ELECTRIC SHOCK!
I'LL DO IT!
THEN LET'S START THE GAME!!
BADUM BADUM
¥500,000!!
I'M ALMOST TO THE GOAL!!
NO TIME LEFT!
TIPTIP TIP
GOAL
GOTTA RUN!

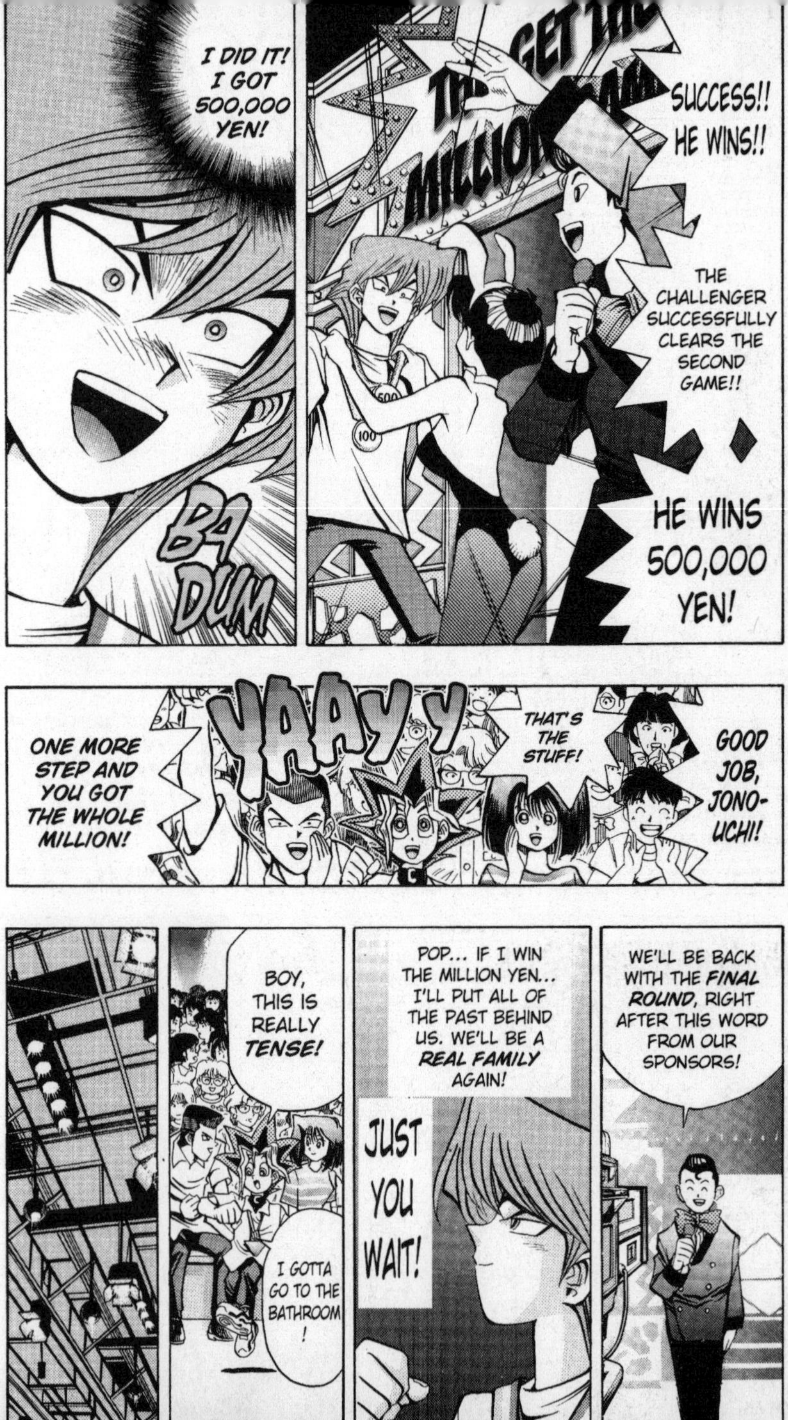
SUCCESS!! HE WINS!!
THE CHALLENGER SUCCESSFULLY CLEARS THE SECOND GAME!!
HE WINS 500,000 YEN!
I DID IT! I GOT 500,000 YEN!
BA DUM
GOOD JOB, JONO-UCHI!
THAT'S THE STUFF!
YAAYY
ONE MORE STEP AND YOU GOT THE WHOLE MILLION!
WE'LL BE BACK WITH THE *FINAL ROUND*, RIGHT AFTER THIS WORD FROM OUR SPONSORS!
POP... IF I WIN THE MILLION YEN... I'LL PUT ALL OF THE PAST BEHIND US. WE'LL BE A *REAL FAMILY* AGAIN!
JUST YOU WAIT!
BOY, THIS IS REALLY *TENSE!*
I GOTTA GO TO THE BATHROOM!

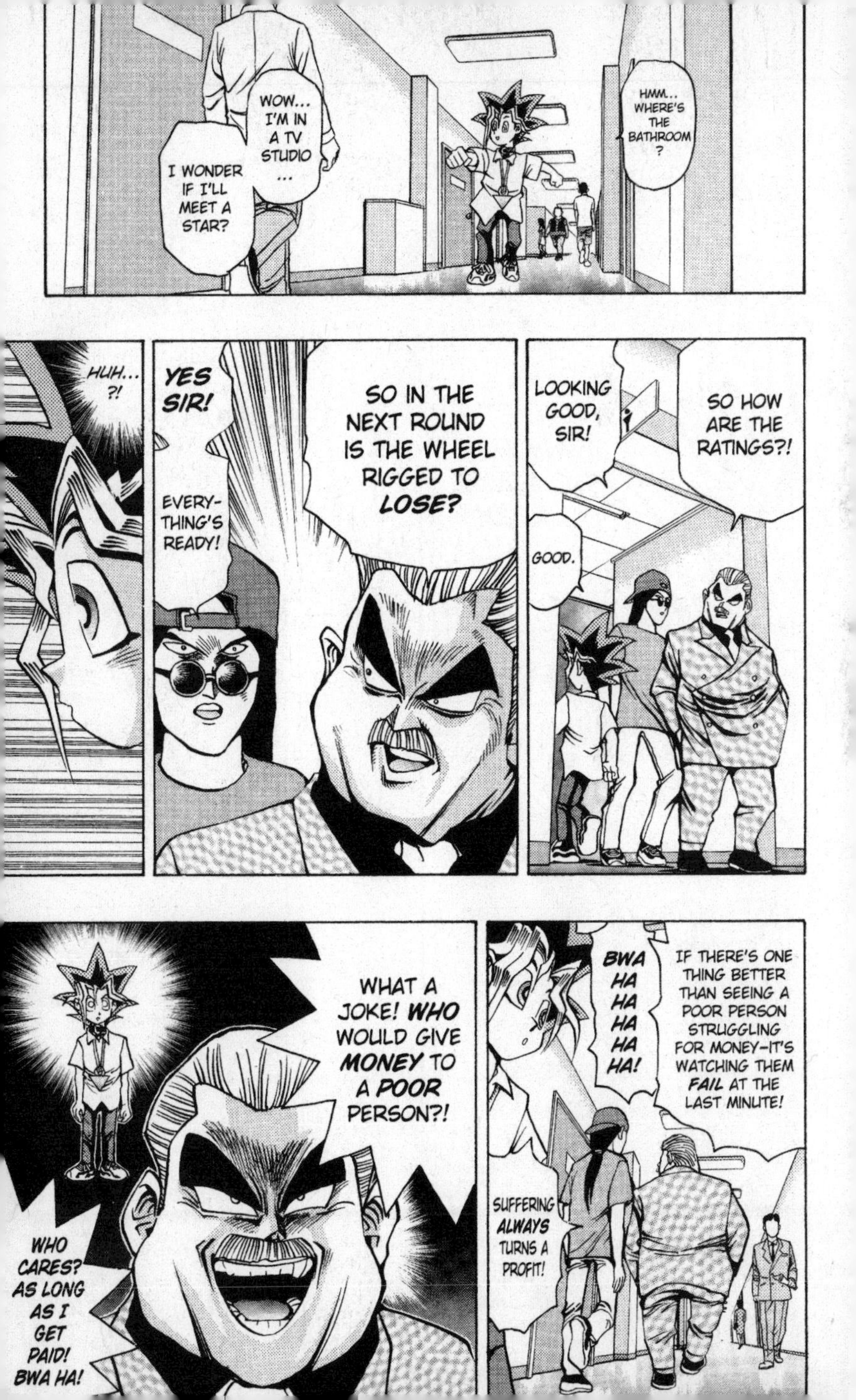
HMM... WHERE'S THE BATHROOM?
WOW... I'M IN A TV STUDIO...
I WONDER IF I'LL MEET A STAR?
SO HOW ARE THE RATINGS?!
LOOKING GOOD, SIR!
GOOD.
SO IN THE NEXT ROUND IS THE WHEEL RIGGED TO LOSE?
YES SIR!
EVERY-THING'S READY!
HUH...?!
IF THERE'S ONE THING BETTER THAN SEEING A POOR PERSON STRUGGLING FOR MONEY—IT'S WATCHING THEM FAIL AT THE LAST MINUTE!
BWA HA HA HA HA HA!
SUFFERING ALWAYS TURNS A PROFIT!
WHAT A JOKE! WHO WOULD GIVE MONEY TO A POOR PERSON?!
WHO CARES? AS LONG AS I GET PAID! BWA HA!

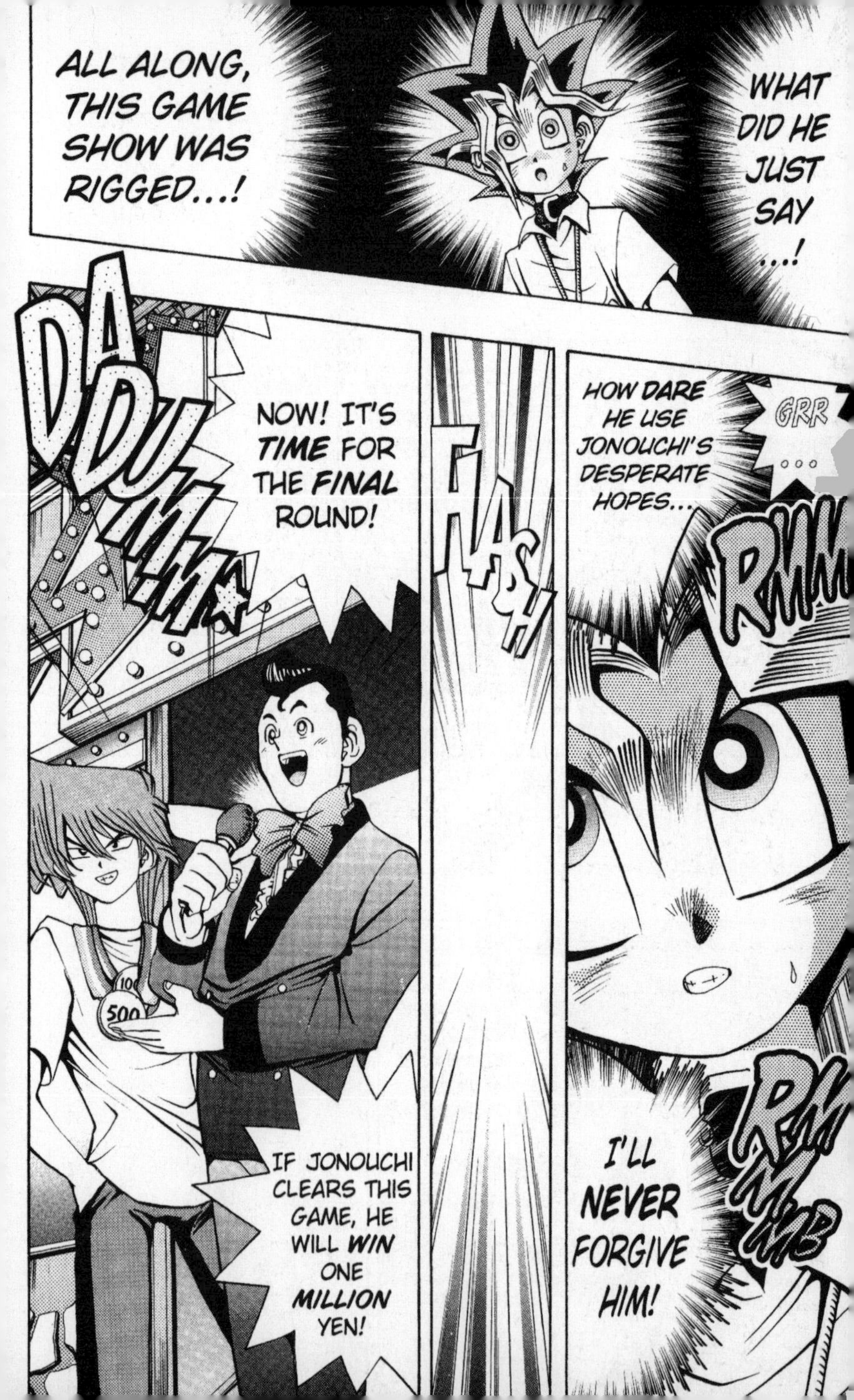
WHAT DID HE JUST SAY ...!
ALL ALONG, THIS GAME SHOW WAS RIGGED...!
HOW DARE HE USE JONOUCHI'S DESPERATE HOPES...
GRR...
I'LL NEVER FORGIVE HIM!
FLASH
NOW! IT'S TIME FOR THE FINAL ROUND!
IF JONOUCHI CLEARS THIS GAME, HE WILL WIN ONE MILLION YEN!

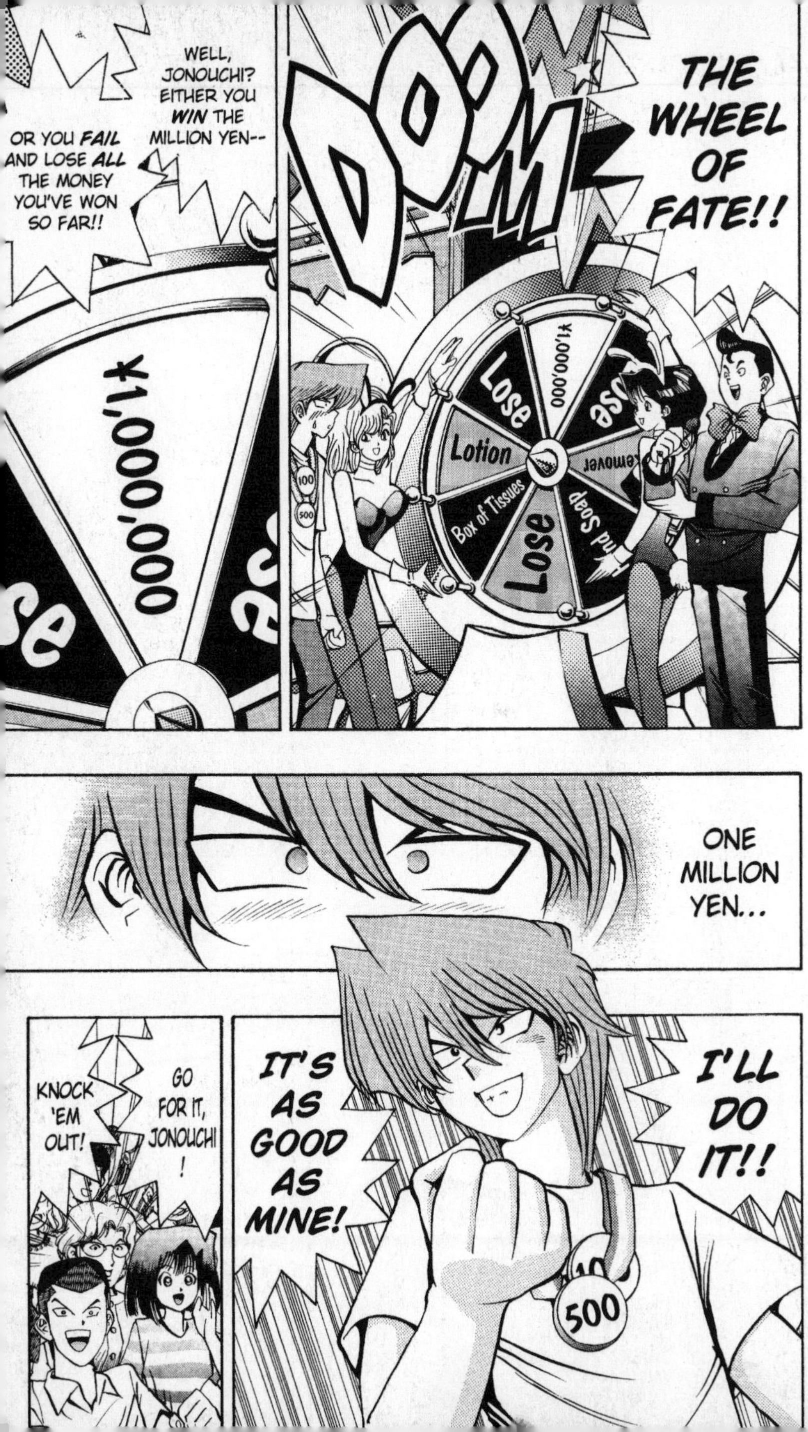
THE WHEEL OF FATE!!
DOOM
¥1,000,000
Lose
Lotion
Box of Tissues
Lose
WELL, JONOUCHI? EITHER YOU WIN THE MILLION YEN--
OR YOU FAIL AND LOSE ALL THE MONEY YOU'VE WON SO FAR!!
ONE MILLION YEN...
I'LL DO IT!!
IT'S AS GOOD AS MINE!
GO FOR IT, JONOUCHI!
KNOCK 'EM OUT!

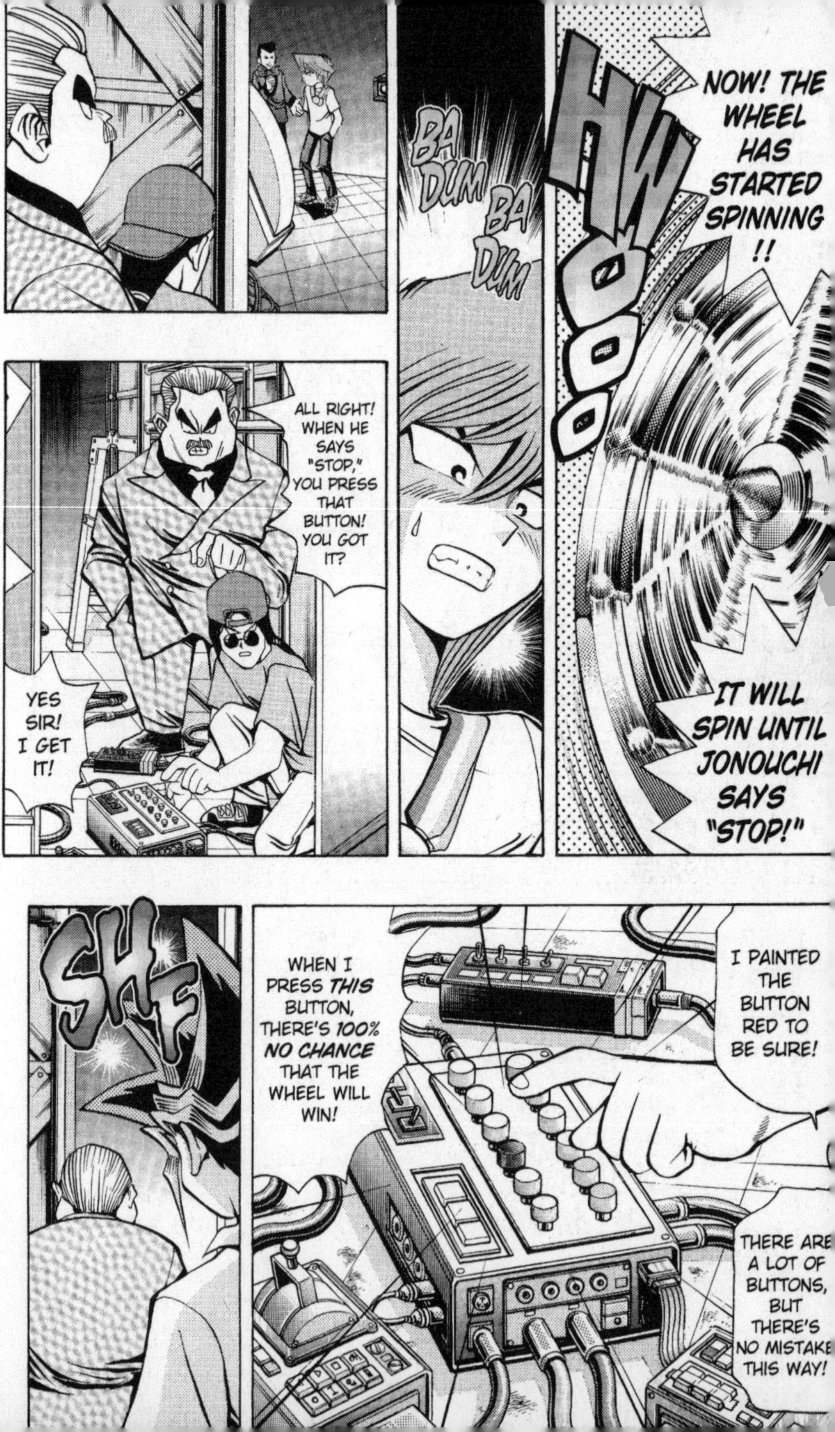
NOW! THE WHEEL HAS STARTED SPINNING!!
HWOOOO
IT WILL SPIN UNTIL JONOUCHI SAYS "STOP!"
BA DUM BA DUM
ALL RIGHT! WHEN HE SAYS "STOP," YOU PRESS THAT BUTTON! YOU GOT IT?
YES SIR! I GET IT!
I PAINTED THE BUTTON RED TO BE SURE!
WHEN I PRESS THIS BUTTON, THERE'S 100% NO CHANCE THAT THE WHEEL WILL WIN!
THERE ARE A LOT OF BUTTONS, BUT THERE'S NO MISTAKE THIS WAY!
SHF

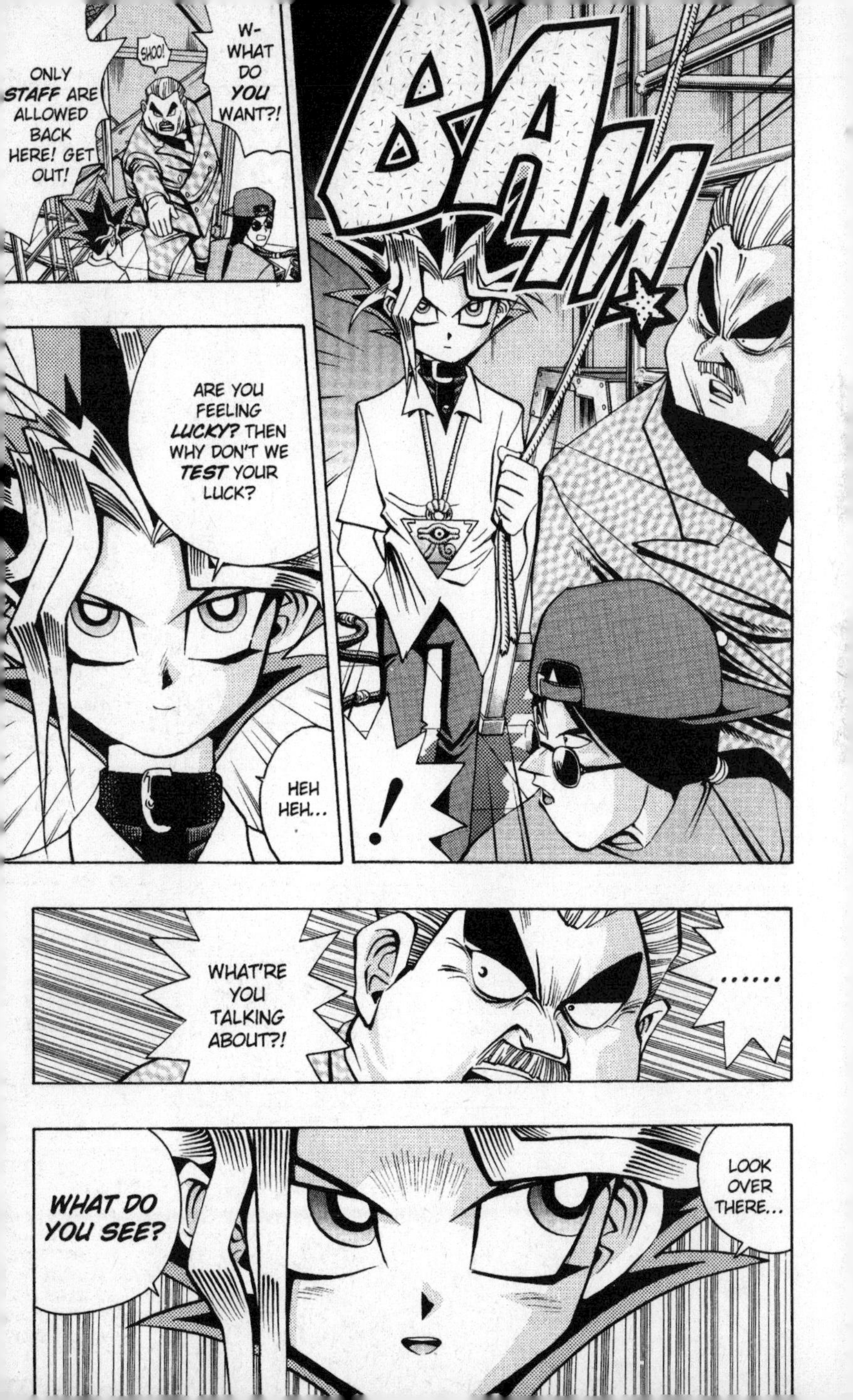
BAM
!
W-WHAT DO YOU WANT?!
SHOO!
ONLY STAFF ARE ALLOWED BACK HERE! GET OUT!
ARE YOU FEELING LUCKY? THEN WHY DON'T WE TEST YOUR LUCK?
HEH HEH...
......
WHAT'RE YOU TALKING ABOUT?!
LOOK OVER THERE...
WHAT DO YOU SEE?

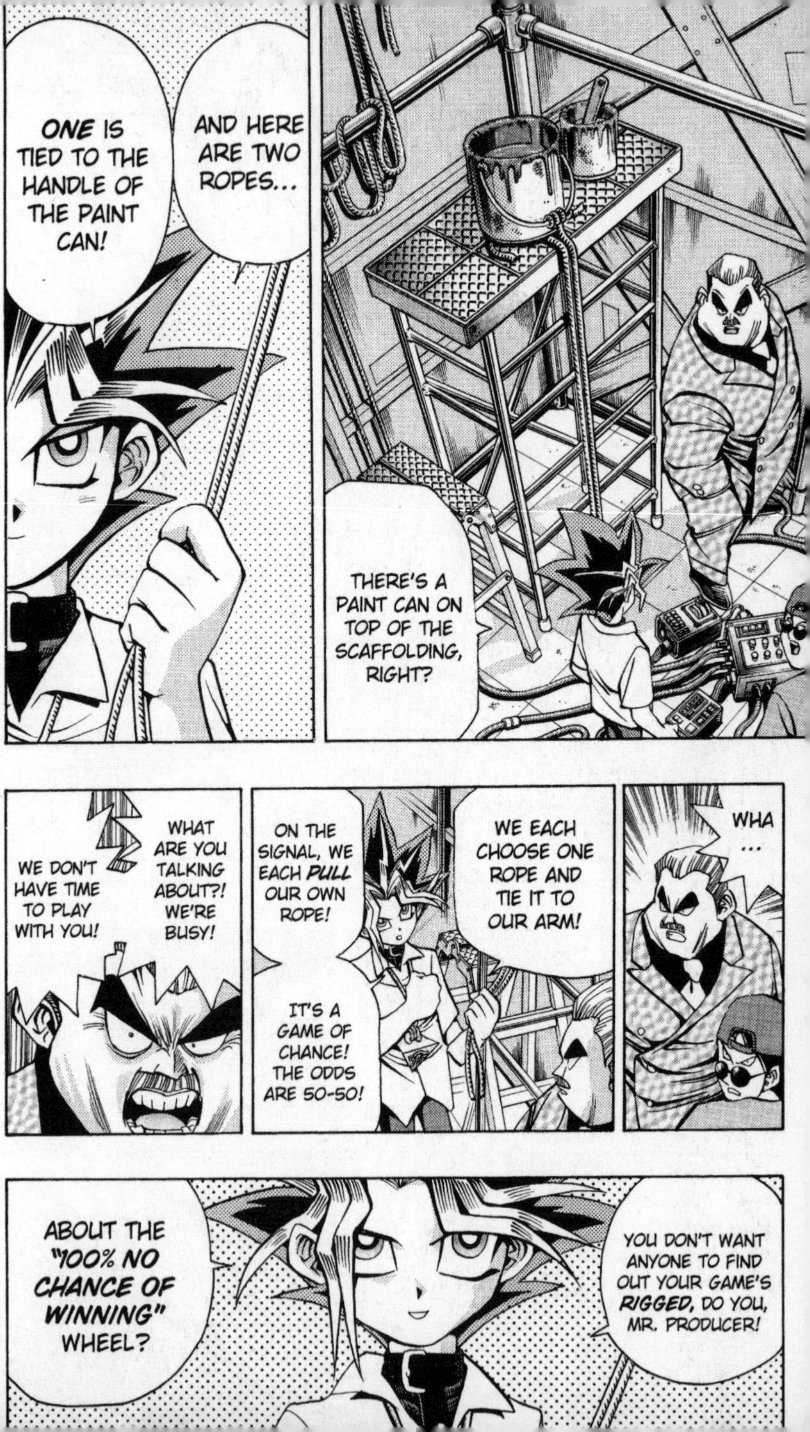
THERE'S A PAINT CAN ON TOP OF THE SCAFFOLDING, RIGHT?
AND HERE ARE TWO ROPES...
ONE IS TIED TO THE HANDLE OF THE PAINT CAN!
WHA ...
WE EACH CHOOSE ONE ROPE AND TIE IT TO OUR ARM!
ON THE SIGNAL, WE EACH PULL OUR OWN ROPE!
IT'S A GAME OF CHANCE! THE ODDS ARE 50-50!
WHAT ARE YOU TALKING ABOUT?! WE'RE BUSY!
WE DON'T HAVE TIME TO PLAY WITH YOU!
YOU DON'T WANT ANYONE TO FIND OUT YOUR GAME'S RIGGED, DO YOU, MR. PRODUCER!
ABOUT THE "100% NO CHANCE OF WINNING" WHEEL?

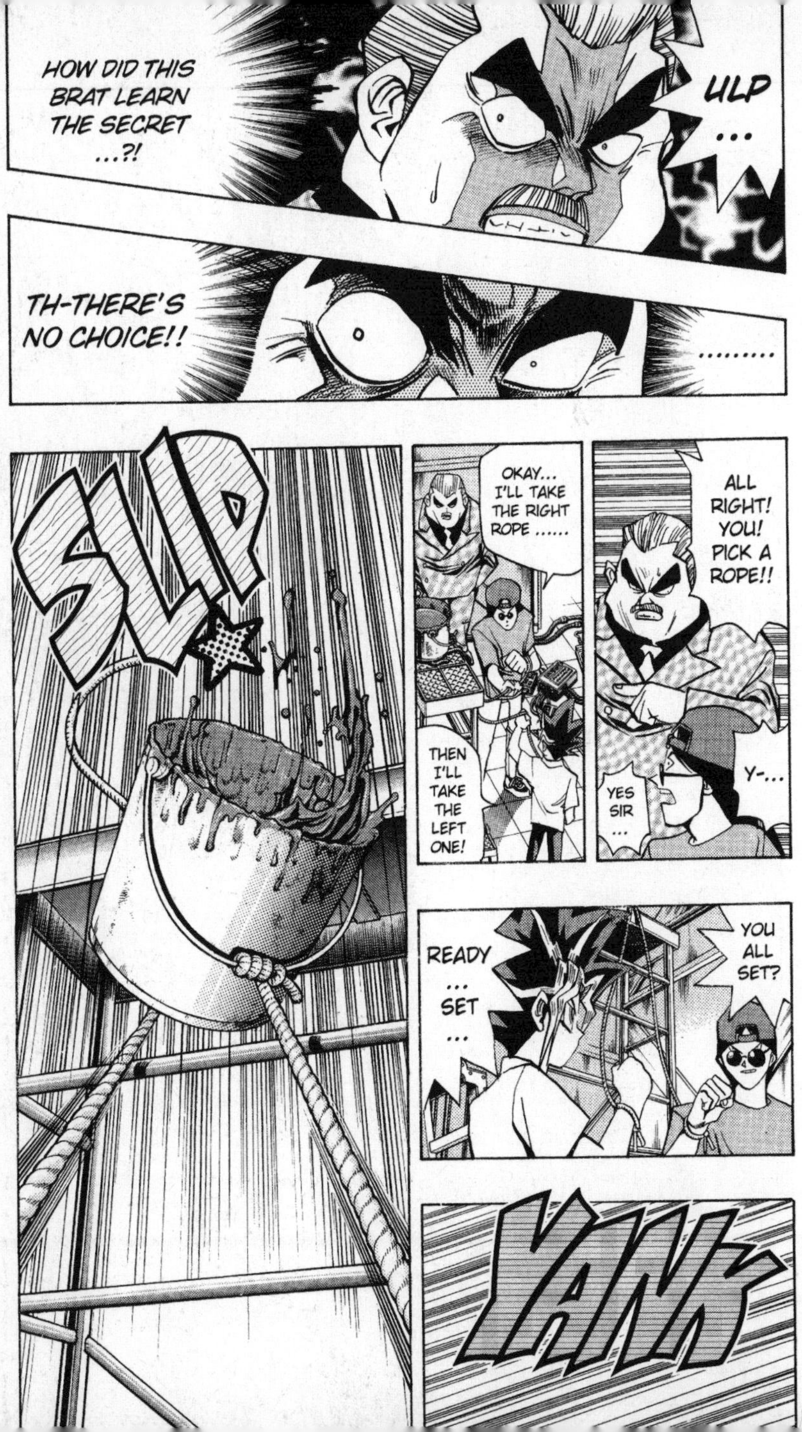
ULP ...
HOW DID THIS BRAT LEARN THE SECRET ...?!
....
TH-THERE'S NO CHOICE!!
ALL RIGHT! YOU! PICK A ROPE!!
Y-...
YES SIR ...
OKAY... I'LL TAKE THE RIGHT ROPE ......
THEN I'LL TAKE THE LEFT ONE!
YOU ALL SET?
READY ... SET ...
YANK
SLIP

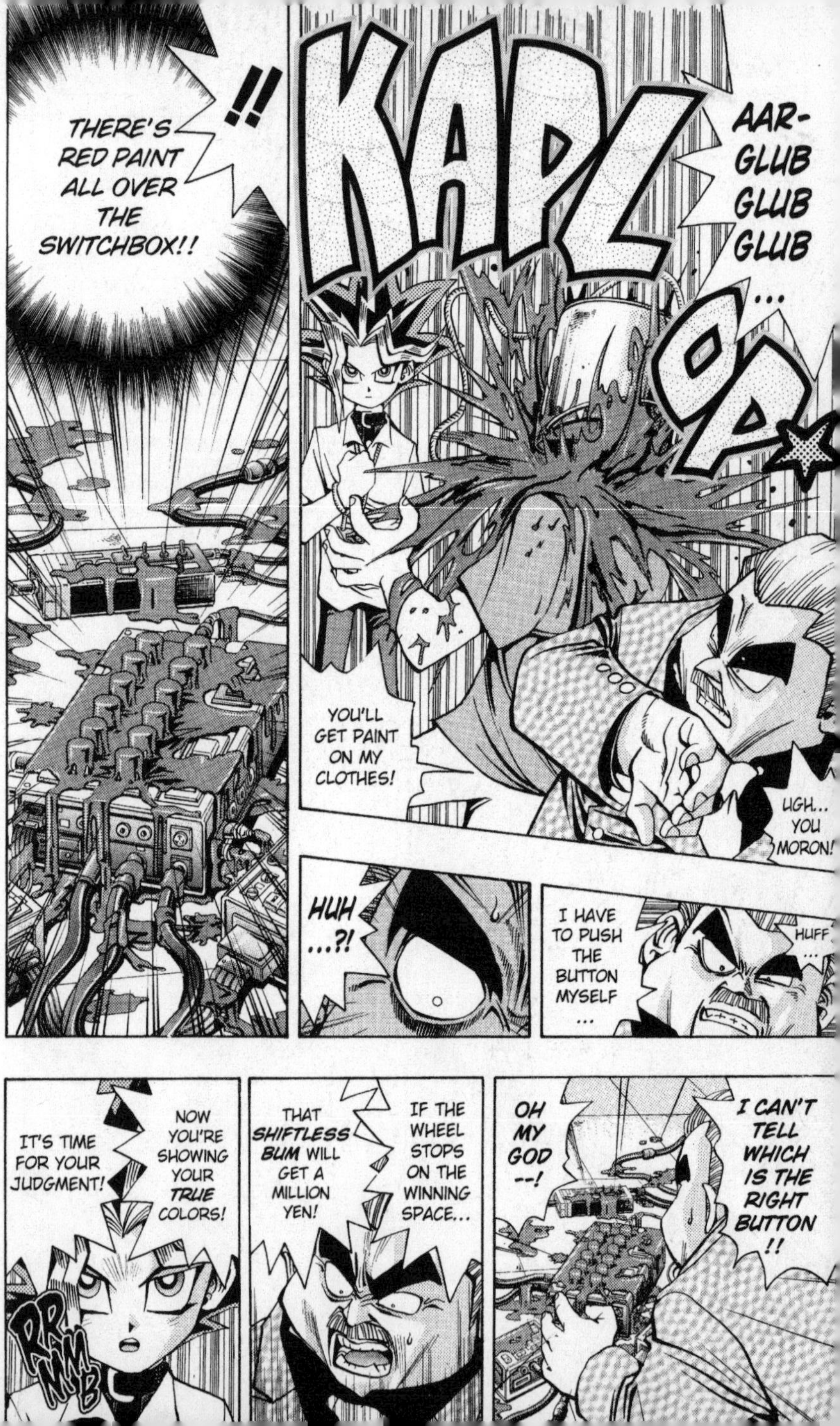
KAPLOP
AAR-GLUB GLUB GLUB...
UGH... YOU MORON!
YOU'LL GET PAINT ON MY CLOTHES!
HUFF...
I HAVE TO PUSH THE BUTTON MYSELF...
HUH...?!
!!
THERE'S RED PAINT ALL OVER THE SWITCHBOX!!
I CAN'T TELL WHICH IS THE RIGHT BUTTON!!
OH MY GOD--!
IF THE WHEEL STOPS ON THE WINNING SPACE...
THAT *SHIFTLESS BUM* WILL GET A MILLION YEN!
NOW YOU'RE SHOWING YOUR *TRUE* COLORS!
IT'S TIME FOR YOUR JUDGMENT!

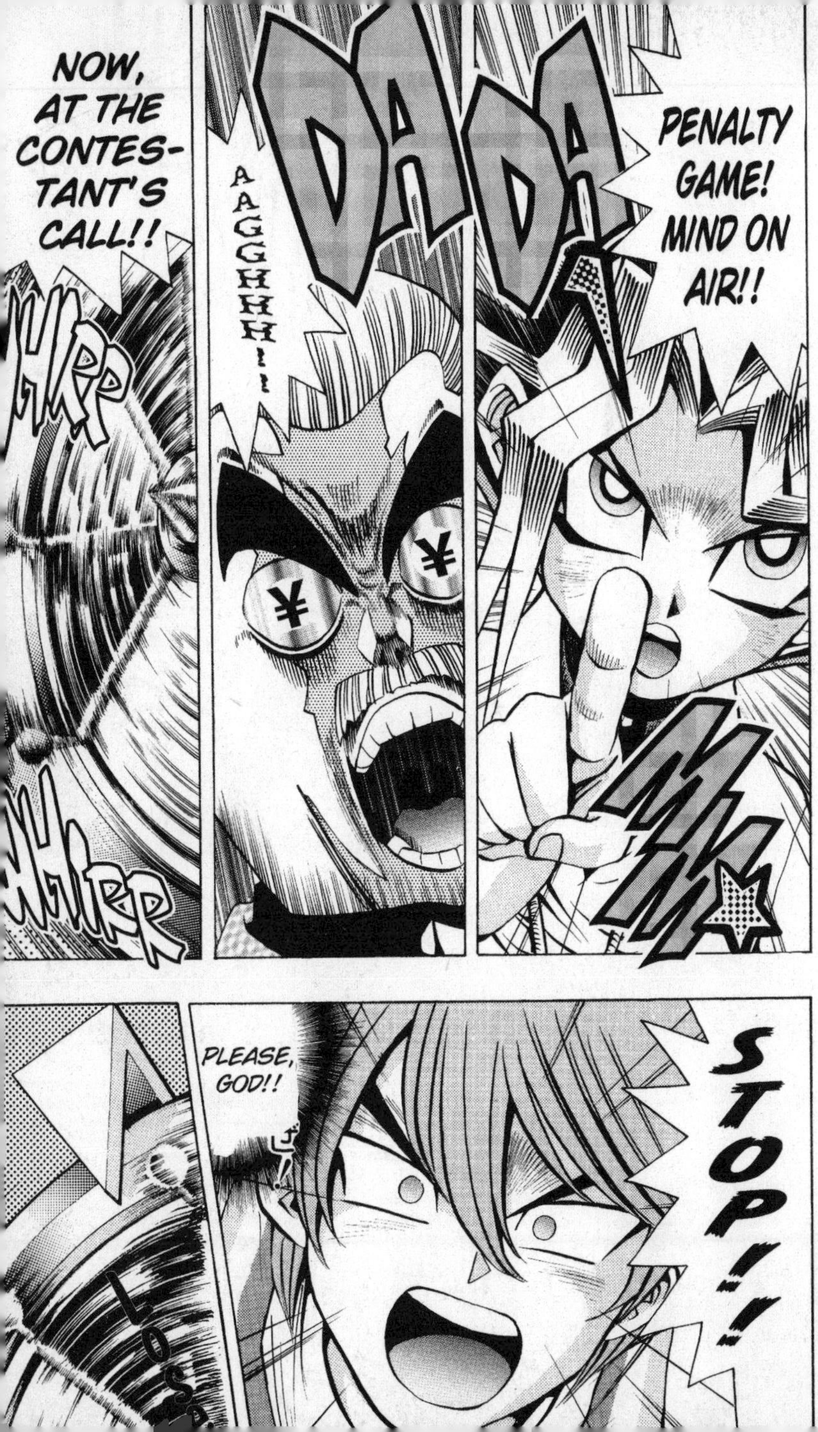
DADA
PENALTY GAME! MIND ON AIR!!
AAGGHHHH!!
NOW, AT THE CONTES-TANT'S CALL!!
WHIRR
WHIRR
STOP!!!
PLEASE, GOD!!

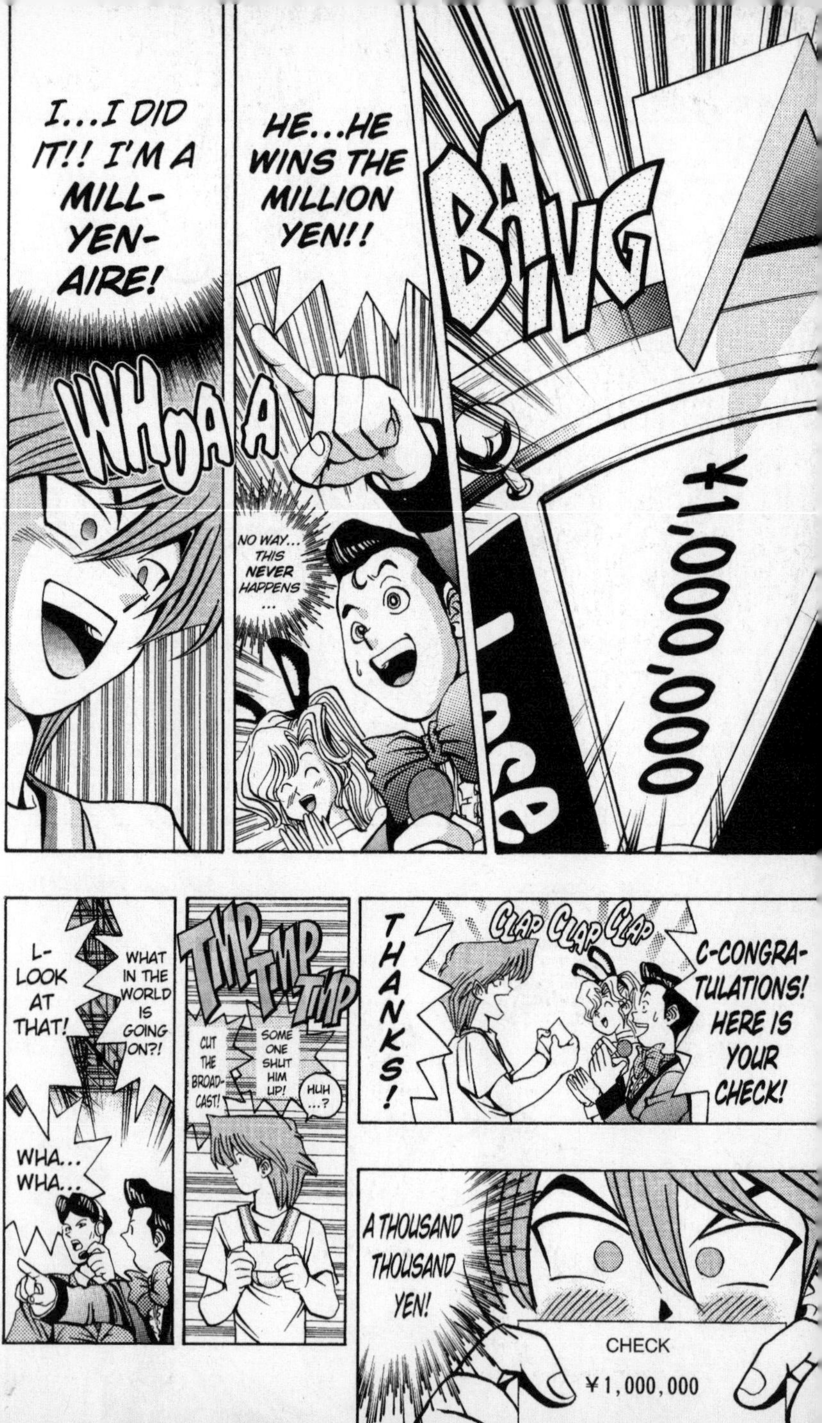
BANG
¥1,000,000
HE...HE WINS THE MILLION YEN!!
NO WAY... THIS NEVER HAPPENS...
I...I DID IT!! I'M A MILL-YEN-AIRE!
WHOA A
CLAP CLAP CLAP
C-CONGRATULATIONS! HERE IS YOUR CHECK!
THANKS!
A THOUSAND THOUSAND YEN!
CHECK
¥1,000,000
TMP TMP TMP
SOME ONE SHUT HIM UP!
CUT THE BROADCAST!
HUH...?
WHAT IN THE WORLD IS GOING ON?!
L-LOOK AT THAT!
WHA... WHA...

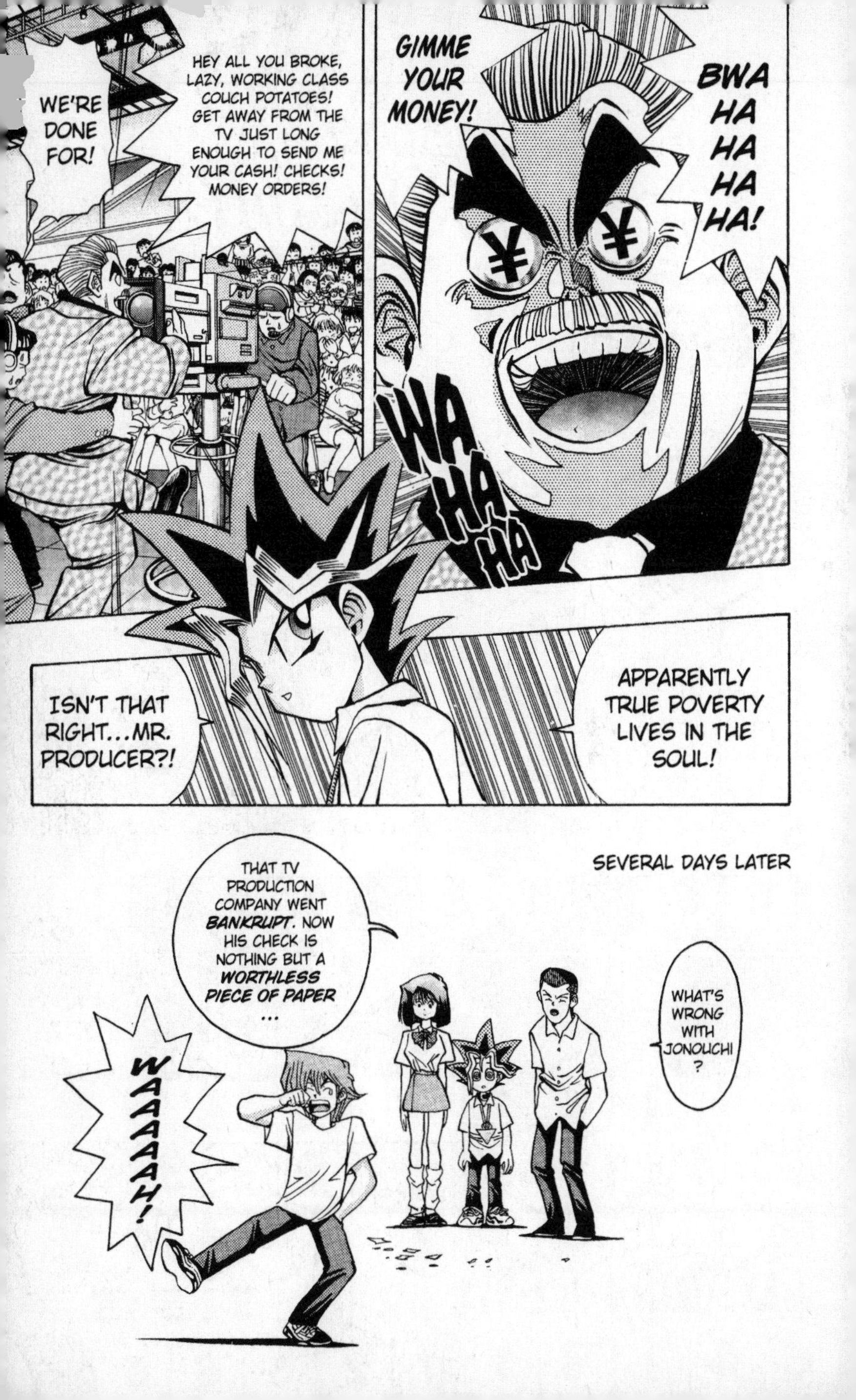
BWA HA HA HA HA!
GIMME YOUR MONEY!
WA HA HA HA
HEY ALL YOU BROKE, LAZY, WORKING CLASS COUCH POTATOES! GET AWAY FROM THE TV JUST LONG ENOUGH TO SEND ME YOUR CASH! CHECKS! MONEY ORDERS!
WE'RE DONE FOR!
APPARENTLY TRUE POVERTY LIVES IN THE SOUL!
ISN'T THAT RIGHT...MR. PRODUCER?!
SEVERAL DAYS LATER
WHAT'S WRONG WITH JONOUCHI?
THAT TV PRODUCTION COMPANY WENT BANKRUPT. NOW HIS CHECK IS NOTHING BUT A WORTHLESS PIECE OF PAPER...
WAAAAAAH!

BUZZ BUZZ

SPECIAL BONUS!

HONEYCOMB BOARD GAME!☆

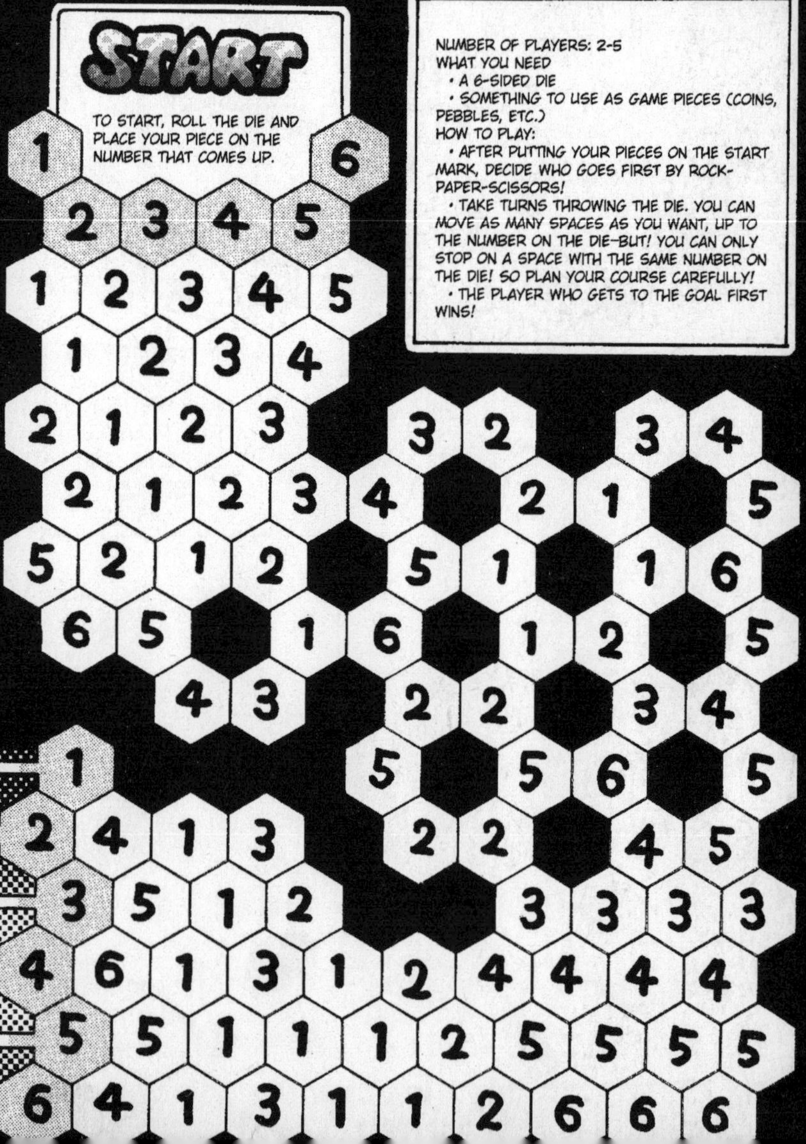
START
TO START, ROLL THE DIE AND PLACE YOUR PIECE ON THE NUMBER THAT COMES UP.

NUMBER OF PLAYERS: 2-5

WHAT YOU NEED

- A 6-SIDED DIE
- SOMETHING TO USE AS GAME PIECES (COINS, PEBBLES, ETC.)

HOW TO PLAY:

- AFTER PUTTING YOUR PIECES ON THE START MARK, DECIDE WHO GOES FIRST BY ROCK-PAPER-SCISSORS!
- TAKE TURNS THROWING THE DIE. YOU CAN MOVE AS MANY SPACES AS YOU WANT, UP TO THE NUMBER ON THE DIE—BUT! YOU CAN ONLY STOP ON A SPACE WITH THE SAME NUMBER ON THE DIE! SO PLAN YOUR COURSE CAREFULLY!
- THE PLAYER WHO GETS TO THE GOAL FIRST WINS!

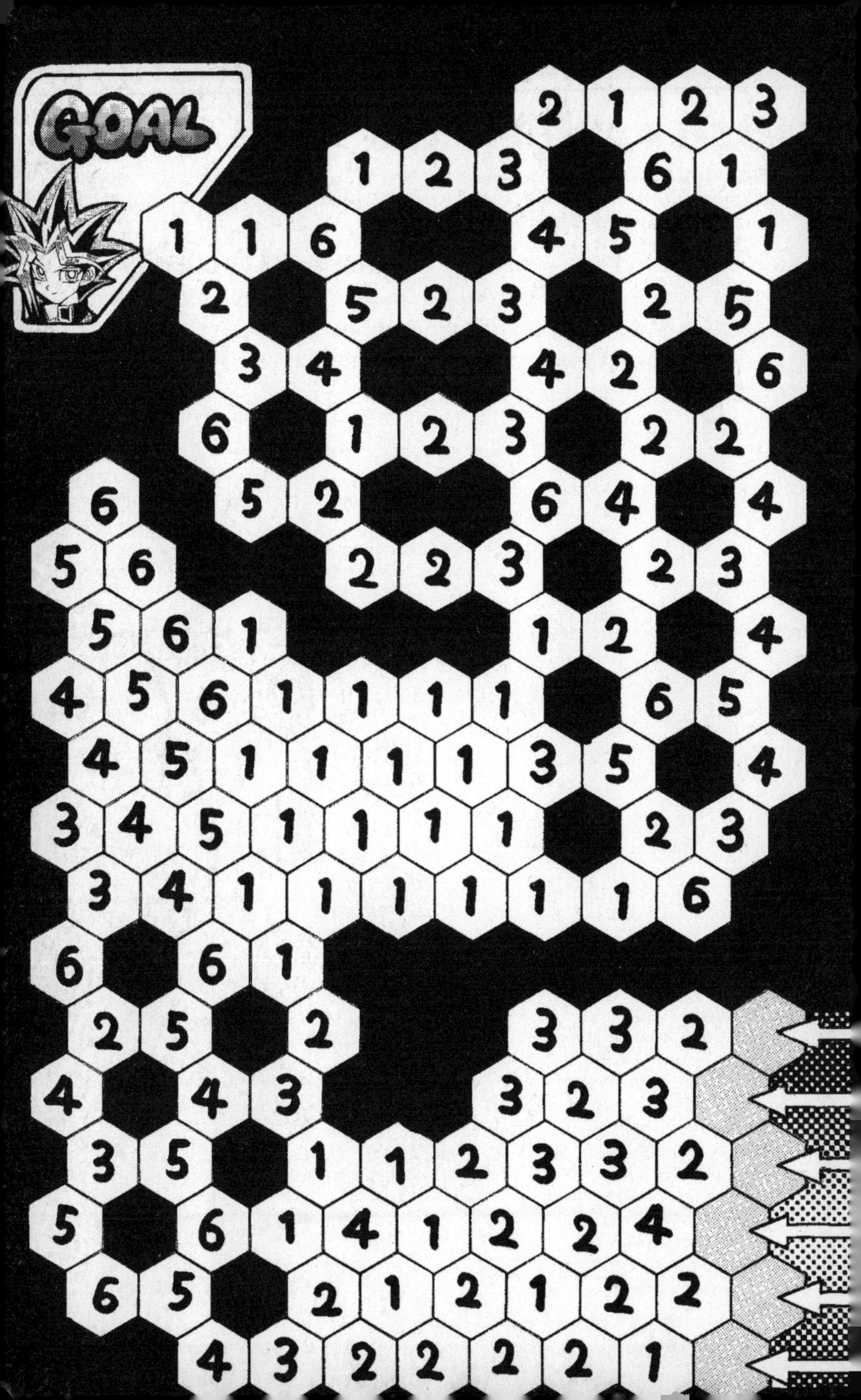
GOAL

MASTER OF THE CARDS

In Yugi's second duel with Kaiba, many classic **Yu-Gi-Oh!** cards appear for the first time. As **Yu-Gi-Oh!** fans know, the manga and anime version of the card game has simpler rules than the real-world version. Also, many of the card names are different between the English and Japanese versions. Here's a rundown of the cards in this graphic novel.

1. Hitotsu-me Giant
Known as "Cyclops" in the original Japanese. "Hitotsu-me" is Japanese for "one-eyed."

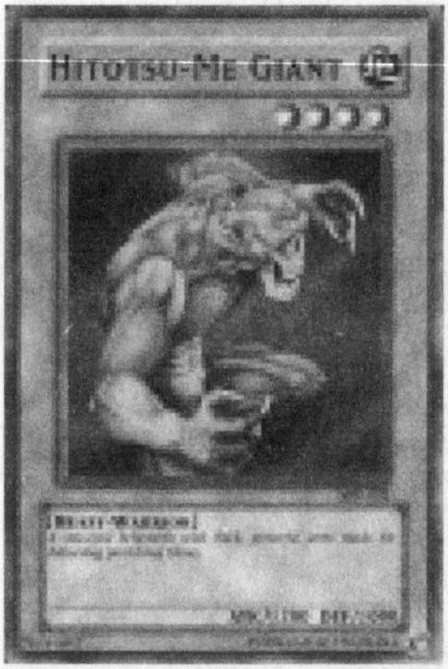
HITOTSU-ME GIANT

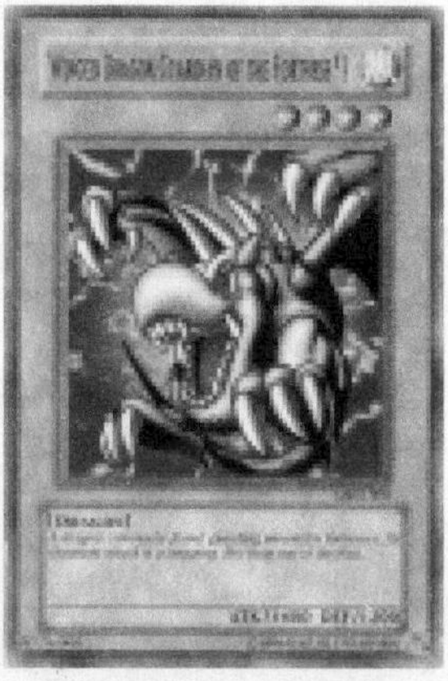

2. Winged Dragon, Guardian of the Fortress
This name is a literal translation of *toride o mamoru yokuryû*. In Japanese and Chinese mythology, dragons don't necessarily have wings, so it's understandable why this card is specifically called a *winged* dragon—or in Japanese, a *yokuryû*. (Dragons are *ryû* in Japanese and *long* in Chinese.) It doesn't have the same powers in the card game that it does in the manga.

3. The Wicked Worm Beast
This name is a literal translation of *jaaku naru worm beast*.

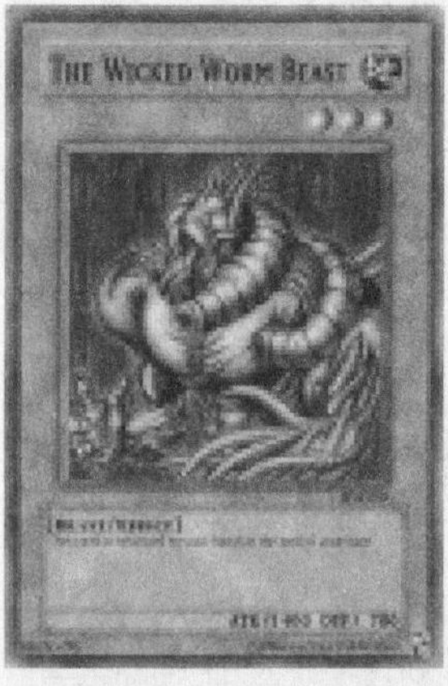
THE WICKED WORM BEAST

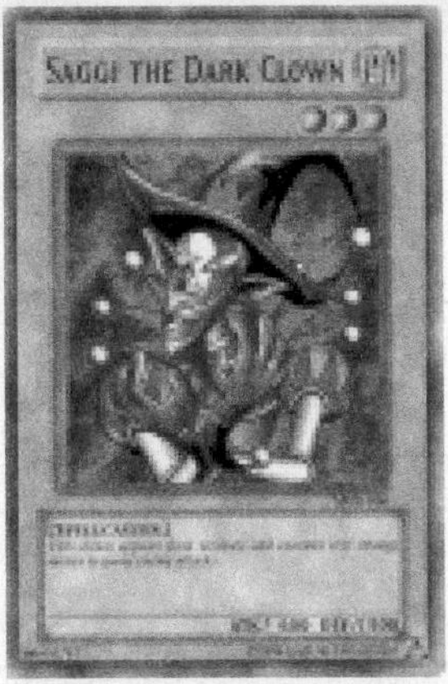
SAGGI THE DARK CLOWN

4. Saggi the Dark Clown
This name is a literal translation of *yami dôkeshi no saggi*.

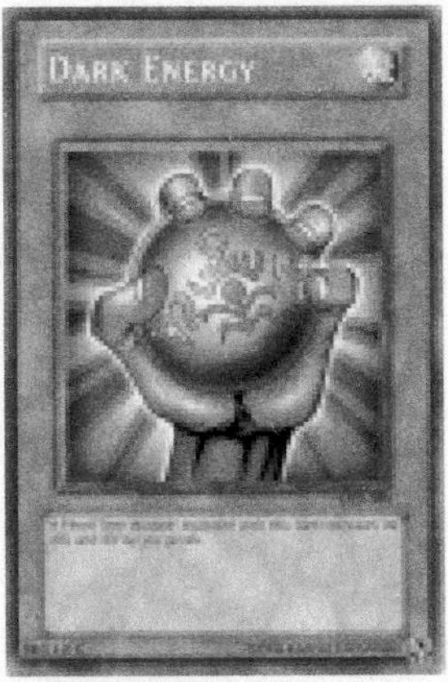
DARK ENERGY

5. Dark Energy
In the real-life game, this card is less powerful than in the manga, maybe because it'd be unbalanced otherwise.

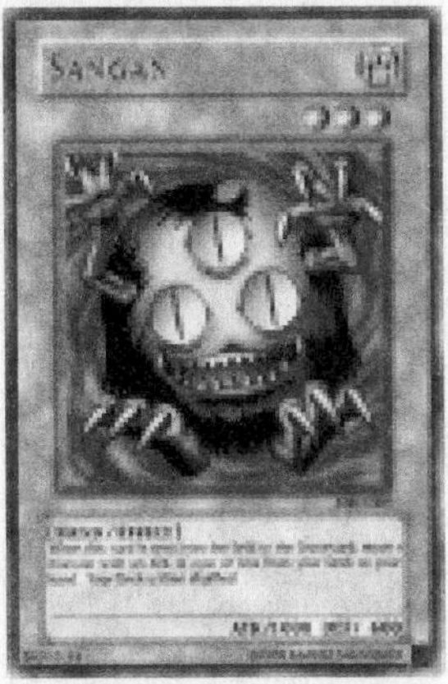
SANGAN

6. Sangan
Known as "Critter" in the original Japanese, "Sangan" could mean "three eyes" in Japanese. This card doesn't have the same powers in the manga that it does in the actual game.

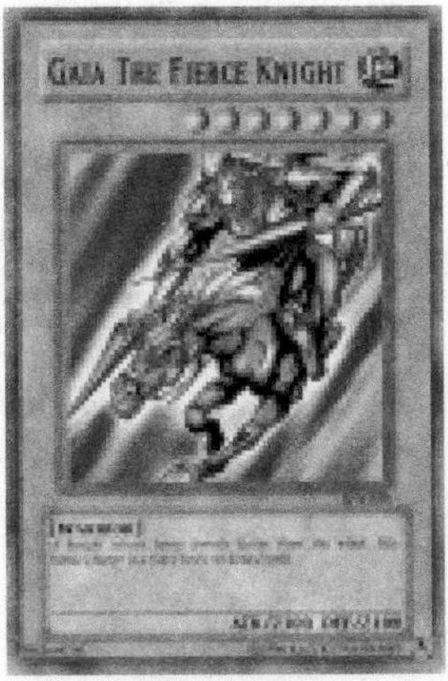
GAIA THE FIERCE KNIGHT

7. Gaia the Fierce Knight
Known as "Gaia the Dark Knight" in the original Japanese.

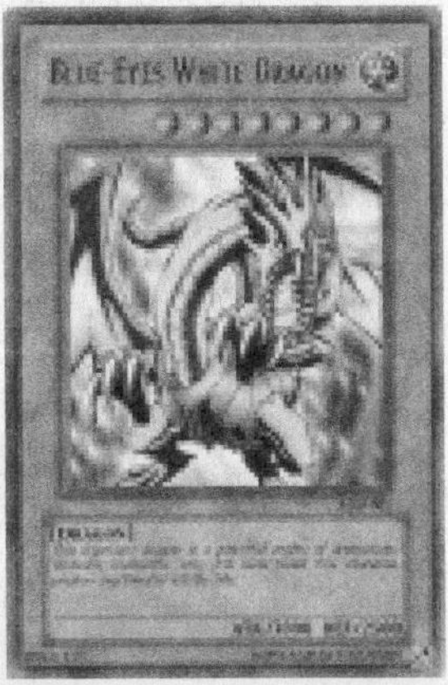

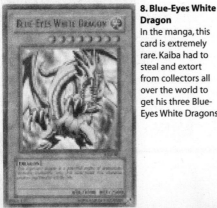

8. Blue-Eyes White Dragon
In the manga, this card is extremely rare. Kaiba had to steal and extort from collectors all over the world to get his three Blue-Eyes White Dragons.

9. Swords of Revealing Light
Known as *hikari no gofûken* ("Swords of Binding Light" or "Swords of Sealing Light") in the original Japanese.

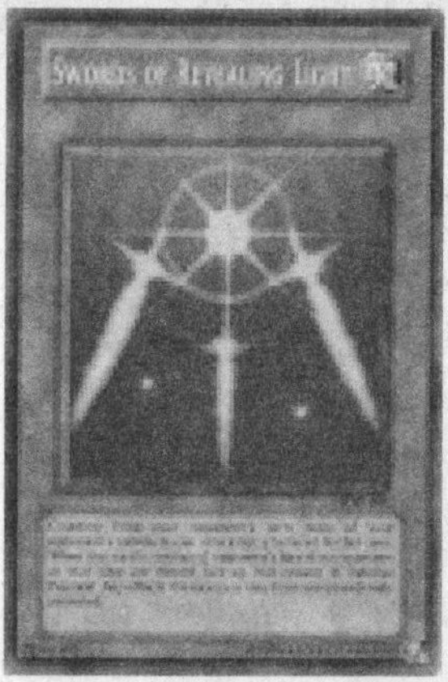

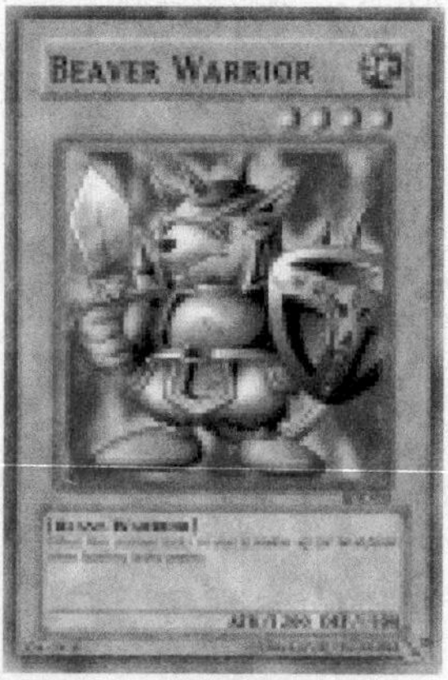
BEAVER WARRIOR

10. Beaver Warrior
Known as "Ruizu" (or, to use another pronunciation, "Louise") in the original Japanese.

11. Judge Man
This name is the same in the American and Japanese versions.

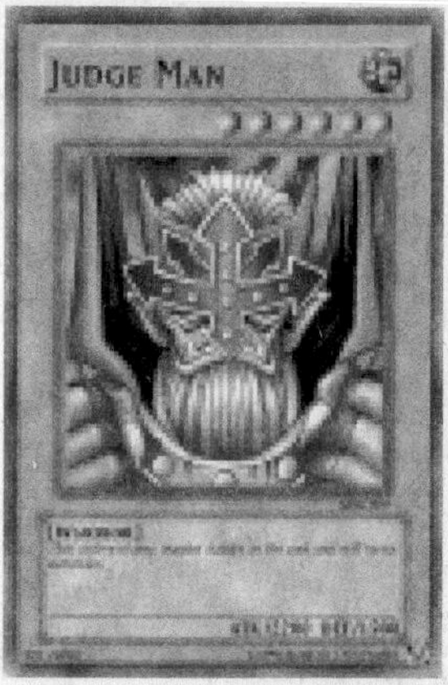
JUDGE MAN

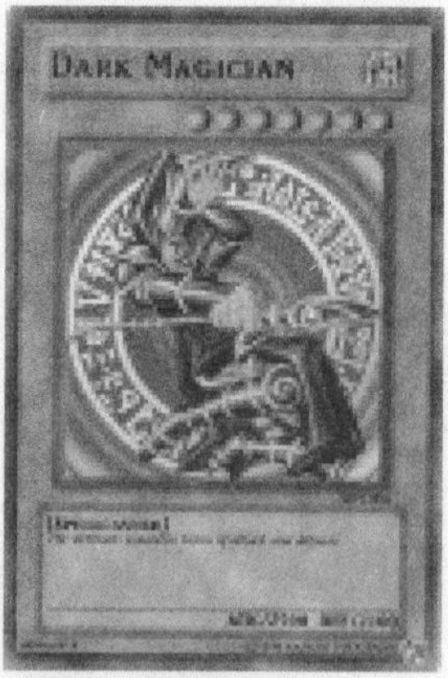
DARK MAGICIAN

12. Dark Magician
Known as "Black Magician" in the original Japanese.

13. The Exodia Cards
In the manga, according to Yugi's grandfather, no one has ever managed to use all five Exodia cards in a game. Perhaps they're rarer in the manga? Or perhaps deck-building skills aren't as advanced in Yugi's world?

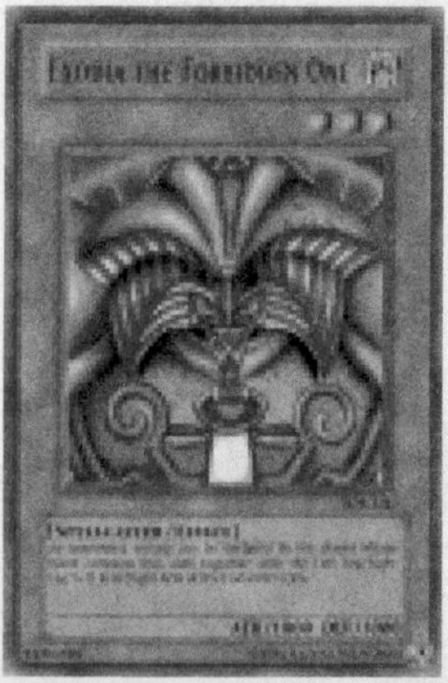

IN THE NEXT VOLUME...

They say the King of Games never loses...but can even Yugi beat these tough new opponents and weird games? "Monster Fight" takes dueling action figures to a new level! A sinister classmate challenges Yugi to a magical game of "Dragon Cards"! Jonouchi and Yugi face the peril of death by yo-yos! But Yugi may have finally met his match when he meets his new classmate Bakura, a game master with a secret who invites him to join a role-playing campaign...

AVAILABLE NOW!

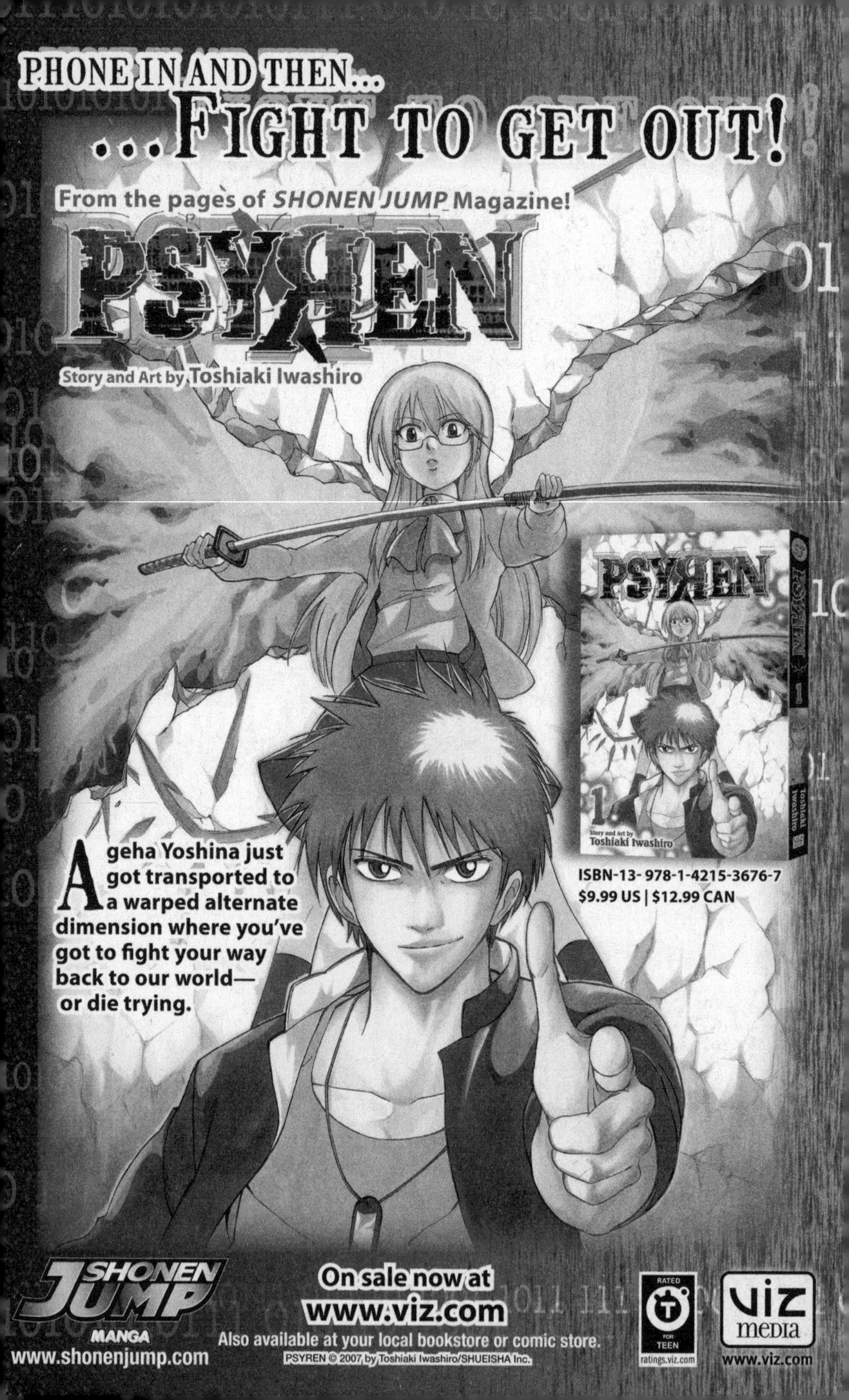
PHONE IN AND THEN...
...FIGHT TO GET OUT!
From the pages of SHONEN JUMP Magazine!
PSYREN
Story and Art by Toshiaki Iwashiro
PSYREN
Story and Art by Toshiaki Iwashiro
1
ISBN-13- 978-1-4215-3676-7
$9.99 US | $12.99 CAN
Ageha Yoshina just got transported to a warped alternate dimension where you've got to fight your way back to our world—or die trying.
SHONEN JUMP MANGA
www.shonenjump.com
On sale now at
www.viz.com
Also available at your local bookstore or comic store.
PSYREN © 2007 by Toshiaki Iwashiro/SHUEISHA Inc.
RATED T FOR TEEN
ratings.viz.com
viz media
www.viz.com

You're Reading in the Wrong Direction!!

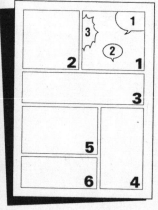

Whoops! Guess what? You're starting at the wrong end of the comic!

...It's true! In keeping with the original Japanese format, **Yu-Gi-Oh!** is meant to be read from right to left, starting in the upper-right corner.

Unlike English, which is read from left to right, Japanese is read from right to left, meaning that action, sound effects, and word-balloon order are completely reversed...something which can make readers unfamiliar with Japanese feel pretty backwards themselves. For this reason, manga or Japanese comics published in the U.S. in English have sometimes been published "flopped"–that is, printed in exact reverse order, as though seen from the other side of a mirror.

By flopping pages, U.S. publishers can avoid confusing readers, but the compromise is not without its downside. For one thing, a character in a flopped manga series who once wore in the original Japanese version a T-shirt emblazoned with "M A Y" (as in "the merry month of") now wears one which reads "Y A M"! Additionally, many manga creators in Japan are themselves unhappy with the process, as some feel the mirror-imaging of their art alters their original intentions.

We are proud to bring you Kazuki Takahashi's **Yu-Gi-Oh!** in the original unflopped format. For now, though, turn to the other side of the book and let the games begin...!

–Editor